T0329648

THE ECONOMICS OF RACE IN THE UNITED STATES

The **Economics** of **Race** in the **United States**

BRENDAN O'FLAHERTY

Harvard University Press

CAMBRIDGE, MASSACHUSETTS & LONDON, ENGLAND / 2015

Third printing

Library of Congress Cataloging-in-Publication Data

O'Flaherty, Brendan.
   The economics of race in the United States / Brendan O'Flaherty.
       pages   cm
   Includes bibliographical references and index.
   ISBN 978-0-674-36818-7 (alk. paper)
   1. Race—United States—History.   2. Minorities—United States—
Economic conditions.   3. Minorities—United States—Social conditions.
I. Title.
   HT1521.O33   2015
   305.80973—dc23   2014041999

For **Frank Hurtz** *and* **Ed Lewinson,**
who were never afraid to do what was right.

Contents

THE ECONOMICS OF RACE IN THE UNITED STATES

1

What Is This Book About?

In the summer of 1832, cholera struck New York City. Cholera starts with an attack of diarrhea and vomiting, progresses to severe abdominal cramps, and then ends with acute shock from the collapse of the circulatory system. In 1832, most victims died within a day. Five Points, the notorious Irish and African American slum, was hit hardest. Some of the city's wealthier residents were not unduly alarmed: one of them described the epidemic as "almost exclusively confined to the lower classes of intemperate dissolute & filthy people huddled together like swine in their polluted habitations." In all, 3,515 New Yorkers died in a few weeks—the equivalent of 100,000 deaths in today's larger city (Wilford 2008).

New Yorkers today don't worry much about cholera or blame it on the intemperance and dissolution of its victims. But we still have hospitals and research centers, even if they don't concentrate on cholera, and no one maintains that disease in general is yesterday's problem. Indeed, we devote more resources than ever before to studying and treating disease, even though we suffer from less disease than ever before. That's not irrational: investing more in effective practices than in ineffective practices makes a lot of sense. Rehydration does a better job of treating cholera than tobacco enemas (one of the mainstays of 1832), and clean water is a better way to prevent cholera than abstaining from cold water and ardent spirits. That's why we invest in clean water and rehydration.

The problems of race in the United States today are also different from what they were in 1832 or 1960 or 1990. That doesn't mean that they've gone away or that we should ignore them, any more than we should ignore disease because cholera is now rare in New York. On the contrary, these problems are worth studying harder because we have better tools and better data than social scientists did a generation ago. And in a country where eventually most of the population will come from races that America's dominant families once despised (and in a world where members of those races are already close to a majority of literate, middle-class, Internet-savvy people), even small reductions in the impediments to cooperation, production, and fulfillment that race now presents can have big payoffs.

So it wasn't silly or nostalgic to write this book.

I call this book *The Economics of Race in the United States*. That's deliberate. I could have called it many other things, but I didn't. You'll understand the book better if you understand the title.

First, this is an economics book. I'll use the tools of economics: equilibrium, rationality, incentives, information. I'll ask economic questions: Who wins? Who loses? What do people know? Is there a way to do it better? I'll look at regressions and worry about reverse causality.

Because this is economics, I'll also look at people in a particular way. Economics doesn't try to label people as heroes or villains. Everyone responds to the incentives he or she faces, and we try to understand behavior by understanding those incentives. Like trees and mosquitoes, the people that economists think about do what they do, and economists don't have methods for deciding whether they will go to heaven or not. In the long history of race in America, many evil deeds have been done (and some saintly ones too), but our job is not to assign praise or blame. We want to understand what is happening and why and how improvements can be made.

Looking for incentives and not for heroes is what got economics labeled the "dismal science." The first use of that term is in Thomas Carlyle's 1849 essay "Occasional Discourse on the Negro Question." This essay is an attack on John Stuart Mill for supporting the emancipation of Jamaican slaves. Carlyle thought the emancipated slaves were lazy, but Mill argued that the former slaves would act more responsibly if they found themselves in an environment where responsibility was better rewarded. Carlyle labeled Mill's view "dismal" because Mill did not understand the innate superiority of white men and how they could gallantly whip Afro-Jamaicans into good behavior.

This book follows Mill, not Carlyle. I don't mind being "dismal." That's why "economics" is in the title.

The next part of the title indicates that this book is about the United States. I'll pay some limited attention to other countries, but only to help understand the United States. My hands are full just trying just to understand the United States.

"Race" is the third ingredient in the title. In Chapter 3, I'll explain what race is and get you confused about it. Because race means different things in different countries, I had to say "United States" before I said "race."

Races in the United States mean African Americans, whites, Hispanics, Asians, Native Americans, Hawaiians, and Pacific Islanders—much more than blacks and whites.* But the literature is mainly about blacks and whites: that's been a crucial discussion in this part of America for the past four centuries. The future may be different, but we're not yet in the future.

Finally, this is a book that I wrote, nobody else. I'm an old white guy from New Jersey. Does being an old white guy from New Jersey disqualify me from writing a book about race? I don't think so, obviously. For one thing, I have a race (in the traditional American conception, races are like noses: everybody has precisely one), and figuring out how whites act and why they act that way (why, for instance, so few white households search for housing in predominantly minority neighborhoods) is crucial for understanding the economics of race in the United States.

I can't write a book that is not written by an old white guy from New Jersey, so if I was going to write this book, that's what it had to be. An economist with a different race would probably write a different book. It would emphasize different points, focus on different questions, interpret some results in different ways. It might be a better book too. But a lot of it would be the same, because economists are trained a certain way and think a certain way.

That's why I called the book *The Economics of Race in the United States* and called myself the author.

You can also get some idea of what the book is like by considering a few titles that I rejected. If you're looking for something that would be in a book with one of these titles, you won't find it here.

---

*Technically speaking, Hispanics are an ethnicity, not a race. We will discuss this in Chapter 3.

The first title I rejected was *What's Wrong with African Americans (or Hispanics or Asians or Native Americans) and What They Should Do about It.* I wanted to write an economics book, and that's not economics. I also rejected *What's Wrong with White People and What They Should Do about It.* The reasons are the same. I'm not trying to make you think that no one has ever done anything morally reprehensible, but as I stated, my job is not to assign either blame or praise.

Another title I rejected was *How to Become a Good Person in a Diverse Society.* Your parents and friends should have taken care of this long before you had the ability to read a sophisticated book like this.

I also rejected as a title *The Economics of Discrimination.* Discrimination is both too broad and too narrow to be the sole focus of the book.

It's too narrow because discrimination is not the only concern in race relations or the only explanation for racial disparities. How important discrimination is and what should be done about it are major questions for this book, but not the whole thing. These are questions, not answers, for now.

Discrimination is too broad a topic because many nonracial kinds of discrimination in the United States matter, but we won't be concerned with them. There is substantial evidence of discrimination on the basis of sexual orientation, age, and gender. But these are different (for instance, practically every man has a mother who is female, but very few whites have mothers who are black) and are the proper subjects of other books.

For the same reason, I didn't call the book *The Economics of Poverty.* Again, poverty is an important topic and I'll discuss it often. But in every race most people are not poor, and lots of the issues in this book affect people who are not poor.

Finally, I didn't call the book *How to Make Students Feel Bad in Class.* I want readers to be emotionally comfortable and intellectually uncomfortable.

I wouldn't have to say something like that if this book were about some other part of economics like macro or econometrics. But race is different: race is personal. There is a long history of race determining who should be treated with respect, who was truly human, whose rights should be protected, who was boring or clever or wily or criminal or dumb or sexually profligate or lazy or untrustworthy or athletic or had rhythm. People often care whether or not these labels attach to them and whether other people are trying to attach these labels to them or their families.

Race is a dangerous topic, and I have to be careful. But not too careful: I don't want to go so far in making this book emotionally comfortable that it's intellectually comfortable too. My editors will help me. If I mess up, I apologize.

I'll also rely on conventions to help me keep things comfortable. Specifically, I'll use the conventions of the *Chicago Manual of Style* and the federal government's Office of Management and Budget for current writing, but I quote older documents exactly even when they go against those conventions. The Chicago style is to capitalize names of ethnic groups and nationalities (but not to use hyphens) and to use lower-case letters for colors. I'll discuss the Office of Management and Budget conventions in Chapter 3.

The plan of the book is to introduce race in the first several chapters and then to look at a series of different areas, see how race impinges on those areas, and think about what policies might be appropriate for them.

I start by looking backward. Race has long been a contentious issue in America, and over the years many brilliant people have said wise and insightful things about it. (An awful lot of nonsense has been spouted too, of course.) Chapter 2 summarizes several major statements from the past century and a quarter, tries to think about them in modern economic terms, and outlines some of the questions that these statements raise about race in the United States today. They also let us see the challenges and opportunities that writing in the twenty-first century presents: the issues are not always precisely the issues that matter now and the analytic methods are often crude by today's standards. I come back to these questions again and again in the rest of the book. They put this book in historical context and link the chapters together.

Chapter 3 goes back even further—millions of years further. This chapter tries to explain what race means, so it has to look at how our species, *Homo sapiens sapiens*, got to be what it is, how members of the species differ from each other, and why. The variation that biology explains, however, is not the entire story of what race means today or what it has meant in American history. So this chapter has to move away from natural science and look toward decision theory, philosophy, and more recent history to understand what people mean when they talk about race today.

After these two introductory chapters come ten chapters on specific areas: health, labor, immigration, education, social interaction and marriage, housing and neighborhoods, homeownership, crime, businesses and entrepreneurship, and wealth. Each of these chapters follows roughly a similar format. I begin by looking at racial disparities, then I consider explanations (benign or not) for the racial disparities, and finally I examine policies that might alleviate the disparities that should be alleviated.

I don't cover every aspect of race in the United States today. I leave out politics, for instance—not because it's unimportant or color blind but because many other works cover politics far better than I could. There is a literature on discrimination in consumer markets—cars, for instance—that doesn't seem to fit in well with anything I cover. The racial implications of an aging white population that is supported in many ways by a minority working-age population are also beyond the scope of this book; I just don't understand yet what this will mean (though I hope to live long enough to become part of the problem). Despite these omissions, the book discusses most major racial issues in the United States today.

The last substantive chapter (Chapter 14) is about reparations. You can't claim to have thought seriously about race in the United States unless you've wrestled with ideas of reparations.

The conclusion returns to the questions the classic texts raised and tries to answer them. It brings the book full circle.

2

Classic Texts

The main reason why people want to study race in the United States is because they think about it as a problem, not just as a curiosity. I could write a book about left-handedness and it would be fun but nobody would really care.* Nobody would be passionate and there would be no need to be explicit about conventions and rules the way I was in the last chapter.

If you subscribe to the idea that race in the United States is a problem—or disagree with it—you have to be able to articulate what kind of problem race is. What's wrong? Why should we be upset or ashamed or outraged or worried or even complacent? Why should you devote your valuable time to reading a book on race?

One way to start thinking about these questions is to read what brilliant people over the last century or more have said about the problem of race in the United States. That's the purpose of this chapter.

We're not studying race in a vacuum. You aren't the first smart people to have landed on this planet. But times change and we need to think about how things are the same and how they are different. And we have three great advantages: hindsight, computing power, and lots of data.

---

* According to Goodman (2014, 94), left-handed people "score . . . lower on measures of cognitive skill, and . . . have more emotional and behavioral problems, have more learning disabilities such as dyslexia, complete less schooling, and work in occupations requiring less cognitive skill."

This chapter is about six texts written long ago. If you study race in America, everyone will presume that you've read them. They give you some rough historical context and some humility—a lot of bright ideas that you thought of yesterday were really around a century ago.

These classic statements introduce this book's main questions. They give possible answers as well. Reading these texts seriously is a good way to start thinking about race in the United States.

Booker T. Washington's Atlanta Address (1895)

By 1895, Booker T. Washington had become the unquestioned leader of African Americans in the United States. He was a self-made man who was born into slavery but rose to become the head of the Tuskegee Institute, a historically black college in Alabama; he was a best-selling author; and he was the first of his race to dine (officially) with the president of the United States. The occasion for the speech was the opening of the Cotton States and International Exposition in Atlanta, to which Tuskegee had contributed an exhibit. The speech is only about the South.

Washington was speaking to an audience mainly of white men, and probably these were the people he most wanted to hear his message. But ostensibly he was talking to blacks; talking to whites was above his station: "To those of the white race . . . , were I permitted, I would repeat what I say to my own race" (Washington [1895] 2012, 61).

What problem was Washington talking to black people about? They didn't have enough education or skills or property. The reason was that thirty years earlier, at the end of the Civil War, black people had almost nothing: "As we present . . . an exhibition of our progress, you must not expect overmuch. Starting thirty years ago with ownership here and there in a few quilts and pumpkins and chickens . . . remember the path from these . . . has not been trodden without contact with thorns and thickets" (61).

In other words, the lack of wealth and education thirty years before was a sufficient explanation for why blacks weren't rich and successful in 1895. The implication was that if blacks had been as educated and skillful and wealthy as whites had been thirty years before, blacks would have been as educated and skillful and wealthy as whites in 1895. Take two families in 1865, one black and one white, who were the same in education, health, and wealth. They would still be the same in 1895.

Your parents matter, not your race, according to Washington. This is a testable proposition and one that you hear in many contexts today—advanced, for instance, by the proponents of class-based rather than race-based affirmative action.

Accordingly, Washington thought that black people should concentrate on the activities and goals that were appropriate for their current endowments and stage of development; the rest would come in time. They should work their way up the skill ladder: "No race can prosper until it learns that there is as much dignity in tilling a field as in writing a poem. It is at the bottom of life that we must start and not at the top" (61).

Washington saw social segregation as nothing to worry about in 1895 because it didn't impede progress up the skill ladder: "The opportunity to earn a dollar in a factory just now is infinitely more worthwhile than the opportunity to spend a dollar in an opera house. . . . It is important and right that all privileges of the law be ours, but it is vastly more important that we be prepared for the exercise of these privileges" (64).

Washington's call for prioritizing the factory over the opera house assumed that access to and success in the factory was independent of access to the opera house. He made this assumption explicit in his famous analogy of the hand: "In all things purely social we can be as separate as the fingers, yet one as the hand in all things essential to mutual progress" (62).

What should blacks do? First, he thought they should stay in the South: "To those of my race who depend on bettering their condition in a foreign land or who underestimate the importance of cultivating friendly relations with the Southern white man, who is their next-door neighbor, I would say: 'Cast down your bucket where you are'—cast it down in making friends in every manly way of the people of all races by whom we are surrounded. . . . When it comes to business, pure and simple, it is in the South that the Negro is given a man's chance in the commercial world" (61).

The question of where black people should live remains a contentious issue today. You hear it, for instance, in the debate about whether black people should return to New Orleans and how gentrification in New York City and Washington, D.C., should be treated.

In the South, the key to black progress was education, according to Washington. This education should be practical—courtesy and hygiene, not Latin and Greek. Whites should support this education because they would gain from more productive and disciplined workers and neighbors: "We shall contribute one-third to the business and industrial prosperity of the South, or we shall prove a veritable body of death, stagnating, depressing, retarding every effort to advance the body politic" (63).

Once again, implicit in Washington's argument is that educational progress could occur in the South, even without social or political equality. His answer would be that since southern whites would benefit from black education, they would support it.

Washington's view of the world is simple, powerful, and consistent and remains popular today. Race is not very important any longer in this view; all that matters is a person's education and character, and these can be produced in a setting where history matters but not race. Not even migration can do much to better a person's education and character. Everything else is "ornamental gew gaws," and racial restrictions in those spheres are not important in the long run: "No race that has anything to contribute to the markets of the world is long in any degree ostracized" (61, 63).

W. E. B. Du Bois's Niagara Movement Speech (1905) and Open Letters to Woodrow Wilson (1913)

The Niagara Movement, which started in 1905, and the National Association for the Advancement of Colored People (NAACP), which was founded in 1909, rejected many aspects of Washington's worldview and almost all of his political approach. W. E. B. Du Bois was a leader in both of these groups.

For Du Bois, race mattered *today*. The Niagara Movement speech cited *current* vote-stealing and *current* discrimination in travel, not something that happened before 1865: "In the past year . . . the work of stealing the black man's ballot has progressed and the fifty or more representatives of stolen voting still sit in the nation's capital. Discrimination in travel and public accommodation has so spread that some of our weaker brethren are . . . simply whispering for ordinary decencies" (Du Bois [1940] 2007, 45).

In a 1913 letter to Woodrow Wilson, Du Bois said that the solution to the race problem was "to see that no man is denied a reasonable chance for life, liberty, and happiness because of the color of his skin" (Du Bois 1913b, 232). Implicit in that statement is the assertion that the race problem existed *in 1913* because some people were being denied reasonable chances *in 1913*. Notice that the statement did not ask for either ex ante or ex post equality, just a floor on inequality.

What Du Bois was saying about the United States in 1905 or 1913 was that your parents matter and your education matters, but your race matters a lot too. Of the two otherwise identical families in 1865 or 1875, the white one will be better off in 1905. Since there were not a lot of otherwise identical families of different races in 1865 or 1875, deciding whether Du Bois or Washington was right is not a trivial econometric problem. Notice that for this controversy it doesn't matter whether the year that race stopped affecting people directly is 1865 or 1875 or 1965 or 2008, as long as that magic year is in the past.

Du Bois rejected Washington's assertion that the spheres of life were independent: "With the right to vote goes everything: freedom, manhood, the honor of your wives, the chastity of your daughters, the right to work, and the chance to rise, and let no man listen to those who deny this" (Du Bois [1906] 1995, 368). In the Wilson letter, he stated, "You cannot make 10,000,000 people at one and the same time servile and dignified, docile and self-reliant, servants and independent leaders, segregated and yet part of the industrial organism, disfranchised and citizens of a democracy, ignorant and intelligent. This is impossible and the impossibility is not factitious; it is in the very nature of things" (Du Bois 1913b, 232).

Du Bois also differed from Washington about which sphere of life was key. Instead of education, Du Bois emphasized voting: "First, we would vote" (Du Bois [1906] 1995, 368). Even within education, Du Bois wanted academic education: "Education is the development of power and ideal. We want our children trained as intelligent human beings should be, and we will fight for all time against any proposal to educate black boys and girls simply as servants and underlings, or simply for the use of other people. They have the right to know, to think, to aspire" (ibid.).

Du Bois did not argue that white people would be better off if blacks were educated like this. That's why voting was necessary in Du Bois's scheme but superfluous in Washington's.

On one point Du Bois and Washington agreed: they don't appear to have cared whether blacks and whites were social friends or whether whites changed their attitudes toward blacks. They thought it would be nice if white attitudes improved but did not think it likely. Du Bois wanted the *right to have* white friends, but he didn't care whether he had any: "No man has the right to choose another man's friends, and to attempt to do so is an impudent interference with the most fundamental human privilege" (Du Bois [1940]

2007, 46). In the letter to Wilson, he made this "the right to choose one's own wife and dinner companions" (Du Bois 1913a, 236). (Notice that he said nothing about choosing one's husband.)

But while neither Du Bois nor Washington called for white attitudes to improve, Du Bois had an explicit agenda for political action that would mainly involve whites: "We want to vote. We want our children educated. We want lynching stopped. We want no longer to be herded as cattle on street cars and railroads. We want the right to earn a living, to own our own property and to spend our income unhindered and uncursed" (ibid., 237). To Du Bois, the problem of race was that the legal structure was permitting or forcing these things to happen.

Thus, Du Bois, like Washington, had a consistent picture of the world and an agenda that arose naturally from that view. Du Bois's picture is no less popular today than Washington's. But the two pictures are very different, and the tools of modern economics can do a lot to sort out the differences.

In the long run, many of the measures that Du Bois called for were adopted; nothing in the Du Bois agenda is controversial today. Washington's agenda, on the other hand, was ignored: black people did not stay in the South and white southerners did not open their purses to educate them. Thus we can ask a question about Du Bois's agenda that we can't ask about Washington's: Has it worked out the way he thought it would?

Gunnar Myrdal's *An American Dilemma: The Negro Problem and Modern Democracy* (1944)

Gunnar Myrdal was a Swedish economist. He won the 1974 Nobel Memorial Prize and also served for a time as Sweden's minister of trade and commerce. In 1938, the Carnegie Foundation asked him to come to the United States and lead a team of social scientists working on "the Negro problem." He began his work by traveling through the South, alone, talking to people. His book, *An American Dilemma,* summarizes the results of this large study.

What was "the Negro problem" that Myrdal studied? There were three main aspects. First, for blacks, there was the problem of intellectual cramping. Myrdal quoted James Weldon Johnson: "And this is the dwarfing, warping, distorting influence which operates upon each and every coloured man in the United States. He is forced to take his outlook on all things, not from the view-point of a citizen, or a man, or even a human being, but from the view-point of a *coloured* man" (Myrdal [1944] 1996, 30).

Second, also for blacks, was the problem of poverty: "Except for a small minority enjoying upper or middle class status, the masses of American Negroes . . . are destitute." But poverty per se was not the problem; the problem was lack of equal opportunity (205, 214).

Finally, the Negro problem was a problem for whites too, because of the hypocrisy, evasiveness, and bad conscience that the condition of black people caused. Myrdal quoted both Du Bois and Washington approvingly on this point. Du Bois said of white people that they "cannot cite the caste-leveling precepts of Christianity, or believe in equality of opportunity for all men, without coming to feel . . . that the present drawing of the color-line is a flat contradiction to their beliefs and professions" (42). Myrdal also quoted James Weldon Johnson: "The race question involves the saving of black America's body and white America's soul" (43).

Thus Myrdal followed Washington's Atlanta Address in identifying the race problem as something that was holding back the full human development of both blacks and whites, but he defined human development more broadly than making money. He followed Du Bois's Niagara Movement speech by identifying the problem as something occurring in the present, not something that ended in 1865. For Myrdal, race mattered in 1940, not just parents.

Myrdal differed from both Washington and Du Bois in that he did not identify any single key sphere on which to focus. Instead, he worked with the "principle of cumulation," or vicious and virtuous circles. He presumed "a general interdependence between all the factors in the Negro problem. White prejudice and discrimination keep the Negro low in standards of living, health, education, manners and morals. This, in its turn, gives support to white prejudice. White prejudice and Negro standards thus mutually 'cause' each other" (75).

Myrdal thus differed from both Washington and Du Bois. He rejected Washington's independence of the spheres and Du Bois's primacy of the political. He also introduced a new concern, white attitudes, that was absent from both older texts, at least explicitly.

On policy, Myrdal differed little from Du Bois, even though he was writing three decades later. The principle of cumulation gave him a theoretical basis for rejecting panaceas and emphasizing change on many fronts. The new element in Myrdal's policy prescription was a call for a change in white attitudes, although he was not explicit on how to make this happen. But he spent several chapters examining in great detail what whites believed and why they believed it.

Myrdal's view raises many empirical questions. How strong are the links between spheres? Is progress in one sphere always complementary to progress in other spheres, or could it be a substitute? Has progress been in the same direction in all spheres, as Myrdal's theory implies?

Martin Luther King's "I Have a Dream" Speech (1963)

King delivered his "I Have a Dream" speech, probably the most famous American speech of the twentieth century, before a huge crowd, mainly but not exclusively black, at the March on Washington, which was called to press Congress for civil rights legislation.

The problem King identified was injustice—something closer to Du Bois than to Washington and Myrdal. He argued that injustice was a current and ongoing problem, not the diminishing residuum of something that had happened a while ago. There was only a small hint that whites would be better off if justice were done.

Injustice came in many forms: "The life of the Negro is still sadly crippled by the manacles of segregation and the chains of discrimination. . . . There are those who are asking the devotees of civil rights, 'When will you be satisfied?' We can never be satisfied as long as the Negro is the victim of the unspeakable horrors of police brutality. We can never be satisfied as long as our bodies, heavy with the fatigue of travel, cannot gain lodging in the motels of the highways and the hotels of the cities. We cannot be satisfied as long as a Negro in Mississippi cannot vote and a Negro in New York believes he has nothing for which to vote" (King 1963). Like Du Bois and Myrdal, then, King was concerned about different spheres, although he made no effort to link them causally.

King differed from Du Bois in his view on social integration. Unlike Du Bois, King wanted blacks to have white friends and companions, not just the legal right to such friends: "I have a dream that one day on the red hills of Georgia the sons of former slaves and the sons of former slaveowners will be able to sit down together at the table of brotherhood. . . . I have a dream that . . . one day right down in Alabama little black boys and black girls will be able to join hands with little white boys and white girls as sisters and brothers."

The importance of actual friendships followed from Myrdal's principle of cumulation: other spheres could not make progress without progress in the social sphere. But Myrdal did not emphasize this implication.

King also envisioned a world in which, at least in some spheres, race did not matter: "I have a dream that my four little children will one day live in a nation where they will not be judged by the color of their skin but by the content of their character." None of the earlier texts imagined such a world. King did not specify which spheres race would disappear in (would his children be considered as spouses by race-blind potential partners?) or whether race blindness could operate equitably and efficiently in one sphere if other spheres were not race blind.

Of course, King was giving an inspirational speech, not writing an economics book, so he didn't have to consider these questions. But we do.

Malcolm X's "The Ballot or the Bullet" Speech (1964)

Malcolm X gave his "Ballot or Bullet" speech in Cleveland shortly after he broke with Elijah Muhammad. Congress still had not passed the civil rights laws that the peaceful, nonviolent March on Washington had demanded the year before. Parts of the civil rights movement were becoming angrier.

Like Washington's Atlanta Address, this speech was directed to black people, and like Washington, Malcolm said that the problem to be addressed was a failure of black people. But for Malcolm, the problem was that black people had sought too little, not that they had sought too much:

> It's time for you and me to stop sitting in this country, letting some cracker senators, Northern crackers and Southern crackers, sit there in Washington, D.C. and come to a conclusion in their mind that you and I are supposed to have rights. There's no white man going to tell me anything about my rights. Brothers and sisters, always remember, if it doesn't take any senators and congressmen and presidential proclamations to give freedom to the white man, it is not necessary for legislation or proclamation or Supreme Court decisions to give freedom to the black man. (Malcolm X [1964] 2009, 411)

For Malcolm, as for Du Bois, Myrdal, and King, the problem was on-going, not just a residuum of history, and as with Du Bois and Myrdal, he saw spheres as linked. Tightly linked, in fact: social, political, legal, and economic activity were all controlled by white people whose interests were fundamentally antagonistic to those of blacks: "The same government that you go abroad to fight for and die for is the government that is in a conspiracy to deprive you of your voting rights, deprive you of economic opportunities, deprive you of decent housing, deprive you of decent education" (407). It made no sense to Malcolm, therefore, to attempt integration in any sphere.

The solution was for blacks to establish their own social, political, and economic domain:

> The political philosophy of black nationalism means that the black man should control the politics and politicians in his community; no more.
>
> The economic philosophy of black nationalism is . . . that we should control the economy of our community. Why should white people be running all the stores in our community? Why should white people be running the banks of our community? . . . Our people have to be made to see that any time you take your dollar out of your community and spend it in a community where you don't live, the community where you live will get poorer and poorer and the community where you spend your money will get richer and richer. . . .
>
> The social philosophy of black nationalism only means that we have to get together and remove the evils, the vices, alcoholism, drug addiction, and other evils that are destroying the moral fiber of our community. We ourselves have to . . . make our own society beautiful so that we will be satisfied in our own social circles and won't be running around here trying to knock our way into a social circle where we're not wanted. (410)

Thus Malcolm was echoing Washington and Du Bois on the unimportance of interracial friendships. But he went further and was in a sense more consistent: he was not seeking close interracial cooperation in any other sphere of life either. For over three centuries, white people had shown themselves to be deceitful, untrustworthy, and exploitive toward blacks and continuing this arrangement made no sense for blacks:

> I'm not going to sit at your table and watch you eat, with nothing on my plate, and call myself a diner. Sitting at the table doesn't make you a diner, unless

you eat some of what's on that plate. . . . Being here in America doesn't make you an American. . . . No, I'm not an American. I'm one of the 22 million black people who are victims of Americanism. . . . When you take your case to Washington, D.C., you're taking it to the criminal who's responsible; it's like running from the wolf to the fox. They're all in cahoots together. (406)

Malcolm's argument has a great deal of intellectual coherence. For some context, think about the many nations of the world. Few economists advocate one-world government. For markets to operate well in a world of imperfect information, participants have to have at least a modest level of trust in each other and in the operations of a legal system that will settle disputes among them. Legal systems need some degree of public cooperation—victims have to report crimes voluntarily and at least a few witnesses have to testify voluntarily and truthfully. Governments can't undertake worthwhile projects unless there are at least a few common interests that almost all citizens recognize. Thus, for instance, in South Asia today no one wants to put India and Pakistan back together. According to Malcolm, the integrationist enterprise was as foolhardy and wasteful as trying to reunite India and Pakistan.

Nationalism doesn't require the full trappings of nationhood such as armies, Olympic teams, currencies, embassies all over the world, and tariff barriers. Monaco, Luxemburg, Quebec, the Basque Autonomous Region, and Scotland are all evolving experiments in nationalism. (And a black or Hispanic America would dwarf all these entities—and the rest of Canada and the combined nations of Scandinavia—in terms of trained military personnel, population, income, world cultural impact, and athletic achievement.) Malcolm didn't have any precise plan, but he raised a serious question about whether the integration that King called for was a reasonable goal.

Both King and Malcolm were trying to estimate what the future would look like. We're now living in that future, and we have good data. We should have better information on the impact of civil rights laws and other innovations of the 1960s and whether the black nationalist route is, or would have been, a better one.

Black nationalism per se has not been especially popular in recent decades. Large numbers of Hispanics and Asians want to leave Hispanic and Asian nations and come to the United States. So do many blacks from Africa and nations of the African diaspora. But Malcolm's mercantilist ideas on black business and community development still exert considerable influence. More important, on an intellectual level his theory is solid and we will examine how it has fared.

The Kerner Commission's *Report of the National Advisory Commission on Civil Disorders* (1968)

In the summer of 1964, riots broke out in Harlem; in 1965, Watts; in 1967, Newark and Detroit and many other communities. People were killed; property was destroyed. In these riots, blacks attacked stores and other establishments in their neighborhoods. These riots were smaller and less deadly than the riots of the early part of the twentieth century, when whites attacked blacks and black neighborhoods. Nevertheless, the 1960s riots created anxiety in the white population, particularly among the owners of downtown real estate in major cities. Harlem, after all, is only one express subway stop from midtown Manhattan. Unrest among young people over the Vietnam War probably added to this anxiety.

Soon after the Detroit riot, President Johnson appointed the National Advisory Commission on Civil Disorders to examine the riots and tell him what should be done. It was a distinguished commission: headed by the governor of Illinois, Otto Kerner, it included the mayor of New York City, the police chief of Atlanta, several members of Congress, and leaders of national unions, corporations, and civil rights organizations. There was even a woman member. Two members were black and one was a Native American. They hurried through their work, afraid of another outburst of violence the next summer, and produced a report in March 1968, a month before Dr. King was assassinated.

This report, then, like Myrdal's book, was addressed to the government (including the Federal Reserve Board) and to opinion leaders—primarily white people. It was also entirely about the North, especially northern cities. This is the opposite of the geographical focus of Washington, Myrdal, and, indeed, King, all of whom concentrated on the South. There is little mention of the 1964 Civil Rights Act, since that was seen largely as a southern issue.

The problem the report addresses is obviously the riots, but at this time many people thought the riots would keep going every summer unless something were done. Such a future would be a disaster: "Our nation is moving toward two societies, one black, one white, separate and unequal." Continued violence and continued separation "leads to the destruction of basic democratic values" (National Commission on Civil Disorders 1968, 1). To translate this prognosis into twenty-first-century images, the United States was becoming a society torn by low-level terrorism—not suicide bombs but arsonists and looters. Cities—the nation's most valuable and most productive real estate—couldn't function under this threat. The concern, then, was maintaining order and letting the economy function. Much of the report was about police tactics.

Notice that this analysis was not far from Malcolm's: a society is not viable without some degree of common feeling and good will, and the United States appeared not to have that degree. The Kerner Commission's view was also close to Malcolm's view about the culprit behind the disharmony.

That culprit was white racism—bad attitudes on the part of whites. The report's language here is often not especially accusatory; the passive voice abounds. You have to read the report carefully and deduce that white attitudes were what was causing the problem. A few sections, however, are more explicit: "In addressing the question 'Why did it happen?' . . . certain fundamental matters are clear. Most fundamental is the racial attitude and behavior of white Americans toward black Americans. Race prejudice has shaped our history decisively; it now threatens to affect our future. White racism is essentially responsible for the explosive mixture which has been accumulating in our cities since the end of World War II" (5).

This conclusion was similar to Myrdal's and Malcolm's, but it carried none of Myrdal's careful analysis. We never learn what exactly these problematic attitudes were or why whites (and not blacks) should have them.

At any rate, the commission thought that these attitudes led to unemployment for blacks, bad policing, bad housing, and bad schools. This list of intermediate concerns was much closer to the concerns of Washington than to those of Du Bois or Myrdal. There was virtually nothing about voting or integrated public facilities (the commission appeared to assume that these were southern issues) or about health and health care (except possibly as ancillary to poor housing). Nor was Vietnam mentioned, although as a demographic group, the young black men who were leading the riots were also being drafted and dying in Vietnam in large numbers.

What should be done? Although the commission's analysis about the problem agrees in many ways with Malcolm's, they didn't go to his final step: they thought that with serious effort harmony could be achieved.

One way the commission members hoped to achieve harmony was through therapy: "increasing communication across racial lines to destroy stereotypes, halt[ing] polarization, end[ing] distrust and hostility" (11). This resembled Myrdal's program of changing white attitudes, but the commission also sought to change black attitudes directly. (Myrdal thought that black attitudes would change indirectly as a result of changes in white attitudes and objective conditions.)

The Kerner Commission also hoped that spending a lot more money would bring more harmony. They were much more specific about spending than they were about therapy, but their plan lacked coherence. You could see a committee at work, one that was operating under tight deadlines.

They began with a careful discussion of whether it would be better to encourage black people to move away from the centralized segregated neighborhoods where they were concentrated in 1968 (and still are, although to a smaller extent) or to try to keep people in place and make the neighborhoods better. Essentially, the question was whether to move the people to the opportunities or move the opportunities to the people. This was a major issue in Washington's time—we've seen his recommendation to keep the people in place in the South—and still is one today. We'll look at it in detail in Chapter 9.

The Kerner Commission concluded that moving people to opportunities was the better strategy; they called this integration. The chapter on this topic was a careful, scholarly piece of work; you would say this even if you disagreed with the conclusion. But then they said that integration wouldn't be achieved in the lifetimes of most black people, so let's enrich the ghetto instead. They didn't say why integration wouldn't be achieved soon or when it would be achieved.

When they got to actual programs, most of the connection with the analysis disappeared. In keeping with the pro-integration conclusion, they recommended an open housing law and reduced segregation in schools, but they didn't say how to achieve the latter (busing, reduced residential segregation, or what?). But they recommended that a lot more money be spent on enrichment programs to keep blacks in segregated neighborhoods, particularly housing construction programs. Finally, they recommended much larger employment and training programs (including public sector jobs) and more

generous welfare payments ("Yet if the deepening cycle of poverty and de-
pendence on welfare can be broken, if the children of the poor can be given
the opportunity to scale the wall that now separates them from the rest of
society, the return on this investment will be great indeed" [256]). Since most
unemployed people and most poor people were white, these programs would
spend most of their money helping white people; it's not clear whether they
were part of either an integration strategy or an enrichment strategy. (But
jobs and welfare may be a good strategy for keeping black people calm and
avoiding riots.)

Notice that affirmative action, either in employment or in education, was
not one of their recommendations, even though the Kerner Commission report is often seen as the epitome of 1960s establishment racial liberalism.

The report also contained no explicit recommendation to the Federal Reserve, but keeping employment high was a constant theme. Standard macroeconomic histories portray the late 1960s as a time when the Federal
Reserve made a serious mistake by keeping monetary policy too expansionary; this led to the inflation of the 1970s and early 1980s. Reading the
Kerner Commission report gives you an insight into why the Federal Reserve may have acted this way: it was scared.

The macroeconomic difficulties this expansionary policy led to, then, can
be seen as part of the cost of the 1960s riots, or, more broadly, as an example
of why a society torn by racial antagonism functions poorly. Washington,
Malcolm X, and the Kerner Commission all worked from this premise, but
they reach different policy conclusions.

Conclusion

Several questions emerge from these texts.

1. Does race matter today or is it just a proxy for history? Are the differences between races we observe today solely a residuum of past
   events or are the events unfolding today amplifying those differences?
   I'll take Washington as representative of writers who say that parents and history are all that matter and Du Bois as representative of
   those who say that race matters today (although the other four of our
   texts agree with Du Bois).

2. How independent are the different spheres of life? Can they be separated? Again, I'll take Washington as representative of the view that connections are weak and separation is easy (the analogy of the hand) and Myrdal and Malcolm as representative of the opposite view.
3. What sphere is key to progress? Some writers identify key spheres—education for Washington, voting for Du Bois—but Myrdal says everything's interrelated and no sphere is key.
4. How important is interracial friendship and understanding? King, Myrdal, and the Kerner Commission want more of it; Washington, Du Bois, and Malcolm don't care.
5. Is a society with many different races, especially a society where one race has exploited another, possible and desirable? Washington, Myrdal, King, and the Kerner Commission say yes; Malcolm says no. Du Bois had many different ideas on this question.

These questions are the major themes this book is built around.

These statements are old, and in all of them nobody has any doubts that races are well-defined—everybody has precisely one and it's obvious what that is. Even the most modern, the Kerner Commission report, refers to "The Negro" as an ideal representation of a mass of disparate people. King uses the same language, while Malcolm refers to "The Black Man" and "The White Man" as if all of his listeners know who these two gentlemen are. There are no Hispanics, Asians, or Native Americans in these texts; that was how the world was then. There are also practically no women.

In the twenty-first century, race is not as simple as these writers thought it was. A sixth question for this book is: Which ideas from these writers will survive the demise of their concept of race? We begin in the next chapter with a serious examination of the concept of race.

3

What Is Race?

Races are labels that have a little something to do with genetics, something to do with culture and social networks, something to do with conventions, and even something to do with individual choice. Exactly what they are today is hard to describe, and I'll spend most of this chapter working at that hard task. Since this is a book about race, I need to begin by discussing what "race" means today. But to do that, I have to start by looking at what "race" has meant in the past. If you want to understand race, you can't ignore the past.

The old story on race reminds me of the miasma theory of disease: it's wrong, but people used to think it was right and it remains influential. In the middle of the nineteenth century, people thought that "miasma"— basically, rotten smells—caused diseases such as cholera and tuberculosis, so they designed sewers that mixed human excreta with storm water runoff in order to move the bad smells into lakes or rivers as quickly as possible. We know now that this is a terrible idea, but New York and other older cities are still stuck with hundreds of miles of combined sewers that empty into major waterways. Just as you can't understand New York's sewers today without the miasma theory, you can't understand "race" today without the old story.

The old story is built around two ideas: species and essence.

The Old Story: Racial Essences

Start with the two pictures in Figures 3.1 and 3.2. The picture in Figure 3.1 is Nell; the picture in Figure 3.2 is Garrett.

You probably don't know either of these creatures. Consider the following questions:

Which one of them is better at reading?
Which one is better at chasing mice?
Do they have the same maternal grandfather?
If they don't, which maternal grandfather is better at reading?

Most of you should consider these questions very easy. But realize what you have done in answering them: you've judged Nell and Garrett by the fur on their faces rather than the "content of their character." You've drawn inferences about their mental abilities from their physical appearances. Not only that: you've drawn inferences about their ancestors' mental abilities from their physical appearances. You've never even seen pictures of their maternal grandfathers and you don't know their names, but you're ready to pronounce judgment on them.

In making these inferences, you've probably relied on the idea of "cat" and the idea of "human." If I asked you to explain your answer on grandfather's reading, you'd say something like this: "Based on their pictures, Nell is a cat and Garrett is a human. So Nell's grandfather is a cat too, and Garrett's grandfather is a human. Humans read better than cats do." You wouldn't go directly from Nell's pointy ears and bushy tail (the features that made you attach the label "cat" to her) to her grandfather's probable reading problems.

All of us can answer these questions easily because we believe that there are very high correlations among cat characteristics and between the characteristics of relatives of cats. That's because there's something distinctive about Nell's family tree—it's all cats. And Garrett's family tree is all humans. If you want to find a common ancestor, you have to go back at least 65 million years. The tradition is that species are defined by the interfertility criterion: two creatures are different species if they can't mate and produce fertile offspring. Because Nell can't mate with mosquitoes (even if she hadn't

Figure 3.1. Nell. (Photo courtesy of Mary Gallagher.)

Figure 3.2. Garrett Augustus Hobart.

been spayed), none of her grandchildren will have wings. (This definition of species, while not unique, is also the most commonly used.)

Despite some high correlations, cats are not all alike. Some are ginger colored, some are cow patterned, some are long haired, some are short haired, some are big, some are little, and some have only three legs. In the seventeenth, eighteenth, and early nineteenth centuries, when Europeans were first encountering the rest of the world and trying to classify what they found, scientists thought that each species had an "essence" that was passed down from generation to generation, starting in the Garden of Eden. The essence was what made cats cats: individual realizations of the essence might differ, but they were all accidental variations on the ideal cat. The ideal cat was something like the cat that Adam and Eve had in the Garden of Eden. So we could talk about "The Cat" as the ideal or essence, even though individual cats differed in one way or another. Plato's influence is obvious.

Because all cats shared the same essence of "catness," they had characteristics that were correlated with the ideal of the cat, so they had characteristics that were correlated with each other. That was how you could reach the conclusion that Nell's grandfather was a lousy reader, even though you had never seen him.

By the nineteenth century, scientists came to believe that races had essences too, just like species. Not just physical characteristics, but also habits of mind and moral attributes. Just as you could say, "The Cat is by nature aloof," so you could say something about "the Negro," or "the Chinaman." Thinking that the world works this way is called *racial essentialism*. (You can see this linguistic construction even in the 1960s in the speeches of King and Malcolm and the report of the Kerner Commission.)

Du Bois (1897, 8) provides an eloquent statement of racial essentialism (although in his later years he moved away from this idea): "Turning to real history, there can be no doubt, first, as to the widespread, nay, universal, prevalence of the race idea, the race spirit, the race ideal, and as to its efficiency as the vastest and most ingenious invention of human progress. We, who have been reared and trained under the individualistic philosophy of the Declaration of Independence and the laisser-faire philosophy of Adam Smith, are loath to see and loath to acknowledge this patent fact of human history. We see the Pharaohs, Caesars, Toussaints and Napoleons of history and forget the vast races of which they were but epitomized expressions."

The Bible story (Genesis 10) of Noah's sons—Ham, Shem, and Japheth—was often part of racial essentialism. Each of the sons started a separate family tree (the so-called ancient candelabrum) and the separate family trees support separate essences: whatever it is that started with Ham passed down to all Ham's descendants. All Ham's descendants share this essence.

As science progressed, various versions of racial essentialism in the nineteenth century moved beyond the Bible and maintained that the races were created separately—that there were many different Gardens of Eden around the world. This idea is called polygenesis. Polygenesis also maintained that while different races could produce offspring, these offspring were infertile or substantially less fertile—not virile—like mules (otherwise frequent interracial mating would render polygenesis irrelevant over time). Supporters of polygenesis included major scientists like Louis Agassiz.

When we refer to people with parents who look different from each other as "multirace" we presume something like the combination of two essences. This expression is left over from racial essentialism. No one is any purer version of anything than anyone else, really—Barack Obama is pure Barack Obama just as Xi Jinping is pure Xi Jinping. The idea of "blood"—as in "one-quarter white blood"—is also generally essentialist. Some of the arguments for some varieties of reparations also resemble essentialism—that certain moral obligations or rights adhere in the essence of a race and so are passed down from generation to generation, like Ham's curse. (There are also non-essentialist approaches to reparations, which I'll discuss in Chapter 14.)

What Do Scientists Now Believe about Racial Essentialism?

What do scientists now believe about racial essentialism? Bottom line: they believe it's wrong.

What we know about genetics now is not consistent with racial essentialism. The human genome consists of a large number of individual discrete pieces or words. Eye color, nose shape, resistance to AIDS or malaria, handedness, tooth shape, whether you have teeth, the number of fingers are all determined by the genome. We don't fully understand all of it yet. But each little piece corresponds to some little trait (often in some combination with other pieces), and most things are inherited pretty much discretely. Some of this genetic material controls structure of the brain—contributing to schizophrenia and developmental disorders, for instance.

Sex characteristics are different. In mammals, the presence of a Y chromosome in a blastocyst causes the production of large amounts of testosterone, and in a fetus, this testosterone causes the development of a panoply of distinct organs. As a result, there are strikingly high correlations among some characteristics. By contrast, no hormone or any other mechanism causes all the characteristics associated with any race. If, for instance, dark skin and curly hair are correlated, it is not because some gene turns on an Africa-hormone in fetal development. Thus the saying: "No race gene." That's why it's easier to operate a Women's NBA than a white boys' NBA.

All humans are the same species—they can mate and produce fertile off-spring. But "*can* produce fertile offspring" is different from "*have* produced fertile offspring." There haven't been a lot of marriages between Norwegians and Maoris. So if Norwegians and Maoris have gone many generations with almost no intermarriage, it's plausible that they have developed different hereditary characteristics, and the racial essentialist story is approximately right—if you knew something about one characteristic that was part of the Norwegian essence and not part of the Maori essence, you could infer other characteristics that were also part of the Norwegian essence.

Why do populations that have had little intermarriage in a long time have different characteristics? Geneticists say the reasons are random variation, sexual selection, and natural selection. Malaria resistance is a well-known case of natural selection. We don't know whether skin color variation was produced by natural selection or sexual selection. Fingerprint styles are probably an example of random variation.

How different humans are from each other is an empirical question. If there's really been a lot of geographic separation and endogamy (reproducing within the same group) and different groups of humans have been subjected to considerably different evolutionary forces, then geographically separated groups of humans would be like different species, or at least like different dog breeds. (Different evolutionary forces are important—Bornean and Sumatran orang utans have been separated for about 1.4 million years yet can interbreed and produce fertile offspring.) If not, then you can't get a lot of natural science information from knowing where someone is from or observing a few characteristics.

What do the majority of physical anthropologists today say? All modern humans—the shorthand is AMH, for anatomically modern humans—are descendants of a handful of people who lived in East Africa about 200,000 years ago. For most of human history, we all lived in Africa, although maybe some groups became relatively isolated in Africa. For most of human history, we were hunter-gatherers. There weren't many of us; before agriculture was invented, maybe about 5 million humans were alive at any time. That's about the population of Singapore (Zimmer 2013a).

Anatomically modern humans started leaving Africa about 100,000 years ago, but the timing of the migrations is controversial. AMHs were in the Levant 115,000 years ago, and there was at least one more exodus from Africa after that. One exodus from Africa went to the Middle East and Europe. A later group went to Asia. About 10,000–20,000 years ago, another band went to Australia and the Pacific Islands, possibly from Asia. People from Asia went across the Bering Strait and spread out across the Americas between 15,000 and 25,000 years ago.

This process could have happened in two different ways. One possibility is that the leavers could have left Africa and never gone back. Or they could have left the Middle East for China and never gone back. Then you would get a tree or candelabrum, as in the story of Noah's sons.

Alternatively, there could have been a lot of movement and gene flow back and forth. If you can walk from Africa to Europe, you can walk from Europe to Africa.

A lot of evidence suggests that the second story, the two-way gene flow, is what happened. If you had a tree, you'd expect Chinese and Europeans to be equally distant from Africans genetically, like Mbuti and Bayaka pygmies (who are equally distant from other Africans genetically). But they're not; Europeans are closer to Africans than Chinese are. In fact, genetic distances between groups are correlated very closely with physical distances, as two-way gene flow would imply.

One of the accidents that happened during these migrations is that anatomically modern humans encountered Neandertals somewhere near the Middle East or in Europe and they encountered Denisovans in Southeast Asia. Neandertals were hominins whose ancestors left Africa between 400,000 and 700,000 years ago and thrived for many hundreds of thousands of years in Europe and the Middle East before going extinct about 30,000 years ago. They were not anatomically modern humans, but they are closely related—that's why they're called hominins. Similarly, Denisovans probably left Africa about the same time and lived in Siberia and Southeast Asia. (Everything we know about Denisovans now comes from part of a pinkie and part of a tooth.)

AMHs interbred with Neandertals and Denisovans, and as a result, most non-Africans carry some Neandertal genetic material and most Melanesians carry some Denisovan genetic material. Among non-Africans, about 2.5 percent of genetic material is Neandertal, and for several groups of Melanesians, about 5 percent of genetic material is Denisovan. This mixture doesn't reflect a great deal of interbreeding; it likely represents a Neandertal and an AMH producing a child about every 30 years (Zimmer 2013b).

Africans don't appear to carry any Neandertal or Denisovan genetic material, as two-way gene flow would seem to imply, but current methods are too crude to answer this question definitively. The proportion of Neandertal material in European and Asian genes is so small that it would be hard to tell whether anything that looked Neandertal in African genes came in during the last few centuries or predated the Neandertal exodus from Africa. The Neandertal genes that survive in Europeans and Asians, moreover, might be well suited for survival outside Africa but not in Africa—they could have been picked up when Neandertals first left Africa and then passed on to later AMH immigrants from Africa.

You should think of these encounters (romantic or not) as just another kind of shock that groups of our ancestors experienced, like encountering cold winters or malaria germs. The encounters don't change the basic picture of a species that originated in Africa, spread over the world, and in the process became different in many ways—but not different enough to start any new species.

Incidentally, DNA differences say that Melanesians are more different from Africans than anybody else is. This provides evidence for the two-way gene flow theory. But Melanesians have dark skin and curly hair. So you can't expect skin color and hair texture to mean much. Similarly, the epicanthic fold (the skin of the upper eyelid covering the inner corner of the eye) is one of the most conspicuous traits of East Asians, but is shared with the Khoisan people of southern Africa, who are genetically quite distant.

So throughout history, on most of the African and the Eurasian land masses, there was a lot of travel and interbreeding. A few groups like the Khoisan and the Mbuti pygmies became more isolated, but isolated groups did not thrive. Invasions and empires such as the Roman Empire, the Indus Valley civilization, and the Tang dynasty brought people together and stirred up the gene pool.

After 1500 there were great migrations that we're aware of: Europeans and Africans to the Americas, Europeans to Australia and New Zealand, Zulus to southern Africa, Asians to Africa and the islands of the Pacific and Indian Oceans. Because of better technology, more mixing and travel occurred after 1500 than before that time.

If you look at the world of 1500, some correlations can be found between genetic traits and geography, hence among genetic traits. Within continents, there's a lot of geographic and genetic variation on a smaller basis too, particularly within the older continents (Sicilians are different Saami, even though they are both Europeans; Ethiopians differ from Gambians). But you'll find almost nothing discrete or automatically correlated, such as sex characteristics.

Still, there are definite correlations. When a person is murdered and the vultures come and eat the flesh off the bones, forensic anthropologists can do a pretty good job of using the body to figure out where most of the body's ancestors were living around 1500. They're close to 90 percent accurate; most of their information comes from the skull. They can also figure out sex.

But in order to be a forensic anthropologist you have to go to school for a few years. You learn about noses and palates, teeth, and ratios between measurements such as head width and head length. If these were all perfectly correlated, you'd only have to learn one or two of them. Weak correlations are what makes forensic anthropology hard. Table 3.1 shows some of the basic correlations that forensic anthropologists work from. Notice that there are no Hispanics in forensic anthropology (although there have been some very recent attempts to include them).

The shape of incisors (East Asians are more likely to have shovel-shaped incisors), blood type (Europeans are more likely to have A or O type blood, Native Americans to have type B), hair, sweating patterns, consistency of ear wax, and color blindness are also correlated with 1500 geography. Some genetic traits are particular to groups defined by smaller regions than continents. The Inuit in North America and Australian Aborigines, for instance, have whorly fingerprints. Many sub-Saharan Africans carry the sickle-cell trait, but not Xhosas, who developed no immunity to malaria because they lived in the more temperate southern tip of Africa. When it comes to malaria resistance, Nelson Mandela, who was Xhosa, looked the same as Bjorn Borg. Tay-Sachs disease, cystic fibrosis, phenylketonuria, and lactose tolerance are also largely confined to particular populations.

So far geneticists have been able to figure out very little about complex conditions, abilities, and traits, such as diabetes, hypertension, running fast, height, intelligence, and impulsiveness. To the extent that there are genetic components to these things, and there probably are, they involve many genes and a lot of interaction. Some of these genes might be correlated with continent in 1500, such as the shape of incisors, and others may not, such as type of fingerprint. Similarly, there are genetic components to how people react to various drugs, and these may have some correlations with 1500s geography. Or they may not.

All of these complex things also involve significant environmental components. Consider height, which we think of as almost purely genetic and pretty simple. But about forty different areas of DNA that affect height have been identified, and these areas can explain less than 5 percent of the

Table 3.1. A partial listing of generalized nonmetric differences among "East Asian," "European," and "African" skulls used in forensic analyses in the United States.

	"East Asian"	"European"	"African"
Vault			
Cranial sutures	complex	simple	simple
Postbregmatic depression	not present	not present	present
Jaws and teeth			
Incisors (maxillary)	shovel-shaped	blade-form	blade-form
Dentition	not crowded	crowded, freq impacted M3	not crowded, large M
Palate shape	parabolic/elliptic	parabolic	hyperbolic/parabolic
Palatine suture	straight/jagged (NA straight)	jagged	arched/jagged
+Mandible	wide & vertical ascending ramus	pinched &slanted/vertical ascending ramus (others—medium, intermediate ramus)	pinched/narrow & slanted ascending ramus
Chin projection	moderate/blunt	projecting/square [bilobate]	blunt/median/retreating
Overall face and orbits			
+Facial height	lesser	greater (less so in Mediterraneans)	greater
Facial and alveolar prognathism	moderate + profile intermediate	little or none + profile straight	marked + profile projecting

Facial width	very wide (a bit less in NA)	narrow	narrow
Zygomatics	projecting, robust (with tubercle)	retreating, small	retreating, small
Zygomaxillary suture	angled	curved	curved/angled
+Orbits	rounded (NA rhomboid)	angular/rhomboid, sloping	rectangular (Gill, Krogman)
Interorbital distance	variable	narrow	wide
Nose			
Aperture	medium	narrow	wide
Nasal bridge	flat/low (NA medium-tented with depression at nasion)	high, arched, steeple-like	low, Quonset hut–like
Nasal sill/lower border	medium, sill to gutter	sharp, sill	guttered, sill very dull or absent
Nasal spine	medium (NA medium/tilted)	prominent, long, large, straight	small, little/none

Sources: This partial listing is drawn from Bass (2005); Gill (1986); Krogman and Iscan (1986); Novotny, İşcan, and Loth (1993); St. Hoyme and İşcan (1989); and White, Black, and Folkens (2011), who in turn draw on older work. It is important to note that not all researchers rely on all of these criteria. Features that are less frequently cited in a cursory review of the extensive literature are indicated with "+." Also, keep in mind that the charts of these various researchers use Native American (NA) or Asian so that one must take care in combining these data. Used by permission of Professor Jill Shapiro, Department of Ecology, Evolution, and Environmental Biology, Columbia University.

heritability of height in humans (Currie 2011). The environmental influence on height is huge. The average full-grown English man in 1790 was 5 feet, 5 inches tall and the average French man was 5 feet, 3.5 inches tall and 110 pounds. Modern-day eighth-graders in Japan are taller than adult army recruits a century ago.

Similarly, world records in track and swimming keep falling at a prodigious rate, much faster than random variation could explain. Scores on IQ tests have been rising about 2.5 points per decade for descendants of Europeans and about 4.5 points per decade for descendants of Africans in the United States (Dickens and Flynn 2006). But the gene pool has not been changing.

Technology also makes a difference. I was born near-sighted, but because of glasses I'm not near-sighted now. Surgery now allows for permanent correction of this condition.

Of course, there probably is a genetic component to many mental abilities, not just whatever it is that IQ tests have been measuring. Similarly, trustworthiness and patience may have genetic components. But we don't know what they are, and in the world in general today they might be swamped by environmental variation.

Take, for example, speaking Mandarin. There's a correlation between observable traits—epicanthic folds, shovel-shaped incisors, straight black hair—and speaking Mandarin. Could there be a genetic component? Sure—some sort of inborn inclination to put words together in a certain way. But it's probably not worth pursuing. Variation in the environment—homes and schools where Mandarin is taught—is enough to explain an awful lot.

So we can pay attention to these correlations without being essentialists.

Possibly more important is the fact that many nongenetic facts are correlated with easily observable genetic characteristics. In the United States, people with dark skin and curly hair are more likely to be Baptists and to have Baptist parents than people with epicanthic folds. People with Tay-Sachs disease are more likely to read Hebrew than the average American (although Tay-Sachs disease is not confined to Jews in the United States; it's present in Pennsylvania Dutch and Cajuns too). The experiences of life in general are likely to be different for people who have different appearances.

There's nothing natural about this and it could change, but it's the way things are now. Similarly, there's nothing natural or foreordained about the correlations of physical characteristics we observe now. They would be different if economics or transportation had been different, they are different now than they were in 1500 or 1900, and they will be different a century from now. God did not decree that Norwegians and Maoris could not produce fertile offspring, but for a long time such dating has been difficult. The correlation between the presence of breasts and the presence of ovaries is in this sense "natural"; the correlation between dark skin and curly hair is not.

Correlations

I'm spending all this time talking about correlations of traits because of two separate types of reasoning: individual inference and social inference. Individual inference means using the characteristics of a person to make inferences about other characteristics or behavior of that person. Social inference means using the characteristics of a person to make inferences about the behavior of other people.

Individual Inference

If I care about whether you have trait A (being trustworthy, for instance) but that trait is difficult or costly or impossible to observe, then if trait B (having a postbregmatic depression, for instance) is correlated with trait A and is easy to observe, then I can base my observations on trait B. More interestingly, if I care about whether *I* have trait A (the potential to be a great basketball player or a great mathematician) but that trait is difficult or costly or impossible to observe, then if trait B is correlated with trait A and is easy to observe, I can base my observations on trait B.

Notice that this is a very restricted model. If there are more than two traits and two different correlations and observation and computation are not absolutely free, it doesn't always follow that you should use a simple correlation. In more complicated circumstances, following simple correlations can lead you to make poor decisions.

Example: Suppose there are three traits: skin color (red or black), incisor shape (shovel-shaped or not), and imagination (imaginative or not). The world looks like this:

Skin?	Shovel-shaped?	Percent imaginative
Red	No	10
Red	Yes	30
Black	No	20
Black	Yes	40

Each of these four groups is 25 percent of the population.

Suppose you want to hire imaginative people but you can't observe who is imaginative. If you look only at skin, you get information because skin is correlated with imagination: 20 percent of red-skinned people are imaginative and 30 percent of black-skinned people are imaginative. If you hire only people with black skin, you will get 30 percent imaginative. Seems like a good idea. But it really is not.

You could do better. If you hired only people whose incisors were shovel shaped, you would have 35 percent imaginative people. And if you hired only black-skinned people with shovel-shaped incisors, you would have 40 percent imaginative.

So the fact that there's a correlation—in this case, between skin color and imagination—doesn't mean that it's optimal to use that correlation, in general.

Will good inference drive out bad? Perhaps in a competitive market; we'll study this later. But good inference will almost certainly not drive out bad in individual life decisions. If you decide to follow the wrong career path in high school you can't turn around twenty years later, fire the person who made that decision, and try again and keep trying until you get it right.

Social Inference

If I care about how people will act toward you and they act as if trait B matters, then I can base my observations and decisions on trait B. (I and you can be the same here too.) For example, suppose that I think that Bank of America is too big to fail and will always get bailed out when it's in trouble. Then I can lend freely to Bank of America even if I think it's incompetently managed. I can base my actions not on my belief about the bank's competence and soundness, which are hard to observe, but on its size, which is easy to observe, and my beliefs about how the government will react to its size.

It's even less clear that good inference will drive out bad here. Note again that correlation is not enough to show that all is well. Suppose I'm a school looking to enroll people whom advertising firms will eventually hire. My payoff depends on my placement record. Suppose I believe firms think skin color matters, not tooth shape. Then I will be reluctant to admit red-skinned people and will not pay attention to teeth. The correlation between skin color and hiring doesn't show that the system is working well.

What does this analysis of correlation say we should be looking for when we classify people? Some fairly easily observed traits that it seems like a lot of people think that other people think that other people think . . . are correlated with something they care about. That gets close to what we mean by race.

How Does the U.S. Government Measure Race?

Classifying people by some easily observable traits is thus not totally inappropriate. However, essentialism would do the same thing, so the process is fraught with difficulties.

Let me explain how it's done in the United States—not to defend, but so you understand the data. The Office of Management and Budget (OMB) makes the rules. They were first issued in 1977 and have been revised several times since then.

Here are some important principles for how the government measures race:

First, race is self-described. Before 1960, all classification was done by interviewers, but for the major surveys that is no longer the case. Thus classification in the United States is pretty far from the genetic division, although it is somewhat correlated with it. Although the system is officially self-described, many exceptions exist. The following groups are usually described by someone else: kids, people who are not at home at the time of the survey, dead folks, prisoners, and babies. Comparisons often become a problem. For instance, the Hispanic mortality rate is the number of deaths of people whom doctors describe as Hispanic divided by the number of people who describe themselves as Hispanic (more on this in Chapter 4).

Second, race is not unique. You can check more than one box. Very few people do outside of Hawaii, and most of those who do are Hispanics.

Third, the classification is two-dimensional. First, you classify your "ethnicity": either Hispanic or not. I'll come back to explain why Hispanics are an "ethnicity." Then you classify your "race": American Indian or Alaskan Native, Asian, black or African American, Native Hawaiian or other Pacific

Islander, white, or "some other race." (If you check "some other race" you are supposed to fill in a blank that says what that race is.)

Essentially, you put yourself in one or more boxes in this grid

	Hispanic	Not Hispanic
American Indian or Alaskan Native		
Asian		
Black or African American		
Native Hawaiian or Pacific Islander		
White		
Some other race		

But if you put yourself in more than one box, all the boxes have to be in the same column.

Precisely, the categories are defined this way:

- *American Indian or Alaskan Native:* A person having origins in any of the original peoples of North and South America (including Central America) and who maintains tribal affiliation or community recognition.
- *Asian:* A person having origins in any of the original peoples of the Far East, Southeast Asia, and the Indian subcontinent, including Cambodia, China, India, Japan, Korea, Malaysia, Pakistan, the Philippine Islands, Thailand, and Vietnam.
- *Black or African American:* A person having origins in any of the black racial groups of Africa. Terms such as "Haitian" or "Negro" can be used in addition to "Black or African American."
- *Hispanic or Latino:* A person of Cuban, Mexican, Puerto Rican, South or Central American, or other Spanish culture of origin, regardless of race. The term "Spanish origin" can be used in addition to "Hispanic or Latino."
- *Native Hawaiian or Other Pacific Islander:* A person having origins in any of the original peoples of Hawaii, Guam, Samoa, or other Pacific Islands.
- *White:* A person having origins in any of the original peoples of Europe, the Middle East, or North Africa.

It's hard to claim that this system represents some uniquely enlightened way of classifying people, especially when other countries such as South Africa, Brazil, and France have very different systems. It's easy to see puzzles and inconsistencies in the U.S. system.

For instance, the definition of black uses the word "race" but no other definition does; is black the only race? The definition of white includes people from the Middle East and the Maghreb. Does that mean Afghanistan? The definition of Asian is about geography; why is India there, when most Indians are genetically closer to Europeans than to Chinese? To be an American Indian you need ties to a tribe. So if you're white do you need ties to a hockey team? The definition of Hispanic is about language and culture. Why is this term but no other tied to language and culture? What about Indonesians, Brazilians, and Australians? How are they classified?

Notice that this classification makes almost no attempt to tell a genetic story. For the U.S. government, "races" are not racial essences. Perhaps the way to think about the system is that to the U.S. government, "race" means where your ancestors were in 1500 and "ethnicity" means where they were in 1900.

People often change classifications; race in this sense is not immutable. For instance, the American Indian population tripled between 1960 and 1990, largely because of changes in how people identified themselves or were identified (Nagel 1995). There are significant differences between how teens report their race at home and how they report it at school (Harris and Sim 2002). And incarceration makes people less likely to report themselves as white and makes interviewers less likely to classify them as white. A substantial number of people who look white outside a prison look black inside it, even to themselves (Saperstein and Panner 2010). Something as changeable as this could hardly be a racial essence. No matter how she might misbehave, no one will ever mistake my cat Nell for an elephant, and she'll never think that she's an elephant, either.

What Are These Things?

Since the categories the federal government uses aren't racial essences, what are they? Probably the most accurate names would be racial identities or racial identifications. Philosopher Kwame Appiah (1995, 76) tells the story of these terms (but leaves out Hispanics, of course):

> At any time in this history [of the United States] there was, within the American colonies and the United States that succeeded them, a massive consensus, both among those labeled black and those labeled white, as to who, in their communities, fell under which labels. (As immigration from China and other parts of the Far East occurred, the Oriental label came to have equal stability.) . . . The result is that there are at least three sociocultural objects—black, white, and Oriental—whose membership at any time is relatively, and increasingly, determinate. These objects are historical in this sense: to identify all the members of these American races over time, you cannot seek a single criterion that applies equally always; you can find the starting point for the race . . . and then apply at each historical moment that criterion of intertemporal continuity that applies at that moment to decide which individuals in the next generation count as belonging to the group. There is from the beginning a simple rule that few would dispute even today: where both parents are of a single race, the child is of the same race as the parents.

Labels are both social and individual. They're individual in the sense that they shape what people think about themselves and how they should act. They're social in the sense that they shape how people act toward those who have them. The two different aspects of labels show up in the question of the process for determining the race someone belongs to. Self-identification (how the census is taken now) emphasizes the individual role of these labels. Having the interviewer attach the label (how the census was taken up to 1960) emphasizes the social role of these labels.

Are there correlations between having a label and having hard-to-observe traits? Just as you used the label "cat" to go from a picture of a little furry creature with whiskers to a grandfather who didn't read well, you can use these labels to remember correlations. But every step that's added weakens a correlation, unless a social aspect strengthens it. Even if Nell's grandfather was a great potential reader, he is unlikely to have learned how because schools don't enroll cats.

Hispanics

Appiah doesn't talk about Hispanics, but it's clear why not. The label is not a historical one; it dates from around 1970. The genetic story is not very strong because the ancestors of Hispanics were living all over the world in 1500.

The other labels are the result of historical processes, and a historical process also produced this label. The story is long.

It begins with the Treaty of Guadalupe Hidalgo on February 2, 1848, which ended the Mexican American War and transferred most of the southwest from Mexico to the United States. The treaty said that Mexicans living in these territories could become U.S. citizens and have the rights of U.S. citizens, although the Senate made the negotiated treaty a little complicated. In 1848, only whites were eligible for citizenship, which was seen as part of white identity, and the Treaty of Guadalupe Hidalgo made Mexicans "sort of white" but not fully white. In 1849, Mexican delegates to the Texas constitutional convention fought to keep the word "white" out of the state constitution, fearing that they would lose the vote.

In the early twentieth century, Mexican immigration increased and legal segregation and disenfranchisement of blacks was very strong in Texas. At the time, four races were recognized in the United States—black, white, Indian, Oriental—and only whites had anything like rights or votes, especially in Texas.

The League of United Latin American Citizens (LULAC) formed in 1929 in response to this. It soon found itself fighting to have Mexicans classified as white. For instance, a big controversy arose in Galveston in 1936 when an Anglo health official classified Mexicans as colored when recording infant mortality. LULAC prevailed in this controversy. But in the 1940s, it started losing cases when it wanted Mexicans to be treated as white.

The turning point occurred in 1954 with the Supreme Court decision in *Hernandez v. Texas* (347 U.S.475, 1954). Pete Hernandez was a Mexican American who appealed his conviction for murder in Texas. His appeal was based on the fact that the jury that tried him had no Mexican American on it. Moreover, in the county where he was tried, no Mexican American had served on a jury in twenty-five years, even though there was a substantial Mexican American population. Hernandez won.

The most important question before the court was whether Mexican Americans were a class that was subject to the protection of the Fourteenth Amendment. The state of Texas argued that they were white and so were not subject to Fourteenth Amendment protection. Chief Justice Earl Warren said no: to decide whether a group should be protected, you have to look at what's actually happening in a community or area. He cited several pieces of evidence:

1. Residents of the community distinguished between "Mexicans" and "whites."
2. Until recently, Mexican kids had attended a segregated school for the first four years.
3. At least one restaurant had a prominent sign that said "No Mexicans served."
4. At the courthouse, there were two toilets: one unmarked and one labeled "colored" and "hombres aqui."

Notice that none of this evidence was based on genetics.

So you see a change: as minority groups came to be protected, the legal advantages of being white diminished. This change created conflict in the Mexican community between old-timers, who want to be hyphenated whites, and members of the Chicano movement, who wanted to be a minority group. Ethnic group is a realistic compromise, since it carried no genetic story.

Given U.S. history, this compromise makes good sense, but if you just arrived from Mars, it would look crazy.

So once again, history gives us labels that may influence how we live our lives.

Do Labels Matter?

Do labels matter? Appiah says that they do: "Once the racial label is attached to people, ideas about what it refers to, ideas that may be much less consensual than the application of the label, come to have social effects. But they have not only social effects but psychological ones as well; and they shape the ways people conceive of themselves and their projects" (1995, 78).

That's an empirical statement. So it should be testable. In fact, a number of tests have found that Appiah's statement is fairly accurate. Two of these tests involve baseball umpires in the United States and kids working puzzles in India.

Umpires

Parsons et al. (2011) look at all the pitches in Major League Baseball for a couple of years, especially the probability that a pitch was a called strike. Their first major finding is that a pitch is more likely to be a called strike if it is thrown by a pitcher of the same race as the home-plate umpire, holding many things constant. The labels that attach to the umpire and the pitcher matter to the umpire. They seem to matter more when the pitch is not crucial or when the umpire is not being monitored closely, but they matter. Racial identity affects how we act.

More interestingly, strikeouts are more likely when the pitcher and the home-plate umpire are of the same race. But not strikeouts where the third strike is called—instead, swinging strikeouts (where the batter swings and misses) are more likely. Now it's not the umpire who is acting differently because of his race or even the pitcher who is acting differently. Batters apparently swing at worse pitches because they anticipate that the umpire will call them as strikes. The races of the pitcher and of the umpire matter to the batter, as well they should. In a world that is not race blind, an effective batter is not race blind either.

Puzzles

Like races, castes in India are hereditary and hierarchical. Unlike race, caste is based on your parents' occupation, not on your appearance, so it's different from race. Since Myrdal compared race in the United States to caste, we can learn something about identities from two experiments devised by Hoff and Pandey (2006). These experiments involved several hundred children in Uttar Pradesh.

The first experiment asked children to solve mazes and rewarded them for how many they could solve in fifteen minutes. Some kids were from a high caste, some were from a low caste. Everybody was in groups in a classroom.

Classrooms were set up three different ways:

Anonymous—At the start, the experimenter revealed nothing about the other kids in the classroom.

Caste revealed—The classroom held a mixed group of children from different castes. At the beginning, the experimenter turned to each kid and publicly stated his or her name, father, grandfather, caste and asked the kid to nod if the information was correct.

Single caste—Same as the caste-revealed group except everybody in the classroom was in the same caste.

What were the results?

In the anonymous setting, there was no difference between the castes in the number of mazes solved.

In the caste-revealed setting, the differences among the two caste groups were large: compared with performance in the anonymous setting, low-caste children performed considerably worse and high-caste children did about the same.

In the single-caste setting, no difference between castes emerged but everybody did poorly.

The task itself carried no emotional significance, but when a child's caste identity was brought to his or her attention, it changed how he or she acted. These labels matter.

The second experiment involved solving a difficult puzzle, extracting a toy car from a maze. Kids had an opportunity to practice (to see how hard the puzzle was) and then to decide whether to play for real.

If a child decided not to play for real, he or she got 10 rupees.

If a child decided to play for real, he or she got 20 rupees if they succeeded and nothing if they failed. (Twenty rupees is equivalent to about $15 or $20.)

In one version of the gamble, there was no scope for discretion in getting the reward: the player could see the money inside the car. In the other version of the gamble, the player got a promise of a reward, but adults had discretion about disqualifying players and players couldn't see the money.

Each version of the gamble was repeated in the same three settings as before: anonymous, caste revealed, and single caste.

When adults had no scope for discretion and the setting was anonymous or single caste, children in both castes made the same decisions. But in the caste-revealed setting, a difference opened up. When adults had scope for discretion, high-caste kids gambled more, sometimes a lot more. Once again, labels matter for how people act.

Conclusion

What is race? Races are labels that come from history. Races create a partition of people based (to a great extent) on ancestry, with some genetic correlations, and that partition affects how people think about themselves and how others think about them. Race is a part of a person's identity. It is both individual and social. People base their actions on their race and on the races of the people they encounter.

4

Health and Health Care

Health matters a lot: it's both a production good—you work better if you're healthier and you may not work at all if you're sick—and a consumption good—people want to be healthy even if they're not going to work. That also applies to household production; if you're healthier, your kids will be healthier and happier too. And we'll see in Chapter 7 that the type of care you and your mother get just before you're born and just after affects how well you do in school. Health care is a rapidly rising proportion of national spending, largely because it's getting better and demand is elastic. And it's extremely controversial.

For this book, health is a good place to start for several reasons. First, the discussion of racial disparities in health is fairly new (in recent terms anyway; late nineteenth-century economists were convinced that African Americans would become extinct because of their ill health), so attitudes are not so deeply ingrained (health care is not mentioned in any of the three classic statements from the 1960s). Second, health provides concrete applications of several issues from Chapters 2 and 3. Some explanations for disparities are about the long reach of history and some are about current practices; many discussions attribute health disparities to disparities in other areas like employment or housing; and genetics does play a role (how significant is the question).

The chapter starts with brute facts. Then I'll try to explain those facts. Finally, I'll turn to policy—what should we do about these disparities? For most of the other substantive areas in this book I'll follow the same plan of attack.

Racial Disparities in Outcomes

Survival

The best-measured and most obvious health outcome is survival. Correcting for age differences, African Americans are more likely to die in any year than other Americans, and other minority groups appear to be less likely to die. Table 4.1 shows age-adjusted mortality rates for 2008.

"Age-adjusted" means that you take the actual age-specific mortality rates (the proportion of 35-year-olds who died in 2006) and weight them by the age distribution of the total population in a base year—2000, in this case.

This mortality information comes from death certificates. Doctors fill out death certificates; this is one of those jobs like scratching the middle of your back that you can't do for yourself. The race and ethnicity information on death certificates is not self-assessed. That gives the numerator for the mortality rates reported in Table 4.1 (and everywhere else). The denominator is census information, and so race and ethnicity are self-assessed in the denominator.

Table 4.1. Number of deaths per 100,000 age-adjusted population by race/ethnicity, 2008.

White	750.3
Non-Hispanic white	766.2
Black	934.9
Non-Hispanic black	955.2
American Indian/Alaskan Native	610.1
Asian/Pacific Islander	413.7
Hispanic	532.2
Puerto Rican	639.3
Mexican	565.3
Cuban	553.5
Central and South American	259.9

Source: Miniño et al. (2011).

Table 4.2. Historical data on life expectancy at birth in the United States.

	Male			Female		
Year	Black	White	Difference	Black	White	Difference
2008	70.6	76.1	5.5	77.2	80.9	3.7
2006	69.7	75.7	6.0	76.5	80.6	4.1
2005	69.5	75.7	6.2	76.5	80.8	4.3
2001	68.6	75.0	6.4	75.5	80.2	4.7
2000	68.3	74.9	6.6	75.2	80.1	4.9
1995	65.2	73.4	8.2	73.9	79.6	5.7
1990	64.5	72.7	8.2	73.6	79.4	5.8
1985	65.0	71.8	6.8	73.4	78.7	5.3
1980	63.8	70.7	6.9	72.5	78.1	5.6
1970	60.0	68.0	8.0	68.3	75.6	7.3
1960	61.1	67.4	6.3	66.3	74.1	7.8
1950	59.1	66.5	7.4	62.9	72.2	9.3
1940	51.5	62.1	11.6	54.9	66.6	11.7

Sources: Arias (2004), table 12; Heron et al. (2008, 2009); Miniño, Heron, and Smith (2006), table 6; Miniño et al. (2011).

Thus in mortality rates the denominator is self-assessed race and the numerator is not. Because of this inconsistency, American Indian and Alaskan Native (AIAN) and Hispanic death rates are probably understated, and non-Hispanic white (NHW) death rates are somewhat overstated (doctors tend to label as non-Hispanic white some people who identified themselves as AIAN or Hispanic in the census). The Centers for Disease Control estimates that Hispanic death rates are understated by about 5 percent for this reason. This understatement doesn't change the basic picture in Table 4.1.

Another way of summarizing the information in mortality rates is to look at life expectancy. Table 4.2 shows the data for blacks and whites. The gap is narrowing over time, but not without interruption: the gap increased in the 1990s, for instance.

To see something that might be more relevant to college students, consider the probability of surviving from age 20 to age 65 (Table 4.3). This has important implications for Social Security and for investments in education.

Table 4.3. Probability of surviving from age 20 to age 65 by race/ethnicity, based on U.S. life table for 2004 (percent).

	Male	Female
Black	71.6	83.1
Non-Hispanic white	86.2	89.9
Hispanic	85.4	92.1

Source: Arias (2011).

Going to graduate school is a much better idea if you're going to live to be 80 than if you're going to die at 50.

How much does this matter? Since there are about 38 million African Americans and the difference in mortality rates with NHWs is about 210 per 100,000, reducing the African American mortality rate to the NHW mortality rate would save about 7,400 lives—more than twice the mortality of September 11, 2001—every year. Reducing the African American mortality rate to the Hispanic mortality rate would save over 14,800 lives a year—five times the 9/11 mortality.

In dollar terms, the best estimates are that modern Americans on average are willing to pay about $70,000 for a 1 percent reduction in the probability of death—this is the figure that most cost-benefit studies use. This implies that the average African American would be willing to pay about $15,000 a year to have NHW mortality rates, or about $30,000 a year to have Hispanic mortality rates.

That's crude and doesn't take into consideration the fact that people would be willing to pay different amounts at different ages. Murphy and Topel (2005) do a much more sophisticated job of estimating the value of these differences. Table 4.4 shows what they conclude. It reflects just the value of survival: it omits the value of good health and external benefits. Even at this level, the differences are at least as great as the differences in income and earnings. But the difference between blacks and whites is declining over time.

The first place to start understanding these differences is to look at the relevant causes of death, shown in Table 4.5.

The big sources of the difference in mortality between NHWs and African Americans are heart disease and cancer, which are also the sources of the Hispanic advantage. The greatest relative discrepancies are in homicide, nephritis (kidney disease), septicemia, and diabetes.

Table 4.4. Magnitude of the black-white longevity gap: How much an average black person would be willing to pay to have white mortality (at various years and ages).

	Male		Female	
Age	1968	1998	1968	1998
Birth	$408,753	$263,185	$325,704	$167,539
20	536,280	359,624	405,274	220,522
40	542,920	441,189	500,136	289,337

Source: Murphy and Topel (2005), table 5.
Note: All figures in 1998 dollars.

Table 4.5. Leading causes of death in the United States, 2008.

		Ratios of age-adjusted death rates	
	Adjusted death rate	Black/ white	Hispanic/ Non-Hispanic white
All		1.2	0.7
1. Heart disease	186.5	1.3	0.7
2. Cancer	175.3	1.3	0.6
3. Chronic lower respiratory diseases	44.0	0.7	0.4
4. Cerebrovascular diseases	40.7	1.5	0.8
5. Accidents	38.8	0.8	0.7
6. Alzheimer's disease	24.4	0.8	0.6
7. Diabetes	21.8	2.0	1.5
8. Flu and pneumonia	16.9	1.1	0.8
9. Nephritis	14.8	2.2	0.9
10. Suicide	11.6	0.4	0.4
11. Septicemia	11.1	2.1	0.8
12. Liver, cirrhosis	9.2	0.7	1.5
13. Hypertension	7.7	2.5	1.0
14. Parkinson's disease	6.4	0.4	0.6
15. Homicide	5.9	5.3	2.4
HIV	3.3	9.0	2.6

Source: Miniño et al. (2011).

Table 4.6. Infant deaths per 1,000 live births, 2005.

Non-Hispanic black	13.31
Non-Hispanic white	5.63
Hispanic, total	5.51
Mexican	5.42
Puerto Rican	7.71
Cuban	5.18
Central and South American	4.57
Asian/Pacific Islander	4.78
American Indian/Alaskan Native	9.22

Source: Mathews and MacDorman (2011).

Infant mortality is another important cause of death: see Table 4.6. The ratio of black to white infant mortality rates has not been converging to one. Instead, it has been rising over the past half century or so, definitely since 1980. The black-white disparity in infant mortality is growing, at least in ratio terms.

Morbidity

Morbidity means sickness that doesn't result in death. That's a big problem too, but data are harder to come by. On self-reported health, blacks and Hispanics are worse off than whites and Asians. In 2010, the age-adjusted proportion of people reporting excellent or very good health was 69.7 percent for NHWs, 59.3 percent for Hispanics, and 54.5 percent for non-Hispanic blacks (National Health Interview Survey 2011). The same relationship holds for disability rates; blacks have higher disability rates than Hispanics and whites have higher disability rates than Asians. This disparity matters for work, for instance, and for Social Security disability benefits. But whether someone is sick is not as clear-cut as whether someone is dead—self-reports are not always accurate or objective, and whether people know they have a disease can depend on their access to diagnoses.

Asthma and diabetes are two widespread and serious diseases for which racial disparities are large. The age- and sex-adjusted prevalence of diagnosed diabetes was 13.0 percent for Hispanics, 12.6 percent for non-Hispanic blacks, and 7.3 percent for NHWs. The prevalence of asthma seems more dependent on age. Nine percent of non-Hispanic blacks under the age of 15 reported an asthma episode in the previous year, as did 5.2 percent of young Hispanics and 4.8 percent of young NHWs. The disparity in the incidence of asthma was not as great among adults (National Health Interview Survey 2011).

Height

Economists look at height as a measure of healthful childhood, especially in developing countries. On average, taller people had better childhoods (including in utero experience), suffer less from disabling diseases, and will live longer. Although a lot of the individual variation in height within a population is due to genetics, most of the variation in average height between populations is due to childhood and in utero environment. Whether you're taller than the people you grew up with and went to school with is largely a question of genetics, but whether Dutch people are on average taller than Cameroonians is largely a question of average childhood environment (Dutch men are on average 180.8 centimeters tall, Cameroonian men 170.6 centimeters [Floud et al. 2011, 370]).

Roughly speaking, adult height reflects net nutrition from conception to around age 20. Net nutrition means the nutrition available to you for growing: what you eat (or what your mother eats before you are born) minus the losses from work, stress, and disease, especially digestive diseases. According to Komlos (2010, 59): "Height of a population is a useful indicator of its general biological well-being experienced during the first two decades of its life and correlates negatively with all-cause mortality risk until about 185 centimeters among men and 170 centimeters among women." (These limits are well above anything for population groups in the United States today.)

On average, NHWs are taller than members of other racial and ethnic groups, especially among women. Table 4.7 provides the most current averages for young adults.

For men, the black-white difference in average height has been fairly constant at around a centimeter for most of the twentieth and early twenty-first centuries (Komlos 2010, Table 1); we know little about other races and ethnic groups. But for women the gap in height has grown dramatically: for women born before 1950, blacks and whites were about the same height, but white women born between 1980 and 1986 were about 2.0 centimeters taller than

Table 4.7. Average height of U.S. population 20–39 years old by race and ethnicity, 2003–2008.

	In inches		In centimeters	
	Female	Male	Female	Male
Non-Hispanic whites	64.9	70.4	164.8	178.9
Non-Hispanic blacks	64.3	70.1	163.2	178.0
Mexican Americans	62.5	67.2	158.7	170.6

Source: National Health and Nutrition Examination Survey (NHANES) as reported in McDowell et al. (2008), tables 9–12.

Table 4.8. Historical average adult heights in the United States by birth cohort, gender, and race, 1930–1986 (in centimeters).

	Female		Male	
Birth year	Black	White	Black	White
1930–1934	162.9	163.0	174.4	176.8
1935–1939	163.1	163.0	175.3	176.8
1940–1944	162.5	163.2	176.1	176.5
1945–1949	163.3	163.6	177.2	177.6
1950–1954	163.0	163.8	177.1	177.9
1955–1959	163.8	164.8	177.3	177.7
1960–1964	163.8	164.1	178.0	178.6
1965–1969	164.1	163.7	177.1	178.2
1970–1974	163.8	164.4	177.7	177.8
1975–1979	163.3	165.0	177.7	179.0
1980–1986	162.5	164.6	178.3	179.1

Source: Komlos (2010), table 1.

their black counterparts. In fact, the average height of African American women *decreased* by about 1.5 centimeters from the cohort born 1965–1969 to the cohort born 1980–1986, as shown in Table 4.8. According to Komlos (2010, 64): "Such a deep decline in height is practically unprecedented in modern history except in wartime."

Table 4.9. Percentage of U.S. population over age 20 that was obese, 2007–2008.

	Female	Male
Non-Hispanic white	33.0	31.9
Non-Hispanic black	49.6	37.3
Mexican American	45.1	35.9

Source: Flegal et al. (2010).

Obesity

Minorities are more likely to be obese than NHWs. This is especially true for African American and Hispanic women. Obesity has risen rapidly in the United States over the last few decades in all groups, but it has risen faster for minorities. Obesity is of concern in itself, since obese people suffer from limitations in the physical activity they can undertake; hence I have included it as an outcome. It also contributes to morbidity, especially for diabetes and heart disease, and to mortality.

For adults, obesity is conventionally defined as having a body mass index (BMI) greater than 30. Body mass index is the ratio of weight (in kilograms) to height squared (in meters). A person 6 feet tall is obese if he or she weighs over 221 pounds; a person 5 feet, 4 inches tall is obese if he or she weighs over 175 pounds.

Table 4.9 shows the incidence of obesity in 2007–2008.

Why Are Hispanics Healthier than NHWs?

The reporting problem from doctor-assessed race in the numerator and self-assessed race in the denominator is part of the reason that Hispanics appear to live longer than NHWs, but when that problem is accounted for, Hispanics still live longer. Three main reasons have been discussed in the literature, and I'll consider each of them. Interestingly, nobody has suggested a genetic explanation.

Salmon Bias

Perhaps Hispanics go home to die (like salmon do), so their deaths are recorded in other countries. This is probably not a major piece of the story. For Cubans and Puerto Ricans, it's not a factor. If salmon bias is important for other nationalities, we would expect to find elevated death rates in Mexico or the Dominican Republic or El Salvador, but this is not the case.

Immigrant Selection

About 40 percent of Hispanics are immigrants. Most people migrate for economic opportunity, and if a person is not healthy the lure of economic opportunity is smaller. So you would expect migrants to be healthier on average than other people in the source country. That may make them healthier on average than other people in the destination country. Mexico, Cuba, and other major source countries have lower life expectancy than the United States and higher cardiovascular mortality. So selection would have to be very strong. Hispanic immigrants appear to be healthier than second-generation Hispanics, as selection would predict. But that could also be a lifestyle difference.

Behavior and Lifestyle

Hispanics drink less, smoke less, and eat a better diet than NHWs. Some evidence indicates that acculturation leads to a less healthy lifestyle. That might also explain why the second generation are less healthy than immigrants.

On the other hand, Hispanics don't lead a healthier life in all dimensions. The most complete recent data (Saffer, Dave, and Grossman 2011) indicate that Hispanics do about 10 percent less nonwork physical activity than NHWs. About half of this gap can be explained by education, age, income, and metropolitan area, but about half cannot. Employed Hispanics do about 15 percent more physical activity at work than employed NHWs; about two-thirds of the difference is attributable to education, age, income, and metropolitan area. But the medical evidence indicates that only nonwork physical activity promotes health and reduces mortality; physical activity at work seems to raise mortality. So physical activity is one part of lifestyle that doesn't seem to explain any of the Hispanic advantage.

It seems as though selection and behavior in some combination are probably the story. Behavior and lifestyle could not be the whole story, since the countries of origin are not healthier than the United States (although not a lot less healthy). Many factors might lead you to expect that Hispanics would be less healthy than NHWs: they are poorer, less well educated, and more likely to be uninsured, for instance. Whatever is working in the opposite direction is stronger. Since many Asians are also immigrants, selection and behavior could also be improving Asians' health.

Nothing about any of these explanations is specifically about Hispanics or how people act toward Hispanics. Anyone who had such a lifestyle or who was selected for migration in this fashion would be similarly healthy. Thus we have every reason to expect convergence with NHWs—which in this case would be a bad thing. Because these explanations do not appeal to anything special about Hispanics or the way people treat Hispanics, they are in the tradition of Booker T. Washington and they lead to similar predictions about convergence.

Why Are NHWs Healthier than African Americans?

Why are NHWs healthier than African Americans? The basic answer is "We don't know." Health disparities are now a very active area of research, and major questions are still open. Some answers are known, but what's known is probably not big enough to account for the full size of all the disparities. Some answers have been ruled out, however.

Some explanations are pure Booker T. Washington–style stories that emphasize the "long reach of history;" others point to current disparities in other areas, and some are W. E. B. Du Bois–style explanations that emphasize current racial distinctions. (We've seen that homicide is a major contributor to the racial mortality gap, but we'll postpone discussion of that crime to Chapter 11.)

Health of the Previous Generation

Events that occurred in the Jim Crow South still reverberate today, or at least they reverberated for a long time after the 1960s. In particular, being born with low birth weight (LBW) is associated with many health and developmental problems later in life. Moreover, LBW mothers tend to have LBW kids: Costa (2004) finds that this inheritance explains about 5–8 percent of the racial gap in LBW in the late twentieth century. How your parents were treated in utero affects how healthy you are when you are born, which affects your whole life. Almond and Chay (2006; Almond, Chay, and Greenstone 2003) have studied the desegregation of hospitals in the South in the 1960s. The *children* of black women born in integrated hospitals were healthier.

Thus part of the story is just like the story that Washington told a century ago: things were quite bad a few decades ago; race really did matter a few decades ago; and it will take a long time for the damage that was done then to work itself out. What is new is the hard evidence on this sort of biological transmission of ill health.

But segregated Southern hospitals were probably not worse than Mexican hospitals fifty years ago, so segregated hospitals are not the whole story.

History also matters for height. Most directly, in utero conditions sixty years ago, say, affect the height of people who are 60 years old today. But the reach of history is even longer. As Floud et al. (2011, 38) write:

> Wasting and stunting in a mother are likely to have arisen partially from her own deprivation before and after birth and, therefore, to have been influenced by the nutritional status and standard of living of her own mother. It is therefore in no way fanciful to see the influence of the health and welfare of grandparents in the bodies of their grandchildren and the effect may be even longer lasting. . . . The most graphic illustration of this phenomenon can be found in the Japanese-American and Italian-American populations of the United States. In these communities, it is commonly at least two generations before young people take on the bodily characteristics of the host population.

But history does little to explain the recent decline in height among African American women.

Income and Education

Rich people are healthier and taller than poor people, even in Canada and Britain where medical care is mainly free, and educated people are healthier than uneducated people, holding income constant. Since blacks are poorer than whites and less educated, this explains part of the gap, but not all of it. For instance, rich black women have higher infant mortality rates than poor white women. (And Hispanics are healthier than either non-Hispanic group but are poorer than whites and less educated than blacks.) Figuring out precisely how much of the health difference income is responsible for is difficult because the variable you want to observe is permanent income, not current income. Some studies have estimated that income and education account for about a quarter or a third of the mortality gap. The relationship between income and health is complex: maybe people are healthy because they are rich (and can get good medical care and have less stressful lives) or maybe they are rich because they are healthy (and can work hard for long periods of time). Health improves in recessions, and it is also the case that people who win the lottery become less physically healthy.

Poorer and less educated people are more likely to be obese, but these differences account for little of the obesity gap. (The racial gap in income and education is about the same for men and for women, but the racial gap in obesity is not.)

Notice that this explanation says that black health is worse than white health because of something going on outside the realm of health. This explanation is incomplete because it doesn't explain why blacks are poorer and less educated. Perhaps the reason is something having to do with race today; perhaps the reason is some facet of history. Other explanations that point to something going on outside the realm of health have the same weakness. Right now we'll look at these explanations with an open mind about what is causing the underlying discrepancy. Later in the book, we'll look at most of the underlying discrepancies.

Marriage

Married people, especially men, are healthier than unmarried people, holding age constant, and blacks are now considerably less likely to marry than whites are. But the relationship between marriage and health is complex: does marriage make people healthy or do healthy people marry?

Table 4.10. Health insurance status, 2008 (percent).

	Private	Public	Uninsured
Non-Hispanic white	78.0	24.3	10.6
Black	55.5	33.6	18.0
American Indian/Alaskan Native	43.7	30.4	31.6
Asian	72.6	17.6	14.5
Native Hawaiian/Pacific Islander	67.9	21.4	16.2
Hispanic	45.4	26.6	31.5

Source: American Community Survey data from Turner, Boudreaux, and Lynch (2009), table 2.
Note: "Public" includes Medicare, Medicaid, TRICARE, and Indian Health Service.

Health Insurance and Access

Health insurance helps. A lot of the effects of insurance, however, are picked up in the effects of income or education.

When people qualify for Medicare at age 65, mortality goes down for poorer people. A randomized experiment with Medicaid eligibility in Oregon led to better self-reported physical and mental health for those selected to enroll in Medicaid (Finkelstein et al. 2011). Higher Medicaid rates in California led to better birth outcomes for black women (Decker and Rapaport 2002). Blacks under 65 are considerably less insured than whites. Table 4.10 shows the detail.

Many uninsured people are young and healthy, but blacks are considerably less likely than whites (specifically both Hispanic and non-Hispanic whites) to be insured when they are not healthy, especially in their fifties. The average white person can expect to spend 4.6 years of his or life both uninsured and unhealthy; the average black person, 6.0 years (Kirby and Kanedo 2010).

Wrong Hospitals

There are huge geographical differences in the United States in how medicine is practiced, and some of these differences show up in differences in how effectively medicine is practiced. The worst hospitals are in the states of the New South (Arkansas, Mississippi, and Louisiana especially) and the best are in New England (Vermont, New Hampshire, and Maine especially).

A lot more blacks live in the New South than in New England. Chandra and Skinner (2003) show that if blacks used the same hospitals as whites did, a considerable part of the mortality gap would be removed.

Within the New York metropolitan area, Gray et al. (2009) find that minority patients (black, Hispanic, and Asian) were significantly less likely to be treated at high-volume hospitals for services where volume improves performance. They held many variables constant, including socioeconomic characteristics and insurance coverage. Minority patients in New York still went to the "wrong" hospitals for the services they needed. Liu et al. (2006) has similar results for California.

Housing and Neighborhoods

Exposure to pollutants is bad for your health, and minorities tend to be exposed to pollutants more than NHWs, even holding income and education constant. Exposure in utero is especially damaging. Currie (2011) shows that exposure to toxic releases from industrial plants is responsible for about 6 percent of the difference in the incidence of low birth weight between infants of white college-educated mothers and black high school dropout mothers. There are many other types of pollution, but their effects have not been measured yet.

Minorities tend to live in neighborhoods with more fast food restaurants, reduced access to fresh produce, and less opportunity for safe exercise (Burke and Heiland 2011). These neighborhood conditions may promote obesity. To the extent that lower income is the cause of minority concentration in these neighborhoods, income effects already account for these neighborhood effects. But we'll see in Chapter 9 that income disparities explain surprising little about racial and ethnic residence patterns.

Stress

Cortisol is released in your blood when you are under stress (Aizer, Stroud, and Buka 2009). It can do bad things: in utero damage, higher blood pressure, more heart disease. Poor people generally have more cortisol in their blood than rich people—this is part of the reason for the socioeconomic health gradient and the intergenerational transmission of status. Given income, blacks in the general population have more cortisol than whites. I don't know about Hispanics. In laboratories, racist incidents raise cortisol levels. So racist incidents and stress may explain some of the gap.

Unsafe neighborhoods may have the same effect: worrying about being the victim of crime is stressful, as is witnessing violent crime. A recent experiment called Moving to Opportunity, which is described in Chapter 9, randomly selected residents of low-income housing projects, mainly minorities, to move to wealthier, slightly more integrated neighborhoods. Those who moved enjoyed better mental health, especially in the dimension of calmness, and possibly a reduction in obesity.

Diet and Exercise

Are blacks more obese and less healthy because they eat too much of the wrong things and exercise too little? Recent studies have found some effects of diet and exercise, but they explain less than half of the racial gap in obesity (so the impact on morbidity and mortality is probably even smaller). Food intake and exercise are hard to measure in large surveys: respondents are not always truthful and accurate, and even the best surveys look at only small slices of time when long-run practices are what matter. The Institute of Medicine study on racial disparities in medicine found that blacks and whites had equally poor diets; Hispanics and upper-income blacks had the best diets (Smedley, Stith, and Nelson 2002).

Blacks do about 26 percent less nonwork physical activity than NHWs on an average day, and employed blacks do about 9 percent more work-related physical activity than employed NHWs (Saffer, Dave, and Grossman 2011). Only about a quarter of the gap in nonwork physical activity and half the gap in work-related physical activity is explained by socioeconomic variables and metropolitan area. Since nonwork physical activity is good for longevity and work-related physical activity is not, these gaps are probably one reason why blacks don't live as long as NHWs, controlling for socioeconomic characteristics.

Early papers that tried to explain BMI using inadequate measures of diet and exercise accounted for very little of the racial gap in obesity. However, a recent study by Burke and Heiland (2011) corrected for many errors in the measurement of food consumption; it found that about half of the racial gap in BMI for women and all of the (small) gap for men is attributable to diet and exercise. Almost all of the male difference was due to exercise.

Table 4.11. Age-adjusted mortality rate related to drugs, alcohol, and firearms, 2008 (per 100,000 population).

	Hispanic	Non-Hispanic white	Non-Hispanic black
Drugs	6.5	15.4	9.7
Alcohol	8.8	7.5	6.4
Firearms	6.8	9.2	19.1

Source: Miniño et al. (2011).

For the portion of the female gap that could be explained, exercise was also more important than diet. We are, of course, left with the question of why blacks exercise less than whites.

Diet and exercise may also affect height. Komlos (2010) conjectures that obesity among adolescent girls may explain some of the recent startling decline in height among African American women. Excess weight may induce early puberty, which in turn produces hormonal signals that stop girls from growing taller.

Substance Use and Abuse

Smoking rates for blacks and whites are about the same (though brands are different). So this variable won't explain health differences. (Hispanics smoke less.) Whites and AIANs are the big alcohol consumers, and blacks consume less than Hispanics. Finally, there are no big differences in illicit drug consumption, and blacks are less likely to die from illicit drug use than NHWs, as you can see in Table 4.11. We'll look at this again later, in Chapter 11. Differences in substance use and abuse do not contribute to the black-NHW health gap.

Genetic Susceptibility to Disease

Are African Americans more genetically susceptible to disease than whites? For some diseases, this is clearly true: for instance, African Americans are more likely to have the genotype for sickle-cell anemia. For other diseases, the opposite is true: African Americans are much less likely to have phenyl-ketonuria (PKU) and Tay-Sachs disease, for instance, and they are more likely to have genetic resistance to malaria than whites from northern Europe. None of the diseases where these correlations are known are in the top fifteen, how-ever. The genetic connections of the major diseases are very complex and not well understood.

For instance, a particular chromosome called 8q24 is associated with higher risk of prostate cancer, and men of African ancestry are more likely to carry this chromosome than men of European ancestry. But it is the chro-mosome, not the skin color, that is associated with prostate cancer. Simi-larly, blacks and whites on average have different reactions to some drugs for treating chronic heart failure. But any number of factors, including what you ate for lunch, can trigger different reactions to drugs. (As anyone who has ever trained for a sport knows, the fact that something is physical doesn't imply that it's genetic.)

Genetic Predisposition to Obesity

One explanation for higher black obesity rates that has been advanced is that blacks on average might have lower basal metabolism rates than whites; they get more work done with fewer calories. If this were the case, it would ex-plain why diet and exercise could account for less than half of the racial dif-ference in BMI for women. Of course, this biological phenomenon would have to occur only in women, since diet and exercise can account for the entire gap in men. However, a number of medical studies have looked for a racial difference in basal metabolism and have not found one (Burke and Heiland 2011).

Peer Group Effects

Surveys indicate that the BMI that black women view as ideal is higher than the BMI white women view as ideal. Other studies have found that black women face lower social and economic penalties for being obese (Burke and Heiland 2011). Peer group effects may amplify any obesity gap that exists for other reasons.

Minority Status and Research Costs

Some important aspects of health care are like public goods, for which it's helpful to be like everyone else. For instance, being left-handed in the United

States is difficult because many things in the United States are set up one way, and that is the way that is best for right-handed people. Right-handed people bear no animosity toward left-handed people; the problem is that there are more of them.

This relationship matters in several areas.

Kidney transplants.   Currently, a cadaveric kidney transplant is more likely to be successful if there's a better match on several specific antigens between donor and recipient. These antigens are correlated with where most of your ancestors lived in 1500. African Americans are disproportionately represented among people with end-stage renal disease (ESRD)—people who could use a kidney transplant. But they're not disproportionately represented among cadaveric kidney donors. Thus the antigens that were prevalent in West Africa in 1500 are more common among would-be recipients than among donors.

The rules for allocating kidneys among possible recipients can do better or worse jobs of dealing with this problem. I discuss these rules more in the section on policy. The current rules end up with more black deaths than some other rules might. It's not good to be a minority in this sense, and the problems of being a minority continue every day. (It's not a question of animosity— white people don't go around making sure their kidneys are unusable by blacks.)

This would not be a problem if the United States were Nigeria. But it's not. Or if kidneys could be flown in from Nigeria, which is not impossible.

Induced innovation.   Technological progress is important to the practice of medicine. It occurs because companies and governments decide to invest in research and development. Often the payoff from research and development is greater if more people have the disease or condition that is being studied. It usually doesn't take much more effort to understand a problem that many people have than to understand a problem that few people have. Hence, diseases and conditions that are more common may receive more attention and faster progress may be made in treating and averting these conditions. To the extent that diseases and conditions are correlated with race, those that afflict less numerous races will receive less attention and progress against them will be slower. "Minority" in this case is not just a demographic term; it's also a prediction of where research effort will flow.

Infant mortality is the area where this phenomenon has been most carefully studied. A lot of progress has been made in reducing infant mortality, and a good deal of it has come about because researchers discovered ways of treating different causes of infant mortality. Cutler, Meara, and Edwards (2009) show that researchers chose the causes they would concentrate on in a very reasonable fashion: the more babies were dying from a cause, the more research energy they devoted to that cause. The greater the research energy devoted to a cause, the greater the reduction in infant mortality from that cause—research works.

But the proportions of black infants who die from different causes are not the same as the proportions of white infants who die from those causes. For instance, respiratory distress syndrome is the second leading cause of infant deaths in the total population but the third leading cause for blacks; the reverse is true for congenital anomalies of the heart. Because whites are more numerous than blacks, researchers concentrated on the causes that were most severe for whites and white infant mortality fell more rapidly than black infant mortality. They estimate that innovation induced by these incentives accounted for about a third of the increase in the ratio of black to white infant mortality since the 1970s. (If blacks had the same distribution of infant mortality causes as whites, then the ratio would have risen by two-thirds as much as it actually rose.)

It's plausible that this relationship holds in other areas as well, particularly with pharmaceuticals. The effectiveness of some drugs is greater with some genotypes than with others. Pharmaceutical companies generally do better when they develop drugs that are effective for the most common genotypes in the United States (or the other rich countries). Those genotypes may be less common in the African American (or Asian or Hispanic) population. This is particularly true for drugs that treat heart disease and cancer. But little empirical work has been done on this issue, so my statements here are largely speculation.

Of course, differing genotypes need not be the cause of differential effectiveness of pharmaceuticals by race or differential rates of infant mortality by race. As Kaufman, Nguyen, and Cooper (2010, 116) write, "It is well known that patients respond differently because of innumerable physiological, genetic, dietary, psychological, and cultural factors—everything from obesity to recent consumption of grape juice." What's necessary for the induced innovation story to work is not that African Americans be genetically different from NHWs but that they be somehow different. For this story to explain differences in health, it would need to be true that race matters in many aspects of American life and that African Americans are a minority. Those last two conditions are not controversial.

Racial Health Care Disparities

There is a final possible race-based reason for black-white differences in health outcomes: some physicians may treat African American patients differently because of their race (not their genotype or income or parents or insurance status) and African Americans may respond to physicians in ways that are different because of their race (not their genotype, income, etc.). At the turn of this century, the Institute of Medicine (IOM) undertook an exhaustive study of disparities in health care at the request of Congress, and in 2002, it published a detailed volume of study results (Smedley, Stith, and Nelson 2002). This topic has been a major area of research and discussion since then; that's why I'm devoting a large section to it.

The IOM report provides abundant evidence that minorities—not just African Americans—are often treated differently. There is also substantial evidence that black patients behave differently. There is less evidence that this makes a difference, so it's not clear how much, if any, of the black-white mortality and morbidity disparities are due to different health care. But some proportion of those disparities could be due to physicians' behavior. Doctors treat Hispanics, Asians, and Native Americans differently too, so the effect on mortality is probably not large.

Different behavior doesn't mean that all physicians will burn in hell. We have to be careful about using the word "discrimination." And discrimination isn't present everywhere. For instance, race doesn't matter in bounce-back rates from emergency departments (bounce-back rates give the proportion of patients who have been discharged from emergency departments who are admitted to hospitals in the next few days) (Anwar and Fang 2012).

Evidence of Different Care

The IOM report cites several hundred papers about differences in health care.

More studies have been done about cardiovascular diseases than any other medical problem. Cardiovascular diseases are the major cause of death in the United States, and sample sizes are very big. Cardiovascular care is also an area where a lot of technical progress has occurred.

Many studies in many settings find that blacks are less likely than whites to receive high tech, quite effective treatments such as coronary artery bypass grafts (CABG) and catheterization, holding many variables constant. Some studies show the same for Hispanics too. Simeonova (2008) shows that blacks in the Veterans Health Administration (VHA) system with chronic heart failure are less likely to comply with the drug regimens their doctors order. This matters for mortality.

Quite a few studies look at cancer treatment, but they are not as sophisticated as the cardiovascular studies. Some of these studies show less aggressive care for African Americans and corresponding lower survival rates. For instance, African Americans receive surgical resection, the optimal treatment for early stage lung cancer, less often than whites do and have lower survival rates.

Studies also show that minorities are less likely to receive pain relief. Among elderly nursing home patients with cancer, African Americans were less likely to receive painkillers. Among patients with long-bone fractures in Los Angeles, Hispanics were twice as likely as NHWs to receive no painkiller. Note that here, reducing pain is the relevant outcome, not survival.

Finally, mental health treatments also differ. African American patients get higher doses of anti-psychotic medicines in emergency settings. Whites are more likely to receive anti-depressants.

Looking at Possible Reasons for Treatment Disparities

Why are patient-doctor interactions different? How can we explain what's going on? Is discrimination happening?

Many of the studies have looked at easy answers for the "why" question and found them inadequate. The easy answers explain part of the difference but far from everything. Many of the studies controlled for some of the easy answers:

Income and insurance. In some studies, everyone has the same disease, ESRD, for which everyone is covered, by Medicare or the VHA and

Department of Defense (DoD) systems. Income and education matter to health, so it might matter to treatment and thus should be included as a variable in studies. A few studies held these two variables constant and still found disparities.

Degree of sickness.   Many of the studies didn't have good clinical information about how sick the patients were, but many had such information. The disparities remained.

Co-morbidity.   Many of the studies didn't have good clinical information about what other health problems the patients had, but many had such information. The disparities remained.

Overmedication of whites.   Perhaps the story is not that doctors treat minority patients poorly but that they overmedicate whites and treat minorities appropriately. The one study where survival rates differed contradicts this idea. Many other studies used specific criteria to look for overmedication and found that it did not explain much of the disparity.

Treatment refusal.   Perhaps the problem is that minorities refuse treatment, not that doctors don't offer it. Some studies can observe refusals. African Americans refuse more, and this explains some of the difference in treatment but not most of it. And it doesn't answer the question of why African Americans refuse more.

It's helpful to think about the evidence in statistical terms. Most of the studies are something like a regression. For instance:

$$\text{Log (odds of CABG)} = a + b \text{ [co-morbidity]} + c \text{ [how sick]}$$
$$+ d \text{ [patient's education]} + e \text{ [physician's race]}$$
$$+ r \text{ [race of patient]} + \text{[many other variables]}$$

where race of patient $= 1$ for African Americans or for minorities.

For the most part the results are that r is significant and negative for African Americans and Hispanics. But this doesn't prove that individuals are discriminating. Why not?

Maybe the regression left out some variable that matters and is correlated with race. On kidney transplants, it might be ABO blood type or commonness of antigens. Clearly anyone who runs a regression like this has left out some important things: otherwise you wouldn't need a doctor to order a CABG; you'd just need a regression. What matters is whether the left-out variables are correlated with race. The error that is caused by leaving out important variables that are correlated with race is called *excluded variable bias*.

On the other hand, you can't avoid the first kind of problem by putting everything in the world into the equation. You might have too many explanatory variables. If race is in fact doing the work, you can drive the race coefficient to insignificance by adding variables that are correlated with race but have no real effect—bregmatic depressions or shovel-shaped incisors or time watching hockey on TV, for instance. The errors that are caused by including extraneous variables correlated with race is called *included variable bias*.

Even if you have all the right variables and the coefficient on race is negative, it doesn't indicate that any particular doctor is discriminating. The story could be about sorting—that black patients for some reason go to doctors who don't do CABG much or live in regions where there isn't much of it. This is what Chandra and Skinner (2003), Gray et al. (2009), and Liu et al. (2006) found, for instance. In general this is a problem, but some evidence indicates that sorting is not the complete story with many kinds of medical care.

So regressions by themselves can't *prove* discrimination. Other approaches aren't all that much more foolproof either. Consider a famous study conducted by the Cleveland VHA hospital. Decisions on angioplasty and CABG were made by a committee that reviewed what they claimed was all the medically relevant information, but the committee did not know the race of the patients. The researchers then ran the standard equation to explain CABG decisions and found that $r = 0$. The interpretation that the IOM report gives is that the standard equation doesn't leave out anything important that's correlated with race. I disagree. If you did CABG randomly, you would get $r = 0$. The question is whether the committee in this particular case did a good job of assigning the right people to CABG. I suspect that they didn't because committees like this are generally not used—usually these decisions are made by physicians who do actual physical examinations of the patients. So I'm not convinced by the Cleveland VHA study.

The bottom line is that you can never prove discrimination. You can never prove that other people exist either or that the universe didn't begin yesterday afternoon, complete with memories and pregnant women. What would I conclude from all these studies, then?

"I can't think of any simple story that explains all these results other than that some doctors sometimes discriminate." Or, "The simplest story that I know that's consistent with the bulk of the results is sometimes some doctors discriminate." You can never get stronger than this sort of statement about discrimination—or about practically anything else, for that matter.

Understanding Differential Treatment

So why do some doctors sometimes treat some minorities differently? And why do minorities sometimes act differently from whites in how they react to doctors? What does economics tell us about this behavior?

One possibility is that doctors are consciously hostile to minorities or are consciously racial essentialists or are members of some large conspiracy. In other words, that they show *prejudice*. This is probably not the best story. They're mainly nice people who consciously abhor discrimination. A conspiracy would be detected, and the market would probably keep minority patients away from obviously racist doctors.

More rigorously, Chandra and Staiger (2010) claim to have a way of testing whether doctors are acting in a prejudiced way or in some other way. (The test is actually slightly weaker than they claim. It can show that doctors are prejudiced in some cases when they are prejudiced, but it can't show that they are not prejudiced. It's a necessary but not sufficient condition, like testing whether a creature is a cat by asking whether she has given birth to kittens.) Basically, they say that if doctors are prejudiced, there will be a "Jackie Robinson effect."

Digression on the Jackie Robinson effect: I'm sorry it's another baseball story, but you don't have to know anything about the game. Jackie Robinson was the first black Major League Baseball player in 1947, and he was extraordinarily good. So were most of the other first handful of black major leaguers, such as Monte Irvin. If you looked at Major League Baseball in 1950, the average black player (there were only a few) was way, way better than the average white player (of whom there were a lot). Why were the black players in the major leagues like Jackie Robinson? Because they had to be. Mediocre white players could make it to the majors but not mediocre black players. Because of prejudice, the standard that black players had to achieve before they were accepted in the majors was much higher than the standard that white players had to achieve. The result was that the average quality of blacks was much higher than the average quality of whites.

The question Chandra and Staiger look at is whether patients get catheterization ("cath" for short) after a heart attack. Their picture is that different patients get different benefits from cath and that a doctor will do a cath if the benefits B are greater than some threshold T. In other words, they will do cath if and only $B > T$.

We observe that blacks (and women) are less likely to get cath than white men. Suppose the reason is doctor prejudice and that blacks have the same distribution of benefits as whites. Prejudice would mean a higher threshold for blacks: $T(b) > T(w)$. If so, then blacks who do get cath will have greater average benefits than the whites who do:

$$E(B \mid B > T(b)) > E(B \mid B > T(w)).$$

To measure "benefits," Chandra and Staiger use increases in survival probability. When they do that, they can't reject the hypothesis that average benefits are equal for blacks and whites.

Specifically, they show that if the black and white distributions of potential benefits are the same and you take two people, one black, one white, with the same propensity to be treated, then doctor prejudice implies that the black patient who gets treated will get greater benefits on average than the white patient who gets treated. (He or she will be the Jackie Robinson of cath benefits.)

This doesn't hold in the data. The average black who gets cath does not get greater benefits than the average white who gets cath.

Chandra and Staiger conclude that the distribution of potential benefits for blacks is "less than" the distribution of potential benefits for whites. On average, black patients would gain less from cath than white patients (whether they get cath or not).

Something that reduces benefits from cath is correlated with the label "black." What that something is we don't know. Thus the disparity in treatment in this case does not imply that doctors are prejudiced (or that they are not prejudiced).

A Possible Model

The story that seems right to me, and that seems to be the IOM story, is subtle and not fully worked out. It's about knowledge, stereotypes, and trust. Somehow, clinical encounters involving minorities are more likely to go wrong.

Getting medical care is not like getting soda out of a vending machine. Both parties (or many parties) have to act together, and to do so requires a certain amount of trust and confidence and an assessment of what the other party is going to do. Medical care in this regard is not that different from athletic teams or from classrooms.

Communication takes effort on both sides, as anyone who has ever written a paper or tried to understand difficult lectures can attest.

What about physicians and communication? Data are messy, X-rays and test results can be read in different ways, and there are time constraints. What did the patient say? Language is a problem with some Hispanics and Asians, but even English-speaking people use different dialects and nobody really has a good way of describing pain. So the physician may be asking: Should I ignore entirely what this patient is saying, or what parts of it should I pay attention to? What will the patient do? Will the patient comply with treatment? How will the patient act with staff?

The patient may also be asking questions. Why is this doctor telling me these things? How valuable are they really for me to do? What should I tell her so she will treat me correctly? Is this going to hurt? How will the nurses and staff treat me? Will I feel better? If this doctor is treating a person like me, could she really be competent? Or is she just trying to run up bills?

The interplay between patient attitudes and behavior and doctor attitudes and behavior evokes Myrdal's principle of cumulative causation (Chapter 2). Neither one is the sole "cause" of the other because each affects the other. To make predictions about what will happen we need to look for the equilibrium—the combination of patient and doctor behavior where both parties are satisfying the other party's expectations and both are doing as well as they can, considering the other's behavior.

Start with patients. Think of them as choosing "effort": how hard they will try to explain the problem to the doctor and listen to what she says, how much they will comply with her instructions, how pleasant and cheerful and humorous they will be. How much effort they expend depends in part

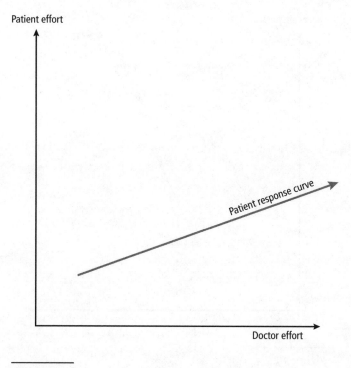

Figure 4.1.

on what they think about the doctor: if they think she doesn't care about them and is not trying to help, they will expend little effort; but if they think the doctor is competent and trying hard, they will expend more effort. We can summarize the relationship between doctor effort and the effort that patients expend in response by a graph, as in Figure 4.1.

Consider doctors next. They choose effort too: how hard they will try to understand the patient's problems, how scrupulously they will follow the patient's wishes in designing treatments, what lengths they will go to in order to cure the patient, what high-tech treatments they will authorize, how hard they will push insurance companies, how pleasant they will be with patients, and how much time they will take to answer patient questions. In part, the effort that doctors choose depends on the effort they foresee patients making. Why answer a question if the asker is paying no attention? Thus we can draw a doctor response curve just like the patient response curve. This is shown in Figure 4.2.

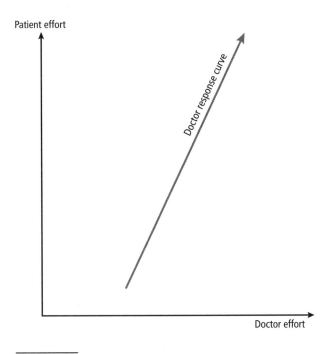

Figure 4.2.

Equilibrium is where the two curves intersect: point E in Figure 4.3. Point E is the only combination of patient effort and doctor effort where the amount of patient effort is consistent with the amount of doctor effort and vice versa. In the long run, you wouldn't expect to see any situation much different from point E.

The important implication of Figure 4.3 is that small differences in either the patient or doctor response curves can cause big differences in the equilibrium combination of efforts. Look at Figure 4.4. The story that goes with Figure 4.4 is something like this. Suppose for some reason patient attitudes toward doctors change in a favorable way: they trust doctors more; at any level of doctor effort they're more willing to comply with directions; they're more cheerful. This raises the patient response curve. Then starting at point E, patient effort rises to F. That's the immediate response. But because patients are making more effort, doctor effort rises to G. This increase in doctor effort begets a further increase in patient effort, and so on. Eventually, the system converges to E* with more doctor effort and with an in-

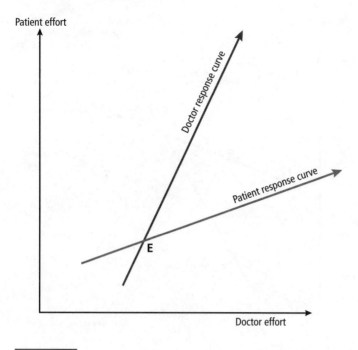

Figure 4.3.

crease in patient effort larger than the original increase that set off the spiral.

Since health outcomes depend on both doctor and patient effort, a small change in the patient response curve can cause a big improvement in health. The spiral amplifies small changes. (This is like the multiplier in Keynesian macroeconomics.)

Obviously the spiral could be set off by a shift in the doctor response curve too, just as Myrdal argued Chapter 2). Any small change is amplified, not just those initiated by patients.

What does this model say about racial disparities in health care? The mechanism works both between groups and over time. Look at Figure 4.5. It's the same as Figure 4.4, but I've labeled the patient response curves differently. Instead of "old patient response curve" the label is "minority patient response curve," and instead of "new patient response curve," the label is "NHW patient response curve." I've already given a few reasons why the NHW patient response curve might be higher than the minority curve. Then

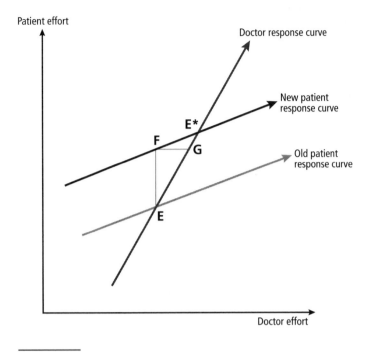

Figure 4.4.

the implication of Figure 4.5 is that the racial difference in equilibrium effort and equilibrium health outcomes will be bigger than the racial difference in patient response curves.

And Figure 4.5 is constructed on the assumption that doctors are color blind. In Figure 4.6, I show what happens if the doctor response curve to minority patients is less favorable than that to NHW patients. Obviously, the differences are greatly amplified. Even though the differences between the response curves in Figure 4.6 are quite small, the two spirals create a large gulf between the minority equilibrium M and the NHW equilibrium W.

The flip side of Figure 4.6, however, is that small changes in the response curves might be able to bring about a rapid convergence in health care quality.

Notice that these stories work only if markets function fairly poorly. Otherwise, some physicians would have an incentive to distinguish themselves as great for minorities. Then these physicians would get all the minority patients and everyone would be happy. The other doctors would still have their personality problems, but it wouldn't matter.

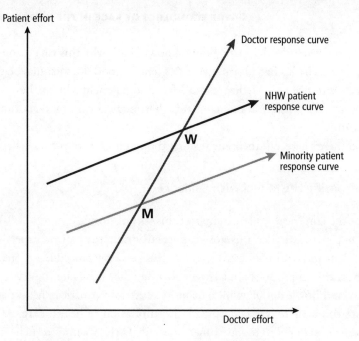

Figure 4.5.

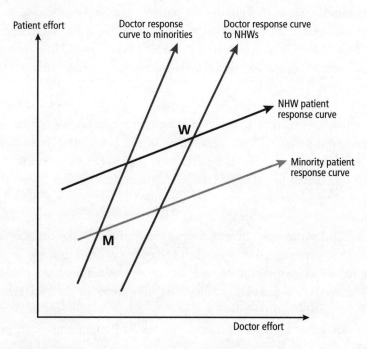

Figure 4.6.

Why doesn't this happen? I don't know. That's why this isn't a complete theory. Maybe it's hard for patients to identify good doctors; maybe third-party insurance and Medicare and Medicaid payment systems have something to do with it. No one contends that medical care markets function smoothly.

So there's a decent theoretical story, though it's far from conclusive.

Confronting the Model with Evidence

Does the empirical evidence support this sort of story?

On patient attitudes, this story requires that minority patients expect worse treatment and trust physicians less and refuse invasive procedures more. Data support this implication: in a survey that Smedley et al. cite (LaVeist, Nickerson, and Bowie 2000), while a majority of African American heart patients didn't think there was widespread discrimination in health care, African American patients were four times more likely than whites to believe that racial discrimination was common. In a random sample of the general population (Lillie-Blanton et al. 2000), 30 percent of Hispanics and 35 percent of African Americans thought discrimination was a "major problem," as opposed to 16 percent of whites. Fifty-six percent of Hispanics and 65 percent of African Americans were "very or somewhat concerned" that they or a family member could be treated unfairly because of race when seeking medical care.

Several studies (Schecter et al. 1996; Sedlis et al. 1997) that looked at patient refusals found that African Americans were more likely to refuse invasive procedures than whites, even holding medical condition constant, and that African American ESRD patients were less likely to want transplants. Simeonova (2008) found that black heart patients complied less with their drug regimens. Some studies that the IOM cited, however, found no difference.

The IOM study reported on a survey (van Ryn and Burke 2000) of physicians that was designed to assess their perception of heart patients. It asked them to rate patients on intelligence, self-control, education level, pleasantness, rationality, responsibility. They were also asked for their feelings toward the patient and their beliefs about the patient's degree of social support, tendency to exaggerate discomfort, likelihood of complying with medical advice, likelihood of drug or alcohol abuse.

Then the investigators surveyed the patients to learn about sickness, depression symptoms, personality traits, socioeconomic status, and so on.

They ran regressions of patient characteristics and race on physician attitudes to find out whether race mattered in explaining physician attitudes toward patients.

Holding the direct survey data on patients constant, African American patients were rated by physicians as less intelligent, less educated, more likely to abuse drugs and alcohol, less likely to comply, more likely to lack social support, less likely to participate in rehab.

In this regression format, African American patients were also rated less likely to be the kind of person that physicians could see themselves being friends with. Physicians rated black patients of low socioeconomic status as less pleasant and less rational.

Because the VHA and DoD systems are different from health care systems in the rest of the country, they can give us a convenient test of this explanation. Generally, health care disparities are less in these two systems than elsewhere. In fact, quite a few studies of VHA-DoD activities find no disparities in how patients are treated. For example, a study of patients admitted to the VHA system for pneumonia, angina, congestive heart failure, chronic obstructive pulmonary disease, diabetes, and chronic renal failure concluded African Americans had somewhat better survival rates than whites.

Why does the VHA treat patients more equally? One possibility is less physician discretion. Doctors are salaried and the VHA clinical decision support system is computerized. Patients are more homogenous in terms of socioeconomic status, and big differences in physicians' racial stereotypes about patients are harder to maintain. Since the doctors are salaried, they don't make more money if the patients have more operations. This may induce patients to trust them more and be more willing to comply with their recommendations.

Thus the better VHA-DoD results are consistent with this model of transaction difficulties and give us some idea of what might be important.

Minority Physicians

What about black and Hispanic physicians?

They might do better at treating all patients equally, but nothing in the model guarantees it. They have stereotypes too, and patients believe they have stereotypes. They watch the same TV shows and undergo the same indoctrination as white doctors.

We don't know much about this topic at this point. Minority patients like physicians of the same race as themselves, especially when they choose them, and many choose them. Minority physicians tend to listen to patients of all races more. But we don't know whether these physicians provide better care. One study (Chen et al. 2001) tried to look at the race of the physician in CABG decisions, but it probably got it wrong. The study looked at the race of the attending physician, but the cardiologist is the one who makes the decisions about CABG, not the attending physician (Smedley, Stith, and Nelson 2002, 134–135). The race of the attending physician didn't matter.

Implicit Bias and Unconscious Racism

Implicit bias and unconscious racism are technical terms that social psychologists use to describe negative attitudes toward racial groups that the holders of these attitudes are not conscious of. These attitudes may explain some of the transaction difficulties I've been discussing.

Two kinds of laboratory tests are used to find out about these attitudes. In priming tests, priming images are flashed too quickly for the subjects to read or recognize them. The images might be black or white faces or the words "black" or "white." Then the subjects are asked to evaluate some ambiguous situation—say, a race-unspecified figure acting in an ambiguously threatening way. The result is that white subjects who have been primed with the black prime interpret the race-unspecified figure as hostile more often than white subjects who have been primed with the white prime, and many black subjects act the same way.

In implicit association tests, subjects are tested on the speed at which they can perform a task. Subjects are shown nonracial words or images and are asked to press one button if the words and images are positive, another if they are negative. At the same time, subjects are shown names or images associated with blacks (or Hispanics) and names or images associated with whites. They are asked to push one button for the minorities and another for the whites. Sometimes the white button and the positive association button are the same; sometimes the minority button and the positive association button are the same. A considerable majority of whites and a noticeable minority of blacks work faster when white and positive are the same button than when black and positive are the same button.

Thus "attitudes" is too strong a word to describe the results of these experiments; I'll use "propensities." Why should we care about these propensities? Because they're correlated with behavior—better correlated, in fact, than what people say they believe (which is known as "propositional attitudes").

To quote Quillian (2008, 9): "In general, studies suggest that implicit prejudice is often manifest in subtle behaviors in interaction that are difficult for respondents to consciously control, such as nonverbal cues to affect and lexical errors in speech. . . . Yet these subtle or quick behaviors are important in many situations and cannot be dismissed: . . . nonverbal behaviors more strongly correlate to perceptions of friendliness by an interaction partner than do verbal statements."

More specifically, Green et al. (2007) find an association between implicit association test results and recommendations that doctors make for heart disease treatment when they're presented with vignettes about black and white patients. Doctors who show more anti-black propensities in the implicit association test are more likely to recommend less invasive treatment for black "patients."

Thus these propensities may underlie some of the interaction problems that this section deals with. Where do these propensities come from? The most common story is that the images that Americans are bombarded with from childhood on often portray blacks and Hispanics as impoverished, illiterate, hostile, or in trouble with the law. If these images create the biases, why don't minorities have exactly the same biases that NHWs have, since they're exposed to the same media? It's plausible that minorities would have accumulated more positive images and experiences to offset the negative ones—their mother's love, for instance, or the good times they have had with siblings and friends.

So we see some support for the idea that two-sided mistrust plays an important role in health care disparities.

Policies

What (if anything) should governments do about health and health care disparities? This is a question that we will come to repeatedly in this book. In other economics classes, you've been taught a way of answering questions like this—deadweight loss triangles, consumer surplus, efficiency, and so on.

You've learned about good taxes and bad taxes, rent control and regulation. But when you hear people talking about race, they don't sound like economists at all; the criteria they appeal to seem to be different. They talk about justice and fairness, not Pareto optimality and utility. What criteria are we going to use, then, to evaluate current conditions and proposed policies?

I don't want to be didactic about this question, and I don't want to arrive at an answer quickly. Instead, I want you to develop an approach over time by looking at specific questions and seeing the general rules you apply to these questions. The plan is to look at specific questions and learn general rules from specifics rather than to start by debating abstractions. It's a slow approach, so in this chapter I'm not going to have time to say much about actual policies on health and health care. The question in this section is really how you should approach policy questions that involve race; we won't get to apply the answers in any depth.

This section looks at four specific areas: the Hispanic-NHW mortality gap, cadaveric kidney transplants, patient-doctor interactions, and race-specific drugs. In each, I first ask what's wrong (if anything). Then I ask what sorts of policies would be good to address the problem, but I look at specific policies only superficially and briefly. A better way of phrasing the question might be "What sorts of policies would not be obviously horrible ways of addressing this problem?" Because this question is so weak, most of the answers will be obvious; the challenge will be figuring out *why* these answers are the right ones. Learning why in this chapter will let us approach other policy questions in other chapters better.

The Hispanic Advantage

Hispanics have lower mortality rates than other ethnic groups, especially NHWs and non-Hispanic blacks. Are you worried that something might be wrong here? What policies does this situation call for?

The obvious naïve reaction is that this is good news and we should try to figure out why Hispanics are healthy and see if we can transfer those lessons to NHWs and African Americans. We should hope that non-immigrants would retain the healthy practices of immigrants, and perhaps we should design policies to encourage this. I think that the naïve reaction is the right one, but why?

The first part of the favorable reaction to low Hispanic mortality is that we don't think it comes at the expense of other ethnic groups. Good health is not a finite resource in our society; Hispanic good health does not reduce NHW good health. Notice that this would not be true in a poorer society: if, for instance, Hispanics were healthy because they controlled the grain supply and other groups starved. And Hispanic good health also does not come from an egregious draw on health care resources. If Hispanics ate more junk food and were less healthy, other groups would not be healthier under any scenario I can imagine.

Non-Hispanics, then, are less healthy because of something in U.S. history that has made them more inclined to engage in poor health practices. Whatever that is, it does not seem to have a large racial component, since it affects all groups who have been in the United States for a reasonably long period of time (including second-generation Hispanics). Studying this issue is important in health economics, but not in the economics of race.

Finally, the (relatively) poor health of NHWs does not seem to be the result of any (racial) injustice; Hispanics have not forced junk food on them or restricted their access to healthy foods and exercise. Nor is there a history in this country of Hispanics attempting to exploit NHWs or denying them what we think of now as basic human rights.

For all these reasons, then, the naïve reaction seems right. (One caveat: if the Hispanic advantage is due to selective immigration rather healthy lifestyles, then there's absolutely nothing to be learned from it.)

What lessons about race and policy can we take from this first exercise? First, disparities by themselves are not reasons for concern; we have to know why they arise. Racial disparities do not automatically imply racial policies. Second, history matters. Even though policies can deal only with the future, we can't pretend that they operate in a world without a past. Third, in this case at least, we don't need any tools that are strange to either economics or to common sense.

Let's move on to more challenging problems.

Cadaveric Kidney Transplants

Cadaveric kidney transplants are a desirable substitute for dialysis for patients with ESRD. Live kidney transplants are even better, and the number of such transplants is growing, but cadaveric transplants are still much more numerous.

On the demand side, a lot of people could benefit from a cadaveric kidney that's right for them, and they wait until they either get such a kidney or they die. On the supply side, cadaveric kidneys pop up whenever someone with healthy kidneys dies and their family agrees to a donation or they have already signed a donor form. When that happens, a semi-public organization takes charge of the kidney and assigns it to the recipient who has the highest score for that particular kidney.

The score for any kidney-recipient pair depends on many things. The interesting ones are geography (how close the recipient is to the kidney), time on the waiting list (how long the recipient has been waiting), and match quality (how close the donor is to the recipient in ABO blood type and antigens, thus how likely the recipient's body is to reject the kidney).

African Americans are less likely than whites to get kidneys because of poor match quality. The proportion of African Americans among donors is less than the proportion among potential recipients, mainly because African Americans are heavily overrepresented among people with ESRD. The distribution of transplant-relevant kidney characteristics is different in the African American population than in the NHW or Hispanic populations.

Money is not a dominating issue here, although it is not entirely absent. This is not a market. The allocation is bureaucratic, and most people want to keep it that way. Donors don't get paid for kidneys, and recipients don't pay for kidneys. ESRD patients are all covered by Medicare, so they don't pay for the operations either. But doctors don't work for free, and you can't do a kidney transplant operation without a donor kidney. Thus doctors have a strong pecuniary interest in seeing that their patients get kidneys. The allocation of kidneys is both big business and a humanitarian concern.

The controversies about cadaveric kidney transplants are over how much weight to put on match quality and how much weight to put on everything else. Because most whites match better with most cadaveric kidneys, the more weight the formula puts on match quality, the better whites do. The less weight on match quality, the better blacks do.

So how much weight should be put on match quality? If you didn't know economics and were myopic, your first reaction would probably be to put a lot of weight on match quality. If you have one kidney, shouldn't you give it to the person who is most likely to be able to use it? Why would you ever take a chance on wasting a valuable kidney on someone who is more likely to reject it?

The naïve reaction here is wrong. There are very good reasons to go against maximizing match quality. The reason is that society should be organized according to comparative advantage, not absolute advantage: kidneys should be matched with recipients for whom they have the greatest comparative match quality, not the greatest absolute match quality.

Let me illustrate with an example.

Example: Mr. A and Mr. B are waiting for a transplant. Two types of cadaveric kidneys show up randomly. Ninety percent of kidneys are type 1. Every time a kidney shows up, the probability that it is type 1 is 90 percent. Type 1 kidneys are very good matches for Mr. A: the match works 100 percent of the time. They're horrible matches for Mr. B: they never work.

Type 2 kidneys are the other 10 percent of the kidneys that show up. They're not great kidneys: 50 percent chance of success with Mr. A and 30 percent chance of success with Mr. B.

Obviously, if a type 1 kidney shows up, it should go to Mr. A. What about a type 2 kidney? Match quality says it should go to Mr. A, since Mr. A can make better use of it than Mr. B can, but is that always the best policy?

It's the best policy if this particular kidney is the last kidney that will show up before the patients die. In that case, there's no sense giving it to Mr. B.

But what if it's not the last kidney ever? Suppose that two random kidneys will arrive serially before the patients die. What should we do if the first turns out to be type 2? The trees in Figure 4.7 illustrate the possibilities.

Suppose Mr. A gets it. Then he has a 50 percent chance of survival now. If it doesn't work, then both patients are around for the second kidney and he's sure to get it, no matter what type it is. So his probability of a successful transplant on the second round, conditional on a failure in the first round, is $0.9(1) + 0.1(0.5) = 0.95$. (90 percent chance of a type 1 kidney, which gives him certain survival; 10 percent chance of a type 2 kidney, which gives him 50 percent chance of survival). Thus overall, his survival probability if he gets this kidney is $0.5 + 0.5 (0.95) = 0.975$.

If Mr. A gets this kidney and it fails, then Mr. B has no chance of survival, because he will not get a kidney on the next and last round. If Mr. A gets this kidney and it works, then Mr. B doesn't compete with him on

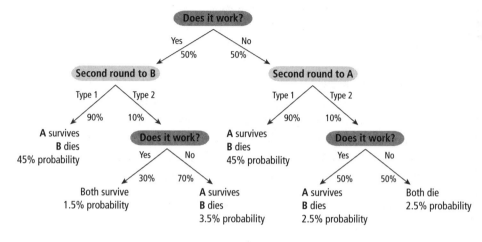

Total probability of survival: A 97.5%, B 1.5%

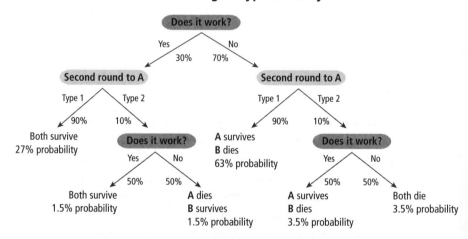

Total probability of survival: A 95%, B 28.5%

Figure 4.7

the next round. On that round Mr. B has a 3 percent chance of survival—10 percent chance of a type 2 kidney, and 30 percent chance of survival if a type 2 kidney arrives. Thus Mr. B's chance of survival overall is $0.5(0.03) = 0.015$.

The expected number of survivors if Mr. A gets this kidney is $0.975 + 0.015 = 0.99$.

Now suppose Mr. B gets the kidney. Then he has a 30 percent chance of survival on this round and none on the next round. So overall Mr. B has a 30 percent chance of survival. Mr. A has no chance on this round but a 95 percent chance on the second round, because he's going to get the second-round kidney no matter whether Mr. B survives or not on the first round.

So the expected number of survivors if Mr. B gets this kidney is $0.30 + 0.95 = 1.25$.

On most reasonable criteria, most people would say Mr. B should get the kidney. (But not on every possible criterion. If Mr. B gets the kidney, the probability that both die is 0.035. If Mr. A gets the kidney, the probability that both die is 0.015. If the criterion is to maximize the probability that at least one of the pair survive—to carry on a family name, say—then Mr. A should get the kidney.) Giving the kidney to Mr. B produces greater total survival that is more equally distributed. Mr. A is worse off if Mr. B gets the kidney, but the gain to him of getting the kidney (0.025) is a lot less than the loss to Mr. B (0.285) from not getting it. Only if you valued Mr. A's life much more than Mr. B's would you reasonably think about giving the kidney to Mr. A. (Similarly, if there were markets and Mr. A and Mr. B were equally wealthy, Mr. B would outbid Mr. A for this kidney.)

Thus in the more realistic case, where many kidneys are likely to become available, match quality should not be the sole driving force.

Reality is more complicated than this simple example. With many kidneys and many possible recipients and an unknown number of kidneys that patients will be exposed to before they die and many different types of kidneys, optimal allocation is a complex dynamic programming problem (for a much more complete discussion, see Ayres 2005). Three important things about this problem:

First, the optimal solution doesn't put all the weight on match quality.

Second, in the optimal solution, people with rare antigens will do worse than people with common antigens, but they will do better than they would do if all weight were on match quality.

Third, in real life, nobody can write this problem down and solve it objectively. The real rule is going to be some sort of an approximation.

Now many African American groups are concerned about the formula for the allocation of kidneys.

Let's think about several questions: First, are you worried about whether the system we are now using might not be the best one? Do you think that a serious examination of the current system is worth doing every several years?

The naïve reaction, and I again I think the right one, is that worrying about the system, examining it, and checking it for biases are worthwhile activities. Why? The first reason for doing this is that the best system isn't obvious (all weight on match quality, say, or no weight on match quality). The more subtle reason is that errors in a simplistic direction, appealing to a naïve and myopic analysis, are correlated with a history of injustices. Go back to the example. If instead of weighting the two lives equally, the planners considered Mr. A's life to be more valuable than Mr. B's, they would opt for pure match quality even though it reduced the unweighted total survival probabilities. So in the example, the pure match quality criterion could prevail either because of poor mathematics or because of disregard for Mr. B's life, and if you were on the outside, you could not tell which reason was the real one. In either case, you would want to check the calculations.

In the United States, there has been a history of injustices against minority people. This history makes the case for checking stronger: since disregard for minority lives has motivated official policies in the past, it is quite conceivable that such disregard could be motivating policies now—or at least blinding officials to the subtleties of the calculations. To sharpen your intuition on this question, suppose that rare antigens were correlated with left-handedness instead of with apparent African ancestry and that something about left-handedness made people disproportionately susceptible to ESRD. Would you still be just as strong about the desirability of checking the calculation? (The proportion of lefties in the U.S. population is about the same as the proportion of African Americans.)

Now suppose we have all the information and great dynamic programming capability, what sort of weights should be set up? Probably your answer here is nonracial: the popular answers would be maximizing long-run expected average survival probability or maybe guaranteeing everyone some minimum survival probability and then maximizing the average. Very few people at this stage would want to weight lives based on race or ethnicity. But race blindness in deciding how to weight lives does not prevent us from being race conscious when we decide whether it's worthwhile to treat existing rules skeptically.

In particular, to sharpen your intuition, let's think of several allocation rules that everyone thinks are horrible and explain why they are horrible. First consider segregation: separate queues by race. Why is this a bad idea? Because it will almost certainly result in more deaths (and most of these deaths will be of blacks). Adding constraints can't make the result of an optimization problem better. Second, consider the rule of equalizing expected survival rates by race. Again, it costs lives (most of the lives here would be of whites), and most people would turn away from it for that reason.

Finally, what if I said: "Yes, there's been a history of injustice, but let's just pay reparations and forget about whether the kidney allocation formula is the right one or not"? You would stare at me. The question of the right allocation formula is forward looking, not backward looking, and thus is independent of the question of reparations. Whether or not reparations have been paid, getting the right kidney allocation formula is something that has to be done, and it has to be done carefully. Compensating someone for wrongs your ancestors did to their ancestors doesn't give you the right to kill them.

All of these arguments for careful scrutiny and a nonracial objective function assumed that the number of cadaveric kidneys was fixed. These arguments are generally strengthened if potential donors care about what happens to their kidneys. If saving lives is the major motivation of most potential donors, then there will be more potential donors if the rules do a better job of increasing average long-run survival probability. Incremental African American donors may be the more valuable for saving lives than incremental donors of other races, and their willingness to donate may be fairly closely tied to their beliefs about whether the allocation system is subtly rigged against people like them.

What can we take away from this? First, the fact that a question is phrased in a nonracial way ("how much weight should match quality have?") doesn't prevent it from being a question for the economics of race, and the fact that a practice is described in nonracial terms doesn't mean that it has no racial intent or racial consequences. Second—to repeat the lesson from the Hispanic advantage discussion—history matters, even when the question is forward looking. Third, normal economic criteria such as efficiency, equity, and comparative advantage do a pretty good job of judging policies, but they have to be used in context.

Patient-Doctor Interactions, Especially Related to CABG

The problem is fairly simple to express: patients want treatment, and doctors generally want to treat (prejudice doesn't seem to be a major issue), but the two sides don't trust each other enough to expend the effort that high-quality treatment requires. Doctors are less effective than they could be, and patients are treated less well than they could be. Both would be better off if they could agree to cooperate better.

Expressed this way, the problem is standard in economics: it's prisoners' dilemma. The basic economic criteria of efficiency and equity don't need any embellishments here. History is present in the sense that it is history that created the mistrust and stereotypes that prevent optimal cooperation. It's not all right that Hispanics and Asians are treated poorly because they have no legacy of slavery in the United States.

Policies, however, are hard to design. Standard civil rights measures such as anti-discrimination laws are too blunt; the interactions are too subtle and are two-sided: Should doctors be able to sue minority patients for not taking their medicines because of racial distrust? Affirmative action is similarly unworkable: hospitals should not have the goal of giving minority patients CABG. The arguments against these measures are standard economics: they wouldn't work and they would be costly. I like the idea of doctor rating services, where ratings can be specific to minority patients. Large insurance companies and information technology may actually be moving in this direction. The converse would be patient rating services, where patients can be certified for their cooperative qualities, but I don't see how such a system would work.

One possible interpretation of this problem is that in a modern well-functioning society, people can expect a certain minimum amount of respect and kindness from one another (notice the similarity here with the minima that Du Bois talks about). They don't have to be absolutely certain of it; a reasonable expectation is probably sufficient. People don't have to love each other, but most of them need enough respect for the humanity of the others that basic trust and weak promise-keeping are what people expect. It's not impossible to have a society, even a modern one, in which a group is not accorded basic respect. But the costs are great, both to the pariah group and, on net, to everyone.

Race-Specific Pharmaceuticals

If medicines designed for the general U.S. population don't work as well on average for African Americans, should medicines be designed specifically for African Americans or other minority groups? This is a policy question because the federal government must approve pharmaceuticals before they can be used, and it can approve them for use only by specific populations—for instance, women or adults. The issue came to the fore in 2005 when the Food and Drug Administration approved BiDil, a drug for treating chronic heart failure for use by African Americans but not by anybody else.

BiDil had first been tested for the general population in a randomized controlled trial in the 1980s. It failed that test. But if you isolated the African Americans in that test, it would have passed. So BiDil's owners then arranged another randomized controlled trial, but this time only with African American subjects. BiDil passed.

The argument for BiDil is straightforward. In two randomized controlled trials, BiDil on average helped African Americans with chronic heart failure. Thus it's likely to continue doing so on average.

Notice that the argument for BiDil is not racial essentialism. We don't know why BiDil tends to work better for African Americans, and it doesn't work better for all African Americans. Maybe there's a genetic correlation—a chromosome that's more common among people with a lot of West African ancestors—or maybe there's an environmental correlation—perhaps some food or some experience that's more common among African Americans than among other people who grew up in the United States. Scientists are working to understand why BiDil appears to work well for African Americans, but the only hard information that the FDA had in 2005 was that it worked well (Brody and Hunt 2006).

The FDA, however, clearly engaged in racial discrimination, and it asked prescribing physicians and pharmacists to engage in racial discrimination too. That's what made the FDA decision controversial.

Objections to BiDil come in two varieties. One objection is that BiDil is "lazy medicine." The FDA precedent allows drug companies to market drugs such as BiDil without any real understanding of whom the drugs work for. Something that's correlated with being African American in the United States now makes BiDil work better, and if we knew what that was, BiDil could be targeted more effectively, and not using such a medically irrelevant criterion as self-assessed race.

The approval of BiDil can also be labeled lazy medicine because it lowers the standards for FDA approval by giving each drug multiple tries to be approved. By chance, a completely ineffective drug is almost certain to pass statistical significance tests for some group if drug companies are allowed to make up enough groups after the fact. Raising the probability that an ineffective (or even harmful) drug will be approved (and lowering the probability that an effective drug will be rejected) might not be a bad idea (this is not a book about the FDA), but it would not be a trivial decision.

The response to the argument that BiDil represents lazy medicine is also obvious: it may be lazy, but it's the best medicine we have to treat African Americans with chronic heart failure right now. Knowing more would be nice, but refusing to treat people who need help now would be cruel.

Notice that the lazy medicine argument, on both sides, is not about race. If I were to substitute "left-handed vegetarians" for "African Americans," nothing substantive would change.

The racial objection to BiDil is that it "sends the wrong message." A racially essentialist government would approve different drugs for different races, and by acting in the way that a racial essentialist would act, the government and the medical establishment are telling people that racial essentialism is good science. According to a 2005 editorial in *Nature Biotechnology,* "Pooling people in race siloes is akin to zoologists grouping raccoons, tigers, and okapis on the basis that they are all stripy" (Illuminating BiDil 2005: 903). Notice that this would not be an argument against approving drugs for left-handed people; only because of the history of racial essentialism is there a danger that actions might be interpreted as supporting racial essentialism.

I am not sure how seriously one should take the wrong-message argument. Perhaps all it means is that the FDA should have issued a statement explaining why racial essentialism was wrong and why its actions were not based on racial essentialism when it approved BiDil.

Race also enters the story of BiDil at the end. African American patients and their doctors did not embrace BiDil. Although some analysts predicted that annual sales would be in the $500 million to $1 billion range in 2010 when BiDil was first approved, they didn't even come close to $20 million in 2007, and Nitromed, the drug's owner, ceased marketing efforts in 2008 and failed in 2009 (BiDil was its only product).

Why? I don't know. It might be that BiDil was just not a good enough drug. It has many side effects, and it's really just an expensive combination of two generic drugs that can be purchased much more cheaply separately. But it could also be that many African Americans remembered the quality of seats on buses that were labeled specifically for African Americans, or seats in schools, and didn't take such labels as a welcome sign. History doesn't go away.

Lessons about Policy

For now, I can only summarize what we have learned about judging policies, not any particular policies for health care. These are the important lessons.

We don't have to invent new and strange criteria for this book. Basic individualistic efficiency and fairness seem to have done pretty well so far. We have to apply these familiar criteria in light of history. The particular history of the United States matters. Many policies are worth thinking about, not just anti-discrimination laws and affirmative action. Appearances can be deceiving: some racial disparities have no racial content, and some apparently race-neutral policies have a lot.

Conclusion

Health differs among races and ethnic groups. Hispanics have higher age-specific survival rates than Asians and NHWs, who in turn have higher survival rates than African Americans. Outcomes differ for other conditions too, such as asthma, height, and obesity. Many factors explain part of these disparities, but no one has a full picture. As Booker T. Washington would emphasize, some of the disparities arise from history, as people's bodies today are influenced by the height and health of their grandmothers. As Myrdal and the Kerner Commission would emphasize, disparities in other areas such as education, income, insurance, and neighborhood safety spill over into health. As Du Bois, King, and Malcolm X would emphasize, race per se makes a difference in medical care and research. The classic texts themselves say almost nothing about health and health care, but they foreshadowed all the explanations we see today.

5

Employment and Earnings

Money does not buy happiness, but it buys many other good things. Most people get most of their money from the labor market. For many people, work is a source of fulfillment as well as money: what you do is a big part of who you are. Blacks, Hispanics, and Native Americans get less money from the labor market than whites and Asians do. Understanding why is important. (We don't know much about whether they get less or more fulfillment, although job satisfaction is correlated with earnings.)

Labor markets are one of the core subjects in the economics of race. Many of the most useful econometric techniques were developed for studying labor markets, as were the first rigorous models of race in markets. When I first started teaching my course, many of my colleagues thought race was a branch of labor economics.

Race is, of course, a much broader topic than my colleagues thought—Du Bois and Malcolm, for instance, barely mention labor markets. But the amount of money that people make clearly matters an awful lot for their lives and those of their kids. So we need to study labor markets early.

Disparities in Employment and Earnings

Trying to make a simple statement such as "Blacks make less money than whites" is hard. "Average wage" is a complex idea and a construct that's hard to measure. It's amazing how economists can take an idea that looks very simple and make it very complicated. But it really is very complicated.

Employment

Begin with employment. You can't earn a wage unless you have a job. You can't get a job unless you look for one.

The first question then is what proportion of adults are either working or looking for work; this is called the labor force participation rate. Table 5.1 shows labor force participation rates for races and ethnic groups. The highest rates are for NHWs and NHPIs (Native Hawaiians and Pacific Islanders), and the lowest rate is for blacks. (The Current Population Survey and the American Community Survey are the usual sources of information about employment status. I'm using the census because those two surveys look only at the "household population"—people who live in houses or apartments.

Table 5.1. Employment status of population 16 and over by race and ethnicity, 2000.

	Percentage of total population in labor force	Percentage of population employed	Percentage of labor force unemployed
Total	63.9	60.2	5.7
Black	60.2	53.4	11.4
American Indian/ Alaskan Native	61.1	57.0	12.0
Asian	63.3	60.1	5.1
Native Hawaiian/ Pacific Islander	66.2	62.4	10.6
Hispanic	62.1	55.7	9.1
Non-Hispanic white	64.9	62.1	4.3

Source: 2000 Census of Population from American Fact Finder, http://factfinder2.census.gov /faces/nav/jsf/pages/index.xhtml.

Note: "Labor force" includes armed forces.

Only the census includes the "group quarters" population—people who live in places such as prisons, jails, college dormitories, convents, military barracks, homeless shelters, and nursing homes.)

Not everybody who wants a job has one. Table 5.1 gives two sets of numbers about jobs: employment-population ratios and unemployment rates. The employment-population ratio is the proportion of adults who have jobs. This is probably the most important number for this table: you make money only if you have a job. The pattern is the same as the pattern of labor force participation, but the differences are greater. The final column is the unemployment rate—the proportion of adults who want jobs and can't find them. NHWs and Asians have the lowest unemployment rates, AIANs (American Indians and Alaskan Natives) and blacks have the highest. Almost always since the 1950s, the black unemployment rate has been twice as high as the white unemployment rate. Most of the numbers in Table 5.1 move around a lot in the course of the business cycle.

The black employment rate at any point in time could be lower than the NHW rate either because blacks leave jobs more quickly or because they leave unemployment more slowly. It appears that both things happen (Lang and Lehmann 2012, 965–966).

How much of the differences in Table 5.1 are explained by educational attainment? Some, but not all. Table 5.2 shows unemployment rates by educational attainment in 2007 (for the household population only) (I used the last year before the Great Recession began). The disparities within educational

Table 5.2. Unemployment rates by educational attainment, 2007 annual average (percent).

	Total	Less than high school diploma	High school graduate	Some college	Bachelor's degree or more
White	3.3	6.5	3.9	3.2	2.3
Black	6.2	12.0	7.3	5.5	3.0
Hispanic	4.6	6.0	4.4	3.6	2.2
Asian	2.8	2.9	3.2	3.7	2.4

Source: U.S. Census Bureau (2008), table 607.

attainment groups are smaller than those within the labor force as a whole, especially for better-educated groups, but the disparities remain. Studies using many standard characteristics, not just education, also fail to explain much of the racial unemployment differential, at least for men (Stratton 1993).

Earnings

Tables 5.3 and 5.4 give information about earnings, but only of select groups of adults. Table 5.3 is about full-time year-round workers, and Table 5.4 is about full-time workers. Part-timers, unemployed people, people outside the labor force, and people in group quarters are all excluded from this calculation, mostly for obvious practical reasons.

As with employment, NHWs and Asians do better than other groups, but earnings show some different patterns. The median Asian earns more than the median NHW, and the median black earns more than the median Hispanic. The gap between NHWs and Asians on one hand, and blacks, Hispanics, and AIANs on the other, is big, especially for men.

The picture on earnings changes when we look at earnings by educational attainment in Table 5.4. Everyone is closer together, and the patterns are different. Black men make less than Hispanics, not more, and Asians usually make less than whites. (Part of the difference between these two tables is that the denominator is whites in Table 5.4 and it is NHWs in Table 5.3.)

Table 5.3. Median annual earnings of full-time, year-round workers in 2006 (ratio to non-Hispanic white median in same gender category).

	Male	Female
Non-Hispanic white only	1.00	1.00
Black only	.72	.86
American Indian/Alaskan Native only	.68	.78
Asian only	1.05	1.10
Native Hawaiian/Pacific Islander only	.73	.89
Hispanic	.57	.70

Source: 2007 American Community Survey, American Fact Finder, at www.census.gov.

Table 5.4. Median weekly earnings of full-time workers over 25 years old, fourth quarter 2008.

A. Ratio to white median in same gender category

	All	Male	Female
Black	.80	.75	.85
Hispanic	.70	.65	.76
Asian	1.19	1.21	1.16

B. Ratio to whites of same gender and educational attainment

| | Men | | Women | | All |
	Black	Hispanic	Black	Hispanic	Asian
Less than high school diploma	.89	.94	1.01	.95	.90
High school graduate	.79	.82	.90	.90	.88
Some college	.77	.84	.89	.93	.93
Bachelor's degree or more	.73	.80	.90	.89	1.03

Source: Current Population Survey data from U.S. Bureau of Labor Statistics (2009).

Of course, earnings depend on many factors beyond education: for instance, region (wages are lower in the South), age and experience, the difficulty of doing the job and the strength and exertion it requires, and the number of hours worked. Some of these can be measured and some can't (or aren't). As Table 5.4 shows, some of the disparities in median earnings are due to differences in education (as Booker T. Washington would emphasize), and differences in other aspects of employment are also likely to contribute to observed disparities (possibly making them bigger as well as smaller—look at how Asians compare with whites once education is accounted for). Regression equations should help us account for these other differences. But before we can start looking at these equations, we need a little more mathematics.

Mathematics for Earnings Disparities

Economists almost always talk about the logarithm of wages, not absolute wages. For small x, ln x is approximately $x - 1$. So ln (black wage/white wage) is approximately (black wage/white wage) $- 1$: the percentage difference in wages. Economists will often measure wage differences in "log points," which are approximately percentages.

With the idea of log points, you can understand Blinder-Oaxaca decompositions. This is the most common technique for netting out the impact of nonracial factors to find out whether any racial differences remain and estimate how big they might be. It was first used, independently, in the early 1970s by economists Alan Blinder and Ronald Oaxaca.

Blinder-Oaxaca decompositions rely on fitting two wage regressions, one for each race. (This is a two-way technique; there is no obvious extension to more than two racial groups.) I'll talk about black and white as the two races.

Why not just fit one regression, as we did in Chapter 4, on health and health care? Two reasons (closely related): included variable bias and possibly different coefficients. Fitting one regression, for instance, forces education to act on black wages the same way it acts on white wages. Maybe it doesn't. (Table 5.4 suggests as much.)

With two regressions and different coefficients, how do you conveniently summarize your results? The Blinder-Oaxaca decomposition is a way to do this.

Consider black and white log wages as a function of some variable x, such as education. (It's easy to expand this to many other explanatory variables and an intercept, but the algebra is messier.)

So

$$\ln w_b = \beta_b x$$

is the equation for blacks, and

$$\ln w_w = \beta_w x$$

is the equation for whites. From the basic properties of ordinary least squares regressions:

$$\overline{\ln w_w} = \beta_w \overline{x_w}$$

$$\overline{\ln w_b} = \beta_b \overline{x_b}$$

where the lines on top indicate averages.

We can think of two kinds of comparisons to make, and there are two different Blinder-Oaxaca decompositions.

The first comparison is what I call the *enrichment experiment.* Suppose blacks had the same average education as whites. How much of the gap between average wages would be eliminated? If blacks had the same education as whites but continued to be treated the same way in the labor market, their average log wage would rise to $\beta_b \overline{x_w}$. Now let's write everything out:

$$\overline{\ln w_w} - \overline{\ln w_b} = \beta_w \overline{x_w} - \beta_b \overline{x_b} = \beta_w \overline{x_w} - \beta_b \overline{x_w} + \beta_b \overline{x_w} - \beta_b \overline{x_b}$$
$$= (\beta_w - \beta_b)\overline{x_w} + \beta_b(\overline{x_w} - \overline{x_b}).$$

The first expression is the part of the difference due to differing coefficients and the second expression is the part of the difference due to differing education (think Booker T. Washington). The first expression is sometimes called the *residual* or the *unexplained part,* or the part that education can't explain (think W. E. B. Du Bois). Often it's given in percentages. That's one Blinder-Oaxaca decomposition.

The other Blinder-Oaxaca decomposition is what I call the *civil rights experiment.* Suppose the labor market treated black education the way it treated white education. How much of the gap between average wages would be eliminated? If blacks continued to lag in education but were treated in the labor market the same way whites were, their average wage would rise to $\beta_w \overline{x_b}$. Then we can write everything out the same way.

$$\overline{\ln w_w} - \overline{\ln w_b} = \beta_w \overline{x_w} - \beta_b \overline{x_b} = \beta_w \overline{x_w} - \beta_w \overline{x_b} + \beta_w \overline{x_b} - \beta_b \overline{x_b}$$
$$= (\beta_w - \beta_b)\overline{x_b} + \beta_w(\overline{x_w} - \overline{x_b}).$$

Once again the first expression is the *residual* and the second expression is the part of the difference due to differing education.

You can also do this exercise with pictures instead of algebra. Suppose that the white return to education is greater than the black. Then the regression lines would look like Figure 5.1.

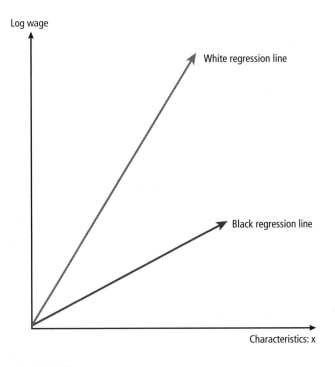

Figure 5.1.

Suppose that average white education $\overline{x_w}$ is greater than average black education $\overline{x_b}$. Then the actual difference D in average log wages is shown in Figure 5.2.

$$D = \beta_w \overline{x_w} - \beta_b \overline{x_b}$$

The average black worker is at point B in Figure 5.2; the average white worker is at point W.

Now think about how to move from point B to point W: What would it take to make blacks like whites on average? There are many routes between B and W, but the Blinder-Oaxaca decomposition concentrates on two obvious ones.

The enrichment experiment moves along the black regression line first— to point E, as shown in Figure 5.3.

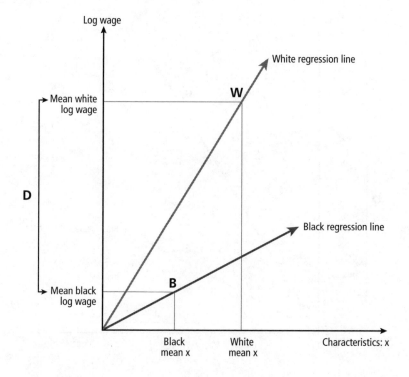

Figure 5.2.

Point E shows what black wages would be if blacks had the same characteristics as whites but those characteristics were rewarded the same way. The difference between wages at E and wages at B is the part of the total wage gap due to education. The difference between W and E is the residual: the part of the wage disparity that would not go away if you conducted the enrichment experiment.

The civil rights experiment takes a different route: it moves between the regression lines first. Figure 5.4 illustrates.

Point C shows what black wages would be if existing black characteristics were rewarded the same way white characteristics are rewarded. The difference between wages at C and at E is the part of the disparity due to education. The residual here is the part of the disparity that would not go away if white education fell to the level of black education.

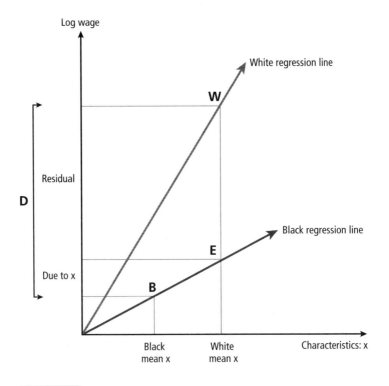

Figure 5.3. The enrichment experiment.

Standard Blinder-Oaxaca Decomposition Results

What do Blinder-Oaxaca decompositions look like when researchers use standard characteristics such as age, education, gender, and region—characteristics that are available in almost all large data sets? They show that characteristics explain a lot of the wage disparities, but residuals remain.

Table 5.5 gives the results from Altonji and Blank (1999), a standard study of wage disparities using household data from the Current Population Survey. In 1995, the wage gap between blacks and whites was roughly 21 percent (21 log points, to be precise) and the wage gap between Hispanics and NHWs was roughly 30 percent (30 log points). Altonji and Blank conduct the civil rights experiment. Of the 21 log points in the black-white difference, 8 are due to characteristics and 13 are residual. Of the 30 points in the Hispanic-

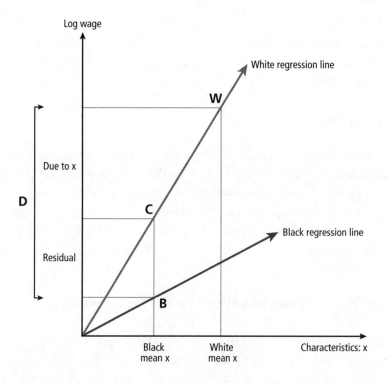

Figure 5.4. The civil rights experiment.

Table 5.5. Log wage gap from Current Population Survey data, both genders.

	1979	1995
Raw gaps		
Black-white	−0.165	−0.211
Hispanic-white	−0.126	−0.303
Due to characteristics (not including job characteristics or AFQT score)		
Black-white	−0.063	−0.082
Hispanic-white	−0.086	−0.193
Residual		
Black-white	−0.102	−0.134
Hispanic-white	−0.041	−0.112

Source: Altonji and Blank (1999).

NHW difference, 19 are due to characteristics and 11 are residual. Standard characteristics can't explain most of the black-white earnings difference among employed people, and they can't explain over a third of the Hispanic-NHW earnings difference.

Bottom Line

Booker T. Washington was partly right about earnings: a major reason why blacks and Hispanics make less than NHWs do is that they are less educated and blacks live in low-wage places. Over time, this part of the wage gap has been eroding for blacks. But a large part of the wage gap cannot be explained by standard, nonracial characteristics. Maybe W. E. B. Du Bois is still relevant today.

Empirical Studies of Labor Market Discrimination

The previous section showed that Hispanics and African Americans and Native Americans and Native Hawaiians did not do as well in the labor market as NHWs or Asians and as a result have less income on average. Standard characteristics don't explain this entire difference. The residual could arise for many reasons: for instance, something important for wages such as health could have been left out of the studies. But one reason could be that employers and customers treat blacks and Hispanics differently than they treat whites with the same productive characteristics. This is what is called *labor market discrimination*, and it's received lots of attention.

This section is empirical: it asks what research has shown about differential treatment and its implications. The following section asks why employers might act this way.

Disparate Treatment and Disparate Impact

First, though, I want to make a distinction between *disparate treatment* and *disparate impact*. These are legal terms, but we need them in order to be precise about what might be going on and what is going on. I'll introduce them and use them in a nonlegal sense first, before we get to legal usage. They refer to different kinds of discrimination.

Start with things that everyone can agree on. Consider the same firm employing a bunch of otherwise identical people doing the same thing but paying Hispanics less than whites. Everybody calls this discrimination. Or turning away large numbers of blacks while hiring productively identical whites. Or a little bit more difficult: hiring identical whites and Hispanics and placing whites in jobs that are clearly more desirable. This is the picture most people have of discrimination. To be precise, I call it *disparate treatment* discrimination. The difficult questions here are: What are productive characteristics and what is otherwise identical? How do you think about soft skills, such as confidence and getting along with co-workers?

For the most part, economists measure something else. The typical study measures disparities in wages or employment of otherwise equivalent people, no matter where they're employed. These studies use the results of household surveys: the census, and the Current Population Survey that we saw above; the National Longitudinal Study of Youth, which I'll discuss in this section; and several special smaller surveys. These studies look for *disparate impact,* or market-wide discrimination.

Let me try to be precise. In disparate treatment discrimination, a particular employer treats (or would treat) people of different races (or ethnicities) differently because of their race. In disparate impact discrimination, something happens that produces worse results for otherwise identical people of different races.

You can have disparate treatment without disparate impact, and you can have disparate impact without disparate treatment.

Disparate treatment without disparate impact: minorities might be segregated into nondiscriminatory firms that do very well. American whites are discriminated against (disparate treatment) in employment in North Korea, but they still do okay (no disparate impact).

Disparate impact without disparate treatment: suppose Hispanics believe (maybe wrongly) that high-paying firms discriminate, so they don't apply there. Or suppose that high-paying firms, deliberately or not, locate where few blacks or Hispanics can find them or firms base their actions on criteria that happen to be correlated with race but not with productivity: for instance, hiring friends and relatives of the owner.

So these are distinct ideas. But they could be linked, obviously.

Which one do we really care about it? It depends. If all we worry about is the well-being of Hispanic and black people, conventionally measured, then disparate impact is the story. If we're worried about psychological harm or the kind of society we're living in, then disparate treatment is what matters. If disparate impact is occurring, then knowing whether or not disparate treatment is also occurring might help in the design of policies.

Disparate Treatment Studies

With disparate treatment studies, the evidence is less controversial (although it's still controversial). These are field experiments; they're often called "audits."

In traditional audits, the researchers send people to employers and see how the employers react; in a recent study by Bertrand and Mullinaithan (2004), they sent resumes. When you run a traditional study, you hire a bunch of people of different races (generally college students in the summer). They're called "auditors." You pair them, one minority with one white. (One recent study sent trios of whites, blacks, and Hispanics.) In setting up the pairs, you try to make the two people as alike as possible. You then train them on how to answer questions and how to act when they go looking for jobs. You don't want them to get jobs; you want to find out what happens when they look for jobs.

Then you get the newspaper (I said traditional), go to the help-wanted ads, and dispatch your pairs to apply for randomly selected jobs. More recent studies have used both Craigslist and newspapers. Sometimes the minority auditor goes first, sometimes the white auditor. They're very similar but not identical. Then they report back on what happened and go to the next job.

What do these audit studies generally find? First, most of the time nobody gets a job. Since this is most of the results, it's important how you think about them. My inclination is to ignore such cases: they weren't qualified. The employers may have been biased or not.

Second, the rest of the time, either one or both get offers. More often than not, if only one gets an offer, it's the white auditor. Some numbers are in Table 5.6.

In the study by Pager, Western, and Bonikowski (2009) in New York City in 2004, young men applied for unskilled jobs. When nobody had a criminal record, whites got the most call-backs, then Hispanics (no significant difference from the NHW applicants), then blacks. When the white guy had

Table 5.6. Types of job offers auditors received contingent on at least one offer being made (percent).

	Both	White only	Minority only
Black and white, Chicago	44	38	18
Hispanic and non-Hispanic white	41	44	15

Sources: Black-white data from Urban Institute audits as reported in Heckman (1998), table 1; Hispanic–non-Hispanic white data from Kenney and Wissoker (1994).

a criminal record (prison time for selling cocaine), the white guy still got more call-backs than his minority counterparts with clean records, but the difference was not significant.

Sometimes the disparate treatment comes from a categorical, quick refusal to deal with the minority auditor. More often it comes in the interpretation of qualifications. The glass is half-full when the white guy brings it, half-empty when the black guy brings it.

Pager, Western, and Bonikowski also found that blacks were more likely to be "channeled down" and whites were more likely to be "channeled up." Channeled down means you apply for a job as a waiter and the employer offers you a job as a busboy. Channeled up is the opposite.

What are the correlates of turndowns? In one study, Hispanics did worse in high-income areas but whether the job involved customer contact didn't matter. In other studies, African American males and Hispanic females were less likely to suffer discrimination. Moss and Tilly (2001) talked with employers: employer statements were highly disparaging of black males and praised Hispanics. But the worse they talked about blacks, the more they hired them.

Traditional audit studies have several drawbacks. Heckman (1998) has two criticisms. First, sorting: it's not clear how these discriminatory employers actually affect anyone in real market transactions, since minorities might just steer clear of them. Second, unobserved characteristics: employers care about more than the characteristics that auditors were matched on. Things such as drive and initiative, a pleasant personality—all those good mushy words. Even if the two auditors have the same mean of these characteristics, if they have different variances employers will act differently. Another criticism is biased auditors: they know the purpose, this is not a serious job interview for them, and they can shade their behavior to get the desired result.

Pager, Western, and Bonikowski tried to address Heckman's criticism about unobserved characteristics by training and recruiting very carefully, experimenting with auditor-fixed effects, and pointing out that in a very large proportion of interviews, there is no meaningful contact with the employer.

Bertrand and Mullainathan (2004) addressed both Heckman's unobserved characteristics criticism and the biased auditor criticism. They just sent resumes. They first manufactured a list of white-sounding names and a bunch of black-sounding names that they got from Massachusetts birth certificates at the relevant time. Then they manufactured a set of resumes from actual resumes. They attached names to the resumes and formed pairs.

The beauty of this experiment is that the "auditors" didn't differ in unobserved characteristics because they didn't have any unobserved characteristics. Auditors couldn't consciously or unconsciously bias the results because there were no auditors.

What did Bertrand and Mullainathan find? First, most employers, over 80 percent, didn't call back. But those who did called "auditors" with white-sounding names 50 percent more often than the "auditors" with black-sounding names. At the extremes, 15.9 percent of employers called Brad, but only 2.2 percent called Aisha. Better characteristics led to more call-backs for whites, but not for blacks.

Notice, however, that by answering one of Heckman's criticisms of audits, Bertrand and Mullainathan move further away from addressing the other criticism. All they learned is whether the auditors got called back for interviews. Since there weren't any real auditors, no one went for the interviews and we never find out more. We don't know about hiring. Clearly, getting called back for an interview can make a difference to your life, but we don't know how much. All the Brads might have been rejected, since all they had going for them was their first name, and Aisha may have gotten the job.

Fryer and Levitt (2004a) raise some additional problems for how you interpret the Bertrand and Mullainathan experiment. They have data on real people with African American names in California. They find, first, that people with African American names don't do worse than people of similar background without African American names. You don't blight a child's life by calling her Aisha. This may explain why parents choose these names.

But children with African American names come from worse backgrounds. So employers may be using the name as a signal about background. Is this discrimination? Yes—but discrimination about background, not about race.

Disparate Impact Studies

The idea in disparate impact studies is to run regressions and see if race makes a difference to wages or employment once you've controlled for everything you're supposed to control for. Sometimes this is done with one regression; sometimes it's done with two. This procedure allows us to see if something is making minorities worse off that the audits can't tell us about. But the procedure can't tell us what that is, if anything.

As we saw in the medical care case, it's hard to get the right explanatory variables. To the extent that we can't agree on the right explanatory variables, we can't agree on the existence or extent of disparate impact discrimination.

All of the problems from the medical care case—excluded variables and included variables—are present in the labor market case. Labor brings up one new variety of included variable problem: endogenous included variables. Say we include years of actual experience in a wage regression. Clearly experience can be related to productivity. But holding age constant, blacks have fewer years of experience on average because they have lower employment rates. So including actual experience reduces the estimate of discrimination. Should it be included?

My answer: it depends on what you're looking for. If you're looking at a particular firm, include it. If you're looking at actual discrimination right this minute, include it. If you're looking for how the labor market affects the lives of minorities, exclude it.

Other variables like this include health, marital status, industry, and occupation.

What did these studies find? Recent studies—based on 1990s data—generally find something like the Altonji and Blank results. Leaving out controls for occupation and AFQT (which we'll discuss in a little while), you get an "unexplained gap" of

Black males	12–15 percent (occasionally up to 20 percent)
Black females	less than this
Blacks overall	around 11–13 percent
Hispanics overall	around 11 percent

Notice the contrast with the audit results.

For future reference when we look at theory, these studies find no difference in rate of return to education—again in contrast to the audit studies.

Before going on to discuss how AFQT affects these results, let me discuss two related topics in disparate impact analysis: skin tone and beauty.

Beauty. A substantial body of literature in which researchers run regressions similar to the standard ones for race finds that beautiful people get paid more, holding the usual characteristics constant, just like white people. The wage difference for two standard deviations in beauty—one standard deviation above the mean compared with one standard deviation below—is about 10–15 percent, just like the standard racial wage gaps.

The beauty premium doesn't seem to be due mainly to directly productive characteristics. Jobs with customer interaction, where worker beauty might increase employer profit, aren't much different from other jobs.

We'll come back to think about the beauty premium when we talk about theory and policy.

Skin tone. Since people with very different complexions are usually classified (using U.S. conventions) as African American, a few studies have looked at how complexion affects wages. (I'm not aware of any results on how skin tone affects the wages of Hispanics, but I haven't looked too hard.) Several small special data sets have information about skin tone (usually poorly measured).

At this point, I don't think this literature tells us much. The main result is that light-complexioned people do better, with little difference between medium complexion and dark complexion. Light-complexioned people have higher wages and more education. Holding education and a rich array of other variables constant still leaves light-complexioned people making more money on average, but this difference is not always significant. The data sets involved are small.

This difference is not explained by beauty.

I don't think there are any big conclusions to draw yet. These groups are different on average in both observable and unobservable ways. That they are paid differently is no surprise.

The AFQT controversy. The 10–15 percent gap is where things stood until the mid-1990s when researchers started looking at a new variable: AFQT—the person's score on the Armed Forces Qualifying Test. This variable is available in a particular data set called the National Longitudinal Survey of Youth (NLSY). This is a federally funded survey that started with several thousand young people in the late 1970s, collected a great deal of information about them and their families then, and has been following them (and now their children) ever since. The NLSY started with 12,686 people born between 1957 and 1964.

The AFQT is a paper-and-pencil test like the SAT that the armed forces developed to help them place people in the right jobs. The NLSY people took the AFQT in 1980.

All the economists who write about the AFQT describe it as a measure of skills or achievement or what you learned in high school. Coaching can improve your score, and your score rises as you get more education. The standard term for what the AFQT measures is "pre–labor market conditions." Unfortunately, in *The Bell Curve,* Herrnstein and Murray (1994) call what the AFQT measures "intelligence." This is not accurate.

The AFQT has four subtests: arithmetic reasoning, word comprehension, paragraph comprehension, and numerical operations.

The Department of Defense and the National Academy of Sciences have tried to remove racial bias from the AFQT for DoD purposes. They've been fairly successful: various parts are good predictors of how well you will do at various military tasks.

When you add AFQT total scores to a standard wage regression, a large part of the gap for black men is removed and all of the gap for other groups. Some results show small premiums for some minority groups.

Neal and Johnson (1996) is the most definitive paper that uses the AFQT and gets results like this. The wage data come from the early 1990s when the NLSY people were in their late 20s.

The basic Neal and Johnson results use a single equation and control only for age, AFQT, and AFQT squared. They find that for Hispanics and black women, AFQT explains almost all or more than all of the wage gap with whites. AFQT reduces the wage gap for black men from 24 log points to 7. See Table 5.7.

The conclusion that Neal and Johnson draw is that for the most part, wage disparities are determined before people enter the labor force. In their phrase, "pre–labor market" factors are responsible for almost all of the wage gaps. To understand the wage gaps or do anything about them, you have to

Table 5.7. Neal and Johnson results on wage gap and AFQT scores.

	Raw gap (log points)	Adjusting for AFQT score
Black men	−24.2	−7.2
Hispanic men	−19.6	−2.5
Black women	−18.5	+3.5
Hispanic women	−2.5	+14.5

Source: Neal and Johnson (1996).

concentrate on education, health, and parenting. Race may matter before you go to work, but once you start looking for jobs, your skills (as measured by AFQT) are all that matter.

Of course, it should be clear that these are results about only a particular labor market variable—hourly wages—for a particular age group—young adults—at a particular historical moment—the 1990s. When Johnson and Neal (1998) looked at earnings rather than wages, they found that black men earned 27 percent less than whites, holding age and AFQT scores constant. Since earnings are the product of wages and hours worked, most of this difference comes from non-employment. Tomaskovic-Devey, Thomas, and Johnson (2005) looked at the participants in the NLSY when they reached the age of 40 and found that a much larger wage gap had opened up, controlling for AFQT scores. They couldn't tell whether aging or the changing U.S. economy was responsible.

The results for black men started a large controversy. Selection issues make comparisons of women's wages difficult, and since everyone in the NLSY was living in the United States in the 1970s, the sample is not representative of the current Hispanic population. When Neal (2004) corrected for selection, he found the wage gap for black women to be about the same as that for black men.

Neal and Johnson have answered some of the objections to their methods. The AFQT is an unbiased test, and it is for the armed services. When Neal and Johnson ran black and white regressions separately (the Hispanic sample is too small to get meaningful results), the rate at which higher AFQT increased wages seemed to be about the same on average for blacks as it was for whites; thus AFQT scores don't appear to be like sunblock. The sample in their study is restricted to people who were earning wages, but when later studies tried to account for people without wages, the results didn't change much.

Some other objections have proved more durable. For instance, Rodgers and Spriggs (1996) find that the math part of AFQT predicts wages for whites while the verbal part predicts wages for blacks. This is not consistent with the idea that the market is responding to the same set of skills for blacks and whites. Neal and Johnson's result, then, that blacks and whites have the same rate of return to AFQT depends on the weighting of the verbal and math parts of the test, which is arbitrary. If the verbal part is weighted more, blacks have a higher rate of return to AFQT than whites do; if the math part is weighted more, blacks have a lower rate of return.

Several other papers have argued the Neal and Johnson's results suffer from omitted variable bias. Neal and Johnson deliberately used only age and AFQT instead of the large number of variables researchers usually use when they fit wage regressions. They argue that this spare approach is the best way to find out how much of the wage gaps are due to pre–labor market factors and how much are due to labor market functioning. Standard explanatory variables such as region and experience don't belong in the equation because they're endogenous, given a person's skills when he or she enters the labor market. If you compared two people who entered the labor market at the same time with the same AFQT scores and one lives in Mississippi and the other lives in New York, that was something the labor market did, so current region should not be an explanatory variable for Neal and Johnson's purpose.

Goldsmith, Darity, and Veum (1998), in contrast, added a number of variables that measure psychological traits at around the time the NLSY members took the AFQT. Presumably, an individual's psychological attributes—like being able to plan ahead and get along with other people—should matter in how she navigates the labor market over her life, not just the kind of knowledge measured in the AFQT. If you compare men with the same AFQT, black men are better psychologically adjusted than white. When Goldsmith, Darity, and Veum added psychological variables, the unexplained wage gap rose to traditional levels that studies without AFQT usually find, even when they held AFQT scores constant.

When Lang and Manove (2011) and Carneiro, Heckman, and Masterov (2005) added education to the Neal and Johnson equation, the gap between black and white men also widened to the traditional size. Again, if you compare people with the same AFQT, blacks get more education than whites: if you compare two individuals, one black and one white, with the same AFQT score in their late teens, the black individual will on average end up with about a year and a half more education than the white person. However, when you compare men with the same education and the same AFQT scores, you will find that blacks earn less. Black men don't appear to be compensated for the extra education they get.

The same result doesn't hold for Hispanic men: adding education to the AFQT equation doesn't make the unexplained gap bigger.

Neal and Johnson considered adding education to their wage equation, but they rejected the idea for two reasons. First, they said, education was endogenous: skills and labor market opportunities, not color, determine how much education a young adult will get, so everything interesting about education is already in AFQT. Lang and Manove reject this argument. Holding AFQT constant, race matters in determining education. Blacks need more education than equally able whites to demonstrate their ability and productivity to skeptical employers, so they get more education. The labor market, in Lang and Manove's view, induces blacks to get more education than whites to earn the same wages; this effect shouldn't be considered a pre–labor market factor.

Neal and Johnson's second argument against using education is that blacks on average get lower-quality education. Employers care about the output of educational activities, not the inputs into them, so AFQT contains all the information about education that is relevant to productivity. Blacks stay in school longer, but only because the poorer quality of the education they receive means they must persist longer to learn as much as whites do. The market is right to ignore these additional years.

Lang and Manove respond empirically by including measures of school quality in their wage regressions. These reduce the size of the gap for men, but not by much. On the theory side, they argue that lower quality doesn't necessarily increase time in school (dropouts are associated with bad schools, not good ones).

My take on this controversy is that it's probably not over. Goldsmith, Darity, and Veum, and Lang and Manove, are probably right to add more variables to the spare Neal and Johnson equation. When they enter the labor market, people bring attributes such as health, strength, endurance, and the ability to charm a reluctant customer, and employers rightly care about these attributes. Region of birth influences the cost of being in a region where jobs are plentiful and wages are high; being born in the New York area or in the Bay area makes it easier for you to find and keep a high-paying job. These are pre–labor market factors, and they are not the same as the skills AFQT measures. When Black et al. (2009) added location to the basic equation, the estimated wage gap increased.

The more serious question that both Lang and Manove and Rodgers and Spriggs raise is whether a distinction between pre–labor market experience and labor market experience is relevant when children (or their parents) can anticipate what will happen in the labor market. If employers treat every characteristic or set of characteristics at the margin the same for blacks as for whites, then you can make a clean distinction between pre–labor market experience and labor market experience because only differences in pre–labor market conditions such as schools will cause people to make different decisions about pre–labor market investments. The return to every possible pre–labor market investment will be independent of race. But both Rodgers and Spriggs and Lang and Manove show that the return to some pre–labor market investments is different for blacks than it is for whites. So different labor market reactions to their investments would cause blacks and whites to make different pre–labor market investments even if their pre–labor market conditions were identical. Thus the Rodgers and Spriggs and Lang and Manove results indicate that a clean distinction between labor market operations and pre–labor market investments is not meaningful. You have to assume either no discrimination or a very particular kind of discrimination in the labor market for a distinction between pre–labor market investments and labor market operations to make any sense.

Theory

When I talk about theory in an undergraduate class, about 60 percent of the students go to sleep and most of the rest wonder why I'm doing it. So I'd better start off telling you why I'm doing it.

The world is very complicated. We want our beliefs about it to be consistent and we want to be able to assess our beliefs against the evidence we have. Economic theory is a crutch to help us to do that. If we were smarter or if the world were simpler, we wouldn't need it.

In economic theory, we start with a simple story about how people interact and draw as many implications as we can from it so we can see whether the story makes sense.

If I tell you a story about why minorities get paid less or work less, economic theory lets us think systematically about this story and probe it for weaknesses. Why would you want to know why minorities get paid less? Because different reasons have different implications for policy, as we'll see below.

In this section, I'll discuss several separate classes of theories about discrimination: Marxian theories ("discrimination for profit"), Beckerian theories ("taste-based discrimination"), community pressure theories, statistical discrimination theories ("discrimination from ignorance"), and transaction-based theories. This is roughly the historical order of the appearance of these theories. Along the way I'll say something about why beautiful people get paid more.

Each model of discrimination sounds good when you start but then runs into problems. Most of them probably describe some part of what's going on or has gone on, but none by itself is a complete picture. That's why this section is so long.

Marxian Theories ("Discrimination for Profit")

Marxian theories are the oldest. Capitalists as a class gain in several ways if white people generally dislike black people. First, this makes workers disunited and prevents a strong workers' movement from forming; such a movement would either get a larger share of revenue or overthrow the capitalists. Second, it allows capitalists to pay black workers less and to have a reserve army of unemployed blacks.

Even assuming that these benefits are real, the story is still weak. First there is the collective action problem—every individual capitalist has good reason to deviate and break the cartel—to act like a free-rider, in other words. Second is the mechanism problem: if the capitalist class can get itself together to do this, what mechanism do they have to make whites dislike blacks? Third is the motive question: if capitalists can both overcome free-riding and manipulate workers' minds, why don't they just raise prices and cut wages without going through all the white-sheets-and-burning-crosses rigmarole? If they can manipulate white workers' attitudes, why don't they make white workers love high prices and low wages instead or at least make them love tranquility and exempting capital gains from taxation? If capitalists as a class have all these powers, is it reasonable that the only thing they could use them for is beating up on blacks? The capitalist class is better off when I leave my umbrella home on a rainy day too, but I don't think that the Rockefellers and the Gateses sit around plotting distractions so I will forget my umbrella. People can profit from a condition without causing it.

Taste-Based Theories

Taste-based theories are the oldest formal discrimination theories in economics; they were first proposed by Gary Becker in 1957. Essentially they say that the wage differential arises because some whites dislike doing something with blacks. Exactly what that something is—being near, working with, eating a hamburger served by—differs in different versions. There is no story about why whites (or anyone else) have these preferences. The economics is about the consequences of these preferences.

Discrimination by identical capitalists. In the simplest Becker model, every employer is the same and becomes worse off for every hour of work that a black person does in his firm. The employer doesn't maximize profit; instead, he maximizes profit minus the disutility of his being around black workers. Black and white workers are perfect substitutes in production. The employer loses d in utility for every hour a black worker works in his firm, even though black workers work just as hard and produce just as much as white workers. Let w_w denote the wage of a white worker and w_b denote the wage of a black worker. If both black and white workers are employed, the first-order conditions for profit maximizing are

$$\text{Marginal revenue product of labor} = w_w$$
$$\text{Marginal revenue product of labor} - d = w_b.$$

Hence

$$w_w = w_b + d.$$

Blacks are paid less.

The prejudice d could be nepotism too—how much employers are willing to pay for working with their friends and relatives who are of the same race.

Capitalists who differ. What happens when capitalists differ in their distaste for having blacks work for them? Assume many capitalists, competition, and constant returns to scale in production. Let $d_1 < d_2 < d_3 < \ldots$.

Capitalists who have lower numbers have less taste for discrimination.

Suppose $w_b <$ Marginal revenue product $- d_1$. Then employer 1 will make money and gain utility every time he hires a black worker. He should expand and expand. All blacks will work for him and he'll be rich. (This is reminiscent of Schindler in *Schindler's List*.) Employer 1 is doing well by doing good. So the wage is

$$Marginal\ revenue\ product - d_2 = w_w - d_2 = w_b.$$

The second least discriminatory employer sets the standard.

Suppose there are a few employers who are fair: $d_2 = 0$. Maybe they're black or maybe they're absentees who see only green, not black and white. Then the wage differential disappears. This is an example of disparate treatment without disparate impact.

In this sense, Becker's theory of discrimination is about why disparate impact discrimination can't persist. But it has persisted.

This is interesting: it says that your naïve ideas about discrimination don't work. It doesn't say that discrimination doesn't occur or doesn't persist; it says that we have to think hard to understand why. What's wrong with this model?

There are many ways to tweak the model. Some work and some don't. For instance, monopoly by itself doesn't get rid of the problem of disparate treatment without disparate impact. Suppose there is a monopolist or a monopsonist who discriminates and pays blacks lower wages. She would make more money by paying whites lower wages and hiring more blacks, until the wages were equal. What happens? If the stock is publicly traded, a raider can come along and buy her out or do a leveraged buyout. If the raider is less discriminatory, she will make more money. If the firm is private already, a less discriminatory raider can buy her out directly because the raider will offer her more than the present value of the profits she would make. Then she can retire to someplace where she will never see blacks.

Discrimination by workers. An alternative story is that white workers, not capitalists, dislike black workers and require a wage premium to work along-side them. Suppose black and white workers are perfect substitutes for each other and both are reasonably plentiful. Then the result will be segregation: no firm employing black workers would want to hire a white worker (since another black worker would not require a wage premium), and no firm employing white workers would want to hire a black worker (since the white workers would demand a wage premium or quit). But black and white workers will be paid the same: if black workers were paid less, the firms that employed them could make output more cheaply than the firms that employed whites, and either the black-employing firms would expand or the white-employing firms would decide to replace their entire work forces with blacks. We would observe disparate treatment (blacks would not be hired at some firms), but no disparate impact.

As with the models with discriminatory capitalists, models with discriminatory capitalists do a poor job of explaining the observed wage and employment disparities.

For examples of taste models that don't fall apart, see the next two sections.

Customers who discriminate. Suppose that customers are identical and that they prefer hamburgers flipped by whites to hamburgers flipped by blacks: in particular, they are willing to pay only 90 percent as much for a hamburger flipped by a black as for a hamburger flipped by a white. If both types of hamburger are actually sold, the wage of black hamburger-flippers has to be lower than the wage of white hamburger-flippers.

What about heterogeneity? Here relative numbers matter. If there are only a few hamburger customers who feel this way and not many black hamburger-flippers, then in equilibrium there will be segregation but no differential in pay. The discriminatory customers will all go to the place where all the flippers are white, and everybody else will go to the other restaurants, where the flippers will be of all races. This is like my dislike of the British royal family: I would never eat a hamburger they served (or any other hamburger, actually), but they don't care. This is another example of disparate treatment without disparate impact.

But if there are many discriminatory customers and many black hamburger-flippers, then all of the black guys will be employed (as they must be in equilibrium) only if some of them are serving discriminatory customers. And since all of them must get the same wage in equilibrium, that wage has to be lower than the white wage. But if customers differ in how discriminatory they are, it is the marginal discriminatory customer who is actually served by a black flipper who matters.

There is evidence of customer discrimination in some markets: basketball, baseball, baseball cards. But not in other jobs: basketball coaches, domestic service. And many jobs do not involve customer contact: you don't know the race of the person who put the lead in your pencil or who answered the call you made to a call center. But some people have a comparative advantage at jobs that involve customer contact and they will not do as well at the next-best job if they can't do what they do best. And jobs involving personal interaction seem to be becoming more important over time as the U.S. economy moves in the direction of less manufacturing and more services.

Search models with heterogeneous discriminatory employers.   Discrimination can also persist when there is labor market friction, even if some employers are nondiscriminatory.

Suppose some fraction of employers dislike blacks and will never hire them. But you can't tell who they are. Workers search for jobs because each worker-employer pair has an uncertain nonpecuniary value that they can learn only after applying for the job. Employers have some monopsony power: once a worker is standing in front of the employer, a worker who turns down the wage offer will have to spend more time and energy searching and may not find a better job. If the offer is very high, the worker is likely to agree—the match is unlikely to be terrible and the worker isn't likely to need to do further searching to find something better. A lower offer leads to more profit for the employer but a lower chance of acceptance. The optimal offer for the employer trades off the two forces—just as a monopolist trades off sales volume for margin.

If all workers look alike, nondiscriminatory employers will make the same offer to all of them. But suppose black workers look different from white. An unprejudiced employer knows that blacks have worse prospects than whites in future job searches because they may encounter prejudiced employers and have to search longer. So she knows that continued searching is less attractive to blacks than to whites and that blacks are thus more likely to accept an offer. So unprejudiced employers make lower wage offers to blacks. Blacks end up with lower wages and more unemployment (they have to search longer).

What about firm profits? Unprejudiced firms make more profit. Why can't they expand and put prejudiced firms out of business? The supply of entrepreneurial talent is not infinitely elastic: fewer prejudiced firms operate, but some do. You can't expand your firm infinitely.

Notice that if potential entrepreneurs are more prejudiced, the wage differential is bigger. Also, if there are more black workers relative to the supply of unprejudiced firms, the wage differential is bigger.

This model assumes that firms can't advertise themselves as unprejudiced or develop reputations, workers can't look at the existing work force, and the capital market is not perfect. Otherwise the discriminatory employers would be out of business because they have higher costs.

Empirical. Charles and Guryan (2008) review the Becker models—actually, the last two Becker models. Suppose either that customers discriminate or that some employers discriminate but workers have to search for jobs. Then the black-white wage disparity will depend on how prejudiced the marginal employer or customer is—that is, the most prejudiced employer or customer who actually engages with a black worker. If there are more blacks, the marginal employer or customer will be a more prejudiced person, since an additional black worker requires that another employer or customer willing to deal with a black worker must be found, and all the less prejudiced ones are already engaging with black workers. How prejudiced the most prejudiced guys are won't matter—they're out of the game.

Charles and Guryan compare U.S. states. First they calculate the distribution of prejudice in each state over time from the General Social Survey, using answers to questions such as whether you think interracial marriage should be permitted as a proxy for prejudice. There are big regional differences in the direction you would expect—New England and the West are the least prejudiced, the New South the most prejudiced. Prejudice is declining over time too. (Perhaps measures of unconscious rather than propositional racism might have been more useful, since the former often predict behavior better [Bertrand, Chugh, and Mullinathan 2005; Rooth 2007; Van der Bergh et al. 2010], but Charles and Guryan didn't have a large national sample of such scores.)

Then they calculate the unexplained portion of the wage gap for workers—pretty much the standard regression. Then they regress the wage gap on the proportion of blacks and several measures of the distribution of prejudice. How prejudiced the most prejudiced whites are makes no difference, as Becker predicts. The proportion of blacks matters—more blacks results in a bigger wage gap, as predicted. And how prejudiced the least prejudiced whites and "marginal whites" are also matters, as Becker predicts.

This sort of prejudice accounts for about a quarter of the wage gap, which is something, but not everything.

You should still have some questions about prejudice, however. Your first reaction may be this: "Of course—prejudice is greatest in the New South, where it was greatest historically." Sounds nice. But prejudice in the Becker model is aversion to being with people of the other race. Then how do you account for the fact that these states passed anti-enticement laws in the early twentieth century to prevent recruiters from luring African Americans to the North? If the whites in those states dislike being around blacks, why do they live in some of the states with the highest proportion of black population?

Community Pressure Stories

Community pressure is implicit in Myrdal, and it comes up in several empirical studies that examine the impact of civil rights legislation in the 1960s. But I don't know of any rigorous theoretical exposition. Think of community pressure, first of all, as a model of the mid-twentieth-century South. The idea is that employers outside agriculture are afraid of reprisals from customers, other workers, suppliers, or local governments if they employ blacks.

The first implication is that however community pressure works, it produces lower profits for non-agricultural firms; essentially it's a tax on black employment. So it leads to less investment, less development, and industrial land that is less valuable. This implication is consistent with the fact that the South was an industrial backwater in the mid-twentieth century.

How does it work? Possibly local governments (without black voters) could organize community pressure. Who gains? Agricultural landowners and employers gain because of lower wages for blacks in agriculture; white workers might possibly gain from reduced competition in non-agricultural jobs. These gains to agricultural landowners are consistent with anti-enticement laws. Does it pay to implement community pressure? Possibly, if some white workers gain from higher wages as a result of excluding blacks from industry. But it may result in lower wages on net because of general underdevelopment.

Information-Based Theories—Statistical Discrimination

The first statistical discrimination theory was put forward by Edmund Phelps in 1972.

The stories I told about races when we were trying to define them were about beliefs, not values. I don't hate salamanders; I think I'm smarter. I love my two cats and would accept a pay cut if they could be with me at work, but I wouldn't go to them if I needed an appendectomy.

So if employers think minorities are less competent, given education and everything that is easily observable, it's not surprising that they hire them less often and pay them less. (To the extent that the propensities shown in the unconscious racism experiments are like beliefs, discrimination that arises from them can also be labeled statistical.) But if this belief is wrong, we get back to our old problem: Why don't smarter employers put the dumb guys out of business?

Several different approaches produce several different kinds of statistical discrimination stories.

Maybe minorities are less productive. Hispanics are more likely to be illegal immigrants than Anglos, and it's difficult to tell who is really legal. If the government finds out that employees are illegal, the employer is likely to lose money. Bansak and Raphael (2001) show that laws against hiring illegal immigrants reduce Hispanic wages.

Poor perception and self-fulfilling prophecies. Suppose that employers can't observe the skill level of blacks as well as they can observe that of whites. Then blacks will have a lower rate of return to skill than whites. Hence blacks will invest less. Then most blacks will be unskilled.

These models have two problems. Empirically, blacks don't seem to have lower rate of return to education than whites. Theoretically, why can't the smarter firms put the dumber firms out of business?

Getting stuck with self-fulfilling prophecies.   Several theories about discrimination rely on rational, self-fulfilling beliefs about blacks' qualifications—stereotypes, essentially. According to these theories, no single employer can get rich by being smarter or more mercenary than other employers because even the smartest and most mercenary employer will discriminate.

These theories use Bayes' theorem, which is stated and discussed in Appendix A. This theorem lets economic theorists reason about a world in which, on the one hand, people's minds are not blank slates, but on the other, experience forces people to modify their beliefs. For instance, if you asked me to estimate the average height of Estonian men (which I've never looked up), I would guess something—I wouldn't just stare at you. But I would revise that estimate upward if you also told me that the Estonian national men's basketball team placed second in the European championships. But if I originally thought Estonians were very short, I might attribute their success to clever play or dishonest referees, not height, and my final estimate of Estonian height would be less than if I was originally mainly agnostic. Bayes' theorem gives an explicit formula for carrying out this sort of reasoning.

The first complete model where employers use Bayesian reasoning was developed by Glenn Loury and Steven Coate. This model is a circle. Employers have prior beliefs about workers, employers give tests and interpret those tests in light of their prior beliefs (and Bayes' theorem), employers hire based on the updated beliefs, workers decide whether to invest based on the results they see, workers' investment decisions produce different proportions of qualified workers, and employers' prior beliefs are consistent with the proportions of qualified workers that investment decisions produce. You can start anywhere in this circle and keep going around. Economic theory requires consistency all the way around.

Assume that employers' prior beliefs are that blacks are less likely to be qualified than whites. Then when they interpret the test results, they require a higher score from black applicants before they will deem these applicants qualified. We saw this happening in New York City in 2004 with the Pager, Western, and Bonikowski audit studies. Thus blacks are less likely to be hired for the skilled job and go into the unskilled job more often and get lower wages. Blacks see that investment does not pay off as well for them as it does for whites, hence they invest less than whites (this step is not necessary, as we will see in the Moro-Norman model below: substitution effects say less

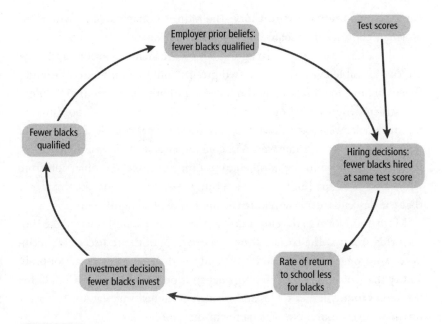

Figure 5.5.

investment but income effects say more). Thus they are less likely to be qualified. Employers' prior beliefs that blacks are less likely to be qualified are justified.

(What about implicit bias? It depends on how employers' discriminatory propensities arise. If the unconscious propensity arises from experience and that experience is updated in Bayesian fashion, then nothing in the Coate-Loury model needs to be changed; it wasn't necessary that employers be conscious of what they were doing. But if the employers' unconscious racist propensities are idiosyncratic or fail to respond to new information in Bayesian fashion, then Bayesian employers, who will be conscious racists, will put the unconscious racists out of business over time.)

Figure 5.5 illustrates this circle, and Appendix B gives a numerical example.

One problem with this model is that it requires that the return to education be less for blacks than it is for whites. Empirically that does not appear to be the case.

Putting some teeth in Coate-Loury: The Moro-Norman model.   Moro and Norman consider the Coate-Loury and similar models and point out that they don't have any teeth. Blacks and whites are identical groups and there are two possible equilibria. The two groups could be on separate islands. Blacks are in a low-investment, low-wage equilibrium, whites are in a high-investment, high-wage equilibrium, and it's a shame. It's a coordination failure: blacks wear snowshoes and parkas for formal occasions, and whites wear business suits without ties. As a consequence, it's a Pareto improvement for blacks to move to the good equilibrium: let's do it. No objection from whites, no need for Jim Crow or anything else. And it's just a coincidence that the descendants of slaves are the ones in the bad equilibrium.

Moro and Norman develop a different twist on Coate-Loury where they turn this around. The basic setting is the same, but the test score is continuous. Your wage in the skilled job depends on the employer's posterior probability that you're qualified, so wage depends on test score and race. Higher test scores imply higher wages and whites get higher wages at any test score if whites invest more. No big change in this story so far.

The big change is that skilled and unskilled labor are inputs into a standard diminishing marginal returns production function, like Cobb-Douglas. So forgetting about race and information for a moment, if the ratio of skilled to unskilled labor goes up, the relative wage of skilled labor goes down. Scarcity matters.

Now think about what happens when the proportion of skilled blacks goes up for some reason. For blacks, two effects offset each other. First, employers change their prior belief on blacks being qualified, which implies higher wages for all blacks. Second, more skilled workers lead to a lower premium for having high skill, and hence lower wages for all skilled workers.

The size of the minority group matters (as in Charles and Guryan). For a small group, the first effect (better prior beliefs) is larger than the second (lower premium on skill). For a large group, the opposite holds. So, for instance, for Asians in the United States, more skilled workers unambiguously implies higher average wages because the skill premium changes little, but for blacks in South Africa, the skill premium would shrink.

Now consider the effect on whites of the presence of more skilled blacks. Only the reduction of the skill premium matters for them; the prior beliefs employers hold about them don't change. So whites are worse off unambiguously. This produces a conflict between races. In the Coate-Loury model, unilateral re-coordination is possible, but not here. Blacks and whites are not on separate islands in the Moro-Norman model: blacks invest little because whites invest a lot and vice versa. Moving blacks away from the bad equilibrium is no longer a Pareto improvement.

Beauty: Why does beauty matter? Can we learn something about race? Mobius and Rosenblatt's (2006) study of beauty gives a species of a circular stereotype model, except that some of the words are changed around.

Investment in this story is not in skills but in confidence. Usually, confidence makes you more productive, especially if it's well placed. Confidence is something that you develop as a child and adolescent. The key assumption is that the beautiful and the unbeautiful have different costs for developing confidence. In childhood, it's easier for the beautiful to develop confidence because adults and teachers treat them better (there's good social psychology evidence for this).

Confidence plays out in the labor market in two ways. First, more confident workers get employers to pay them more because employers rationally believe that more confident workers will do better. This is an effect that should survive when people deal over the phone: more beautiful workers who apply by phone should do better.

Second, employers who see their workers should pay beautiful workers more because they believe these workers are more confident on average and therefore better workers on average.

Mobius and Rosenblatt's research is based on a series of clever experiments to see how important these various effects are. "Workers" solve mazes (a task that has no obvious link to beauty) and "employers" have to estimate how well they'll do. Sometimes employers see the workers, sometimes they talk on the phone. Mobius and Rosenblatt conclude that 15–20 percent of the premium is due to confidence. Half of each remaining part is attributable to audio information and half to visual information.

What do we learn about race from this research? It seems entirely possible that this sort of phenomenon could be at work if you substitute "white" for "beautiful." So these results are in keeping with the literature on circular stereotypes. But there are differences in investment cost—unlike a lot of the circular stereotype models, where whites and blacks are absolutely identical and so whenever you find an equilibrium where whites earn more you can also find an equilibrium where blacks earn more.

Is statistical discrimination really different from taste-based discrimination? The distinction at first appears obvious: taste-based discrimination is about the discriminator's preferences, statistical discrimination is about her beliefs, and preferences and beliefs are different. Thus new information can affect statistical discrimination but not taste-based discrimination.

But discrimination based on implicit bias doesn't seem to fit well into either category. Anti-minority propensities in priming and implicit association tests can hardly be called beliefs, because beliefs are something you know you have. But they're not preferences, either, since they probably arise from experience and respond to certain kinds of new information.

In general, the distinction between preferences and beliefs is a lot less clear than economists like to think. Just observing that you drink large quantities of whiskey can't tell an observer whether you like it or you think it's good for your health, and if someone asks you whether you think it's good for your health, your answer may be either what you want them to believe, what you want yourself to believe, or something like the truth, if you know it. Thus, for instance, when Charles and Guryan used responses to questions on the General Social Survey to measure preferences for discrimination, they were really measuring a combination of preferences and beliefs. White people could oppose intermarriage, for instance, because they didn't like black people or because they believed that intermarriage would reduce the quality of hockey or classical music in the United States.

The relevant distinction, I think, is much less grand. The distinction is between models that try to explain the discriminatory impulses they contain—statistical discrimination—and models that don't explain discriminatory impulses—taste-based discrimination. The latter models don't need to maintain that discriminatory impulses are immutable or mysterious, only that they are best studied by someone else or at some other time.

The implicit bias experiments thus suggest that a strong claim is implicit in the statistical discrimination literature and a possible weakness. This is the assumption that in the long run employers' beliefs about race in the labor market reflect only experiences in the labor market (or possibly only their own experiences in the labor market). You don't even need to accept implicit bias to question the relevance of this assumption. Suppose employers are good Bayesians and use all the information available to them (this is the common assumption about investors). In the modern world, that information includes a continuing barrage of news about minority and nonminority individuals—

public and private information about celebrities and nobodies, crime and politics, sports and business, good and bad. Then they will update their prior beliefs with this information. Only with very strong restrictions on the content of this information will it be irrelevant to the long-run equilibrium in the labor market. We will see an example of how this might work in the empirical results on drug-testing laws that I discuss in the next section.

Once again we will see that spheres are linked together.

Transactions Difficulties (Not Well-Developed)

Language is sometimes a barrier for Hispanics and Asians. Transactions between people are more difficult when they don't speak the same language well. No surprise. Can this be generalized?

Remember medical care. Subtle, complex transactions involving trust were difficult, even when both parties wanted them to work out. Jobs are sometimes like this too: getting hired, getting along with co-workers and customers, figuring out when you can get the afternoon off to take care of family business, negotiating raises, and so on. Trust is important. If medical care transactions sometimes fail, labor market transactions may also fail sometimes. This theory has not been well developed yet or tested empirically.

Conclusions about Discrimination and Second Thoughts

In this section, we've seen researchers try to answer the following questions: suppose you start with two completely otherwise identical groups of people who differ only in racial label. Can you end up in an equilibrium with different wage distributions? That is: If history had never happened and we started off with a clean slate today, could you get a racial wage differential? Under what conditions?

For empirical work, the question is: Suppose we hold everything relevant to production constant, so econometrically we project ourselves into a world where the slate has been wiped clean, would there be a wage differential?

In both cases, we've seen that these are difficult questions. They seem to ignore Booker T. Washington entirely and try to describe the world in extreme W. E. B. Du Bois terms.

Perhaps these aren't the right questions. The interesting question for today should be something like this: Given the particular existing disparities, does the operation of the labor market today make the disparities bigger or smaller? The problem with this natural question is that the disparities you start off with—AFQT score or years of education, say—are measured one way and the disparities you end up with are measured another way—wages or earnings or employment rates. In general, you can't compare them—with one exception.

The exception is when the disparity you start off with is zero. Then, however you measure it, if the disparity you end up with is greater than zero, the labor market is making the disparity bigger. Because zero has this convenient property, theorists and empiricists keep using it.

But this isn't the only way researchers could operate. In education and in crime, we'll see a few ideas closer to the question, starting with present non-labor disparities. This is also why this is a book about race, not about labor or education.

Since policy is ultimately our concern, maybe it would be better if researchers concentrated directly on policies, not on the intermediate step of attaching the word discrimination to different activities. So instead of theories about discrimination, we would have theories about civil rights laws or affirmative action and test them against data on civil rights laws or affirmative action. That would be another way to approach research in this area.

Policy

Very few policies for dealing with minority problems in the labor market have been tried and even fewer have been studied rigorously. Most of this section will be about civil rights laws and affirmative action programs, since these have received almost all the attention. But I will say a little about some alternative approaches.

Traditional Policies: Civil Rights and Affirmative Action

"Civil rights" is the shorthand I'll use for anti-discrimination laws. The most important of these laws happen to be called civil rights acts.

History and description. The key piece of legislation is the Title 7 of the Civil Rights Act of 1964. This was preceded by the Equal Pay Act of 1963.

Title 7 was a key demand of the March on Washington. It forbids employers from hiring, promoting, firing, and so forth on the basis of race (or on the basis of gender; age was added later). It explicitly states that it does not require preferential treatment on account of numerical or percentage imbalance. It is enforced mainly by complaints: complainants can sue for and receive jobs, back pay, or attorney's fees. The 1972 Equal Opportunity Act lets the federal government initiate some complaints, and the Civil Rights Act of 1866 provides punitive damages in some cases. The Civil Rights Act of 1991 made punitive damages bigger and easier to obtain.

The initial litigation under Title 7 involved what lawyers now call *disparate treatment* cases: a plaintiff tries to show that in a particular instance an employer did something that hurt her *because* of her race. The legal use of the term is slightly different from the economic one, but it's the original use. In these cases, the plaintiff has to show motive. That's easy if employers just post signs or advertise in newspapers or publish a manual that says, "Don't hire Hispanics." It's tough if employers don't do obvious things or write smoking-gun memos. Motive is usually very hard to prove or disprove. By the 1970s, the courts had worked out a three-part test for disparate treatment (the important case is *McDonnell Douglas Corp. v. Green* [1973]).

The first of the three parts is the plaintiff's prima facie case: for example, she applied, was qualified, was rejected, is a member of a protected class, and the employer continued to look for applicants. Or the employer promoted somebody else of a different race or hired someone to do substantially the same work.

The employer then explains why he rejected the plaintiff for some legitimate nondiscriminatory reason. (Customer discrimination is not a legitimate nondiscriminatory reason. A discriminatory hamburger restaurant can't say it hires white hamburger-flippers because that's what its customers want, even if that's true.)

The final step is for the plaintiff to get another chance to show that the employer's reason was in fact pretext. Statistics are relevant here.

Notice, first, that rarely will evidence be overwhelming in one direction; thus standards and burdens of proof matter a lot in how these cases are resolved. Moreover, whatever standard of proof is adopted, it's likely that a lot of cases will be decided wrongly. The question that disparate treatment cases try to answer is: If this person were some other race (usually white), would he or she have been treated like that? The answer is inherently unknowable. An equally tough question is what reasons are legitimate.

Second, this setting is somewhat unusual in that employers must justify to the government what they do. It seems to go against stupid, fun, or quirky decisions: hiring somebody so you can carry on an affair with their spouse, for instance, or because you want to laugh at them. Epstein (1992) emphasizes that civil rights laws are meddlesome. The *New York Times* Sunday business section runs a regular series on how executives manage companies. Often the CEO of a trendy start-up company will talk about how he chooses employees based on whether he would like to go out to dinner with them. That is nice. It's also a lawsuit waiting to happen.

Third, civil rights laws are not race blind. You have to establish what your race is, what the employer's race is, what the race of the person who got promoted is.

Fourth, being sued is not pleasant for the employer, since defending himself is expensive and he may lose whether or not he's actually discriminatory. So employers will take steps to avoid being sued. One way to avoid being sued is by being extra nice to minorities. Another way is to avoid coming into contact with minorities. Since it takes plaintiffs to sue, one way to avoid suit is to reduce the number of potential plaintiffs—using location to cut down on minority applicants, for instance, or not hiring minorities to cut down on cases related to promotion and termination. Unsuccessful applicants are unlikely to sue—they have very little information about how their application was handled and very little to gain since they're looking at many companies. Internal plaintiffs are more likely to be formidable legal opponents: they have useful information and they have a lot to gain or lose. So you minimize your chances of an expensive suit by minimizing the number of potential internal plaintiffs—you don't hire minorities. Empirically, hiring cases are much less common than promotion and dismissal cases.

That's disparate treatment in the legal sense.

Disparate impact cases evolved later because of the difficulty of proving motive in disparate treatment cases. The idea of disparate impact in the legal sense (again, this is slightly different from the sense I've been using it in economics) is that a business procedure—usually a test for hiring or promotion—is invalid if it disproportionately hurts minorities and if its use can't be shown to be a "business necessity." The key case is *Griggs v. Duke Power* (1971).

Congress explicitly incorporated disparate impact into the Civil Rights Act in 1991 after some court decisions raised questions about it.

Duke Power Company required a high school diploma for certain positions, such as shoveling coal or sweeping floors. A lot more whites who applied had high school diplomas than blacks. Duke couldn't or didn't show a "demonstrable relationship to successful performance of the jobs." They lost. Intent didn't matter. Warren Burger, the chief justice, a Republican and a Nixon appointee, wrote this in the majority opinion: "The act proscribes not only overt discrimination but also practices that are fair in form, but discriminatory in operation. The touchstone is business necessity. If an employment practice which operates to exclude Negroes cannot be shown to be related to job performance, the practice is prohibited."

For employers, *Griggs* gives a formula for not being sued. Notice Epstein's point: "business necessity" and "legitimate reasons" are, potentially at least, intrusive meddling.

The 2010 New Haven firefighters' case, *Ricci v. DeStefano,* is a case about civil rights, not affirmative action, and is about a possible conflict between disparate treatment and disparate impact. New Haven gave a promotional exam for firefighters. The results indicated that very few minorities would be promoted. New Haven feared that black firefighters would file a disparate impact lawsuit if the results stood. Therefore they rejected the results and essentially called for a new exam. Firefighter Ricci and other firefighters who had done well on the exam filed a disparate treatment lawsuit. The Supreme Court agreed with them.

Notice that the Supreme Court's decision is a tightening of disparate treatment law for employers. In *McDonnell-Douglas* terms, the court is saying that avoiding a disparate impact lawsuit is not a "legitimate non-discriminatory reason." So they are giving employers less scope to run their own businesses and making disparate treatment law more meddlesome. In his opinion, Justice Scalia said that he would like to see a constitutional challenge to disparate impact, but he was alone.

Affirmative action in labor markets has a more amorphous history. There were two sources. The first was Executive Order 11246 in the early 1960s forbidding racial discrimination by government contractors; the second was disparate impact litigation, especially the litigation involving building trades unions, fire departments, and police.

Suppose Mr. C is a federal contractor and Mr. B is a federal bureaucrat, and they both want to avoid the trouble and the costly motive-seeking that civil rights laws entail. There is an obvious agreement: if Mr. C hires enough minorities, Mr. B won't have to worry about whether Mr. C is discriminating and Mr. C won't have to worry about whether Mr. B will go rummaging around trying to impugn his motives. Seems like a better way to operate. It's called affirmative action.

In the building trades case (*Contractors Association of Eastern Pennsylvania v. Secretary of Labor*, 442 F.2d 159 [3d Cir. 1971]), the judge effectively said: "I'm not going to tell you how to recruit carpenter apprentices and plumber apprentices. I can't run your union business. But these are the goals: if you meet them you're okay."

Nixon was president at the time; affirmative action wasn't a radical invention. In a lot of ways it blurs with disparate impact. But it's distinct from disparate impact: *Ricci* says nothing about affirmative action.

Affirmative action gives employers (and unions) more room to maneuver, which can promote efficiency in many ways. Courts or bureaucrats telling employers that they will leave them alone if they hire enough minorities is like parents telling high school students that they can go out as much as they want as long as they maintain high grades.

Notice also that affirmative action has never been a policy for the labor market as a whole (unlike anti-discrimination laws). Affirmative action affects building trades workers, federal contractors, police, and firefighters—that's about it. These are all areas where workers get rent—that is, where wages don't adjust downward to clear the labor market. So a labor market with affirmative action should not be compared to a competitive labor market, because I don't know of any instance where it has been implemented in one.

Empirical results of anti-discrimination laws.   Little work has been done to study empirical results of anti-discrimination laws.

The chief consensus is that Title 7 and the rest of the civil rights revolution raised black wages in the South in the 1960s. The original long survey of black male earnings (Smith and Welch 1989) did not come to that conclusion, but subsequent work (Chandra 2003) overturned this conclusion for the South by carefully considering selection and nonparticipation.

Two studies by Heckman provide more detail on what happened. Heckman and Payner (1989) show that the breakthrough in manufacturing employment in South Carolina came in 1963 in textiles. Before that, very few blacks worked in manufacturing, which was a high-wage occupation in the South at that time. Many South Carolina textile makers had DoD contracts and thus were covered by Executive Order 11246. Donahue and Heckman (1991) find that civil rights complaints and activity before 1975 were the precursors to relative wage increases.

Oyer and Schaeffer (2000) find that the 1991 Civil Rights Act caused employers to shift from firing blacks to laying them off.

In a totally negative direction, a number of articles (for instance, Acemoglu and Angrist 2001) about a nonracial civil rights law have shown it to be a failure. The Americans with Disabilities Act (ADA) requires employers to provide reasonable accommodation for disabled workers and prohibits discrimination based on disability status. ADA reduces the employment of disabled workers and does not increase their wages. This effect is strongest in middle-sized firms (small firms, which are exempt, have not reduced employment of disabled people).

Almost no work has been done on the efficiency effects of civil rights laws. Taste-based or community pressure theories would lead you to expect that innovations in civil rights coverage would raise the stock prices of the companies involved. Marx would probably predict the opposite. The stock market responds positively when the Department of Labor gives a firm the Exemplary Voluntary Efforts Award for its actions to reduce discrimination, but settlement of discrimination suits has a negative effect on the market price of the affected stock. You could interpret these results as saying that the stock market likes nondiscrimination (the Department of Labor award is a signal of nondiscrimination and the discrimination suits are a signal of discrimination) or that the stock market likes firms that don't have the government meddling with their business.

Empirical results on affirmative action in the labor market. There was a positive correlation between black employment and federal contractor status in 1974–1980. It's modest, though (and of course it doesn't imply a net gain in employment; black workers may just have been shifted from one employer to another). In general, wages of contractors are higher today. Prakash's (2009) research on affirmative action in India shows that it does not increase employment but that it increases overall consumption expenditures for scheduled castes (a lot of whom live in cities) but not for scheduled tribes (almost all of whom live in remote areas).

Holzer and Neumark (2000) find that firms covered by affirmative action mandates act differently: they recruit more, pay less attention to visible negatives, screen more intensively, and train more intensively. Notice that all of these activities have positive externalities for other employers, in theory. Holzer and Neumark don't establish causality, though.

They also look at supervisor ratings of performance. They take a difference in differences approach. The difference between supervisor ratings of white males and supervisor ratings of minorities and women is the same in affirmative action firms as it is in non–affirmative action firms (except for Hispanic males). This means either that affirmative action does not result in worse workers or that supervisors in affirmative action firms don't tell the truth. There's some reason to suspect the former.

Theoretical comments.   Some results hold no matter what kind of discrimination is occurring.

First, consider the costs and benefits of civil rights and affirmative action no matter what discrimination (if any) is like. Both policies have the first-order effect of sometimes placing the wrong person in a job. This is probably less of a problem in affirmative action than in civil rights, because affirmative action specifies only race, while a civil rights suit specifies a person.

Both policies also appear to increase screening and general training. This probably promotes efficiency, since screening and training create positive externalities in most markets. But it's not clear that affirmative action and civil rights are the most effective ways to increase screening and general training.

Both policies have avoidance costs: for instance, firms that move to different locations or don't hire protected classes in order to avoid promotion, accommodation, and termination disputes. These are efficiency costs. The case of ADA indicates that sometimes these costs can be large.

Other results hold when only a certain kind of discrimination is occurring.

For instance, if employers discriminate because of community pressure, then both civil rights and affirmative action promote efficiency. They give employers an excuse to do what they want to do—hire qualified blacks. Thus they promote efficiency (leaving aside the external cost, if any, to people who prefer to see blacks do poorly). Civil rights does better than affirmative action because it allows employers to do exactly what they want, unless they are under community pressure not to use their discretion.

You should be careful in how you think about this argument. First, I'm not arguing that civil rights in this case is a Pareto improvement. For instance, agricultural employers in the South became worse off when manufacturers in South Carolina started to hire blacks. Civil rights is a *potential Pareto improvement:* the winners could compensate the losers, even if they don't. Most uses of efficiency in applied economics are about potential Pareto improvements, not Pareto improvements—for example, the famous arguments against tariffs. Second, I'm not counting racial animosity. There are two arguments for doing this. The first argument is that if you start caring about meddlesome preferences that people might have, economics as we know it falls apart. Suppose the world includes one sadist who is better off whenever anyone else is worse off and worse off whenever anyone else is better off. Then everything is always Pareto optimal and there is nothing for economics to say. Second, we don't know how strong racial animosity is—how much a racist would be willing to pay to have something bad happen to the object of his animosity—and maybe you can think that that amount is not that different from how much other people would be willing to pay to see the racist's desires frustrated. Once you get to this remove, you see why I don't want to go down this way.

The Heckman papers on the South argue that the civil rights laws in the 1960s were acting against segregation due to community pressure. The implication is that they enhanced efficiency. The civil rights revolution of the 1960s in the South may have been a one-time event, but it is the only one ever studied rigorously.

That result is about discrimination as a result of community pressure. On the other hand, if taste-based discrimination is occurring, the effects of civil rights and affirmative action depend on whose tastes matter.

Consider discrimination by firms. If every firm is equally discriminatory, then discrimination causes no loss of output and no efficiency loss. Neither civil rights nor affirmative action can make efficiency gains. If a civil rights law is instituted and equal wages are required, then no firm will hire blacks. Civil rights laws will raise black unemployment. (This is a testable proposition, but it's never been tested to my knowledge.)

If firms differ in how discriminatory they are (and for some reason discriminatory firms survive), then more discriminatory firms (that hire some blacks) will be producing too little and less discriminatory firms will be producing too much, relative to the optimum. If civil rights policies are a tax on hiring white workers in discriminatory firms, then the efficiency loss will be exacerbated. On the other hand, if affirmative action forces discriminatory firms to hire minorities, this doesn't happen. It could create an efficiency gain under some conditions. So in this case, affirmative action improves the allocation of labor and civil rights makes it worse.

Next consider customer discrimination. I won't talk about affirmative action here because it's difficult to model affirmative action and it isn't seen in these markets. With identical customers, civil rights forces minorities out since they can't get lower wages. With differing customers and enough non-discriminatory customers for there to be no racial wage differential, civil rights is a tax on consumption by discriminatory customers; if demand is elastic, it creates deadweight loss.

With differing customers and a racial wage differential, the civil rights laws are effectively a tax on white-flipped hamburgers that has two effects: it is a new tax on discriminatory customers and so creates deadweight loss; and it evens the playing field for the marginal customer between minority-produced goods and white-produced goods and reduces deadweight loss. This is a standard second-best problem (like how to set the optimal subway fare when car transportation has to be undertaxed). The solution is an intermediate tax. So civil rights could have efficiency-enhancing effects here if it sets something like the right level of tax. But it might not.

What happens in labor markets with rent? Even without any kind of discrimination, affirmative action in these markets might enhance efficiency. Why? Because without affirmative action the people who enter these occupations are *over*qualified. With the right parameters, affirmative action reduces overqualification and enhances overall efficiency. Remember that resources should be allocated on the basis of comparative, not absolute, advantage.

To see this, suppose that for some reason security guards at Columbia University were paid $5 million a year. Many highly talented and highly skilled people would apply for the job, and those who were hired would be extraordinarily talented. The world would gain some wonderful security guards who would do their jobs very well. But it would also lose some talented doctors, engineers, teachers, lawyers, and entrepreneurs because they would be security guards. On net, the world would lose. Starting from this situation, if an affirmative action program drew a slightly less talented group of people into the security guard business, it would set free a group of highly talented people to be great doctors, lawyers, engineers and entrepreneurs. It would be easy to design an affirmative action program that promoted efficiency by reducing overqualification in this way.

Thus in markets with rent—the type of markets where affirmative action is found—it's entirely possible that it promotes economy-wide efficiency even if there's no prior discrimination.

We should also think about what policies do if statistical discrimination is occurring. Probably the most important question for policies when statistical discrimination is present is how people look at each other and think about each other. The other important questions about policies are what they do to trust and to incentives to invest in education, job searches, and other skills. Unfortunately, little evidence exists on these questions.

But economists have some enlightening theory on some of these questions. The best-developed model on part of this question is Coate-Loury. We looked at the predictive part above: how you could get an equilibrium where blacks invested little and got low wages and whites invested a lot and got high wages. It's obvious that this equilibrium is inefficient: indeed, it would be a Pareto improvement in the Coate-Loury model for blacks to move to the better equilibrium. The second part of Coate-Loury asks whether affirmative action can move the black equilibrium in that direction.

The basic idea is that affirmative action in hiring for one cohort can increase minority incentives to become qualified and thus break the cycle. The problem in the original situation was that minorities didn't have enough incentive to invest because employers believed (rightly) that a positive test outcome was not good enough information about their abilities. If you force employers to hire minorities with good test outcomes, the employers will lose money with this cohort, but the next cohort of minorities will invest just like whites and will be qualified just like whites. Some affirmative action can incentivize minorities to invest more. The problem is that affirmative action of the wrong strength can incentivize minorities to invest less. There is a happy medium.

Appendix C continues the example in Appendix B and gives a numerical example of how affirmative action in the Coate-Loury model can be designed to work and how it can be designed to fail. Thus good affirmative action is good and bad affirmative action is bad.

To summarize what we know about the traditional policies: civil rights produced fairly clear efficiency gains during one very important historical episode. There's some decent evidence of more careful screening associated with affirmative action and civil rights, and some reallocation of minority employment, but nothing else very strong. There is no clear ranking of civil rights and affirmative action in terms of which is "better." Both—done wrong—have serious weaknesses, but both—done right—can sometimes produce large gains. This theoretical ambiguity makes the relative scarcity of empirical work more disturbing.

Nontraditional Policies

Civil rights and affirmative action thus don't appear to be perfect remedies for labor market discrimination. Might there be better approaches? Very little work has been done on this question, but some intriguing possibilities should be considered. Some of these alternatives have had some popularity, but not all.

One alternative would be to *add* to the information that employers and others use. Traditional civil rights essentially asks employers to operate with less information than they have. With imperfect markets that's sometimes a good idea—for instance, it's probably better if professors grade student essays anonymously and students write course evaluations anonymously. But it goes against the grain of history at this time.

One alternative would be for the government to subsidize screening programs for employers and the development of better employment tests. Employer screening has positive externalities because one employer can observe the results of another employer's screening efforts. (If employer A has a really accurate screening test, then employer B can take advantage of it: employer B can infer from employer A's actions that people who are hired by A are qualified at a certain level and those who are not hired are not qualified; employer B has less reason to buy her own screening system.)

Autor and Scarborough (2008) studied a firm that switched to using a more accurate test. Better screening didn't change the proportion of those hired who were minorities, even though minorities did worse on the test. Why? The firm had been statistically discriminating before it switched to the new test. In the long run, better tests provide better incentives for minorities in skills and education. Thus better testing could remove statistical discrimination in the short run and lead to higher minority skills and wages in the long run.

Subsidies aren't the only policy that promotes better tests. Anti-trust laws could be relaxed to permit employers to form hiring consortia that would internalize externalities and develop better tests on their own. The danger, of course, is monopsony.

One class of policies that alter the information that employers gather about job applicants are those that deal with drug testing. Some states have adopted laws that encourage employers to use drug tests, some have adopted laws that discourage it, and some have done neither. Wozniak (2014) has studied the impact of these laws and derived a very strong result: laws that encourage drug testing increase black employment, especially for low-skilled men and especially in the types of companies that are likely to use drug testing—big firms with good benefits. The story is similar to that of Autor and Scarborough: without drug testing, many employers have a stereotype of African Americans as drug users and therefore don't hire them. Thus drug testing allows non-drug-using African Americans to prove that they are clean. The increase in employment from drug testing is consistent with the idea that the stereotype overestimated the prevalence of drug use among African Americans. This could be an example of the phenomenon I alluded to in the discussion of statistical discrimination: a belief that employers have that arises from general media bombardment, not from their own experience, and one that is inaccurate (at least for long periods of time, if not for eternity).

Employment problems persist after hiring, of course, and similar approaches might be applied to the problems of workplace conflict. Knowledge of good management practices is a public good. The government helps farmers with the agricultural extension service; perhaps it should establish a "diversity extension service" to help employers manage a diverse work force and do research into better management techniques. This may be more effective than waiting for trouble to occur and responding with expensive litigation.

Another alternative is to forget about correcting problems in the labor market and concentrate on outcomes—income in this case. If you changed the income tax code and taxed minority workers less, then you could make up for any discrimination problems and forget about all the meddlesome legal problems and litigation connected with civil rights and affirmative action. If all that matters are outcomes, this is the obvious path to take. I've tried this proposal on numerous audiences and have yet to find anyone who likes it; many people actively dislike it. The distaste for the income tax remedy tells me that minority income isn't the sole criterion that anyone uses in evaluating programs in this area; efficiency and fairness seem a lot more important.

A final set of proposals draws on the insights of Becker and Malcolm. If whites dislike minorities a lot, then separation may be the best course. Mild versions of this idea call for expansion of minority businesses so that minority workers don't have to face discrimination by employers; this is the subject of Chapter 12. Stronger versions call for minorities to take advantage of existing residential segregation by establishing as many institutions of their own as possible so that minority workers can escape both employer and customer discrimination; these ideas are discussed in Chapter 9. The strongest versions call on minorities to separate deliberately in new political entities.

Many Hispanics and Asians and a significant minority of blacks are immigrants and have implicitly rejected the idea of separatism: the advantages of living in a unified, wealthy, capital- and knowledge-intensive economy are so great that they have opted to leave their home countries to experience them. The losses from discrimination in the United States, which we have measured in this chapter, are nowhere near as great as the losses from living in Haiti rather than in Brooklyn or Michoacan rather than in Los Angeles. That seems like a very reasonable choice. Thus at the present time it is not surprising that the stronger forms of separatism have lost much of the appeal that they held in the 1920s or 1960s.

Conclusion

Blacks and Hispanics make less money than whites and Asians because they are less likely to be employed, and when they are employed, they earn lower wages. Less education and lower AFQT scores account for a good part of the disparity in wages (though less of the disparity in employment), especially for Hispanics, but not all of it in most regression studies. Audit studies also show that employers on average tend to treat blacks and Hispanics worse, although it's not clear whether or how this leads to differences in labor market outcomes. Civil rights laws appear to have raised black earnings in the 1960s South, but very little else is known about how anti-discrimination laws and affirmative action work. They don't work perfectly.

Two other kinds of ideas for raising minority wages in the United States have received a lot more attention in the last decade than civil rights laws or the nontraditional policies that I discussed. These are restricting immigration and improving education. I'll discuss these areas in the next two chapters.

Appendix A: Bayes' Theorem

Bayes' theorem, which dates from the 1770s, is one of the great results of the application of probability theory to practical problems. It tells you how to use evidence to update your beliefs.

The basic formulation and proof is very simple. Suppose there are two events, A and B. Write $P(A)$ as the probability of A; $P(B)$ as the probability of B; $P(A|B)$ as the probability of A conditional on B (that is, the probability of A if B happens); $P(B|A)$ as the probability of B conditional on A; and $P(AB)$ as the probability of both A and B.

Common sense and Venn diagrams tell you

$$P(AB) = P(B)\,P(A\,|\,B)$$
$$P(AB) = P(A)\,P(B\,|\,A)$$

so

$$P(B)\,P(A\,|\,B) = P(A)\,P(B\,|\,A)$$

which implies

$$P(B\,|\,A) = [P(A\,|\,B)\,/\,P(A)]\,P(B).$$

This is Bayes' theorem.

Think of B as the proposition you are interested in (it's winter) and A as some piece of information that has some bearing on this proposition (there's a lot of snow on the ground). $P(B)$ is called your *prior probability* of B—it's what you believed before you got the evidence in A. $P(B|A)$ is called your *posterior probability* of B—it's what you believe after you have seen the evidence in A. So Bayes' theorem is a formula for updating your original beliefs with new information. The same information gives you a different posterior belief if you start with different prior beliefs.

Appendix B: Numerical Example of the Coate-Loury Model

Workers can be either qualified or unqualified. If an employer hires an unqualified worker for the job in question, it will cause the employer to lose $1,000. If she hires a qualified worker, she will make $1,500. She is risk-neutral. Thus she will hire a worker if and only if she thinks the probability that the worker is qualified is at least 40 percent.

Employers can't tell who is qualified and who is not. They can give a test, though, which is an imperfect indicator of qualification. The test has three grades: A, B, and C. Qualified people are more likely to get better grades on the test, but the relationship between qualification and score is imperfect. Specifically: If you are qualified, here is your probability distribution of grades:

A—50 percent
B—50 percent
C—0 percent

If you are not qualified, here is your probability distribution of grades:

A—25 percent
B—37.5 percent
C—37.5 percent

The next step is where Bayes' theorem comes in. The employer is going to see a grade and then come to posterior probability that the worker is qualified. So let P denote the prior probability that the worker is qualified and $P(q|grade)$ denote the posterior probability that a worker with that grade is qualified. The prior probability of a grade is:

P^* [*probability of that grade if qualified*]

$+ (1 - P)$ [*probability of that grade if unqualified*].

Thus from Bayes' theorem we can derive the posterior probabilities of qualification that an employer believes after she has seen test scores:

$$P(q \mid A) = [0.5/[0.5P + 0.25(1 - P)]] \; P = 2P/[P + 1].$$

$$P(q \mid B) = [0.5/[0.5P + 0.375(1 - P)]] \; P = 4P/[P + 3].$$

$$P(q \mid C) = 0.$$

Now suppose that the employer has different prior beliefs about the probability that black and white applicants are qualified. In particular, her prior
beliefs are that half of whites and a quarter of blacks are qualified. Don't ask
me why now; we'll see later.

Then in the above formulas, $P = 0.5$ for whites and $P = 0.25$ for blacks.
So the employer's posterior beliefs will be different for different races for the
same grade. In particular:

For applicants who got an A on the test:

$$P(q \mid A, \text{white}) = 2/3$$

$$P(q \mid A, \text{black}) = 2/5.$$

For applicants who got a B on the test:

$$P(q \mid B, \text{white}) = 4/7$$

$$P(q \mid B, \text{black}) = 4/13.$$

But for applicants who got a C on the test

$$P(q \mid C, \text{white}) = P(q \mid C, \text{black}) = 0.$$

These are derived by plugging into the posterior probability formulas.

Now some economics. We observed a while ago that the employer will
hire an applicant only if her posterior probability that the applicant is qualified is at least 40 percent. Then who gets hired? Easy to see: blacks who got

A's and whites who got A's or B's. Those are the only instances where the posterior probability is at least 40 percent.

Now add on a new element to think about: What proportion of workers will in fact become qualified? Suppose that getting hired is worth 1 to every worker (otherwise the workers will have to do a less-desirable job). To become qualified you have to go to school, and going to school is costly for you. The cost of going to school varies for different people. In particular, I assume that the cost of going to school and becoming qualified is uniformly distributed between 1/8 and 5/8. This is the same for both blacks and whites.

Who goes to school? It depends on the increased probability of getting the good job that going to school gets you. This is different for blacks and whites.

For blacks, if you're qualified, you have a 50 percent chance of getting an A and getting the job. If you're not qualified, you have a 25 percent chance of getting an A and getting the good job. So getting an education increases your probability of getting the good job by 25 percent—from 25 percent to 50 percent. Since the value of getting the good job is one, you will get educated if the cost of education to you is less than 0.25. That means that blacks with a cost of between 1/8 and 1/4 will get educated, and blacks with costs of between 5/8 and 1/4 will not get educated. In all, one-fourth of blacks will get educated. Thus I have constructed an example where employers' prior beliefs about the proportion of qualified blacks is correct.

For whites, if you're qualified, you have a 100 percent chance of getting an A or a B and getting the job. If you're not qualified, you have a 62.5 percent chance of getting an A or a B and getting the good job. So getting an education increases your probability of getting the good job by 37.5 percent—from 62.5 percent to 100 percent. Since the value of getting the good job is one, you will get educated if the cost of education to you is less than 0.375. That means that whites with costs of between 1/8 and 3/8 will get educated and whites with costs of between 5/8 and 3/8 will not get educated. In all, half of whites will get educated. Thus I have constructed an example where employers' prior beliefs about the proportion of qualified whites is also correct.

Appendix C: Affirmative Action in the Coate-Loury Model

Suppose that blacks and whites are equally numerous in the population. An affirmative action program is set up. To keep things simple, assume that it takes a generation for educational decisions to be made and that each cohort's decisions are based on what it sees in the previous cohort.

Suppose that an affirmative action program is set up. The government can't observe test scores (or the employer can lie about them). In the original equilibrium, you can calculate what proportion of people are getting each grade on the test. For blacks, the grade distribution is:

A—10/32
B—13/32
C—9/32

For whites, the grade distribution is:

A—12/32
B—14/32
C—6/32

Thus, originally, 10/32 of blacks get hired and 26/32 of whites—there are 2.6 whites for every black.

Suppose an affirmative action program comes along and mandates that the employer hire 23 blacks for every 26 whites she hires. This reduces her profit, but assume that she complies and doesn't reduce total employment. Then she will hire all blacks who got a B as well as all blacks who got an A. Many of these new hires will be unqualified.

But in the next generation, blacks will have the same incentive to get educated as whites do, and the same proportion of blacks will be educated as whites. Employers will then voluntarily hire all blacks with a score of B and affirmative action will no longer be needed.

This happy result depends on picking the right number for the quota. Suppose that instead of mandating 23 black hires for every 26 white hires, the government requires 32 black hires for every 26 white (somebody wrote the quota numbers backward). Then the firm hires all blacks and blacks have no incentive to become qualified. Affirmative action makes blacks less qualified and never ends.

6

Immigration

In Chapter 5 we saw that beautiful people were paid more; there was discrimination against the unbeautiful. An interesting policy question is whether the protection of anti-discrimination laws should be extended to the unbeautiful. Proponents of such an extension argue that it's wrong to base hiring and promotions on criteria other than job-related qualifications, and this argument has great appeal to Americans today. (Opponents might point out the costs of anti-discrimination law and want it reserved for cases of overwhelming historical injustice.)

Despite the appeal of the idea that hiring and promotions should be based entirely on job-related qualifications, the United States today has lots of regulations *requiring* discrimination based on country of birth or citizenship, which is hardly ever a job-related qualification. And most of the people who are directly adversely affected by this sort of legally mandated discrimination are minorities. So a book about race has to consider immigration and immigration policies.

Specifically, the questions for this chapter are: How does immigration affect minorities in the United States (and potential members of U.S. minority groups), some of whom are natives, some of whom are immigrants, and some of whom are only potential immigrants? And how does it affect NHWs (who also fall into the same three classes)? How would different policies make a difference to these groups? Because this is economics we have to try to look at a full set of costs and benefits, no matter what the current residences are of the people affected.

I'll start with some basic facts and numbers, then look at some economics, and finally turn to policy discussion.

Numbers and Facts

First, most immigrants are minorities. You can see this in Table 6.1. Less than a fifth of the foreign-born population of the United States are now NHWs; the rest are minorities, mainly Hispanic. When you talk about immigrants, you're talking about minorities.

Moreover, the controversial people and the people to whom the most aggressive policies are addressed are almost all minorities. The Department of Homeland Security estimates that in 2012 about 11.4 million foreign-born residents of the United States were "unauthorized"—they did not fit into any of the authorized categories such as permanent residents, tourists, refugees, or students. Of these 11.4 million, 10.9 million were born in North America (including Central America and the Caribbean), Asia, or South America and were probably either Hispanic, Asian, or black (Baker and Rytina 2013). Enforcement actions are also almost all directed against

Table 6.1. Distribution of the U.S. foreign-born population by race and ethnicity, 2000 and 2012 (percent).

	2000	2012
Black	6.8	8.5
American Indian/Alaskan Native	0.4	0.4
Asian	22.5	24.7
Native Hawaiian/Pacific Islander	0.2	0.3
Non-Hispanic white	22.0	18.7
Hispanic	45.5	46.2

Sources: Decennial census for 2000 from Malone et al. (2003), figure 5; American Community Survey one-year estimates for 2012 from American Fact Finder, http://factfinder2.census.gov /faces/nav/jsf/pages/index.xhtml.

Table 6.2. Percentage of foreign-born in U.S. population, 2000 and 2012.

	2000	2012
Total	11.1	13.1
Black	6.1	8.8
American Indian/Alaskan Native	5.4	5.6
Asian	68.9	66.5
Native Hawaiian/Pacific Islander	19.8	21.4
Non-Hispanic white	3.5	3.9
Hispanic	40.2	35.6

Sources: Decennial census for 2000 from Malone et al. (2003, figure 5); American Community Survey one-year estimates for 2012 from American Fact Finder, http://factfinder2.census.gov/faces/nav/jsf/pages/index.xhtml.

minorities. The Department of Homeland Security lists the top ten countries of origin for immigrants subject to apprehension, detentions, and removals. These countries account for between 94 and 97 percent of these actions and are all in Latin America, except for occasional appearances of China, Jamaica, and Brazil (Simanski and Lapp 2013).

Second, many minorities are immigrants, and most Asians are immigrants. You can see this in Table 6.2. Over a third of Hispanics are immigrants, and the proportion of immigrants in the black population is about twice the proportion of immigrants in the NHW population. In some major cities this relationship is much stronger: in New York City in 2007–2009, 32 percent of the black population was foreign born. When you talk about minorities, you're talking about a group that contains many immigrants.

Finally, the immigration to the United States for the past few decades has been different from previous immigrations. First, it is large: the number of foreign-born people in the United States is greater than it has ever been, and the proportion of the population who are foreign born is approaching the peak level of 1890 (see Table 6.3). Immigrants and their children comprised 24 percent of the U.S. population in 2010 (Grieco et al. 2012, 16). Second, immigration is coming from different places: Latin America and Asia especially rather than Europe (see Tables 6.4 and 6.5). Finally, within the United

Table 6.3. Foreign-born population in the United States, 1850–2010.

	Percent of U.S. population	Number of people (millions)
1850	9.7	2.2
1860	13.2	4.1
1870	14.4	5.6
1880	13.3	6.7
1890	14.8	9.2
1900	13.6	10.3
1910	14.7	13.5
1920	13.2	13.9
1930	11.6	14.2
1940	8.8	11.6
1950	6.9	10.3
1960	5.4	9.7
1970	4.7	9.6
1980	6.2	14.1
1990	7.9	19.8
2000	11.1	31.1
2010	12.9	40.0

Source: U.S. Census Bureau (n.d.).

Table 6.4. Distribution of foreign-born population by region of birth, 1960 and 2010 (percent).

	1960	2010
Europe	75	12
Northern America	10	2
Latin America	9	53
Asia	5	28
Other	1	5

Source: U.S. Census Bureau (n.d.).

Table 6.5. Top ten countries of birth of foreign-born population, 1960 and 2010.

1960	2010
Italy	Mexico
Germany	China
Canada	India
United Kingdom	Philippines
Poland	Vietnam
Soviet Union	El Salvador
Mexico	Cuba
Ireland	Korea
Austria	Dominican Republic
Hungary	Guatemala

Source: U.S. Census Bureau (n.d.).

Table 6.6. Distribution of the U.S. foreign-born population by region, 1960 and 2010 (percent).

	1960	2010
Northeast	47.0	21.6
Midwest	23.4	11.2
South	9.9	31.9
West	19.8	35.3

Source: Grieco et al. (2012).

States, immigration is directed more to the South and West than to the Northeast and Midwest, as previous immigration was directed (see Table 6.6).

Effects of Immigration: Some Theory and Some Empirical Data

Changes in the volume of immigration and in immigration policies affect many different people, many of whom are minorities. Not all of these people are in the United States now. So to assess these effects and to set the stage for policy discussions, we have to look at many different groups.

Effect on Immigrants

Immigration is usually great for immigrants. In 2000, the average 23–27-year-old man with five to eight years of education made $1.80 an hour in Mexico and $8.19 an hour in the United States. The then-standard border-crossing fee of $2,000 could be made back in eight weeks (Freeman 2006). Clemens, Montenegro, and Pritchett (2008) estimate that the real earnings gap for observably identical low-skill workers in the United States and in countries such as Haiti and Nicaragua is around 1,000 percent. Immigrants who aren't successful often return to their home country. The benefits of immigration can be seen in the queue for green cards; if immigration weren't good for immigrants, few people would want green cards.

The big real wage gain is an efficiency gain; immigrants make more money in the United States because they are more productive in the United States than they were in their home country. A basic principle in trade theory is that the size of the efficiency gain depends on the difference in prices across countries. The differences in the price of labor are bigger than the differences in the prices of goods. Clemens (2011) presents recent estimates of the size of the efficiency gains for the world that would occur if various kinds of restrictions on mobility were eliminated. The efficiency gain to removing all barriers to the international movement of goods (total free trade) would be between 0.3 percent and 4.1 percent of world GDP. The gain from removing all barriers to capital flows would be about the same size, maybe a little smaller. But estimates of the gains from removing all existing barriers to migration run from about 67 percent to about 147 percent of world GDP.

Immigrants are often positively selected: the most enterprising and industrious people in many societies have the most to gain from moving to the United States. When that happens, the United States adds people who are not at all representative of the society they were born in. For instance, on many dimensions, West Indian immigrants and their children do better than African Americans (they are heavily overrepresented among blacks in elite colleges, for one thing). Model (2008) tried to find out why and concluded that positive selection was the main reason. (If positive selection is strong, you can't forecast the wage gains of people who might move to the

United States if immigration were easier from the wage gains of those who have actually moved.)

Positive selection occurs often but not always: immigrants from Mexico to the United States are probably not positively selected in recent years (people in the middle are migrating the most), and there's some evidence that immigrants from Norway to the United States were not positively selected in the nineteenth century. (That means that estimating potential wage gains for Mexicans from actual wage gains does not introduce a large error.)

Effect on Origin Countries

Not a lot is known about how immigration affects the countries that immigrants leave. Remittances are a major source of income for some countries (about 19 percent of the income of Honduras, for instance, and 15 percent of the income of Haiti before the earthquake), and remittances from the developed world are a larger source of money for the developing world than foreign aid (Yang 2011). Remittances appear to be a good source of insurance for developing countries: Clarke and Wallsten (2004), for instance, found that increased remittances made up for about a quarter of the damage that Hurricane Gilbert did in Jamaica in 1992.

A great deal of controversy has surrounded the "brain drain" issue: whether and to what extent developing countries are hurt when their most skilled citizens such as doctors and engineers migrate to developed countries. Firm empirical evidence has not established any great harm: different studies come up with different answers about whether migration of doctors affects health in the origin countries (McKenzie and Gibson 2011).

The skills of returnees also help the home country, and many immigrants return. Immigration affects the distribution of skills in the home country, and change in skill distribution affects different people different ways; for instance, the loss of the most enterprising could hurt. Emigration may change politics in the origin country: many independent countries such as Ireland, Czechoslovakia, and Israel have been nurtured by diaspora communities in the United States. But the fact that dissidents can leave may make it easier for tyrants to consolidate their rule.

In all, it is hard to pin down the net effect of emigration on the origin country, aside from remittances.

Effect on U.S. Natives

Most attention is paid to the issue of how immigration affects the native-born population of the United States. This is a complex general-equilibrium question because immigration affects many aspects of life simultaneously: immigrants affect the supply of labor and the demand for goods simultaneously, for instance. But very little general work on equilibrium has been done. Most research has been done on the labor market, but the strongest results are for the housing market. Some work has been done on public goods and crime too. (The bottom line on crime is this: immigrants are extremely law abiding, mainly because of selection [Butcher and Piehl 2007].)

Effect on housing markets.   Saiz (2007) found that immigrants drive up housing prices: 1 percent more immigrants (as a proportion of city population) in a city causes 1 percent higher housing prices. How he did this is interesting.

In the cross-section, you want to see whether cities with more immigrants have higher housing prices. But you can't assign immigrants to cities randomly, and if immigrants just go to cities with lower housing prices, you won't find anything. Fortunately for econometricians, though, immigrants don't behave like that. They tend to go to cities where they have fellow countrymen and countrywomen. This makes sense: in a strange country, you want to stay close to people you might know and who speak your language. The number of immigrants in a city from a particular country in 1970 predicts the number of immigrants from that country in that city in 2010 pretty well. So it's a good instrument.

Thus using instruments for national and international changes, Saiz can identify the causal results of an increase in immigrants.

Saiz also used information about the Mariel boatlift, a famous incident that took place in 1980. For about six months in that year, Fidel Castro let any Cuban who wanted to leave do so from the port of Mariel. About 125,000 Cubans left, many on totally inadequate watercraft, and almost all went to Miami—a huge, unexpected influx of immigrants. Saiz estimated that the boatlift raised rents in Miami by about 8 percent.

The increase in rents is a gain for native landowners and homeowners, a loss for native renters.

The standard theory is that immigration is an exogenous shock to demand for housing. The size of the price effect then depends on the elasticity of housing supply (things such as topography and zoning regulations matter), the elasticity of capital supply, the demand for amenities by natives (if natives are very sensitive to housing prices, they'll move to offset immigrants and prices won't change). Immigration could also affect housing prices if immigrants fill jobs that complement housing: if there are a lot of immigrants around, it will be easy to get your lawn mowed or your basement waterproofed, so you're more willing to pay for a lawn and a basement.

These housing market effects are much bigger than anything found in the labor market. It's not impossible that the restrictions to immigration in the early 2000s contributed to the bursting of the housing bubble in 2006 and 2007.

Effect on labor markets.   Immigration's effect on labor markets is the area where the vast majority of work has been done. The answers remain murky and controversial.

Start with theory. The traditional simple theory about immigration is like trade theory. Think of two countries—to be concrete, call them the United States and Mexico. Assume that the total number of workers in the two countries is fixed but that workers may be able to move across the border. So we can draw the total number of workers as a fixed distance on the horizontal axis. For now, assume that the two sets of workers have identical skills.

In the United States, you can draw a "demand-for-labor curve." This is shown in Figure 6.1. For each number of workers in the United States, it gives the wage that workers will get. Wage equals the marginal product of labor.

The reasoning behind this curve is much different from the reasoning behind a standard microeconomics labor-demand curve for a firm. That's why I put quotation marks around "demand-for-labor."

The curve in Figure 6.1 is more complex than a standard demand curve in microeconomics because it allows other markets to make a full adjustment to the labor supply—it doesn't hold other prices fixed the way a demand curve usually does. When more labor enters a country, demand for goods in the country changes and so does the return to capital. In the limit, if every input in the world were completely mobile, the "demand curves" in the United States would be flat because immigrants could just create miniature versions of the pre-immigration U.S. economy, where the prices of every-

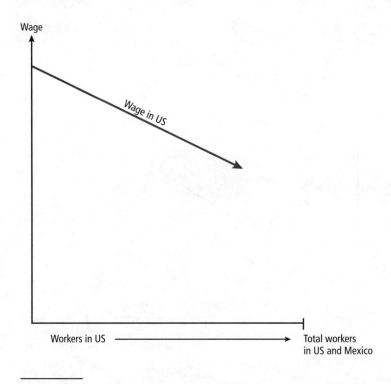

Figure 6.1.

thing, including labor, would be the same, and the United States could go on replicating itself ad infinitum. So the "demand curve" in the United States depends on how much more capital is forthcoming, on how much more land can be put into use, and on export-import markets.

Why then did I draw this curve sloping down? Because some factors of production are in limited supply in the United States, even in the long run. Examples are land, the electromagnetic spectrum, possibly entrepreneurial talent. How much these fixed resources matter and over what period of time is an empirical question that we will discuss in a little while.

We can draw a similar curve for Mexico. But since for this exercise we are assuming a fixed labor supply, more workers in Mexico will mean fewer workers in the United States and vice versa. So instead of drawing separate diagrams for the United States and Mexico, I can use the same diagram but with the curve sloping up instead of down. This is shown Figure 6.2.

Then we can put Figures 6.1 and 6.2 together in Figure 6.3.

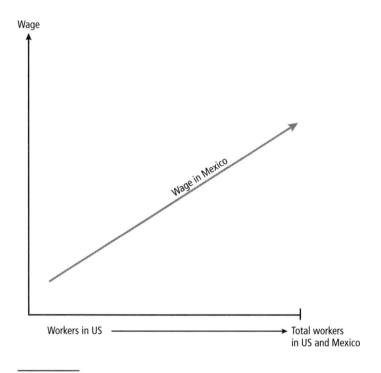

Figure 6.2.

If there were no barriers to migration, the system would end up at point E, where wages would be the same in both countries; only then would no one have an incentive to move. However, migration restrictions in the United States keep the number of workers in the United States below the equilibrium, at point R. We know that these restrictions are binding because wages in the United States (U in Figure 6.3) are higher than wages in Mexico (M in Figure 6.3) and people try to migrate from Mexico to the United States. People whose marginal product would be U if they were allowed to enter the United States produce instead at the lower level M.

What would happen if migration barriers disappeared—if the United States and Mexico reverted to the nineteenth-century idea of open borders? Both countries would gain on net, although some individuals in each country would lose. Figure 6.4 illustrates.

First, think about the United States. Wages would fall from U to W. This would be a loss for U.S. workers (meaning workers who were in the United States before open borders). They number R, so the total loss for U.S. workers

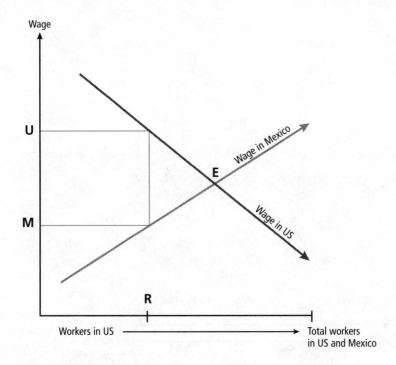

Figure 6.3.

would be in the region A. What about U.S. consumers, capitalists, and land-owners? They would get the "consumer surplus triangle"—the difference between the value of total production in the United States and the wage bill. So they would gain twice from open borders: they would get region A as a simple transfer from workers, and they would get region B as a result of increased production in the United States. So the total gain of consumers, capitalists, and landowners would be $A + B$. So the total gain for U.S. people would be region B.

On net, open borders would make people who now live in the United States better off. The simple reason is that they would gain something from the added production Mexican immigration would foster within U.S. borders. Some people in the United States would be worse off, but the winners could compensate the losers.

What about Mexico? The result would be the same, but the reasoning is reversed. All Mexican workers (meaning workers who were in Mexico before open borders) would gain when their wage rises from M to W. The total

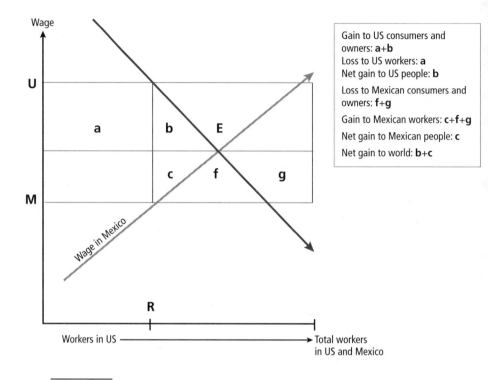

Figure 6.4.

gain for this group would be $C + F + G$. But Mexican consumers, capitalists, and landowners would lose. The region of their loss would be $F + G$. So the net gain to Mexican people would be region C. In simple terms, open borders would mean that Mexican people would produce more, so Mexicans, on net, would gain.

The total net gain for the world would be $B + C$: this is the value of the additional production that occurs because workers would be allowed to go where they could be most productive.

This is the simplest analysis. One of the major weaknesses of the analysis is the assumption that all workers are the same. In fact, workers differ a lot in skills and immigrants don't have the same skill distribution as natives. Relative to natives, immigrants are about equally likely to be college grads; more likely to have advanced degree; much more likely to be high school dropouts; and much less likely to be in the middle (people who have high school diplomas or who have some college). Immigrants to the United States tend to be at the extremes in terms of skill levels, not in the middle.

So a first guess might be that immigrants would depress wages for native-born high school dropouts. But theory doesn't compel this answer. If immigrant dropouts are substitutes in the labor market for native-born dropouts and if immigration doesn't increase the demand for goods made with dropout labor in the United States, then immigration will drive the real wages of native-born dropouts down. But immigrants might be complements in the labor market for native-born dropouts, not substitutes: crews of immigrant house-painters, for instance, might need native-born organizers to negotiate with homeowners on their behalf and drive them to jobs, so a native-born house-painter might end up with a small crew instead of working alone. Or immigrants might shift demand for output: an influx of immigrants with children to a small town might create jobs for native-born women in the school cafeteria.

Thus the effect of immigration on the wages of various kinds of native-born workers is an empirical question. And a controversial one too.

What do the empirical results look like?

The cross-section results are not controversial. In the cross-section, labor economists have looked at wages with the same sort of instrumental variable approach that Saiz (2007) used for housing prices. (In fact, Saiz imitated labor economists, who used this technique first.) Simple correlations are likely to be misleading because immigrants might naturally be expected to gravitate toward higher-wage cities.

So are wages for dropouts (or anybody else) worse in metropolitan areas with a lot of immigrants? No. Many cross-section regression studies have found this result.

The Mariel boatlift experience confirms this finding. Card (1990) looked at wages and unemployment rates for low-skilled natives in Miami after the boatlift. Relative to other southern cities that did not were not affected by the boatlift, wages and unemployment did not change.

The latest research on this question is by Monras (2014). He looked at immigration from Mexico induced by the Mexican peso crisis of the mid-1990s. He found that the immediate effect was a substantial reduction in wages for low-skill jobs in the states that were most affected, but that this effect wore off in a few years. (He found similar results for migration of low-skilled workers to other states from Louisiana and Mississippi following

Hurricane Katrina in 2005.) Why the difference with the Mariel boatlift results? Part of the reason may be sample size: Monras had a much bigger sample than Card did, and Card's results had a larger sampling error. The boatlift group may also have been substantially different from the Mexican peso crisis immigrants: they did not have much time to figure out what they would be doing in the United States, and some were rumored to have been released from prisons and mental hospitals (this rumor may have been exaggerated, but the group did include people who were outcasts in Cuba such as Seventh-day Adventists and Jehovah's Witnesses).

Why is the effect after a few years so small? (All the research agrees on this.) This question has not been resolved. The first response from economists was that maybe the presence of immigrants reduced the native-born population, either through a lack of in-migration ("Who would leave Iowa for Miami when they don't speak English?") or the encouragement of out-migration ("Let's leave Miami and go to Omaha, where they speak English"). Monras (2014) supports this explanation, but other evidence contradicts it. In particular, rents don't respond the way we'd expect if natives were offsetting immigrants. Saiz shows that they go up, and they would not go up if natives were leaving. More directly, Card (2005) shows that the immediate effect of one more immigrant dropout increases the population of dropouts in a metropolitan area by one, but his data set is not as large as Monras's.

Another possible answer is trade: cities with a lot of dropouts may start making goods that use a lot of unskilled labor (like China or Thailand do). Evidence doesn't support this explanation either. Capital may flow into the cities to which immigrants come. One possible story is that within industries, firms adjust how they produce their goods so they can use more dropouts. For metropolitan areas, in other words, the "demand curves" are virtually flat.

If immigration affects wages, then, the effect would have to be national. The way to look for a national effect is in the time series. This is controversial— and time-series evidence will always be weaker than cross-section evidence because we don't have a lot have as many observations with time as we do in a cross-section.

Where you should see the effect in the time series is in the wage ratio of dropouts to high school graduates, since immigration is increasing the number of dropouts relative to high school grads. Card (2005) points out that this wage ratio has been stable since 1980. But Borjas, who generally takes a more negative view of immigration than Card, says that in the absence of immigration this ratio would have gone up, since the number of native-born dropouts is decreasing. More seriously, both Card and Monras provide evidence that dropouts and high school graduates are substitutes in the U.S. labor market, so a supply shock such as increased immigration or more schooling for native-born residents should have no effect on the wage ratio; even if the ratio had moved it would tell us nothing about immigration.

Borjas (2003) also does an analysis where he looks at many different education and experience cells and regresses immigrant change on wage change. The question about this calculation is whether the experience and education of immigrants is really a substitute for the experience and education of native-born people. Borjas concludes that for 1980–2000, immigration reduced the wages of dropouts by 8.9 percent, it reduced the wages of college graduates by 4.9 percent, and it did approximately nothing for the group in between. The research of others implies considerably smaller effects.

Little of this work has concentrated on the effect of immigration on native-born minority workers, as opposed to native-born workers in general. The major exception is a controversial study by Borjas, Grogger, and Hanson (2010) that looked at how immigration affected black men. No work that I know of concentrates on women, Hispanics, or Asians.

Borjas, Grogger, and Hanson, like the other Borjas studies, divided data on the national population into a multitude of cells representing education, experience, and years resident in the United States and regressed various labor market outcomes for black and white men on the proportion of immigrants in these cells. As do the other studies that use this method, they found that greater immigration reduced wages for both blacks and whites at about the same rate. Immigration also reduced employment rates and increased institutionalization rates for blacks (but not for whites). Institutionalization for men in the age range studied mainly refers to incarceration. Borjas, Grogger, and Hanson interpreted this result by hypothesizing that when immigration lowers wages in the legitimate labor market, black men turn to crime and therefore tend to go to prison. White men don't have similarly good criminal contacts, so they keep working in the legitimate market.

Raphael and Ronconi (2008) raised several serious questions about this paper, especially the presumed (but not demonstrated) direction of causality. As we will see in Chapter 11, the immigration-wage-crime-prison story has serious problems. The effect of wages on crime is weak and appears to hold almost entirely for property crimes. Property crime accounts for considerably less than a majority of prisoners. More seriously, incarceration trends in the United States appear to be driven almost entirely by policy decisions about probation, sentencing, severity, and parole; changes in prison population are almost entirely unrelated to actual crime.

Institutionalization rates should thus be considered exogenous. If they are, then the correlation between institutionalization and immigration in the national data would be a coincidence. This would lead to a different interpretation of the relationship between immigration and lower wages. Groups with higher incarceration rates plausibly have lower wages and lower employment—employers don't like hiring former prisoners, and at any moment former prisoners are going to look about the same demographically as current prisoners. So one explanation for lower wages in the cells with more immigrants is that these are also the cells with more former prisoners.

Policy

So what? Suppose (a big suppose) immigration depresses the wages of black and second-generation Hispanic dropouts. Is this a good policy reason to restrict immigration? Computers also reduce the wages of dropouts. Should we ban computers? If you want to manipulate the labor force to maximize the wages of minority dropouts, why not expel white dropouts?

We know that we should look at questions of race not just in terms of gains and losses but also in the terms by which policies are normally evaluated.

Let me be broader here and not confine my attention to efficiency for a little while. Three public philosophies dominate American thought about how societies should operate: utilitarianism (Bentham and most economists), libertarianism (Nozick and Hayek), and prioritarianism (Rawls and maybe all Christians). Nobody accepts all three of these philosophies (that would be inconsistent), but most thinkers stay close to one or another. What's interesting is that if you adopt any of these ways of analyzing policies on immigration, the only defensible policy is open borders.

Utilitarianism we've already seen: that's the efficiency argument.

Libertarianism: if Joe in Nebraska wants to hire Jose in Mexico to mow his lawn, and both Joe and Jose agree to this voluntarily and knowledgeably, the government has no right to interfere. The rights to enter into contracts and to travel to better yourself are core libertarian values.

Prioritarianism: immigration of poor people from poor countries helps poor people.

So generally, only if we are fairly hypocritical can we consider immigration a problem or something to be regulated. I'm not going to be elected president on that platform.

Moreover, even if you thought immigration was a problem, you wouldn't set up a regime like ours where entry is rationed and the border is heavily policed.

For one thing, border blocking misses the point and causes serious problems of its own. If wage losses are what you're concerned about, entries are not the problem; immigrant-days in the United States are the problem. You want to charge immigrants a fee per day in the United States, not try to block them at the border. Border blocking discourages reverse migration because once immigrants are in, they don't want to incur the cost of trying to get in again. This means that there are too many immigrants in the United States during bad times (and the winter is always a bad time in agriculture and construction) and not enough in good times. Border blocking creates the worst of all possible worlds—too many immigrants when they shouldn't be here and too few when they should be.

Payment regimes have many advantages. The most obvious one would give native-born workers the right to sell days in the United States to anyone who would buy them. It helps native-born workers, especially those who are not very productive, and it helps immigrants. Given any desired size for the U.S. population, that population would consist of the people who have the most to gain from living here—it gets the right people in the United States. And it can very well be pro-poor.

Even a program that charged for entry on a centralized level and didn't give native-born workers the right to rent out their citizenship would be an improvement on the current system. It would get the right immigrants even if it would not get the right residents overall. It would respond correctly to the business cycle instead of perversely.

Most important, it would promote trust, fair dealing, cooperation, and the rule of law; and it would combat some ethnic stereotypes. Everyone you encountered in the United States would have equal rights; everyone could talk to the police without fear of deportation; employers could hire the best-qualified applicants without fear of being raided; workers could write contracts believing that they could go to court to get them enforced.

One lesson in this book has been that the effects of treating people like pariahs are long lasting and hard to reverse. It's probably not a good idea to start doing it again.

7

Education

We've seen that differences in educational attainment—how many years you've gone to school—and educational achievement—what you learned—explain a big part of the disparities in earnings and employment. The obvious next questions are what explains differences in educational attainment and achievement and what, if anything, should be done about them.

Education is valuable. The average rate of return on education was above the rate of return on bonds almost all of the last century and has been well above the rate of return on stocks for the past decade. Even in normal times, education usually beats most other investments, although it's individually risky (if you invested in becoming a travel agent in 1990, you made a mistake that was hard to hedge against). Individual returns to education are more than pecuniary: holding income constant, people with more education are healthier, live longer, and may live better. Education has external benefits as well: educated people invent and innovate more, commit less crime, participate in civic affairs more and bring more to those affairs, and help educate children around them.

This chapter begins with basic facts about educational attainment (first section) and educational achievement (second section). The third section discusses possible reasons for racial disparities in attainment and achievement. The next section is about possible reforms in elementary and secondary education and their effect on the racial gaps. The last substantive section is about higher education, but it discusses only one policy, affirmative action.

Disparities in Educational Attainment

Educational attainment means how long you went to school and what degrees you got. Of the outcomes associated with education, attainment is easiest to measure, and it is a surprisingly powerful variable. Education is in part socialization and a way to keep you off the streets, so for some outcomes attainment is all that's important. It's also a necessary condition for a lot of achievement.

The basic way to look at educational attainment, for our purposes, is to look at people old enough to have completed schooling but not old enough to have completed it too long ago. You don't want to look at 65-year-olds because their educational attainment reflects what was going on in schools forty or fifty years ago; you don't want to look at five-year-olds because they really don't have educational attainment yet.*

Table 7.1 looks at people between 25 and 29 in the household population (so it omits prisoners and homeless people) and shows the extremes of the educational attainment distribution—those who have not completed high school and those who have completed college. Two numbers stand out: the high proportion of Asians who have completed college and the high proportion of Hispanics who have not completed high school. Blacks and NHWs are between Asians and Hispanics in educational attainment. Even comparing blacks and NHWs, the gap in educational attainment is considerable: almost twice as many NHWs as blacks have graduated from college (proportionately) and almost twice as many blacks as whites have dropped out of high school. But the difference between Asians and Hispanics is much larger.

*Technically, we're looking at "status completion" and "status dropout" rates: how many of the people in the United States of a particular age at a particular time have completed a given level of education or not. Some of these people were not in the United States when they were of high school age, for instance, and some of the people who went to high school in the United States are no longer here because they have died or emigrated. We are not trying to follow particular people over time as they enter or leave different grades or to assess school systems. Some data sets try to do this, but transfers and immigration make these data sets very hard to understand. For a detailed discussion, see Murnane (2013).

Table 7.1. Educational attainment of 25–29-year-olds, March 2011, civilian noninstitutionalized population (percent).

	Less than high school diploma	Bachelor's degree or more
Non-Hispanic white	5.6	39.2
Male	6.6	35.5
Female	4.5	43.0
Black	12.3	19.6
Male	12.5	16.1
Female	12.3	22.9
Asian	4.7	56.1
Male	6.6	51.3
Female	3.3	60.7
Hispanic	28.5	12.8
Male	30.8	9.6
Female	25.7	16.8

Source: U.S. Census Bureau (2012a).

Whether you are a recent immigrant makes a big difference for high school completion among Hispanics. Among 20–24 year-olds in the American Community Survey, only 48.5 percent of recent Hispanic immigrants (immigrants who arrived after the age of 11) had completed high school, while 77.8 percent of Hispanics who were not recent immigrants had done so. (For blacks and NHWs, the proportion of recent immigrants was smaller and the gap between recent immigrants and others was small or negative.)

High school completion rates for blacks and Hispanics who were in the United States before the age of 11 are about the same, and in the first decade of the twenty-first century the rates for these minority groups began to converge to those of NHWs (I don't have data for Asians). For the last three decades of the twentieth century, the gap between NHWs and these minorities on high school completion stagnated. Table 7.2 shows this pattern. (Unlike Table 7.1, this table uses the American Community Survey, so it includes prisoners, college dormitory residents, and military personnel. I look at 20–24-year-olds, since almost everyone who is going to finish high school has done so by that age.)

Table 7.2. Percentage of 20–24-year-olds who have completed high school, 1970–2010.

	1970	1975	2000	2010
Whites	83.8	84.2	81.8	83.7
Blacks	63.7	69.1	68.0	78.2
Hispanics	58.6	64.6	63.9	77.8
Hispanics, including recent immigrants	56.6	54.5	53.3	71.0

Source: Murnane (2013), table 3.
Note: Recent immigrants are excluded from the data except where noted.

Achievement: The Test Score Gap

Educational achievement is worse for minorities, except Asians, holding family background constant.

There are two kinds of educational achievement: cognitive and noncognitive. Cognitive means how well you know academic material. Noncognitive means everything else: how honest and patriotic you are; whether you are healthy and well adjusted; how strong you are; whether you get along well with other people. Sometimes these skills are described using the term "social and behavioral" rather than the bureaucratic and negative term "noncognitive." Not a lot of data on noncognitive achievement by racial groups are available, but what there are indicate a picture similar to that for cognitive achievement.

Minorities, except Asians, almost always get scores on tests of cognitive achievement that are worse than those of NHWs. Generally the ranking is Asians, NHWs, Hispanics, African Americans. Notice that this is not the same as the attainment ranking: Hispanics do better than African Americans on achievement but not on attainment.

Generally, the median score for blacks is below the score of about 75 percent of whites on most standardized achievement tests. Since test scores have no independent meaning and are often forced into conforming to the normal distribution, another way of expressing this is that black scores on average are usually about one standard deviation below those of whites.

The National Assessment of Educational Progress (NAEP) has the longest history of any standardized achievement test. Table 7.3 provides some historical data on NAEP test scores. Generally the black-white gap narrowed

Table 7.3. Long-term trend in black and Hispanic scores on the NAEP, 13-year-olds (absolute point gap with scores of non-Hispanic whites).

	Blacks	Hispanics
Math		
1973	46	35
1978	42	34
1982	34	22
1986	24	19
1990	27	22
1994	29	25
1999	32	24
2004	27	23
2004 revised	30	23
2008	28	23
Reading		
1971	39	na
1975	36	30
1980	32	27
1984	26	23
1988	18	21
1992	29	27
1996	32	28
1999	29	23
2004	22	24
2004 revised	26	24
2008	21	26

Source: National Center for Education Statistics (2005).

in the 1970s and 1980s, stagnated or widened in the 1990s (some economists attribute this deterioration to the crack epidemic), and narrowed a little in the 2000s. The Hispanic-white gap in math scores is about half or three-fourths of the black-white gap and has not changed much since 1980. The Hispanic-white gap for reading scores is about the same as the black-white gap and has also been fairly steady since 1980.

Possible Explanations for the Attainment and Achievement Gaps

In the labor chapter (Chapter 5), when it came to explaining disparities, the emphasis was on contemporary events, especially discrimination; the analysis was more in the W. E. B. Du Bois tradition than the Booker T. Washington tradition. With education, both traditions are important.

For most people, the major thing that your parents (and the taxpayers and teachers of your parents' generation) have done for you is contribute to your education. You may or may not pay them back (probably you won't), and if you don't, they have no legal claim on you for that. Contributions to education are the main way that one generation is linked to the next in our society. Thus studying education lets us see how the past has created the disparities we observe today—the reason Booker T. Washington emphasized in his explanation of current disparities. After ignoring this approach for the last two chapters, we can come back to it again.

Specifically, suppose group B earns less than group A. There are three possible reasons:

1. Group B might have the same level of educational attainment and achievement as Group A but earn less.
2. Group B might have the same level of parental resources as Group A but get less education.
3. Group B's parents might have had fewer resources than those of Group A, and thus group B might have received less education.

W. E. B. Du Bois would emphasize possible reasons 1 and 2. Booker T. Washington would emphasize possible reason 3. We looked at possible reason 1 and found something there when we discussed labor market discrimination in Chapter 5. In this chapter, we'll look at possible reasons 2 and 3.

Possible reasons 1 and 2 determine the speed at which incomes and education levels converge or diverge; possible reason 3 determines the distance to be covered. In 2003, in ruling on the higher education affirmative action case *Grutter v. Bollinger,* Supreme Court Justice Sandra Day O'Connor said, "We expect that 25 years from now, the use of racial preferences will no longer be necessary" because educational levels across race and ethnicity will have converged. To think about what 2028 will look like and evaluate

Justice O'Connor's forecast, we need to answer all three questions: we need to know how far apart the races are now (possible reason 3) and how quickly (if at all) they are converging (possible reasons 1 and 2). (Justice O'Connor's forecast is actually wildly optimistic, as a group of economists from Princeton showed shortly after she made it [Krueger, Rothstein, and Turner 2006].)

Notice that if blacks in one generation get less education than whites in that generation, the gap can close in the generation after that only if black children get *more* education than white children, holding their parents' education constant. So racial convergence in education can occur only if possible reason 2 fails.

Attainment Disparities

We pretty much know why blacks and Hispanics complete fewer years of schooling than NHWs (one of the few questions in this book that seems to be settled): family background. (There are interesting stories about mortality gaps, but they don't seem to be needed.) There is almost no data on why Asian educational attainment is so high.

The basic finding is that blacks, whites, and Hispanics of the same family background get virtually the same amount of education. This has been true for several decades, and it is roughly true of both men and women. A Blinder-Oaxaca decomposition with white characteristics (the enrichment experiment) shows almost no residual, or a negative residual.

There are a few exceptions to this generalization. In the 1970s and 1980s, black men and women with low socioeconomic status (SES) were more likely to graduate from high school and attend college than whites with low SES. This difference disappeared in the 1990s. Hispanic men in the National Longitudinal Survey of Youth in the 1980s were more likely than NHW men to graduate from high school and attend college. But the NLSY may be misleading for Hispanics at this time, since it did not include recent immigrants. High SES blacks and whites almost always look the same.

Thus, for the last several decades, there has been little "catching up" in educational attainment, since "catching up" requires that in the group that is behind, children get more education, conditional on family background, than children in the group that is ahead.

Thus, conditional on family background, minorities spend as much time in school as whites do, and sometimes more.

Moreover, blacks seem to work just as hard as whites and buy into school just as much. I have not seen similar results about Hispanics. For instance, Cook and Ludwig (1997) show that blacks have just about the same expectations as whites regarding school attainment, and about the same attendance. In a study of attitude questions for high school students, Akerlof and Kranton (2000) found that compared to whites, blacks are less likely to "dread English class," less likely to "dread math class," more likely to perceive "school spirit as excellent," more likely to report a "positive attitude toward self," and much more likely to "like working hard." Ferguson (cited in Fletcher 2001) finds that black students and white students spend the same amount of time on homework.

Explaining the Test Score Gap

The disparities in achievement are much more puzzling than the disparities in attainment. Many different explanations have been advanced. A few of them have no merit, but many do. None of the possible explanations, however, is sufficient by itself to explain more than a fraction of the gap, and even all together it's not clear that the explanations are enough. We may be missing something important. We will look at several possible explanations in this section.

Family Background

Family background did a fairly good job of explaining (or even overexplaining) the attainment gap, but it doesn't work as well for achievement. It definitely makes a difference, but it's not the whole story. In almost every study, when you put in family background, the gap gets smaller but it doesn't disappear. Generally, family background can account for about half of the black-white test score gap.

Two studies are exceptions. One exception is Fryer and Levitt (2004b): at the start of kindergarten, holding family background constant, they found no difference in test scores between blacks and whites. But then the gap grows at an almost constant rate throughout the next several years of schooling.

(In all these studies, there are issues about which skills the tests are measuring. If you gave kindergarteners a test on calculus, there would be no gap in test scores.)

The other exception is a study by Rothstein and Wozny (2011). What they do differently is to look at "permanent income" as part of family background, not current income. "Permanent income" is how much income a family usually gets, so it ignores transitory shocks to a particular year's income such as lottery winnings or short spells of unemployment. Permanent income should have more impact on a family's behavior and decisions than current income, especially when the family can save or borrow without too much difficulty. The Gates family, for instance, is rich even in years when it loses a billion or two in the stock market. So permanent income is probably a better measure than current income of the family background a child experiences (and has been experiencing).

Permanent income does a better job of explaining the test score gap than current income. Using the variable of permanent income, Rothstein and Wozny found that family background accounts for about three-fourths of the gap in test scores. But not all of it.

There's also some evidence that the gap is bigger for high SES families. In fact, some evidence suggests that the black-white gap gets quite small late in school for the lowest SES kids, while it grows for the highest SES kids. So the pattern is not that different from the pattern on attainment, although the level is different.

Family backgrounds of black kids have been improving faster than family backgrounds of white kids—better-educated parents and fewer siblings are more important than more single-parent households—and this has been responsible for a part of the convergence in test scores over the last forty years. (The popular impression is that black family background has been deteriorating, but that is not accurate. Single-parent households have been increasing for blacks, as we will see in Chapter 8, but they have been increasing for whites too. Whether a child comes from a single-parent household is not an important determinant of either achievement or attainment. The number of siblings and the mother's education make a big difference, and these variables have been improving for blacks.)

Observable School Inputs

There are some differences between races in measured inputs such as spending and pupil-teacher ratio, but they aren't big enough to explain a lot of the difference (partly because the efficacy of these variables is not unquestioned). The gap exists within school districts and within schools. Stiefel, Schwartz, and Ellen (2007) have data on New York City schools that confirm this picture. In Fryer and Levitt (2004b), there are no racial differences in observable school inputs.

The average black student is in a slightly smaller class than the average white student but with a slightly less experienced teacher. These effects are small.

Unobservable School Inputs

Unobservable school inputs are attributes of schools that are not measured in the data sets researchers are using—the personalities of the principals and teachers, the quality of the school building, the school culture, and so on. The way to look for the effects of unobservable school inputs in regressions that try to explain educational achievement outcomes is to put a separate variable for each school in the regression as an explanatory variable (or a separate variable for each classroom). Researchers who do that are essentially holding constant all of the attributes of the school, whether they can measure those attributes or not. This technique is called fixed effects.

Fryer and Levitt used this technique for the first two years of schooling. The fixed effects of schools reduced the black-white gap by about two-thirds, while measured inputs didn't do anything. So they thought that certain things schools were doing—great principals or good practices or school spirit—made a difference. But when they got to the third grade, school fixed effects and even teacher fixed effects did a lot less. In Fryer and Levitt (2004c), by the third grade, two-thirds or more of the gap was within the same classroom. (That is, within the average classroom, the racial gap was about two-thirds of the racial gap in the entire population; differences between classrooms explained at most a third of the gap.)

Since Fryer and Levitt found almost no test score gap conditional on family background on entering kindergarten, they thought that the growth in the gap after kindergarten was due to unobservable school inputs. Todd and

Wolpin (2007) disagreed. They also found that the test score gap is small in kindergarten and increases up to age 10–12. But they don't accept the Fryer and Levitt picture. Education is a cumulative process, so as kids get more exposed to great or lousy home life, the gap should get bigger. They find that 20–30 percent of the black-white gap—and slightly more of the Hispanic-white gap—is due to home variables, but they have poor information about schools. That leaves 70–80 percent unexplained.

Classmates

The average minority student has classmates who are poorer than the class-mates of the average NHW student. Classmates matter—but not enough to explain a lot of the test score gap. For instance, the effect of classmates is controlled for in Fryer and Levitt (2004b, 2004c).

Genetics

Fryer and Levitt (2006, 2013) find no difference for infants (but tests are not great). Racial differences don't appear until age 2. Black adoptees in white households do well, at least until adolescence. IQ is malleable. We talked about this in Chapter 3.

Reactions to Test Taking

Psychologists have shown that blacks do worse on tests when those tests have certain associations with self-worth and racial identification (Steele 1997). Since what we are calling the achievement gap is based on tests, this reaction may contribute to the gap but it's unlikely to be the whole story. Within race, these exam scores are correlated fairly well with things that are not multiple-choice exams, such as college grades and wages.

"Acting White"

Minority students may be ridiculed by their friends if they attempt to become high achievers. This practice is common among disadvantaged groups: it's been observed among the English working class, Boston Italians in the 1950s, and certain groups in Japan. Trying to achieve is held in disdain.

Or more precisely, activities correlated with high achievement are held in disdain, such as asking questions in class and carrying books. Signals that beget labor market success are signals that induce peer disdain.

Fryer and Torelli (2010) is an attempt to test empirically whether high-achieving minority students in the United States are held in disdain by their peers. It uses data on friendships and grades in high schools. It looks at 175 schools in 80 communities throughout the United States. Students were asked to list ten friends. Fryer and Torelli measured a student's popularity by the number of other same-race students who listed her or him as a friend. Each friend is weighted by the number of friends that he or she had. The restriction to same-race friends is not a big issue for the purposes of this study. The average student had only one friend of another race, and all the results stayed about the same when Fryer and Torelli included all friends, not just same-race friends.

They found that for whites, better grades led to higher popularity. For blacks, better grades led to modest increases in popularity with grades of up to 3.5 on a scale of 4; after that, better grades reduced popularity. A black kid with a 4.0 grade average had 1.5 fewer friends than a white kid with a 4.0.

Among Hispanics, the relationship was flat for grades from 1.0 to 2.5; after that, higher grades reduced the number of friendships. A Hispanic student with a 4.0 was the least popular Hispanic student and had three fewer friends than a white student with a 4.0. Accounting for the number of students at each grade level did little to change the picture.

These relationships between grades and popularity are different in heavily minority schools. The relationships are most salient in schools where fewer than 20 percent students were black.

The result tells us something about the popularity and perhaps the happiness of high-achieving minority students, but it doesn't tell us a lot about achievement. Previous studies of peer pressure found no effect, so even these small effects may be overestimates.

Oppositional Culture

Perhaps peer pressure is tied to oppositional culture and the combination is what holds minority students back. The data don't seem to support this story. Oppositional culture would be strongest in all-black schools, but peer pressure doesn't seem to work against achievement in those schools.

Teacher Expectations or Self-Perception or Something Else

Teacher expectations almost certainly play some role in the test score gap. Figlio's (2005) study about first names in Florida is probably the most convincing evidence for this proposition.

He makes a distinction between "low SES names" and African American names. He defines low SES names according to phonemic rules similar to those used in Scrabble scores. African American names are defined by relative frequency in the population. Dwayne is an African American name; Da'Quan is a low SES name. Whites have low SES names, but it's mainly blacks who have these names. Not many Hispanics are included in this study. Figlio also looks at Asians with and without Asian names.

He makes comparisons within families in order to take out family background effects. So if Ronald and Vivek are brothers, then when you see what happens to Vivek relative to Ronald, it can't be due to family background, since they both have the same family background.

He finds that names cause a test score gap and that the effect of low SES names is bigger than the effect of African American names. Brad does better than everybody else (except Vivek), but Dwayne does better than Da'Quan.

Why? He looks at teacher expectations. Consider the following two questions: Holding grades constant, who gets into gifted classes? Holding grades constant, who gets promoted?

A student of whom teachers expect little would not get into the gifted class (at the margin) but would get promoted (at the margin). Low SES names work that way. Asian names work the opposite way. Thus if Da'Quan and Vivek have the same grades and are on the margin of admission to a gifted class, Vivek will get in and Da'Quan won't. But if they're on the margin of being held back, Vivek will be held back and Da'Quan won't be.

Notice that this suggests that teacher expectations (a teacher's prior beliefs) are one way that names could translate into cognitive achievement. But it's not the only way. For instance, self-perception could matter, as in the caste experiments in Hoff and Pandey (2006) and the beauty experiments I discussed in Chapter 5 (Mobius and Rosenblatt (2006). Vivek might feel confident about his ability to learn, while Da'Quan might not.

Teachers' Unconscious Attitudes

Elementary school teachers interact with their students for long periods every day under circumstances that change rapidly and unpredictably. They may not always be able to control their demeanor and utterances. Students react to teachers' unconscious and nonverbal actions just as much as they react their statements and conscious behavior. Van der Bergh et al. (2010) found that Turkish and Moroccan students in the Netherlands fared more poorly in classes with teachers who showed a greater propensity to link these groups with negative images on implicit association tests. Teacher scores on tests of propositional racism were uncorrelated with their implicit association test scores and did not predict student achievement. I'm not aware of any similar research in the United States.

All of these factors seem to matter but not to matter enough. The standard conclusion (Jencks and Phillips 1998) is that whatever is happening is happening at the level of classroom interactions. Teacher expectations tie into this.

Where have we heard this before? In our discussion of doctors and patients. Learning is not just about getting educational inputs poured into your head. It involves complex interactions between teacher and student and between student and student. Expectations and stereotypes could matter an awful lot, because kids don't know much. As in health care, small differences compound each other.

An expectation of being less than equal may lead to difficulties with interactions. Ogbu (1994, cited in Fletcher 2001) gives the example of Koreans: in Japan they are considered inferior and perform poorly in school, while in the United States they are considered superior and perform very well in school. If people have a lingering doubt about your inferiority or if you think people do or if people think you think they do, it's more difficult for them to help you or for you to trust them. Learning involves trust.

The Figlio and implicit association test results partially support this sort of story. So does the result that two-thirds of the test score gap can be found within classrooms. The story also suggests that integration, segregation, and race-congruent teachers could make a difference to learning. In the next section we'll see that that's true.

Improving Pre-College Education

Even though there's a lot we don't know about the gaps (achievement especially), a lot can be done to reduce them. But reducing the gaps isn't cheap or
fast or even especially popular. Chasing after fads won't do the job, especially fads that promise something for nothing, although even fads contain
some wisdom. And race-blind policies by themselves won't eliminate the gaps,
either. The achievement gap in particular is not fully explained by family
background.

A Blinder-Oaxaca picture of the achievement gap can help us understand
the different kinds of policies that might work. Figure 7.1 shows such a picture, where the horizontal axis is some composite measure of family background. Average black (or Hispanic) educational achievement is below
average NHW achievement for three reasons: (1) because average white

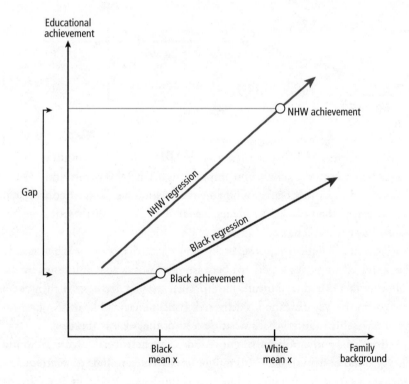

Figure 7.1.

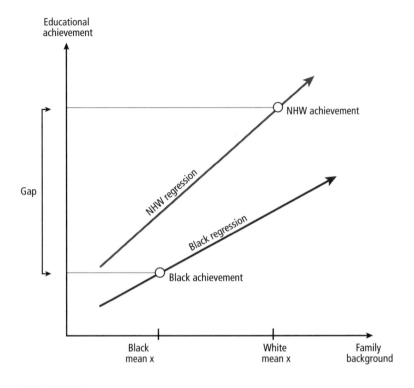

Figure 7.2.

family background is better than average black family background; (2) because better family background implies higher achievement; and (3) because holding family background constant, whites have higher educational achievement than blacks. Reducing the strength of any of these reasons reduces the achievement gap.

Thus, for instance, suppose, as in Figure 7.2, that average black family background improves—perhaps because of reduced discrimination in the labor market or reduced incarceration. Then the gap decreases if there is no change in the way education is delivered. Policies that act like this won't concern us in this chapter; that's what the rest of the book is about.

More relevantly, policies might reduce the educational payoff to family background or help students from poor family backgrounds no matter what their race. An effective policy like this is illustrated in Figure 7.3. I'll call

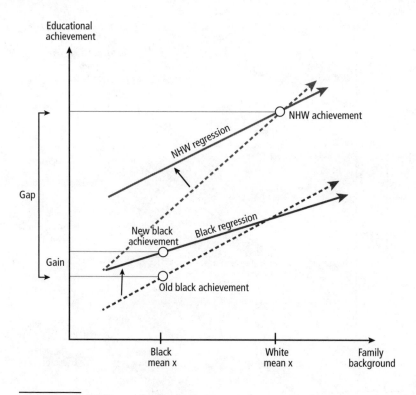

Figure 7.3. Result of a pro-poor policy.

---

policies that are intended to work like this pro-poor policies. As you might expect, pro-poor policies are often color blind.

Finally, some policies might improve minority achievement for all family backgrounds but not affect NHW achievement. Figure 7.4 illustrates. I'll call policies that intend to do this pro-minority policies. Such policies often take color into account.

In this section, I'll look at pro-poor policies first and then pro-minority policies. Two popular ideas—charter schools and vouchers—do not fit comfortably in either box, so I'll consider them separately.

Notice that my search for good policies is more restrictive than one that simply seeks to reduce the gaps. Reducing the gaps is easy: you could just force NHW and Asian kids to eat lead paint chips, for instance, or bar them from attending schools. That's why I'm looking for improvements, not just

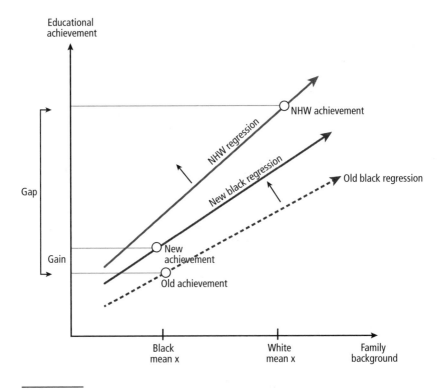

Figure 7.4. Result of a pro-minority policy.

changes, and at pro-poor and pro-minority policies, not anti-rich or anti-NHW policies.

The idea of improvements is that benefits from these changes should exceed their costs, with both benefits and costs broadly conceived. Many worthwhile improvements require greater public budget expenditures—and therefore higher taxes—but that should not be an impediment to their implementation, since benefits exceed costs.

Pro-Poor Policies

Most pro-poor policies keep schools fundamentally the way they are now and intensify students' exposure to motivated teachers.

Early childhood education. This means extending some version of regular schooling to children 3 and 4 years old, younger than traditional kindergarten age. We know a lot now about various forms of early childhood education.

Historically, many early childhood programs, particularly those that poor parents chose, have been of low quality; they were little better than babysitting. Low-quality preschools don't help children much, as you might expect (although they help parents by allowing them to work more in the market). In Fryer and Levitt (2004b), preschool attendance had no effect on cognitive test scores in kindergarten.

At the other extreme, small, very high-quality early childhood education has great benefits—but not exactly the ones you might naïvely expect. In the 1960s and 1970s, a number of intense, expensive, highly professional preschools were established as controlled experiments. (The Perry Preschool Project and the Abecedarian Project were the best known.) Students, almost all of whom were from disadvantaged households, were selected randomly and followed for decades, as was a control group who did not attend preschool.

At the start of kindergarten, the children who had attended preschool showed gains on tests of cognitive skills; the biggest gains were for the students from the most disadvantaged families. But for African Americans, the cognitive gains faded out in elementary school. By the end of elementary school, black kids who had not gone to preschool performed just as well on these tests as those who had. The test score gains of white children did not fade out as rapidly as the test score gains of black children.

But even though the test score gains faded out, other impacts didn't. Children who went to preschool were less likely to be assigned to special education, to drop out of high school, or to go to jail, even twenty years later. Standard estimates of the effect of these high-quality programs find their benefits to be about seven times as great as their costs. Most observers attribute the long-lasting effects to gains in noncognitive abilities such as self-control that preschoolers experience, but there is no solid evidence for this hypothesis.

The major policy question about early childhood education is whether large publicly funded programs are more like the ineffective babysitting preschools or the highly effective boutique preschools like the Perry Preschool. Most evidence indicates that the large public programs are closer to the boutiques than the babysitter preschools, but the jury is still out (and will be for another decade or so).

Head Start, a federal program with local operators, is the largest publicly funded program. It serves about 900,000 students a year, almost all of them from poor and near-poor families. It has been in operation since 1965.

Non-experimental studies of Head Start have shown results similar to those for the boutique programs (see Gibbs, Ludwig, and Miller 2011 for a review). For instance, Currie and Thomas (1995) and Deming (2009) find cognitive test score gains in kindergarten for Head Start alumni and gains at least as large for blacks as for whites. But cognitive gains fade out over elementary school, more rapidly for blacks than for whites. On the other hand, blacks who attended Head Start were less likely to be arrested and whites were more likely to finish high school and attend college. Ludwig and Miller (2007) found that blacks were more likely to finish high school and attend college, but Garces, Thomas, and Currie (2002) did not.

Experimental results about Head Start are just becoming known now as the result of a randomized experiment involving children who enrolled in Head Start (or not) in 2002. The preliminary results are like the non-experimental results: cognitive test scores increase in kindergarten but then the effect fades out. But there are some differences. The rate of fadeout is faster than the non-experimental studies show and is faster for NHWs and Hispanics than for blacks. The real question is what will happen to these children when they reach young adulthood, and we'll have to wait until the mid-2020s to find out.

What are we to make of early childhood education as a way to close the racial gaps? It's hard to see how it could affect the test score gap. The gain that students experience even at its largest, in kindergarten, is relatively small, only about a fifth or a sixth of a standard deviation, and that fades away. If early childhood education is directed at students from low SES backgrounds, however, it might narrow the attainment gap, although the research isn't definitive on this point. Early childhood education has many benefits that probably outweigh its costs, but it's not likely to do much to close the racial achievement and attainment gaps.

Smaller class sizes.   Non-experimental studies of smaller class sizes have been bedeviled by serious endogeneity problems (usually if one class is smaller than another there's a good reason). Experiments and quasi-experiments are thus the key to understanding whether smaller classes are a good way to improve achievement and attainment, but few have actually been conducted.

The best-known controlled experiment was called Project STAR (Student Teacher Achievement Ratio) in Tennessee in the 1980s. It had random selection of students into classes of different sizes, random selection of teachers, lots of testing of cognitive achievement, and a long follow-up period. About 11,600 students participated during their first three years of school. Few Hispanics participated because few Hispanics lived in Tennessee at the time.

The immediate impact was good. Small classes (of thirteen to seventeen students) raised test scores by about 60 percent of a standard deviation—about half of the black-white achievement gap. The gains for blacks and poor-achieving students were somewhat bigger than the gains for whites and better-achieving students.

But many of the gains dissipated after a few years in regular classrooms—just like the gains from early childhood education. And just as we saw with early childhood education, the effects of early experience reappeared much later in life. Dynarski, Hyman, and Whitmore-Schanzenbach (2011) found that the students who were assigned to small classes were more likely to attend college, more likely to graduate from college, and more likely to major in a high-earning field. The effects were much bigger for blacks than for whites.

Several quasi-experiments followed STAR, but didn't fully replicate its findings. In these quasi-experiments, researchers tried to isolate the effects of variation in class size that arose for reasons that seemed to be unrelated to achievement—rounding problems, for instance. These studies, with one exception, found that smaller class sizes improved student performance, but the effects were smaller than those in STAR (see Chingos 2013 for a survey). None of the quasi-experimental studies found that smaller class sizes helped minority students more than they helped NHW students.

Does Project STAR mean that schools ought to reduce class sizes? Not necessarily; remember that STAR was an experiment and not a policy. Most classes in Tennessee stayed the same size, most school districts did not hire new teachers, and the small classes in the project operated for only a few years and under intense scrutiny.

Two kinds of problems could happen in the transition from an experiment to a policy. One problem is teacher effort. If teachers keep their effort at their usual level or higher, smaller classes will produce better students, but what keeps teachers from reducing effort? When my classes get smaller, I don't grade a lot more carefully, I just spend my time on other activities not related to teaching. (Small classes might still help students if they allow more class participation for each student and if they allow teachers to match student abilities and interests more closely.) The STAR teachers may have been aware of the scrutiny, but if small classes become general, teachers will feel no such scrutiny.

The other problem is teacher quality. A large-scale program of smaller class sizes means hiring a lot more teachers and a likely reduction in quality (unless salaries increase considerably). This will cut any gains.

What about the racial gaps? Remember first that the average black student is now in a slightly smaller class than the average NHW student (I don't know about Hispanics). Since the effect of smaller class size is stronger for black students than white on both achievement and attainment, an across-the-board reduction in class sizes would narrow the gaps—if there were no incentive or quality issues. In practice, across-the-board class size reductions don't seem to work this way. Jepsen and Rivkin (2009) found that a California program that reduced class size in the late 1990s caused a significant deterioration in the quality of teachers in predominantly black schools. (Chingos 2012 studied a similar statewide program in Florida, but it brought about only small changes in class size and didn't have noticeable effects.) So once again, even if you think that reducing class size across the board is a good idea, it probably won't reduce the test score gap.

What about reducing class size in predominantly minority schools (since minority students gain the most from smaller classes) while keeping it the same in predominantly NHW schools? It might work, since the quality issues would be less severe, but there's no guarantee. Reducing class size is expensive, and even if it reduced the gap, there might be cheaper ways of doing so.

School leaving age.　　What about both raising the age at which people leave school and lowering the age at which people enter? Currently fifteen states and the District of Columbia have a school leaving age of 18, nine states have an age of 17, and the rest require that you stay in school until you're 16. If you had to wait until you were 18 in every state, say, or had a high school diploma, the black-white and Hispanic-white attainment gaps might narrow by sheer arithmetic. This narrowing would be expensive, however, since high schools, especially high schools in poor areas or with large minority populations, would have to make room for more students. (But any policy that increases attainment will increase the number of students.)

Would the benefits outweigh the costs? There's a good chance that they would. Many studies in the United States have shown that forced schooling produced wage and health gains that have been identified using changes in mandatory attendance laws long ago or differences in birthday. Some studies have shown reductions in later criminal behavior too. UK studies have shown substantial gains in wages but no improvement in health. So students will gain, but how much remains to be seen.

Whether Hispanics and blacks would gain as much as NHWs and thus reduce the attainment gap is also not completely certain. Many Hispanics who will later live in the United States would not be affected by these laws because they are still in their native countries when they attain U.S. school-leaving ages. A smaller proportion of NHWs would be exempted from these laws for this reason. To the extent that minorities are less well prepared academically, compulsion may fail to increase the number of students who *complete* additional years of schooling in the sense of passing the required tests and being certified as having the knowledge. Oreopoulos (2009) found that after recent changes in school-leaving laws, an added year of compulsory schooling increased the number of years the average white student completed by 0.16 but did not have a significant effect on the number of years the average black student completed.

Will it decrease the achievement gap as well as the attainment gap? Probably not a lot. Most of the achievement gap is in place by age 14 and most of the results about achievement tests are about what occurs before age 16. Adult cognitive achievement on tests such as the AFQT may rise a little, but whether the racial gaps will narrow is not clear.

Paying students to stay in school.   Several randomized experiments in developing countries (the best studies were in Mexico and Colombia) showed that if students or their families were paid to stay in school, they did so to some extent. At least one experiment in the United States (Project LEAP, an Ohio program that targeted pregnant teenagers and teen parents on welfare), however, showed no effect (Slavin 2009). The cash rewards may not have been big enough. Paying people to stay in school has considerable advantages over compulsion: the people who really gain the most from leaving school (athletic stars, for instance) can leave and only those who have the most to gain from staying in school remain. But payment is more expensive for the government than compulsion, because most of the money will probably go to people who would have stayed in school anyway, especially in developed countries where the majority of students finish high school.

Paying for achievement.   An alternative incentive program would pay students for achievement, not simply attendance. A program like this, if it worked, might affect attainment as well as achievement: early on, some students might learn more and thus gain more from school by the time they are contemplating dropping out, and later on, school might be more attractive than dropping out because it carries the prospect of winning prizes for achievement.

Most evidence in the United States, however, indicates that these incentive programs don't work. From 2007 to 2009, Fryer conducted experiments in Dallas, New York, and Chicago in which randomly selected students were offered cash prizes for academic performance of various kinds. Almost uniformly, students in the groups that could win prizes did no better than students who were not offered prizes (Fryer 2010). There was one exception: students who were offered prizes for reading a certain number of books increased their academic performance. Apparently, rewarding students for outputs doesn't work because students don't know how to produce those outputs. Rewarding inputs may work better because students know what they have to do to win the prizes.

Intense instruction.   Many schools that have raised cognitive test scores for minority students carry normal school practices to an extreme in four ways (Dobbie and Fryer 2011c). They have longer school days and a longer school year; generally about 20 percent more instructional time than is normal in the United States. Teachers get frequent feedback. Teachers and principals use data to guide day-to-day decisions. And students have access to copious amounts of small-group tutoring. I call this package intense instruction. We don't know whether intense instruction *causes* test score improvements for minorities, but it's at least correlated with these improvements.

Health care and health insurance.   If poor children and their parents are healthier, they can learn more in school. Some of the historical illustrations of this relationship were racial, but most of the applications of this principle in the near future will probably be race blind.

Chay, Guryan, and Mazumdar (2009) looked at forced hospital integration in the South in the 1960s. We've already seen that this caused long-lasting improvements in the health of black kids born then and even in their children's health—the next generation. Apparently, hospital integration also raised the test scores of kids who took advantage of the hospitals in their first few years of life. This cohort of southern black kids is responsible for a large part of the test score convergence that occurred in the early 1980s. They got better health care in their first few years of life, their brains developed better, and they did better in school.

For a somewhat earlier period, eradicating hookworm in the South raised school attendance and literacy (Bleakley 2007).

A lot of other studies (for instance, Figlio et al. 2014) also connect health, pollution, and nutrition early in life to cognitive achievement later on. Focusing on health insurance rather than actual health, Cohodes et al. (2014) found that expansions of Medicaid and other public insurance programs for children raised educational attainment, at both the high school and college levels. The effects on minorities (increases in average educational attainment per percent of youth population newly covered) were bigger than those for whites at the high school level but no smaller at the college level. These expansions also increased educational achievement (Levine and Schanzenbach 2009).

What does this say for today? Health care reform is also education reform. Hispanics are the group least likely to have health insurance, so expansions of insurance and Medicaid could have sizeable effects for them. So could including or excluding illegal immigrants from insurance exchanges. Most of the other ideas we discussed in Chapter 4 might also matter. (If African American life expectancy at age 20 improved, younger people would have a longer time to enjoy the gains in earnings and life satisfaction that education brings and would have greater incentives to invest in education. Evans, Garthwaite, and Moore [2012] speculate that decreasing longevity is one reason why the crack epidemic harmed educational achievement in the 1990s.)

Pro-Minority Policies

Pro-minority policies often take race into consideration explicitly and try to reduce the gap between minority and NHW students with the same type of family background. They start with a story about why that gap exists and then seek to remedy the problem.

Bilingual education. Since the major attainment problem is the Hispanic dropout rate, it's surprising that bilingual education and similar programs targeted toward Hispanics receive very little study by economists.

Bilingual education means that you study most subjects in Spanish and you study English as a separate subject. Schools teach English; they don't teach *in* English. Proponents of bilingual education claim that you learn math and history better if it's taught in your native language; opponents claim that you learn English less well if you are not immersed in it.

Angrist, Chin, and Godoy (2008) examines the claim of opponents, not the claim of proponents. They look at a sudden change that took place in Puerto Rico for political reasons in 1949. High schools stopped teaching in English and started teaching in Spanish with classes in English. (Essentially, they adopted bilingual education.) If the opponents of bilingual education are correct, there should have been a discontinuous drop in the proportion of Puerto Ricans who were fluent in English. Angrist, Chin, and Godoy found no such drop. (They can control for migration because they have plenty of data on Puerto Ricans in the United States.)

Slavin et al. (2011) found a similar result in a randomized control experiment. They randomly assigned kindergarteners to either bilingual education or English immersion education—that is, immersing them in English in regular classes but also teaching them English in a separate class. By fourth grade, the treatment made no difference in how well students used English.

So bilingual education probably doesn't cause the harm its opponents fear. But does it cause the gains that its proponents hope for? Again, the answer appears to be no—provisionally, at least.

Chin, Daysal, and Imberman (2012) look at bilingual education in small, non-urban Texas school districts. By a quirk in state law, some of these districts are required to provide bilingual education and some are not. Students who entered school with limited English proficiency (LEP) in bilingual education districts did no better on reading and math tests than LEP students in districts without bilingual education. The surprising result, however, is that bilingual education helped non-LEP students—students who don't attend bilingual education classes. Apparently, removing LEP students from English-speaking classrooms allowed those classrooms to function more smoothly.

What we don't know yet is whether bilingual education helps the intended beneficiaries over the long run or in noncognitive domains. We don't know whether it improves performance in social studies or music or participation in extracurricular activities. Most important, we don't know whether bilingual education makes LEP students more likely to complete high school. It appears to do no harm, but no one has yet shown that it does anything to reduce the test score gap or the attainment gap.

Integration.   It's funny how the burning issue of *Brown v. Board of Education* has disappeared from most discussions of education today.

Empirical studies of the effect of racial composition on cognitive achievement have a very long history, and for a long time they had very low average quality. In this century there have been a number of good studies and a consensus that integration helps blacks.

Hanushek, Kain, and Rivkin (2002) is one of the better studies. It looks at *school* integration, not classroom integration. They have a huge data set on Texas schools. Holding school and peer achievement constant, they find no effect of percent Hispanic or percent white on anybody and no effect of percent black on low-ability blacks. But high proportions of blacks hurt high-ability blacks—remember that the achievement gap is greatest among students from advantaged backgrounds and students with the highest abilities. The effect is quite large. The average black student in Texas attends a school that has about 25 percent more blacks than it would have if blacks were distributed evenly. Spreading black students evenly through all the schools in Texas for grades 5–7 eliminates about a quarter of the black-white test score gap at grade 7. If integration were maintained longer, more of the gap would disappear.

What about "acting white"? Its effect on the black-white gap in cognitive achievement is probably not large. Maybe it makes top achievers somewhat lonely but still productive.

The Hanushek, Kain, and Rivkin study used school fixed effects, thus eliminating any differences among schools that might have resulted in worse education in heavily black schools. This means that it probably understates the benefits of integration.

Aside from these essentially static reasons, minorities might want integration for a dynamic reason. The quality of schools minority children attend is determined by political processes. In political processes, majorities, especially rich ones, usually count more than minorities, especially poor ones. Integration assures that minority children attend schools no worse than those that NHW children attend. School quality isn't the only variable that's important for education, but it's still important.

As far as attainment goes, Guryan (2004) found that desegregation orders in the 1970s cut black dropout rates substantially: by roughly 11–14 percent. Lutz (2011) found a similar though smaller effect in the opposite direction for ending desegregation orders in the 1990s, especially outside the South. Billings, Deming, and Rockoff (2012) show that the resegregation of Charlotte Mecklenburg schools in North Carolina increased the racial gap in achievement there (although part of this gap was later offset by compensatory education programs for minorities). There are similar results for noncognitive development: court-ordered integration caused dramatic reductions in the rate of homicides of black youth without causing increases in the white rate.

Card and Rothstein (2007) find that metropolitan areas with more residential segregation have greater test score gaps, and that residential segregation is a lot more important than school segregation. They present some evidence that schools that are more integrated have greater within-school segregation—honors classes that have mostly white students, for instance.

What policies can promote integration? Court-ordered desegregation is no longer on the table. Vouchers and charter schools probably work in the opposite direction, as we'll see. The answer may be magnet schools. Magnet schools reduced segregation (relative to what it would have been) in Durham (Billings, Deming, and Rockoff 2012). They may also offset the Card and Rothstein critique that integration at the school level can be undermined by segregation at the classroom level.

On the other hand, the results about magnet schools are not encouraging. These have been studied using regression discontinuity design. Many magnet schools accept students based on some sort of cutoff for an exam score. If magnet schools actually accomplish something, students who just barely pass the exam and get admitted should do noticeably better than students who just barely miss the cutoff and don't pass the exam. Cullen and Jacob (2007) looked at Chicago magnet schools, Deming (2009) looked at magnet schools in Charlotte, and Dobbie and Fryer (2011a) looked at high schools in New York City that required entrance examinations. All of these studies find that magnet schools make no difference on test scores: the reason that magnet school students do better is that they're smarter and were better educated before they went to the magnet school, not because of anything that the magnet school did that other schools don't do. Deming's study of Charlotte magnet schools, however, found noncognitive gains: going to a magnet school makes you less likely to be arrested or to encounter serious disciplinary problems.

As Card and Rothstein emphasize, school segregation is tied to residential segregation. Not completely, but it obviously matters a lot. When a program in Chicago moved a large number of families from segregated housing projects to suburbs with far fewer minorities, children's school outcomes improved. This was not a randomized controlled experiment, however. When the federal government tried to replicate these results in the Moving to Opportunity randomized controlled experiment, children's school outcomes did not improve. But the attempted replication may have missed important pieces of what the Chicago program did. We'll look at neighborhood segregation (and how to measure segregation) and the experiences of these programs and experiments in Chapter 9.

Attitudes, trust, and atmosphere.   Learning involves complex interactions between teachers and students (probably between parents and principals too) in which trust and expectations matter a lot. Teachers do more than pour knowledge into the empty brains of students, and students do more than passively receive that knowledge. These subtle interactions were displayed in Figlio's (2005) study of how first names influenced test scores and teacher attitudes and Van der Bergh et al.'s (2010) study of implicit association tests. In this section we've seen how interventions in early childhood and in the first few years of school mysteriously influence behavior and accomplishments more than a decade later, even though they don't affect test scores in most of the intervening years. Perhaps these early interventions influence trust, communication, and attitude.

Thus reforms that change school atmosphere and create a culture of learning for minority students are potentially a way of reducing the gaps. But how do you do that? In this subsection, I'll look at several different ideas.

1. *Catholic schools.*   Back in the twentieth century, African Americans and Hispanics from cities who attended Catholic schools did better, where "better" refers to high school graduation and possible cognitive achievement. No strong evidence indicated that anybody else did better. Why? If the reason was atmosphere, then it could be replicated. If the reason was the dedication and quality of the staff, then it probably couldn't be replicated. If the reason was peers, then it couldn't be replicated. But some evidence indicates that peers weren't all that different *on observables.*

The Catholic schools of the twentieth century are not the Catholic schools of today or the future. Catholic schools, especially in cities, are now in serious difficulty and are closing rapidly. Expansion is unlikely; this is not a way to reduce the test score gap, although possibly we can learn something from them.

2. *Race-concordant teachers (and principals).*   Some evidence indicates that students perform better when they are matched with teachers of their own race. This could happen because of something that the teacher does (called the active effect) or something students do (called the passive effect). Students might infer from the teacher's race that their race is not a barrier to academic success or they might simply feel more comfortable around someone of their own race and therefore learn better. Since these reactions depend only on who the teacher is and not on anything she or he does (although, of course, race contains an element of volition), they are considered passive effects. Minority teachers might also treat minority students differently than NHW teachers do; these are active effects. They might, for instance, call on minority students more often, speak to them in less condescending tones, or talk to their parents more often.

Dee (2004) finds that race-concordant teachers raise test scores for both NHW and black students. The gains for black students per year of race-concordant schooling are about 10–15 percent of the test score gap, so an increase of several years in the time the average black student is in a classroom with a black teacher would make a noticeable difference. Dee uses data from Project STAR, so the students and teachers in his study were assigned randomly, which removes many selection problems. But STAR was designed to look at class size, not race-concordant teachers, so the experiment wasn't perfect (students and teachers, for instance, were randomized within schools, not across schools).

African American and Hispanic students were also less likely to be labeled "inattentive" or "disruptive" when their teachers were race concordant
(Dee 2005) and more likely to be assigned to specialized school services such
as programs for gifted students (Rocha and Hawes 2009).

While these results tell us that employing more minority teachers and
matching them with minority students would reduce the achievement gap
if these teachers were as able as minority teachers are now, they don't say
anything about how to find or produce teachers like this or how to keep them
engaged in teaching. Teachers are more satisfied with their jobs and turn
over less quickly when they're supervised by race-concordant principals
(Grissom and Keiser 2011), but it's just as hard to think of ways of mass-
producing able minority principals as it is to think of ways of mass-producing
able minority teachers. Nevertheless, these results indicate that improvements
in minority education, to the extent that they result in more minority teachers,
lead to long-lasting external benefits.

The issue of minority teachers brings together the insights of Washington,
Du Bois, and Malcolm X. Minority teachers are scarce now because of history; that's what Washington emphasizes. They are valuable today because
of the way racial identities work now; that's what Du Bois emphasizes. And
Malcolm X would point out that a separate black educational system would
provide race-concordant teachers and principals for every black child. (The
separatist solution, of course, comes at a price that includes some less able
teachers and principals and worse peer effects for students from high SES
families. I don't know of any serious effort to weigh its costs and benefits.)

3. *"No excuses" schools.*   Some schools that enroll many students from poor
and minority families insist on order and discipline, and accept "no excuses"
for academic shortcomings; students are expected to succeed. A few of these
schools have been rigorously evaluated and found to cause large increases in
cognitive test scores—for instance, the Harlem Children's Zone in New York
City and some of the KIPP Public Charter Schools in New England. These
gains were especially large in math. For instance, Dobbie and Fryer (2011b)
estimated that the Harlem Children's Zone raised math scores by over a fifth
of a standard deviation in a year, enough to wipe out the racial test score
gap during elementary school.

"No excuses" schools tend to have schoolwide disciplinary rules, frequent
communication with students about school culture, prohibitions against

students leaving until the teacher dismisses a class, standards for backpack and desk contents, and an expectation that student eyes will be following the teacher (Dobbie and Fryer 2011c, 10). The findings that these schools raise test scores are often based on something close to a randomized experiment: a comparison between students randomly accepted from a waiting list and those who were not accepted. Most of the "no excuses" schools that have been studied are charter schools, but some are quite close to traditional public schools (Fryer and Dobbie 2011d).

The weakness of these studies is that they tell us that *something* about the schools is working, but they don't unambiguously tell us what. It could be, for instance, that schools succeed because they have charismatic principals and charismatic principals just happen to implement "no excuses" practices. Schools with charismatic principals might be successful *despite* "no excuses," not because of "no excuses."

Empirically, the "no excuses" approach to school culture tends to be found (at least among New York City charter schools) in the schools that have what I called an intense approach to instruction: frequent teacher feedback, the use of data as a guide, high-dosage tutoring, and more instructional time (Dobbie and Fryer 2011c).

These five practices tend to be a package. Perhaps the parts of the package fit together in a causal way: the extra instructional time, for instance, might be unbearable for teachers if children were allowed to run wild. Perhaps they don't fit together and are just coincidentally associated.

The evidence does suggest, however, that innovations in school atmosphere and culture are likely to reduce the achievement gap. Whether this can occur in an integrated environment (most "no excuses" schools have heavily minority student bodies) is an open question—surely one that Malcolm X would be interested in.

4. *Small high schools.*   Some evidence from New York City (Murnane 2013) indicates that small high schools promote both achievement and attainment. The story is that smaller schools allow for more cohesion and identification; it's harder for students to "get lost." Atmosphere matters.

High-Stakes Testing

High-stakes testing, which is best known in the form of the federal No Child Left Behind (NCLB) legislation of 2002, entails testing of student cognitive achievement in math and reading and serious consequences for principals and teachers if their students don't perform as well as expected or improve as quickly as expected. The idea is that schools know what to do but they don't have the right incentives to do it. Instead, they take it easy on themselves and don't challenge their students. In economic terms, high-stakes testing arranges carrots and sticks (more sticks than carrots) so workers won't shirk.

The benefits of high-stakes testing would exceed its costs if all it did was reduce inefficient shirking (some shirking is efficient: workers shouldn't work infinitely hard to produce output of infinitesimal value). High-stakes testing would cut the racial gaps if shirking were greater in heavily minority schools or if testing programs changed the allocation of teacher effort in favor of minorities.

Both of the stories about the gap have some plausibility. Minority parents may not be as sophisticated or as confident as NHW parents about monitoring teachers and principals; they may allow more shirking. Since high-stakes testing measures the number of students who pass rather than average score, it may encourage teachers to concentrate on students at the margin between passing and failure. If the marginal students are disproportionately minority, this will increase the attention minorities receive. Explicit goals for minority students may help too.

But there is a limit on the extent to which shirking can be a big problem. To the extent that the test score gap is due to unobservable factors in schools, reducing shirking has a chance of reducing the test score gap. On the other hand, if two-thirds of the gap is attributable to what happens in classrooms, the only kind of "shirking" that could be contributing to the gap is how the teacher allocates attention in the classroom. So there are only very specific places we can look for how accountability programs might reduce the gap.

Even if shirking is a big problem, high-stakes testing may not be a good way of addressing it. Agency theory teaches a basic lesson: strong incentives work when every outcome you care about can be equally well measured and your measures are indicators only of things you care about, but otherwise strong incentives can get you worse outcomes. Paying police for arrests, for instance, will not result in better administration of justice. In the case of education, the greater the rewards for teaching testable cognitive skills, the less time, resources, and energy will be devoted to the other goals schools have. The first hour of music instruction may be more socially valuable than the eighth hour of arithmetic, but the school gets rewarded for arithmetic proficiency, not contributions to social welfare.

High-stakes testing may alter other incentives too. Since NCLB in particular uses more sticks than carrots, it may affect who enters teaching and who stays. If heavily minority schools are more likely to be sanctioned for some reason, teachers would also be discouraged from teaching there. Just in terms of arithmetic, all-white schools have the fewest NCLB goals they can fail to meet and so are relatively the most attractive places to work.

Empirical studies have shown that high-stakes testing does alter behavior in unintended ways. Chicago schools, for instance, increased the number of students in special education, preemptively retained students in lower grades, and reduced time for science and social studies. Virginia schools served high-calorie lunches on exam days.

But the major question is how high-stakes testing alters cognitive achievement. Because clean experiments are hard to find, no answer is definitive yet. When high-stakes testing programs start, scores on the test being used usually improve for the first few years, but that usually indicates teaching to the test, not real learning. The relevant question is whether high-stakes testing raises scores on low-stakes tests such as the National Assessment of Educational Progress.

Dee and Jacob (2011) is the best recent attempt to answer this question. Some states had consequential high-stakes testing programs in place before NCLB was enacted in 2002. Presumably NCLB did not affect these states because they were doing what NCLB called for already. So by comparing changes in NAEP scores after 2002 in states that were affected by NCLB with changes in states that were not affected, Dee and Jacob hoped to ferret out the real effect of NCLB.

Overall they found a modest positive effect of NCLB for fourth grade math—about a quarter of a standard deviation—and positive but statistically insignificant effects for eighth grade math and fourth grade reading. This is a cumulative effect of about five years of NCLB. Some gaps also narrowed in math. The Hispanic-NHW gap decreased in both the fourth and eighth grades, and the black-NHW gap decreased in the fourth grade. Reading gaps were unchanged. NCLB might have cut the black-NHW gap in fourth grade math by as much as a third, but the other gaps decreased by less.

Part of these improvements are probably attributable to the factors proponents envisioned—teachers and principals working harder and focusing more intently. Part may be attributable to the fact that schools neglected other outputs, both cognitive and noncognitive. And part likely is attributable to states appropriating more money for education. In another study with the same research design, Dee, Jacob, and Schwartz (2011) found that NCLB caused states and localities to raise their spending per pupil, increase teacher compensation, and increase the proportion of teachers with advanced degrees. The "shirking" that NCLB may have curtailed was that of state legislators.

Charter Schools

Charter schools are a popular educational reform, probably the most popular form of the current decade, just as high-stakes testing was the popular reform when the twenty-first century began. But they are not very common: in 2010–2011, only about 5 percent of public school enrollment was in charter schools. I'm not sure whether they should be thought of as pro-poor, since they operate, at least on the surface, in a race-neutral way, or pro-minority, since they are generally portrayed as designed for minority students.

What are charter schools? States have different rules, but the basic picture is that they are independent entities that are under a loose contract to educate public school students.

Suppose you and your friends want to start a charter school. The first thing you would do is apply to a charter-granting agency, usually a state education department or a state university. In many states the application is a high hurdle: you have to work hard to convince the grantor that you have the resources, ideas, and people to run a good school. Some states are tougher than others. In tough states, a lot of people who apply never get a charter.

If you got a charter, you could then set up a school. You would hire faculty and staff, usually outside union rules, you would get yourself a building, and then you would get yourself some students.

No one is forced to send her kids to a charter school. Parents have to decide to apply. If you got more applications than you had spots, you would have to hold a lottery. If you didn't get enough applications, you would be on your way to being out of business.

How do you get money to operate? The state pays you a fixed fee per pupil. This is usually somewhat less than regular public schools spend per pupil. If you don't fill all your seats, you don't get all the money you were counting on.

Your charter lasts a fixed period of time, usually three to five years. Then the charter-granting authority evaluates how well you are doing. If you are not doing well—for instance, if your students are doing poorly on standardized tests or if the place is a mess—you are out of business.

Who sets up charter schools? You need a certain level of resources and sophistication to clear the initial hurdles (sometimes you might need some political connections too). If you and your friends tried to do it, you'd probably get rejected. Generally two kinds of groups set up schools: local nonprofits that are well established in other areas besides education and national organizations that run chains of charter schools. Some of these national groups are for-profit organizations (e.g., Victory Education Partners) and others are nonprofit (e.g., KIPP).

Notice that this setup means that charters have a lot more types of accountability than regular public schools or regular private schools. Like regular public schools, they have bureaucrats that see that they conform to state laws and that they produce reasonably good test scores. Like regular private schools, they have to convince enough parents that they are good places for their kids. The organizations that run these schools may also be concerned about their reputations: the national organizations probably want to create a uniformly good product—the way McDonald's or Trader Joe's does—and the local sponsors may worry about their local image. But there is no guarantee that better oversight will result—each group of overseers could become more lax because they do not have full ownership.

Can charter schools improve education? Can they reduce the test score gap?

The theoretical and popular answer to this question has emphasized the possibly stronger accountability. As we have seen in the discussion of high-stakes testing, lack of accountability may contribute to the racial gaps, but it is not the whole story.

But accountability might not be the only way that charter schools work. They can also increase variety, and they may just allow more and better resources to be brought to bear on minority education. Perhaps the charter schools can harness altruism better, or perhaps the national organizations can innovate and standardize good practices faster and think about minorities more. Maybe education should be organized nationally (by these organizations that specialize in minority education) rather than locally by school boards organized by geography. Why organize along nineteenth-century lines when you can use twenty-first-century technology?

What do we know about a charter schools? The conclusion of most large-scale studies is that the average charter school is about as good as the average public school, maybe a little worse. Charter schools also are more seg-regated than public schools. Not much to be impressed about.

Even though the average charter school is mediocre, a number of econo-mists have studied specific charter schools or sets of charter schools in the last several years. These studies find that these charter schools are better than the average public school and in a few cases, a lot better. We have alluded to some of these results in the discussion of intense instruction and "no excuses" schools.

Most of these studies take advantage of the admission lotteries that charter schools have to run when they are oversubscribed. Essentially, the studies compare changes in cognitive achievement between lottery winners and lottery losers.

Hoxby and Murarka (2009) looked at forty-seven New York City charter schools. They found some modest differences: charter school students gain around a tenth of a standard error relative to other students per year in reg-ular public school. Abdulkadiroglu et al. (2011) looked at Boston charter schools that stayed in business and kept good records. They found that the gain is one-quarter of a standard deviation per year in reading and four-tenths of a standard deviation per year in math. Angrist, Chin, and Godoy (2010) looked at a specific KIPP charter school in Lynn, Massachusetts, with a large Hispanic and LEP enrollment: the gain was an eighth of a standard devia-tion per year in reading and a third of a standard deviation per year in math. LEP students did better: the weakest benefited the most. Finally, Dobbie and Fryer (2011c), as we have seen, found similar large gains at the Harlem Children's Zone.

These studies find no evidence of "skimming" in these schools—taking the best students out of public schools. However, the comparison group is other students who applied for admission to charter schools, not all students.

Why do these schools do well? Most of the speculation is about intense instruction and "no excuses." Fryer and Dobbie (2011d) suggest that you don't have to be a charter school to use these practices to get these results.

The presence of some excellent schools among the many charter schools in the country does not tell us a lot about charter schools in general or about a policy of encouraging charter school growth. I could also find a bunch of high-performing public schools with large enrollments of poor minority students. One question is whether such good performance is likely to spread. Charter schools, especially the national chains, may be better at spreading successful innovations than a collection of local school districts. They have good incentives to do so and they have the ability to do so very easily. (If I'm running KIPP and my school in Lynn is doing great, I can easily find out something about why and I want to do so; I also want to spread this practice throughout my network. If I'm running a public school in New Jersey, I'm unlikely to find out about Lynn, I'm unlikely to get the time off to visit the school to see how it's done, the Lynn people have no reason to talk to me.) But this is speculation at this point—there is no data to support it.

Even if this speculation is accurate and charter schools are very good at getting better, they are not likely to have a big role in closing the test score gap any time soon. There are just too few of them now, and many of them are lousy. The process of weeding out the bad ones and expanding the good ones and spreading useful innovations has to take time. McDonald's did not transform the fast-food market overnight.

Moreover, expanding great charter schools will not be a pure educational gain. First, the growth of charter schools in the metropolitan area has been a major piece of the demise of the Catholic schools. In some places, Catholic schools are trying to transform themselves directly into charter schools. Everywhere, the growth of charter schools that have money and are looking for a place to operate has raised the opportunity cost of the real estate Catholic schools have been using. More generally, some of the talent and altruism that go into charter schools would have gone into public schools or Catholic schools if charter schools did not exist. Neither effect has been measured yet.

The interesting question that can be asked about existing charter schools is whether school districts that have more of them have better test scores (and other outcome measures) than school districts that have fewer of them. What economists should be looking at is how charter schools affect the district-wide distribution of educational outcomes, not just the outcomes of the students who happen to attend them.

Vouchers

There are many different voucher schemes. What they have in common is that at least some parents will get some public money to spend on sending their kids to some private schools, which are somehow regulated. I'm being vague so I can cover many different proposals, some of which are quite detailed. Most voucher schemes are not at all like markets because prices are not allowed to adjust to equate supply and demand and parents in most cases can't reduce other consumption to get better schools or send their children to worse schools in order to increase other consumption.

Discussions of vouchers would be easier if kids were parents' possessions, like cars or chairs. But they're not. Voucher proponents believe in public funding; they would not advocate public funding for enhancements of their private possessions, like tires for cars or covers for chairs. They believe that there is a public interest in the education of their children; otherwise there would be no justification for public funding of vouchers.

Arguments for vouchers stress both the accountability problem and the variety problem. Vouchers are like high-stakes testing on accountability, but they are the opposite of high-stakes testing on variety.

Let's start with evidence, most of which is indirect.

There have been a number of small voucher experiments: in Milwaukee, New York City, Dayton, and the District of Columbia. These experiments found no strong evidence that whites or Hispanics do better in school as a result of getting vouchers. There was some evidence that African Americans did better, especially on math scores. The most optimistic evidence is that gains for African Americans were about half the size of the gains from small class sizes in STAR. But this result did not hold up. Large numbers of African Americans left private schools after a year. When Krueger and Zhu (2004) reanalyzed the data, the positive result disappeared.

These results aren't really all that informative because they don't tell us how a real system of vouchers would work: how large numbers of students would sort themselves, how new schools would enter and leave over time, how residences would change. You can't evaluate the impact of a change as big as the Internet by simply comparing it with the older communications technology of the telephone; you have to factor in many other variables.

To get some idea of what happens with large-scale, long-term operation, consider voucher education in Chile and New Zealand. The story there is that not much happened. The new schools weren't much like the existing Catholic schools; they were somewhat cheaper secular schools. There were no big changes in average achievement. But there was more stratification: abler and richer students were more likely to be in schools with other able and rich students (Hsieh and Urquiola 2006). The bottom was worse off. In

New Zealand there was increased segregation of Maori and European students and fewer Maoris in the top high schools. But I have not seen studies that look at Maori achievement in New Zealand directly.

This evidence on stratification in Chile and New Zealand may also raise questions about charter schools; the studies of these countries raised the right questions.

Summary

Minority education can be improved and the gaps can narrow. But there is no magic bullet. And there is no free lunch either, to mix metaphors. Endogamy has consequences. Almost everything that shrinks the gaps modestly costs taxpayer money. Many strategies to shrink the gaps do work. But whether governments will decide to spend the money and spend it effectively, I don't know. Even if they do, it will take a long time for the gaps to narrow. Just as no single strategy alone will eliminate the gaps, education alone will not make race disappear in your lifetime.

Colleges, Graduate Schools, and Affirmative Action

The previous section looked at a long and varied series of proposed reforms in elementary and secondary education. By contrast, almost all discussions of higher education concentrate on admissions policies. That will be the subject of this section, even though there are many other important issues in higher education—the minority graduation rate, for instance, and the future of historically black colleges and universities.

Affirmative action in higher education is limited to a small number of colleges and professional schools. That's because most universities accept all reasonably qualified applicants; they worry about filling up classes, not turning students away. Only about 20–25 percent of people who go to college attend schools that are reasonably competitive—according to Barron's, a little over 200 schools. Kane (2004) finds that only the top quartile of schools appear to give preference to minority applicants. The policies in question affect maybe 5–10 percent of the students admitted to those schools (and probably less at the bottom of the 200 competitive schools), so in all, they affect maybe 1–2 percent of college students, who in turn are not all young people. So this is not a topic that is very important in the scheme of things.

Some people have argued that affirmative action in higher education is more important than the small numbers of people involved would suggest. Kennedy (2013, 14), for instance, writes, "Selective institutions of higher education are far-reaching training grounds for the power-elite," and notes that every member of the Supreme Court in 2013 attended law school at either Harvard or Yale. Most of the people who make this claim have a background at one of the institutions in question (and I do too), so they are probably not unbiased observers. At any rate, since many of the people reading this book think they or their friends have been affected by these policies, I should deal with the topic.

In higher education, affirmative action is confined to a small slice of higher education where markets don't operate You don't get admitted to Columbia by outbidding someone else for the position. Notice that the same is true for labor markets: affirmative action there was also confined to a thin slice where markets were not used. So in both employment and education, affirmative action can't be said to interfere with markets. Where affirmative action operates, there isn't any market to interfere with.

Affirmative Action and Its Varieties

What do I mean by affirmative action in higher education admissions? I mean disparate impact. Specifically, if you run a (logit or probit) regression on the probability of admission given all the relevant nonracial characteristics (SATs, high school grades, quality of high school, athletic ability, leadership, legacy status). If a dummy variable for a minority group is significant and positive or you run two regressions and evaluation at the means gives a significant difference, then I will say there is affirmative action. On these regressions, of course, you could always argue that there were unobserved variables— things like the quality of the essay or the eloquence of the recommendation letters—but you could do the same thing when we discussed disparate impact in the chapters on employment (Chapter 5) or health care (Chapter 4). I don't know of anyone who has a plausible disparate treatment story, because to substantiate one you would have to submit phony applications.

Bowen and Bok (1998) ran a series of these regressions for blacks and for nonblacks for the class of 1989 in a small group of elite schools. They concluded that disparate impact occurred in admissions. If blacks had the same coefficients as whites (the "civil rights experiment"), they would constitute about 2–3 percent of the entering classes rather than 7 percent. Rothstein and

Yoon (2008) reached a similar conclusion for law schools. These results are roughly congruent with the decrease in African American enrollment that UC Berkeley experienced when it was forced to end racial affirmative action.

Thus in my world there are no people who are "affirmative action admits" or "affirmative action rejects," just changes in probabilities.

Also note that affirmative action does not make much difference to the average SAT score of an entering class. There are only a few whites and Asians who would have been admitted if policies were different, and they are pretty weak students. The marginal white or Asian students who were not admitted are not as strong academically as the average white or Asian students who were admitted.

Theoretical Results That Are Pretty Solid

The main theoretical result is that color-blind affirmative action, which is popular politically these days, is a fairly stupid idea, relative to color-sighted affirmative action, which is unpopular.

Color-sighted affirmative action means traditional affirmative action: if you want more African American students, then you look at the race of applicants and admit more African Americans. Color-blind affirmative action means the new style of affirmative action: you look at something other than race in the hope that admitting more students with that characteristic will also admit more African American or Hispanic students. Color-blind affirmative action includes economic affirmative action (preferences for kids from poor families regardless of race) and high school affirmative action (in Texas, the top 10 percent of students in each high school get admitted to top state schools; in Florida, the top 20 percent with some other conditions are admitted to state schools; in California, the top 4 percent are admitted on some campuses).

The basic result is this. Consider a college that wants both racial diversity and high cognitive skills among its students. Then color-sighted affirmative action will get that college higher cognitive skills for any desired level of diversity (or greater diversity for any desired level of cognitive skills) than color-blind affirmative action.

The intuition is quite simple: if you want to find something, look for it. If a college wanted both a few tuba players for its band and generally smart students, it would do much better by asking applicants if they were tuba players than it would by admitting a lot of students from high schools that tended to have a lot of tuba players. With tuba-sighted affirmative action, it could identify the tuba players who had the greatest cognitive skills and admit them. This might cut its average SAT score, but not by much. On the other hand, with tuba-blind affirmative action, the college would fill up with a lot of lousy students from high schools where tuba playing happened to be popular, and it might not even get the tuba players who were the best students.

The same is true with race. If you admit randomly, it's color blind and you get a lot of minorities and you have really terrible academic performance. Color-blind affirmative action is just a slightly improved variant of random admission.

If you take something else, such as income, as a proxy for race, you won't do as well as in getting diversity per low-test-score admit. You have to admit a lot of less-qualified whites to get one minority, and the minority you admit might not be the one you want.

Ray and Sethi (2010) go a little further. They show that unless the distributions of cognitive skills across races are very unusual, the optimal color-blind affirmative action scheme is bizarre: it admits a lot of applicants with high cognitive skills, then it admits a lot of applicants with low cognitive skills, including a lot of minorities. The lowest test score in the group with high cognitive skills is much higher than the highest test score in the group with low cognitive scores; there is a gulf between the two groups. One side effect is that within the class admitted with color-blind affirmative action, you will have a bigger gap between the average cognitive skills of African American and Hispanic students and the average skills of NHW and Asian students than you will with color-sighted affirmative action.

These arguments against color-blind affirmative action don't take incentives and deadweight losses into account. Incentives and deadweight losses make color-blind affirmative action look even worse.

Economic affirmative action carries work disincentives for parents. If you're white or Asian and want to get your kids into good schools, it's much easier to make yourself poor than it is to make yourself black or Hispanic. Or to make yourself appear to be poor. Economic affirmative action is essentially a very steep rise in marginal tax rates for families with children who might attend elite colleges.

Changing your race in order to get your kids into a better college is hard (but not impossible for everybody) now. A future with large numbers of biracial kids is interesting to contemplate and has implications for affirmative action in the future, but not here and now.

High school affirmative action gives parents an incentive to get their child into the weakest high school imaginable. This may cause cognitive gains for classmates in those weak high schools (but at the expense of a worsened probability of college admission) but losses for the student herself in terms of cognitive achievement. It means that strong students in weak high schools have no reason to exert much effort. It also reduces pressure from parents to make high schools stronger. If it induces whites to move to all-minority high schools, it might have beneficial externalities. But these probably are not the people on the margin. The people on the margin may include minority parents whose children would gain from being in more integrated schools (although they might lose a few friends). Some of these parents now make big sacrifices in buying homes in communities they may not be able to afford, in long commutes, and in distances from friends and relatives.

But Why Strive for Diversity and High Cognitive Skills?

This is where most of the literature stands now. *If* colleges want both racial diversity and high cognitive skills, then color-sighted affirmative action gives them the best trade-off between the two goals. Why do they want both? Should they want both?

Notice that these are two separate questions: a positive question about why colleges like affirmative action and high cognitive skills now and a normative question about whether setting up a society where colleges act like this is a good idea. Notice also that colleges are after two things: racial diversity and high cognitive skills. We have to look at both. You may think it's obvious that colleges should seek high cognitive skills, but I don't. For instance, if fairness is the issue, then colleges should admit qualified students randomly, as charter schools do. Or if efficiency is the goal, maybe the best faculty should be paired with the worst students, since the worst students can use the most help. Neither goal is obvious.

Three possible normative answers that don't convince me.   Several possible answers to the question of whether affirmative action should be practiced in admissions to higher education do not impress me.

The first answer that doesn't convince me on a normative basis is fairness or political support. Since the citizens of Michigan or Texas as a whole support the flagship university, maybe every group should have access to it in the name of fairness. This doesn't seem persuasive to me. I don't think every group should have equal access to other public facilities like psychiatric hospitals, nor do I think senior citizens should be allowed to go to kindergarten or that horseback riders should have access to the New Jersey Turnpike. On the other hand, affirmative action might be a wise strategy for state college administrators who want to make sure they have a broad base of political support.

Arguments about long-run efficiency and convergence have not been made clearly enough yet. I think there might be something in these arguments, but I've never seen it developed. We've seen in the rest of this chapter that racial achievement gaps are likely to continue for a long time—most of your working lives at least—and that the rate of convergence is very slow. Possibly affirmative action in admissions to higher education will speed up convergence a little bit. Affirmative action might make convergence more rapid because your children will be smarter if you went to UC Berkeley than if you went to UC Davis. Or because minority students in high school will have more incentive to study if they think they have a shot to get into an elite college. Although I haven't seen data to support these assertions, they aren't implausible. But they aren't terribly convincing either. For instance, because a mother's educational attainment affects children more than a father's does, gap closing implies that affirmative action for minority women (or the future mothers of minority children) should be much stronger than affirmative action for minority men.

Is there a general external benefit from reducing the achievement gap? Yes: reducing stereotypes and everything that come with them, increasing trust, and improving self-confidence and self-perception. So gap closing is a possible reason for affirmative action, but the argument has not been worked out.

Finally, the arguments about symbolic fairness and trust are not complete either. The arguments go something like this: in the long run, the United States will work better if minorities believe that they are treated reasonably fairly. They are more likely to believe that (whether it's true or not) if they see faces like theirs in visible positions of power and responsibility in business, the media, politics, and government. The people who fill these positions are drawn disproportionately from elite colleges. Thus increasing the number of minority students in these colleges will increase the proportion of minorities in visible positions of power and responsibility and will increase the level of trust in the United States (whether it's merited or not).

Again, every link in this chain of reasoning is plausible, but it's a long chain and it's hard to test. It also stretches over decades. And it's not fool-proof. It could be, for instance, that a significant portion of NHWs is also prone to mistrust the fairness of U.S. institutions and that if they learn that NHW students are not being treated in ways they consider to be fair in college admissions, their trust could erode even further.

Reparations.   One argument is that people from racial and ethnic groups that have been treated wrongly in U.S. history (including the fairly recent history of Jim Crow) should receive favorable treatment to make up for wrong-doing. Kennedy (2013, 78–79) writes: "Making amends for the cruel, de-bilitating racially motivated wrongs imposed upon racial minorities, partic-ularly blacks, over a long period is the single most compelling justification for racial affirmative action. . . . Why attempt to redress past wrongs? Jus-tice demands such an effort. An essential element of justice is righting wrongs to the extent reasonable under the circumstances obtaining." To assess this argument, we need to understand the logic of reparations, which is more than we can do in this chapter. Chapter 14 is about reparations, and we will revisit this argument for affirmative action in higher education there.

The diversity argument.   Colleges don't make any of these arguments when they defend affirmative action. They instead argue for diversity. The Supreme Court accepts some diversity arguments. Maybe both are trying to come up with a pretext for a politically popular position. (Kennedy [2013], for instance, generally a proponent of affirmative action, finds many weaknesses in this argument.) But let's try to see if we can make some sense of this and give them the benefit of the doubt.

The diversity argument in some ways turns the gestalt of the civil rights movement on its head. Under this argument, minority students are on campus not to advance their education or even to help their race; they are there to improve the education of white and Asian students. Minority students are "the help," doing what they can to benefit the "real students." Phrased this way, the diversity argument sounds like an insult to minority students at elite colleges. But is it really? As we saw in Chapter 2, for instance, for James Weldon Johnson and Gunnar Myrdal one of the major reasons for ending Jim Crow was to make whites better people. Closer to home, I spend most of my working hours on the campus of an elite university, but I recognize that my purpose there is to amuse my colleagues and students and maybe teach them something. If I didn't do that, I wouldn't be there. I'm "the help," too. I don't feel insulted by this knowledge. I definitely wouldn't feel better if the deans came up to me and told me that I was useless but they liked me, so I could stay.

More generally, in economics, everyone is "the help." None of us should feel bad about that or look down upon others just because they're useful. In this section I'll develop an economic model of universities where everyone is useful to everyone else.

Perhaps you learned in high school that elite colleges existed to reward selflessly the virtue of students who worked hard. That's not what elite colleges do; that's what Santa Claus does.

The university system: A non-racial model.   I want to think about colleges as clubs. A branch of economics called "club theory" is about groups of people who come together for some common purpose: clubs (swim clubs, chess clubs, athletic teams, and gyms, for instance), marriages, towns, and maybe even companies. The basic questions in club theory are about what groups of people should associate with each other.

You can think of Columbia or any other university as a club of people that includes students, faculty, staff, and alumni. You don't have to ascribe an objective function to "Columbia" when you think of it as a club.

When you think about how people join clubs, you can see a few different organization principles.

The easiest to think about is hierarchy. This is easy to think about because a lot of you got it drilled into your heads all through childhood. Suppose only one attribute matters and the more you have of this attribute, the more you gain from being around people with a lot of the attribute. For instance, consider chess playing: the better you are at chess, the more you gain from playing with grandmasters. The faster you are as a runner, the better you become by training with really fast runners. Sometimes this complementarity can arise because of shared equipment: really serious weight lifters and body builders like to go to hardcore gyms (the ones with lots of free weights, no carpeting, and rap and reggae music). Less serious people don't like these things, so serious folks prefer to hang around with each other because they want to be with hardcore equipment.

It is similar with marriage. Suppose there are two kinds of people, alpha and beta, and the joint product of marriages between them looks like this:

	Alpha	Beta
Alpha	5	3
Beta	3	2

Then the economic theory of marriage has two results. First is that *positive assortative matching* is socially optimal. Positive assortative matching means that people match with people like themselves. In this case, alphas marry alphas and betas marry betas. When there are complementarities, it's easy to see that this arrangement is socially optimal. When alphas marry alphas and betas marry betas, the total product is $5 + 2 = 7$, as opposed to $3 + 3 = 6$ when marriages are mixed.

The second result is that people left to themselves will end up with positive assortative matching. Stability requires it. Suppose an alpha is thinking about marrying a beta. Say that that alpha gets 2.5 while the beta gets 0.5. Then another beta can come along and offer the first beta 1 to marry, and both betas will be better off. Or suppose the alpha is getting only 2 while the beta is getting 1 in the original proposed match. Then another alpha can come along and offer the alpha 2.3 for marrying and break the original marriage up that way. By contrast, you can show that nobody can break up the alpha-alpha and beta-beta marriages. Basically, alphas are willing to bid more than betas to marry alphas, so that's what will happen. (There is a lot of evidence that marriages in the United States tend toward positive assortative matching on a lot of dimensions such as education and beauty.)

So for things with quality complementarity, you see hierarchies: chess clubs, running clubs, gyms, and so forth. Maybe businesses too: at least that's what Goldman Sachs and McKinsey and top-tier law firms want you to believe when they are trying to recruit you. Ivy League schools basically operate on quality complementarity, of which there is a lot. Better students get more from really good faculty than worse students do. Better faculty get more from really good colleagues than worse faculty do. Better students get more from really smart peers than worse students would. Better-educated alumni get more from their contacts than worse-educated alumni would. Having gone to school with the attorney general is more valuable to you if you're a high-powered lawyer than if you're an auto mechanic. Having read the same sort of books and attended the same sort of lectures as the Supreme Court justices is more valuable for a high-powered lawyer (even one who does not know them personally) than it would be for an auto mechanic. At universities we like to tell ourselves this, and a good deal of it is probably true.

This is the basis of the hierarchy world. This is why you can rank universities and get something close to agreement, at least at the top. This is why a lot of you are neurotic. Not everything is like this, but some things are.

The hierarchy model is not a complete description of the world, however (thank God). Remember principles of economics and all the good action movies. The hierarchy model depends on having only one attribute matter, but for many purposes many attributes matter. When you put together a team to save the Na'vi, you need a helicopter pilot, a scientist, a bird thing, and a really tough Marine. The complementarity is across different attributes. Four tough Marines would have been useless.

Thus, if you want to be a really well-educated person, you should know micro, macro, and econometrics, not just micro. On the faculty side, you want to put together a team that's diverse, not only for teaching but also for research: applied economists can do better work when they can talk to econometricians—and to historians and neuroscientists. The same is true on the student side: if you want to get good at econometrics, you want some peers who are really good econometricians, even if you like micro or English better yourself. So you want students and faculty with many different talents at the same university. Similarly, companies want to hire people with complementary skills and alumni want to know people with many different kinds of talents and accomplishments. Athletic clubs want goalies as well as strikers and trainers. Many people would like to marry spouses of a different gender from their own.

Sometimes, however, even if you want to bring people with different attributes together, there is complementarity in quality across attributes. If you are a great ski jumper, the gain that comes from having a great doctor to patch you up instead of a mediocre one is greater than it would be if you were a mediocre ski jumper. The gain that comes to a soccer team from improving its offense is greater if the team has a great goalie, and vice versa. Thus you would expect to see the best doctors patching up the best ski jumpers and the best offensive players matched with the best goalies. This arrangement is efficient and the market is likely to produce it.

The same holds true for universities. The research payoff from hiring great econometricians is greater if you have great applied economists, so universities with great applied economists are willing to pay a lot of money to hire some really good econometricians. This is socially optimal. The same is true for alumni. If you are a high-powered investment banker, your gain from knowing a high-powered lawyer rather than a mediocre lawyer is greater than if you were a checkout clerk at Walmart's. You will gain more from going to school with people who are likely to be successful in other domains than your checkout-clerk friend. Similarly, if you are a high-powered academic you will gain more from having your students in important jobs than if you are a nerdy unimaginative recluse. You will also gain more from learning to talk with lawyer types and artist types than your checkout-clerk friend would. This applies in the marriage market too.

But quality complementarity doesn't hold for all attributes. The people who heat my office contribute less to total social output than the people who heat Joe Stiglitz's office, because Joe is a better economist than I am, so they should do a better job of heating Joe's office than they do of heating mine. But the difference to total output from having a great stationary engineer heat Joe's office and having an unskilled but adequate stationary engineer do the job is very small. So Columbia does not try to hire the world's best stationary engineers (or security guards).

That gets us a few basic features of an optimal university system: a rough hierarchy with the best students matched with the best faculty and with top universities that are excellent across many attributes but not all. That may be socially optimal.

Does our actual system approximate this ideal? Think about how marriage partners got sorted out the optimal way. The more attractive partners were able to outbid the less attractive partners. Two problems may keep this from happening in the college market for students: capital markets may shape who goes to the top colleges (really able 17-year-olds may not be able to borrow a few hundred thousand to outbid the less able but richer 17-year-olds); and the private benefits of education (the benefits to the student herself) may be less than the social benefits (the benefits to the student and everyone else), and this difference may differ among prospective students.

The capital market problem may be partially offset by formal loans and by the alumni system. You can look at alumni as students who continue to

pay for their education long after they have graduated. Why do they continue
to pay, since there is no contract that forces them to do so? Maybe altruism
and pride, but also partly because alumni gain from being associated with a
stronger school. That's the subject of a different book.

The externality problem is more serious. Prospective students whose education will produce lots of positive externalities won't be able to bid as much
as other students, so they may get into the best colleges less often than is
socially optimal. I don't see where alumni giving makes up for this.

You can look at admissions as collecting the bids by students to get into
a particular college. That may be why admissions offices pay attention to effort. Then you can think of a socially optimal admissions process as one
that mimics the results of a bidding system if there were no capital market
or externality problems. I have no idea how close we come. The importance
of need-blind admissions at top schools indicates that the situation probably
isn't terrible. But at least we have an answer for why top schools try to get
top students and a yardstick to use when thinking about good or bad admissions processes.

What about race?   Admitting Barack Obama and Eric Holder turned out
to be a pretty good move for Columbia.

Can we make reasonable arguments for taking race into consideration in
admissions in this framework? Yes. (Notice I said reasonable; I didn't say
impeccable.)

The first type of argument appeals to the external benefits for people who
are not members of the college community in question. It's possible that elite
education for minorities has more external benefits than elite education for
nonminorities, so in an optimal admissions world, minority students with
identical credentials to those of NHW students should be admitted before
the NHW students. What kind of externalities? Reducing harmful stereotypes (other minorities gain because people think the average minority is
better educated); role models (younger students see that hard work pays off
and, more important, that people who look like them are not inherently stupid
or athletic); and community leadership.*

---

*Krishna and Tarasov (2013) make a different argument about external benefits. They
assume that the information that admissions officers see depends on both acquired ability
and native ability and that disadvantaged groups generally have less acquired ability
than more advantaged groups (because they attend worse schools, for instance, and

This last—community leadership—takes some explaining. People who are leaders of a particular community—active citizens, members of boards, donors to local charities, wise elected officials—produce external benefits, and, on average, people who are well educated may produce greater external benefits than those who are not well educated. Having several Ivy League graduates on the library board or on the bench should be good for a community—Columbia seriously wants the world to believe this, anyway. There may be diminishing marginal returns within a community, however: the first wise civic leader in Camden is likely to be more valuable than the tenth wise civic leader in Scarsdale. (Or an educated alumnus is more likely to become a community leader in a community that has fewer educated people.) That is a conjecture for which I have no support; it may be false, and it should be investigated. If this conjecture is true, elite schools should admit a student who is likely to be a community leader in Camden over a student who is likely to be a community leader in Scarsdale.

Empirically, Bowen and Bok (1998) find that minority graduates of elite schools were more likely to become community leaders than NHW graduates, so there is a little support for my theory at least. (Communities don't have to be physical things. There is a community of stamp collectors and a community of the A.M.E. Zion Church. Nonphysical communities tend to be racially constructed too.)

The second type of argument appeals to two types of complementarity within the club: complementarity based on experiences before (and during schooling) and complementarity based on experiences after schooling.

Complementarities based on experiences before schooling are the type most often cited in diversity arguments. People gain from talking to others whose experiences and viewpoints are different from their own. We've seen already that race makes a difference in how you experience the world, in how you think about yourself, in how others think about you. Race is also a major issue in American life. Both of these sentences are true today, and they are

---

have less supportive home environments). They also assume that better education applied to native ability produces more social benefits than better education applied to acquired ability. Under these assumptions, admitting students from disadvantaged backgrounds produces social benefits under some conditions. This argument seems more like an argument for economic rather than racial affirmative action in the United States.

likely to continue to be true for a considerable time. So people of different races gain from talking with each other (on both sides), and it's plausible that smart people gain more from interracial dialogue with other smart people than they do with such dialogue with less smart people.

Race is probably not the only difference among people for whom this is true, but the argument for racial affirmative action is not necessarily an argument for looking only at race and grades. It's a plausible argument for taking economic circumstances into consideration, for instance. But the sentences are not true for every type of diversity: for instance, being left-handed or being from Dallas rather than Houston.

These are also gains to faculty, probably more than the gains to students. A lot of faculty really care about understanding the world (and get rewarded for writing about it in interesting ways), so the type of background that students bring to the university is very important to faculty.

Complementarities after schooling may be more important but are cited less often. Start from the likelihood that there will be some Hispanic and African American leaders over the next thirty years and that these are likely to be drawn from among the best educated and most capable African Americans and Hispanics of your generation. They will almost certainly not be drawn from among the best-educated and most capable NHWs or Asians of your generation. There will also be Hispanic and African American leaders in positions not tied to minority communities directly. High-powered NHWs of your generation are going to want to know these people. (So will high-powered academics.) They will be willing to pay more than the NHW checkout clerks of your generation to do so. The same is true for the future African American and Hispanic leaders, turned around: they will be willing to pay more than the African American and Hispanic checkout clerks of your generation to know NHW and Asian leaders.

Notice that this argument is not necessarily about knowing high-powered people personally, as in having shared a beer with them. It may be more important to know what sort of education these people received so you know how to frame your argument when you are appearing before the future Justice Sotomayor on the Supreme Court or trying to persuade the future Richard Parsons to invest with your hedge fund. And when you are having dinner with these powerful people and they ask you what college you went to, you don't want to say "the place that's all white." (This is one way current alumni gain from current affirmative action admissions.)

This argument has nothing to do with beneficence. You might also want to phrase it more cynically: affirmative action is a way for current elites to co-opt future elites. That is why I am not aware of any top university that can legally do so that does not practice some form of racial affirmative action or of any that has renounced racial affirmative action voluntarily. Many universities have become very ambitious at various times and have tried to move up in the ranks of the hierarchy, but none has eschewed racial affirmative action in order to do so.

This argument doesn't apply always and everywhere. Two conditions need to hold, and they don't always hold. The argument only works in an intermediate range of racial separatism.

First, race can't make too much difference. If all blacks are going to be cotton pickers and maids no matter what, there would be little point for white elites to get to know them and little reason for blacks to want to go to elite colleges. The Niagara Movement of 1905 was not demanding that blacks comprise 10 percent of the entering class at Harvard Law School. But today blacks and Hispanics hold some important positions.

Second, race has to make some difference. If there isn't going to be a Hispanic community, there will be no Hispanic community leaders. If the lives of black students before they came to college were the same as the lives of white students, there would be no diversity gain. Similarly, if the career paths of minority Columbia graduates were likely to be the same as the career paths of NHW Columbia graduates, there would be no diversity gain for alumni. But we've already seen and will see again in this book that race does make a difference.

All of this implies that elite schools want the best minority students, not just any minority students, so color-blind affirmative action fails them totally in this dimension.

This theory has many empirical implications that have not been tested. When UC Berkeley and the University of Texas adopted color-blind affirmative action, what happened to their success in recruiting the top white and Asian students, who had a choice of going to schools such as Columbia with color-sighted affirmative action? What happened to faculty retention and faculty salaries? What happened to alumni giving?

Jews and Asians.   The traditional view of affirmative action as a beneficent action (misguided, some would say) on the part of universities raises the question of why these same universities actively discriminated against many Jewish applicants in the middle of the twentieth century. Did they really just shift from being bad guys into being good guys? (Or from bad guys into stupid guys, as opponents of affirmative action might phrase it?)

My answer would be no. They were always self-interested, and they still are. When they believed that few Jews would become the type of society leaders that their graduates would have to know, they did not want to admit Jews. My evidence for this is from alumni interviews. The Ivy League schools instituted alumni interviews when they were inundated by Jewish applicants with stellar cognitive skills. If schools wanted to discriminate outright, they could just look at name and ask religious affiliation (this was before civil rights laws). They did not. Instead, the alumni interview let them find out which applicants were "too Jewish"—too far from WASP ways and appearance to have any chance of making it in elite banks and law firms. Because many elite positions were not open to Jews, the Ivies did not want to waste admissions slots on good students who would not be valuable contacts later in life.

I would probably think of the situation of Asians today or in the recent past in similar terms. But this is pure speculation.

Does Affirmative Action Work?

Does affirmative action work? The simple answer is that we don't know. In recent years researchers have made some heroic attempts to find some of the effects of affirmative action, but no definitive picture has emerged.

Part of the problem that empirical work faces is that "affirmative action" is not a single treatment like a particular dose of pesticide. The argument for affirmative action is that well-administered, correctly calibrated affirmative action can produce net benefits, not that any slapdash program that somebody calls affirmative action will work. It could be that the actual programs that colleges run are horrible but that some other affirmative action program would be great. In that sense, empirical work can produce only a lower bound on the net benefits of a potential affirmative action programs. But since nobody seems to know a good algorithm for improving affirmative action programs or even for figuring out in less than a decade which ones are performing better than others, that lower bound is useful to know and may be more relevant than the benefits an optimal affirmative action program could produce.

The question on which most work has been done is whether attending an elite college actually helps the students (of whatever race) who go there compared to attending a less highly ranked school or whether the success of elite college alumni is due solely to selection. The predominant answer in the literature seems to be that something about elite colleges makes their alumni do better after graduation than they would have done if they had attended less highly ranked schools. Attending a higher-ranked school appears to raise your probability of graduation (Cohodes and Goodman 2012), and most of the evidence says that graduating from a more selective college raises your lifetime earnings profile.

The literature on earnings, however, is not unanimous. Since students who attend more selective schools usually have more to begin with of the traits the labor market rewards, answering this question requires controversial assumptions about what they would have earned if they had attended less selective schools. Researchers also differ on how they measure selectivity, what life stage they see graduates at, and what colleges they include in their sample. Most published papers find large and statistically significant earnings gains for students from more selective schools (Behrman, Rozenzweig, and Taubman 1996; Black and Smith 2006; Brewer, Eide, and Ehrenburg 1999; Hoekstra 2009). Two studies by Dale and Krueger (2002, 2011) are the exception. They find positive effects for attending more selective colleges, but the effects are not statistically different from zero: on average, with their methods, the effect is not big enough, if it exists, to be seen, considering the size of their data set.

Dale and Krueger, however, find an important exception: for blacks, Hispanics, and students whose parents were not highly educated, going to a better college causes higher earnings. Loury and Garman (1995), with less extensive data, come to a similar conclusion—that blacks gain more than whites do from selective college enrollment. A quick reading of Dale and Krueger, then, seems to suggest that the best colleges admit too few blacks and Hispanics: these colleges would contribute more to society if they admitted fewer whites, who gain nothing detectible in earnings from attendance, and more blacks and Hispanics, who gain something. But the preponderance of the literature is silent on this question.

What about quality complementarity, the foundation of my analysis? Quality complementarity requires not just that the gain from attending the best colleges for the students who do so be positive but that it be greater than the gain that the students who did not attend would have realized if they had done so. Gains, of course, should be understood to imply nonmonetary and external benefits too. The literature sheds almost no light on this larger question.

A growing but decidedly weak literature tries to assess whether students gain from affirmative action as it is now practiced or as it was practiced in the late twentieth century. Let's be clear on the relevant question. Suppose a highly selective college enrolls a black student instead of a white student with a higher SAT score. The two students are affected directly (the white student attends a less selective college and the black student attends a more selective college) and the other students at the two schools are affected indirectly (the more selective college has more diversity and lower SAT scores and the less selective college has the reverse). Thus the total impact is the sum of four effects, two direct and two indirect.

No single paper tries to estimate all four effects. However, we've seen that Dale and Krueger (2002, 2011) and Loury and Garman (1995) try to estimate the direct effects. Their implicit answer is that the direct effects of affirmative action are positive on net, since the black student moving up gains more than the white student moving down loses. These results, of course, are controversial and deal only with earnings.

No one has yet explicitly tried to estimate the effect on a less selective school's student body of losing a minority classmate but gaining a classmate with a high SAT score. You might be able to piece together an answer from existing results, but it wouldn't be very reliable.

Several attempts have been made to find the indirect effect at the more selective college. This is an obvious question since the legal discussions of affirmative action recently have centered on the benefits of diversity. The results are inconclusive. Two studies (Black, Daniel, and Smith 2001; Wolfe and Fletcher 2013) find that attending a more diverse school helps white college graduates in the job market, and another study (Arcidiacono and Vigdor 2010) finds no effect at best. Since colleges don't establish affirmative action programs randomly, students don't select colleges randomly, and a college's affirmative action program is probably not the defining experience of the average white student's college years, finding the effect of diversity is very difficult.

Most empirical studies of affirmative action, however, pursue a different question. They look at law schools and ask whether the direct benefits to minorities being admitted to better law schools through affirmative action are positive. These benefits might be negative because of a "mismatch": because these students are so far behind their classmates, they might become discouraged, lose confidence, and fare poorly. If you don't know algebra, placing you in a calculus class is not doing you a favor. Mismatch in law schools was first proposed by Sander (2004), and many studies on this topic followed. The key outcome is passing the bar exam after graduation.

As usual, the econometric problem is difficult. You want to find out how the black students who went to the most selective law schools would have done if they had gone to less selective schools instead. You can't compare them with black students with the same observable credentials before law school who went to less selective law schools because there is some reason why those students didn't go to more selective schools and that reason is likely to affect performance on the bar exam. This comparison is likely to overstate the payoff of going to a better law school because law schools have lots of information about applicants that researchers don't have, as do applicants when they decide which school to attend.

Similarly, comparing black students at more selective schools with white students at less selective schools, even holding observable credentials before law school constant, is likely to understate the payoff of going to a better law school. Because of unobservables, even within the same school, blacks do worse on grades and bar passage than whites with the same observable credentials before law school.

Since one comparison overstates the payoff and the other understates it, if you make both comparisons you can find a range in which the true payoff is likely to lie. Rothstein and Yoon (2009) claim to have found this range. They are pretty sure that mismatch doesn't occur at the most selective law schools.

Arcidiacono et al. (2012) take a different approach to looking for mismatch among undergraduates: they compare graduation rates at the many colleges in the California system before and after the abolition of affirmative action in that state in 1996. They find some evidence of mismatch, but not much.

Summary of Affirmative Action in Higher Education

I wanted to give you a different framework for thinking about these questions. I think I did, but I'm not sure I'm right. Notice that I had to explain the two features of higher education admissions: a lot of weight on cognitive skills and some weight on race.

Affirmative action in higher education is unlikely to survive much longer in its current form. This has almost nothing to do with Supreme Court and everything to do with information technology. Affirmative action will change because higher education will change. An ever-greater part of higher education will take place online.

A naïve prediction might be that in a decade or so who gets admitted to Harvard won't matter because everyone will be able to take Harvard classes on Udacity or Coursera. To me such an outcome seems unlikely. Faculty and other advanced researchers will still want face-to-face interaction with small groups of people. Students too will want to interact with their peers as they learn, and the peers they will want to interact with won't be the whole world. So clubs will still dominate the world of higher education, and these clubs will still be zealous about who their members are. I don't know what the names of these clubs will be or whether they will be physical or virtual, but they will still be clubs.

These clubs will also probably draw their memberships from everywhere in the world, and many more people in the world will get the quality of elementary and secondary education needed to aspire to take part in higher education. The new clubs won't look like the clubs we have today: they are unlikely to organize themselves on the same principles, look for the same complementarities, or operate in the same hierarchy.

How race will matter in the new system I can't even guess. But it will probably matter, if only because attitudes about race evolve much more slowly than technology does. That's why it's more important to understand the general ideas about clubs and complementarity than any particular results about affirmative action now.

Conclusion

Racial and ethnic differences in average educational attainment and achievement are a major cause of many of the other disparities we see. If you asked me to pick one area where equalizing outcomes would have the greatest impact on American life, I would probably pick education. So would most of the writers whose statements we looked at in Chapter 2.

But nobody knows how to equalize average outcomes; the question is not a relevant one for the world we live in. No single brilliant educational innovation is likely to wipe out four centuries of history. But several good strategies for reducing the gaps slowly are known, and with the attention this problem is receiving others are likely to be found soon. Reducing gaps in health, income, crime, the bargaining power of women, neighborhood quality, and wealth should also reduce educational gaps, just as reducing gaps in education should reduce gaps in these areas.

8

Social Life, Friends, Partners, and Children

People looking online or in print for partners or spouses often proclaim their race and ethnicity, and often specify what they are looking for (or not looking for) in their partners. This is discrimination: race matters in how decisions are made. But it's legal, and almost nobody believes it should be illegal (not even the explicit public declaration of discriminatory intent) or that an affirmative action program should be established.

This discrimination is also pervasive. Almost all marriages are between people of the same race; for instance, in 2010, only 0.7 percent of NHW husbands had black wives.

People also tend overwhelmingly to choose same-race children for adoption (except for white couples who adopt Asian babies from foreign countries), even though young children, especially babies, don't have enough variance in personality or accomplishments to make us think that agreement on other grounds may be causing the racial concordance. In 2009–2011, about 4.9 percent of the adopted children who were living with nonblack householders were black, even though 16.1 percent of all adopted children under 18 were black.* (Remember that when I say discrimination I'm not concerned about whether the people who are doing it will go to heaven.)

---

* According to Kreider and Lofquist (2014, table 10), 67,125 black children under 18 were transracially adopted in the American Community Survey. The total number of adopted

Baccara et al.'s (2014, 135) study of an American online adoption facilitator found almost all prospective adopted parents were NHWs who revealed little interest in African American children, even though African American birth mothers had slightly more desirable observable health and behavioral markers than other birth mothers: "For an unborn child of unknown gender, the probability that a given prospective adoptive parent expresses interest in the child is about 13.1 percent if the child is non–African American and 1.8 percent if the child is African American." Baccara et al. calculated that prospective adoptive parents behaved as if they would be willing to pay an extra $38,000 in adoption fees to get a white baby instead of an African American baby. (But they showed little, if any, reluctance to adopt Hispanic babies.)

How important is this? Our whole notion of race is based on endogamy. No endogamy, no races. Social interaction and marriage are also how the next generation is produced, and families are where huge amounts of services and money are transferred across generations. Our society is not color blind in this area, and I don't know many people who think it should be.

Social interaction in our society often leads to marriage or childbearing, but it's also valuable in itself. Friends are fun. What other people think about you matters to you, even if there are no other consequences. Social interaction also influences many other areas of life: job networks (your friends may help you find a job), home repair networks (your friends and relatives may tell you which contractors are reliable), education, housing search, criminal activity (what your friends are like seems to matter a lot). More generally, social interactions are the lubricant that makes a market economy work, especially for difficult transactions such as dealing with a doctor or a chimney contractor.

The classic texts are divided about how we should approach discrimination in social interaction and marriage. Washington and Malcolm X explicitly condoned such discrimination: Washington because he thought it was unimportant and Malcolm because he thought it was irrelevant and inevitable. Du Bois wanted the right to have white friends, but he didn't necessarily want actual white friends. Only King and the Kerner Commission advocated actual interracial friendships, but even they had limits: King's

---

children under 18 was 1,556,706, of whom 1,360,583 were living with nonblack householders (table 4). Of all adopted children under 18, 251,002 were black (table 3a).

dream, for instance, was that "one day right there in Alabama little black boys and black girls will be able to join hands with little white boys and white girls as sisters and brothers," not that adults would be able join hands as lovers or spouses.

An area that is as controversial and important as this needs a full chapter. I begin with some history—Myrdal's picture of legal segregation in the South of the 1930s. Historical perspective is helpful because customs and culture matter a lot in this area and because we should understand DuBois's objection to legal social discrimination. The next section is about the civil rights era and laws against discrimination in public accommodations. Then I turn to modern evidence about discrimination in friendship and marriage. The section after that is a more detailed analysis about the types of households in which children of different races grow up and of the relationships that produce these households. The final substantive section looks in more detail at patterns of racial intermarriage.

The topics may seem to be somewhat scattered, but they really aren't. Social interaction leads to friendship, friendship leads to partnership, and partnership leads to children and provides the much of the environment in which children grow up and in which they find friends. Each step is tied to the others, and in our society each step is deeply colored by race and ethnicity.

Social Interaction in the Postbellum South

To understand the differences in the United States today in the areas in which racial discrimination is acceptable—such as marriage—and those in which it is unacceptable—such as employment—it helps to look at the South before the civil rights movement.

How It Worked

Myrdal wrote about segregation in the South in the 1930s. He found racial laws and restrictions in many areas of life and talked to white southerners at length about why those restrictions were in place. His "hierarchy of segregation" was a listing of areas in order of importance to white southerners of the 1930s. It was more important (according to these white southerners) to restrict black activity in some areas more than in other areas, and often the justification for restrictions at a lower level was to prevent or reduce contact at a higher level. So here is the hierarchy, from least important to most important:

11. Jobs, breadwinning, and relief (These are the traditional topics that those who study the economics of race look at, and the ones that we would probably think about as the most important. But they're the least important in this hierarchy.)
10. Justice
9. Politics
8. Public services such as libraries and tax collection offices
7. Public conveyances such as buses, streetcars, and trains
6. Public institutions where people sleep and change clothing, such as jails, hospitals, mental institutions, and homeless shelters
5. Places where people meet socially, such as hotels, restaurants, and theaters
4. Schools and churches
3. Taboos and etiquettes related to personal contact, such as in public toilets and at water fountains, and forms of address
2. Swimming, dancing, and eating together
1. Intermarriage, especially sex between white women and black men

Throughout the South and in most of the rest of the United States (29 out of 48 states in 1930) there were anti-miscegenation laws (the Supreme Court did not declare these unconstitutional until *Loving v. Virginia* in 1967), but by themselves these laws were not thought sufficient to preserve the purity of white women. And of course, there were lynchings to discourage black men. The lower parts of the hierarchy were often justified by their removal of temptations and opportunities. As you look through the lower parts of the hierarchy, you see they are arranged progressively by their propinquity to dating, marriage, and sex. The closer you get to naked bodies touching, the more important segregation was to white southerners.

Notice that the hierarchy influenced both Washington and Du Bois. Although these two writers disagreed on many questions, they both concentrated their efforts on lower parts of the hierarchy (jobs, for instance) and refused to challenge white southerners on the higher parts (close friendship and marriage). They both implicitly accepted the hierarchy; their disagreement was about how far from the bottom to make their challenge, particularly on issues related to justice and politics.

Does anything of the hierarchy survive today? Apparently yes: it's a fairly accurate guide to the social acceptability of discrimination in modern America. Most people agree that discriminating on the basis of race in hiring is despicable, but few people are upset by discrimination in the choice of spouse, partner, or adopted child. That's why it's worth asking why the hierarchy was arranged the way it was. Americans today don't think like postbellum white southerners, but they seem to be influenced by the conclusions about race that postbellum white southerners reached.

Why "Protect" White Women?

I don't know why postbellum white southerners wanted to "protect" white women, but several reasons are possible. Why weren't white women who wanted to marry black men who wanted to marry them permitted to do so?

One possible answer is that when the "one-drop rule" was in effect, as it was in the United States for several centuries, white parents gained from the protection of their daughters. The one-drop rule (see Chapter 3) is that a person with any African ancestors, no matter how small the proportion, is considered black. Under the one-drop rule, all children of interracial couples are black.

Parents want grandchildren—grandchildren who are accorded respect. White grandparents wanted white grandchildren.

Why doesn't this desire carry over into wanting to protect their sons from black women? Childbearing is something that women do, not men. The opportunity cost for a man of fathering a child is much smaller than the opportunity cost for a woman of bearing a child (especially in the past, when maternal mortality rates were high). If a son fathers a black child, there is almost no diminution in the number of white children he can father; the same is not true for daughters.

This explanation, then, depends crucially on the one-drop rule. There's nothing natural or universal about the one-drop rule. It's not used in most of Latin America, for instance. So for a complete explanation we must explain why the one-drop rule evolved in the United States but not in Latin America.

Fogel (1989) has a good explanation. The one-drop rule helped white land-owners because it increased the number of blacks (who could always be compelled to work) and decreased the number of whites (who could not always be compelled to work). Most of the time when slavery was practiced in Latin America, the rate of natural increase among slaves was negative, but in the United States, it was positive. Slave babies in Latin America (and the Caribbean) did not have a good enough chance of living long enough for their lives to be profitable to their owners. It was cheaper to import slaves than to breed them. Thus Latin American slave owners were not eager to increase the number of slave babies whom they would have to feed and clothe until they were old enough to work. Slave babies were valuable enough in the United States that planters wanted to increase their number. This was especially true after the legal slave trade ended in 1807.

How did the one-drop rule survive emancipation? Southern whites couldn't just reconvene a meeting after the Civil War and decide whether it was to their advantage to change the most fundamental ideas they had about how the world worked. And landowners still seemed eager to increase the number of black workers available to them: recall that anti-enticement laws lasted well into the twentieth century. Indeed, the near-universal willingness to consider Barack Obama as African American, even before his declaration in the 2010 census, shows that the one-drop rule remains pretty healthy in the United States today.

Parents aren't the only ones who could bear external costs from an inter-racial marriage. Bad or unconventional behavior by one family member reflects poorly on all family members. Anti-miscegenation laws helped family members by making it less likely that they would be disgraced by the romantic transgressions of other members. Disgrace for other family members follows only if the transgressions become public. Marriage is always public, so it is equally disgraceful for men as it is for women when the partners aren't considered to be appropriate for each other. Nonmarital sex, however, is more likely to be publicly verifiable for a woman than for a man.

Marriages are also alliances between families. A spouse is expected to help his or her in-laws and to be civil or pleasant with them on numerous family occasions. When one sibling marries a partner who can't or won't perform these functions, the other siblings lose: if the sibling had married someone more conventional, they would have been better off.

The Rest of Jim Crow

The other parts of the hierarchy of segregation were justified in part by their ability to reduce the temptations for interracial marriage and sex (as if anti-miscegenation laws and lynching weren't enough), but they also had costs and benefits of their own. The system of laws designed to enforce segregation is generally called Jim Crow, after a blackface minstrel show that was popular in the late nineteenth century.

Jim Crow laws began to be passed in the 1880s and received a big push from the Supreme Court with *Plessy v. Ferguson,* which held that "separate but equal" did not violate the Fourteenth Amendment. More such laws were passed in the South than elsewhere, but virtually every state had some Jim Crow laws. Mexicans were targeted in Texas, and Asians were targeted in California. By 1930, 31 of 48 states had laws against racial mixing in public facilities such as jails and hospitals, 22 had laws about schools, and 14 had laws about public transit (Anderson and Halcoussis 1996). Oklahoma outlawed integrated telephone booths. As late as 1965, Newark had separate facilities for homeless men.

Myrdal makes the point that all these laws were demeaning to blacks: they were enforced only against blacks, in fact, and part of the point was to emphasize that blacks were not full citizens. (Washington says much the same thing in a 1916 essay on residential segregation laws.)

Blacks also lost in more indirect ways from these laws. Segregation in public accommodations made it hard for blacks to travel because they didn't know where they would be served or what hotels they could stay in or what facilities they could use. (Before the Internet, making arrangements to stay in a town far distant from your home was much more difficult.) Fewer establishments were available to them. This made it more difficult to switch jobs or careers.

These laws also made it less worthwhile for blacks to become educated and to make money. Part of the return from these things is that you become respected and you can spend your money to have fun. If you still have to ride at the back of the bus after you have a PhD and you can't eat at the swankiest restaurants in town after you make a million bucks, you have less incentive to do these things. Anderson and Halcoussis (1996) found lower labor force participation among blacks in more heavily Jim Crow states.

So almost all blacks lost in a major way from Jim Crow (some black entrepreneurs may have gained, but at the expense of other blacks). Who gained? Why did white people do these things?

Again, I don't know; I wasn't around then. Part of the gain was the reduction in opportunities for miscegenation, of course. Prestige-seeking whites gained because they could be seen to have a higher status than other people. (For many of these activities the primary consumption is mental; you do them because they make you feel good, not to survive). Whites who disliked contact with blacks—for reasons of either taste-based or statistical discrimination—also gained.

Another way to think about the gains from Jim Crow is to realize that friendly social interaction is not a bilateral transaction but part of a network. If both B and C are A's friends, then B and C are likely to find themselves in circumstances where they ought to be each other's friends—at a barbeque in A's backyard, for instance. The barbeque might be ruined for everyone (especially A) if B and C can't enjoy it together or pretend that they enjoy it together. Even if A is a white person with no racial animosity, someone who would enjoy having black friends if her white friends didn't enter the picture, she might be better off having no black friends at all. To the extent that friendship is more like a disease than a decision—you make friends by being with people, not by choosing to be friends—A might gain if the laws made it hard for her to come into contact with black people in a setting that would foster friendship. The people who gained from Jim Crow might have been white southerners who were not racists rather than those who were.

Civil Rights Laws

Jim Crow was probably the major issue in the civil rights movement, at least in the early part. Rosa Parks sparked the Montgomery *bus* boycott, and Freedom Rides were about lunch counters and intercity buses. The Civil Rights Act of 1964 prohibited discrimination in public facilities and in private facilities used in interstate commerce, including restaurants, railroads, bars, hotels, and buses.

Nobody talks about this issue any longer. I couldn't find any economics studies about it. Conclusion: the laws were wildly successful. Nobody argues about whether restaurants and rest rooms are or should be segregated. Nobody advocates a return to the old days.

Why have these laws been apparently so successful?

First, they are easy to enforce. You can't have a water fountain in a public place for whites only without a putting a sign on it that says "For whites only." Jim Crow can't work without public communication, and you can verifiably ban public communication. Intent is also obvious. (Employment discrimination is quite different.)

Second, the laws could very easily have been potential Pareto improvements because they might have moved society from one equilibrium to another generally superior equilibrium. Getting rid of Jim Crow allowed businesses (with high fixed costs) to serve more customers and it allowed customers to experience more variety. Having two sets of water fountains and bathrooms was expensive, and so was turning away black customers from a half-empty restaurant.

If Jim Crow was such a bad deal, why didn't businesses get rid of it themselves? In many cases, of course, it was imposed through politics or community pressure and they could not get rid of it themselves. There is also a deeper reason: it may have been advantageous for every business to be discriminatory if other businesses were discriminatory, but it may not have been advantageous if other businesses were not discriminatory.

Consider a town with ten restaurants. Suppose all the restaurants do not serve black customers. Each restaurant owner thinks: "If I allow black customers, all black customers will come to me. But that will make this restaurant unacceptable to white customers, because the number of black customers will be too great. I will lose most of my white customers. On net, that's a bigger loss than the gain I make from getting black customers. I will ban black customers too." Given that the other restaurants are banning black customers, each owner thinks the same way and does the same thing. The fact that all restaurants (or all fancy restaurants) ban blacks is an equilibrium.

But suppose no restaurant is banning black customers. Then each restaurant owner thinks: "If I allow black customers, some will come to me and some will go to the other restaurants. I won't lose white customers much, for two reasons: first, the number of black customers won't be overwhelming, and second, white customers have nowhere to go that doesn't serve black customers. So I should serve black customers too." Since every restaurant owner thinks the same way, the situation where no restaurant bans blacks is also an equilibrium. And a better one, in that all restaurants have more customers and more customers get to enjoy restaurant meals.

But you can't get from the bad equilibrium to the good equilibrium by individual decentralized decisions. A civil rights law does the trick. It assures each restaurant owner that other restaurants will be nondiscriminatory restaurants, and that's enough to make him or her nondiscriminatory too.

Social Discrimination in Current Times

We have not totally escaped the past.

Public Accommodations and Public Spaces

The civil rights movement was concerned about discrimination by *providers* of public accommodations, and there is almost no such overt discrimination today—no signs designating rest rooms or water fountains or bus seats as "whites only." The issue has subsided from where it was in the 1950s and 1960s. But lawsuits and settlements indicate that some degree of covert discrimination still occurs—in fast food restaurants, for instance. Many blacks, especially men, perceive incidents of discrimination, as the poll results in Table 8.1 show. Discrimination usually takes the form of refusal to serve a minority customer. Nonracial reasons are often given, but they are difficult to verify. No hard data are available on how extensive this discrimination is.

Table 8.1. Percentage of African Americans and Hispanics who experienced discrimination in the previous 30 days, 2013.

Activity	Blacks	Hispanics
Shopping	24	19
Dining out	16	15
At work	15	15
Interactions with police	17	16
Getting health care	9	16

Source: Data from Newport (2013).

Consumers of public accommodations and public spaces may also discriminate. For many place—beaches and bars, for instance—a great deal of the appeal is who else is present. For many Americans, of all races, the race of the other people at a beach or a bar matters in terms of whether they want to go there.

There may also be sorting equilibria in venues such as bars and beaches. If every race wants to be the majority, if only a small majority, then the only equilibrium is complete segregation. This may or may not be efficient.

To be sure, in many locations, races mix easily. Elijah Anderson (2011, xiv) calls these places "the cosmopolitan canopy": "settings that offer a respite from the lingering tensions of urban life and an opportunity for diverse peoples to come together. Canopies are in essence pluralistic spaces where people engage one another in a spirit of civility, or comity and goodwill." Examples in Philadelphia are the Reading Terminal Market,

> Rittenhouse Square Park, Thirtieth Street Station, Whole Foods Market, the Italian Market, various local fitness centers, hospital waiting rooms, the multiplex theater, and sporting venues. . . . The atmosphere is calm and relatively pleasant, as a mix of people go about their business, at times self-consciously on good or "downtown" behavior, working to "be nice" or civil to the next person. . . . People are continually encouraged to behave courteously to one another; at times denizens can be solicitous and extraordinarily helpful to complete strangers. (66)

But not every place is a cosmopolitan canopy. Anderson describes the Gallery, a shopping mall not far from some of Philadelphia's cosmopolitan canopies:

> Black people from the neighborhoods ringing Center City . . . found a comfortable place to shop and congregate. At some point in the last decade . . . the Gallery acquired a clear and lasting reputation as a "black place" catering to black patrons from the lower economic classes. Latinos and Asians with similarly low socioeconomic identities create what little diversity there is at the Gallery. . . . That reputation is intimidating to the majority of potential white customers and discourages them from visiting the Gallery and mixing with its clientele. The predominance of black patrons at the mall evokes stereotypes of ghetto violence and criminality; in truth, middle-class blacks avoid

the setting as well. . . . A few [whites] venture into the Gallery only when accompanied by black companions. (73–74)

Almost everywhere, except perhaps in parts of the cosmopolitan canopy, certain types of black people evoke negative reactions from strangers:

The young black male is approached with a deficit model: he must prove himself to be law-abiding and trustworthy, which he is seldom able to do to the satisfaction of his white counterparts in the short time allowed. Unable to make sense of him . . . the strangers distance themselves or avoid any contact. The young black woman with children in tow triggers another set of stereotypes. This figure is simultaneously pitied and despised, rather than simply feared; she is imagined as downtrodden and overly assertive, burdened by motherhood yet hypersexualized. (99)

In short, there is tremendous anecdotal evidence of disparate treatment in public intercourse in many (but not all) venues, but little is known about disparate impact.

Friendship

If people chose friends randomly, most of the friends the average minority person had would be NHWs. But the world does not work like this.

We've already seen that interracial friendships are rare: in Fryer and Torelli's (2010) study of high school popularity and academic achievement, interracial friendships were rare enough that the authors could ignore them. (The average high school student had 0.7 friends of a different race.) Rarity, however, does not imply discrimination; perhaps other reasons such as residence, background, education, or interests can explain the discrepancy between the pattern of actual friendships and the pattern randomness would imply.

Marmaros and Sacerdote (2006) look at friendships at Dartmouth College in 2002–2003 by studying e-mail traffic. E-mail messages appear to have been a good proxy for friendship at this time. The volume of e-mail traffic between a pair of students depends on many nonracial factors: where they have been randomly assigned to live, where they went to high school, whether they are involved in athletics or Greek organizations, what classes they take, and what their interests are, for instance. But race matters a lot too. Holding a large array of other variables constant, a white student has 64 percent fewer interactions with a black student than with an otherwise identical white student; 44 percent fewer interactions with an Asian student; and 20 percent fewer interactions with a Hispanic student.

Marmaros and Sacerdote note that friendship falls off very steeply with distance; Dartmouth students don't look very far to find friends. Essentially, they reason, if these students aren't willing to walk a few hundred feet to try to discover a new friend, they probably are also reluctant to take a chance crossing a racial barrier.

Race, moreover, should matter for Dartmouth students much less than it matters for the rest of the population. The Dartmouth admissions committee has carefully vetted the student body; knowing that someone is a Dartmouth student tells you a lot about the probability of what kind of person she is. The probability that a random student is a criminal, a deadbeat, very stupid, uneducated, or a raving racist is low, much lower than in the general population. Since Dartmouth is isolated, these probabilities are also low for the random student's other friends (the ones that you would have to meet if you became her friend). Because of the admissions committee's work, race should carry fewer stereotypes at Dartmouth than it does at most other places, so it should be a smaller barrier to friendship. That Marmaros and Sacerdote find such large effects in such a carefully selected homogeneous population indicates that race must be a huge barrier to friendships in the general population.

Interracial Marriage

Table 8.2 gives recent data on who marries whom. If there were no intermarriage, all the numbers on the diagonal would be 100 percent and all the numbers off the diagonal would be zero. If race and things correlated with race didn't matter, then every row (or column) would be the same and most married minorities would have NHW spouses. I show different tables for husbands and for wives: the number of wives marrying outside the race or ethnic group doesn't have to be the same as the number of husbands marrying outside, because the number of wives of a race doesn't have to be the same as the number of husbands of that race (although, of course, overall the number of wives has to be the same as the number of husbands).

Table 8.2. Distribution of married couple families by race of husband's spouses, 2010 (percent).

A. Horizontal distribution of wives (percent)

Husbands	Hispanic wives	Non-Hispanic wives				
		White	Black	Asian	Other	Total
Hispanic	83.8	13.7	0.7	0.8	1.0	100.0
Non-Hispanic white	2.6	94.7	0.3	1.3	1.1	100.0
Non-Hispanic black	2.8	7.5	87.1	1.0	1.7	100.0
Non-Hispanic Asian	1.4	6.5	0.2	90.8	1.1	100.0
Other non-Hispanic	6.9	42.4	3.3	5.3	42.0	100.0

For instance, for this table, 13.7% of Hispanic husbands have non-Hispanic white wives.

B. Vertical distribution of husbands (percent)

Wives	Hispanic husbands	Non-Hispanic husbands			
		White	Black	Asian	Other
Hispanic	81.3	2.2	1.3	1.7	6.6
Non-Hispanic white	15.6	95.6	3.3	17.7	43.7
Non-Hispanic black	1.6	0.7	94.3	1.2	6.5
Non-Hispanic Asian	0.5	0.4	0.2	77.6	2.8
Other non-Hispanic	1.0	1.0	0.9	1.7	40.4
Total	100.0	100.0	100.0	100.0	100.0

For instance, for this table, 2.2% of non-Hispanic white wives have Hispanic husbands.
Source: U.S. Census Bureau (2012b).

These data refer only to heterosexual marriages. Remember that race is not objective but rather is self-described in these data (or described by the household member filling out the form); that could cause some serious problems in terms of accuracy in the data.

The basic message of Table 8.2 is that intermarriage is rare, especially intermarriage involving blacks. Intermarriage now is more common than it was several decades ago, but the growth is occurring from a very small base.

Intermarriage is also asymmetric. There are a lot more marriages of black men to white women that white men to black women. (7.5 percent of black husbands have white wives, while only 3.3 percent of black wives have white husbands.) The pattern is the opposite for Asians (6.5 percent of Asian husbands have white wives and 17.7 percent of Asian wives have white husbands). The number of Hispanic husbands and wives with spouses of a different race are about equal. (Intermarriage with anyone but whites is small.)

Is intermarriage rare because different races live in different places, have different educational backgrounds, or are different ages? No. Fryer (2007) simulates what would happen if mates were randomly matched holding characteristics constant: "If people were equally likely to marry . . . people of different races but with the same age, education, and geographic location, then we would see far more racial intermarriage than we actually do" (87).

The Households That Kids Grow Up In

Adults set up and run the households that children grow up in and provide all sorts of resources for children. One major reason to be concerned about courtship, sex, and marriage is that these activities determine how those households are set up and how they operate. The composition and operation of those households in turn has a major influence on what kind of adults children become.

Tables 8.3 and 8.4 show big differences among races in the proportion of children who are being raised by lone parents and in the proportion of children born to unmarried mothers. The two phenomena are conceptually

Table 8.3. Family status of children under 18, March 2011 (percent).

	With both parents*	With mother only	With neither parent
Black	37.7	51.2	7.6
Asian	85.2	10.7	2.5
Hispanic	66.9	26.5	3.9
Non-Hispanic white	77.2	15.9	3.0

Source: U.S. Census Bureau (2011).
*Includes parents who are not married.

Table 8.4. Nonmarital births as a proportion of total births (percent).

	Black	White	Hispanic	American Indian/ Alaska Native	Asian and Pacific Islander	Non-Hispanic white
1940	17					
1960	22					
1969	34.9	4.8				
75–79	51.7	8.2				
85–89	61.8	16.1				
1990	66.7	16.9	36.7	53.6		
1999	68.9	26.8	42.2	58.9	15.4	
2004	68.8	30.5	46.5	61.4	15.3	
2005	69.4	31.7	48.0	62.2	16.0	25.4
2008	71.8	35.7	52.5	66.0	17.0	28.7

Sources: Data before 1990 is from Tucker and Mitchell-Kernan (1995); data for 1990–1999 is from U.S. Census Bureau (2002), table 69; data for 2004 is from U.S. Census Bureau (2008), tables 77, 78, 83; data for 2005 is from U.S. Census Bureau (2010); data for 2008 is from U.S. Census Bureau (2012c), tables 80, 81, 85.

distinct, but for our purposes they're pretty much linked: the main reason for the differences in children with lone parents is the differences in nonmarital births. (In Europe the two phenomena are not as closely linked as they are in the United States; in some countries a large proportion of children are born to cohabiting couples.) Both phenomena are increasing for all races, but they are considerably more common for blacks and Hispanics.

Should we care? A lot of evidence indicates that being raised by two loving parents is better for kids than being raised by one loving parent or none. The evidence is like the evidence that being raised by rich parents is better than being raised by poor parents. Children of single parents often do well, as do children of poor parents. It's not a disaster. But getting more resources like money and attention is better for kids. So in the regressions we've seen for education and earnings, having no father at home usually has a negative coefficient. The effect is not huge, and most explanations of racial differences in these areas don't place a lot of weight on lone parenthood.

Why isn't the effect of not having a father at home huge? Several possible explanations suggest themselves. First, bad fatherhood is a continuum: many fathers who are present in kids' households are pretty bad at fatherhood. The regressions show the difference between no father at home and the average father at home—not the difference between no father at home and a really good father. Second, other relatives may step up their efforts to compensate for an absent father—grandparents, aunts, and uncles but mainly mothers. This substitution is good for the kid but bad for the put-upon relatives. Some of the benefits of having a father around accrue to the mother and other relatives, not to the child.

On the other hand, simple regressions may overstate the beneficial effect of fathers because women are probably negatively selected in single parenthood: these mothers probably have fewer resources on average than mothers with spouses around, so they might have accomplished less on average for their kids even if a spouse were present.

Since nonmarital birth rates are connected to lone parenthood and lone parenthood can have detrimental effects on children, we want to explain the differences in nonmarital birth rates. Accounting tells us that there are three possibilities:

1. A high proportion of unmarried women might be having kids. This is the first explanation most people think of.
2. A high proportion of women might be unmarried. If very few women are married, then a large proportion of children will be born to unmarried women because there are so many of them. In the limit, if no women are married, all children, even if there are very few, will be born to unmarried women.
3. Married women might not be having many kids. Once again, in the limit, if married women don't have kids, all children will be born to unmarried women.

You can see how these three possible reasons fit together from the basic identity:

$$\left(\frac{NMB}{MB}\right) = \frac{\left(\dfrac{NMB}{NMW}\right)\left(\dfrac{NWM}{MW}\right)}{\left(\dfrac{MB}{MW}\right)}$$

Here NMB stands for the number of nonmarital births, MB for the number of marital births, NMW for the number of unmarried women, and MW for the number of married women. You can get from the right-hand side of this equation to the left just by cancelling numerators against denominators. Each of the three terms in parentheses on the right-hand side is one of the three possible reasons.

To find out why nonmarital birth rates differ across races, let's look at each of the three possible answers.

Begin with the rate of births per unmarried woman. Table 8.5 presents data across races and over time. Hispanics have the highest rate of births per unmarried woman, and blacks and NHW are not far apart (and are converging). So births per unmarried woman explains some but not all of the black-white difference in the nonmarital birth rate and doesn't help at all in explaining why the Hispanic nonmarital birth rate is lower than the black. Moreover, the black rate is falling: this is clearly not what is driving the increase in the proportion of nonmarital births among African Americans. The portrait of unmarried African American women as hypersexualized is misleading, and the idea that the African American nonmarital birth rate is rising because of a rising tide of immorality is inaccurate.

Next, look at the marriage rate. Data are in Table 8.6. I used the 20–24 age group just to give a snapshot on the marriage rate: many readers of this

Table 8.5. Nonmarital births per 1,000 unmarried women aged 15–44, 1970–2008.

	White	Black	Non-Hispanic white	Hispanic
1970	13.9	95.5		
1980	17.6	82.9		
1990	32.9	90.5	24.4	89.6
1995	37.0	74.5	28.1	88.8
2000	38.2	70.5	28.0	87.3
2005	43.0	67.8	30.1	100.3
2008	48.2	72.5	33.7	105.1

Sources: Data before 1990 is from Tucker and Mitchell-Kernan (1995); data from 1990 through 2005 is from U.S. Census Bureau (2008), table 83; data for 2008 is from U.S. Census Bureau (2010), table 84, and U.S. Census Bureau (2012c), table 85.

Table 8.6. Women ever married, aged 20–24 (percent).

	Black	White	Non-Hispanic white	Hispanic	Asian
1940	59.6	50.3			
1950	65.7	65.6			
1960	61.9	70.4			
1970	55.8	65.2			
1980	21.6	43.1			
1990	22.5	40.1			
2000	11.4	30.8			
2005	13.4	27.9	25.8	36.1	20.1
2008	10.5	23.2	21.3	31.0	17.9
2011	9.8	21.7	20.5	25.7	15.5

Sources: Data before 2000 is from Tucker and Mitchell-Kernan (1995); data for 2000 and after is from U.S. Census Bureau (2011).

book may be interested in this age group, and divorce and widowhood are generally not big issues yet for this group. Table 8.6 shows that the high birth rate for unmarried Hispanic women gets offset by a relatively high marriage rate. The big story is the difference between the black and NHW marriage rates. Moreover, the big fall in the marriage rate is what's driving up the black nonmarital birth rate over time. Note that the black marriage rate used to be higher than the white (and not just for this age group). The difference in marriage rates is not a legacy of slavery (except in the sense that everything is).

I don't have a table for marital birth rates, but the differences across races are small: marital birth rates are higher for Hispanics and Asians, but not by much. In the long run, the decrease in the marital birth rate is responsible for a big chunk of the growth in the white and black nonmarital birth rates, but the time series is not our main concern.

Bottom line: the marriage rate is the story.

You can see this explicitly in Table 8.7. The basic identity for the three reasons is multiplicative, so if we want to decompose the differences among races in the nonmarital birth rate, we have to change it into something additive. Logarithms are the way to change a multiplicative expression into an additive expression. Taking logarithms of both sides of the basic identity gives us a way of expressing differences in (the logarithm of) nonmarital birth rates as the sum of differences in the three reasons:

$$ln\left(\frac{NMB}{MB}\right) = ln\left(\frac{NMB}{NMW}\right) + ln\left(\frac{NMW}{MW}\right) - ln\left(\frac{MB}{MW}\right)$$

Table 8.7 shows the components of this equation. It's clear from this table that low marriage rate for black is the driving force behind the high non-marital birth rate.

So why is the marriage rate so low for blacks but high for Hispanics, especially in recent cohorts? This is a big question that has been drawing a lot of attention (for instance, in Banks's 2011 book *Is Marriage for White People?*). The low marriage rate is not a direct residue of African culture or a direct outgrowth of slavery; recall that black marriage rates were higher than white marriage rates in the middle of the twentieth century. Nor is poverty alone the culprit, because Hispanics are as likely to be poor as blacks are. Welfare is not the story, either: in all economic classes, blacks are less likely than other Americans to marry (Banks concentrates on the stories of unmarried professionals).

One prominent explanation is the marriageable pool hypothesis. For a woman to get married she must find a man to marry, so she's less likely to get married if marriageable men are harder to find. (I'm looking only at het-

Table 8.7. Decomposition of births to married and unmarried women by race and ethnicity, 2004.

	Nonmarital births/ Marital births	Nonmarital births/ Nonmarried women	Nonmarried women/ Married women	Marital births/ Married women
Hispanic	.870	.085	1.181	.115
Asian	.180*	.026*	0.843	.121
Black	2.208	.064	3.120	.090
Non-Hispanic white	.325	.028	1.045	.090

Sources: U.S. Census Bureau (2008, 2014). See text.

Note: "Women" are females aged 15–44.

*Nonmarital births are Asian and Pacific Islander, not Asian, and marital births are calculated as total births minus nonmarital births.

erosexuals; most of this literature developed before gay marriage was legal.) If the ratio of men to women is very low, many women will not marry. But not just any man will do: men who are dead, too old or too young, incarcerated, or (possibly) without a job shouldn't count in terms of the number of men who could get married. A paucity of marriageable men should lead to a paucity of married women. The ratio of marriageable men to women is lower for blacks than for other groups because of male mortality, incarceration, unemployment, and labor force withdrawal. The marriageable pool hypothesis is that the low ratio of marriageable men to women explains the low marriage rate among blacks.

Charles and Luoh (2010) tested the marriageable pool hypothesis by looking at how women's marriage rates in age and race groups in the U.S. states responded to policy-driven changes in male incarceration rates. They found that greater incarceration among men caused lower marriage rates among women who would plausibly have been their partners. Charles and Luoh estimated that the increase in incarceration among black men accounted for around a fifth of the decrease in marriage among black women in the late twentieth century.

The marriageable pool hypothesis, however, runs into two problems, one not so serious and one more serious.

The not-so-serious problem with the marriageable pool hypothesis is that it implies that marriageable black men should have higher marriage rates than marriageable white men. They don't; they have lower marriage rates. Table 8.8 shows the basic data. These data are from the Current Population Survey, so prisoners and homeless people are excluded. But still black men have considerably lower marriage rates than men of other races and ethnicities. Even when we look at men earning between $75,000 and $100,000 a year—clearly "marriageable" men in any socioeconomic reckoning—blacks are less likely to be married, not more likely. Only for 50–54-year-old men making more than $100,000 a year are blacks more likely to be married than NHWs and Hispanics, but the difference is not big. So the marriageable pool hypothesis is not the whole story.

The marriageable pool hypothesis, however, should probably be interpreted more broadly and less mechanistically; this is what Banks emphasizes and why I said that this objection is not so serious. Sex ratios affect bargaining power within partnerships and marriages, and bargaining power may be more important the legal details of marriage. Chiappori, Fortin, and Mazumder

Table 8.8. Percentage of people who are married with spouse present by gender and income.

	Black	Asian	Hispanic	Non-Hispanic white
Men				
All, 25–29	17.3	25.8	28.6	32.9
All, 50–54	51.2	83.7	63.0	68.9
Earning $75–100K				
25–29	36.3	54.3	52.8	43.6
50–54	66.8	100.0	67.2	79.0
Earning $100K+				
25–29	31.6	46.8	42.4	44.3
50–54	76.2	93.7	57.1	68.2
Women				
25–29	19.9	46.8	42.4	44.3
50–54	37.4	71.5	57.1	68.2
Earning $75–100K				
25–29	46.3	35.8	40.8	54.2
50–54	55.6	72.5	55.9	69.8
Earning $100K+				
25–29	18.9	3.3	23.7	58.6
50–54	55.4	68.6	56.7	64.8

Source: U.S. Census Bureau (2011).

(2002) and many other studies have shown than in any (heterosexual) pairing, the bargaining power of the woman is less if marriageable males are rarer.

What does bargaining power mean in this context? A number of different ideas have been proposed.

Charles and Luoh show that women get more education and spend more time in the labor force when incarceration drives the supply of men down. The less that women can rely on men to help them, the more they have to be prepared to rely on themselves.

Banks (2011) emphasizes that men use their bargaining power to *avoid* marriage; they can enjoy both freedom and companionship without the constraints that marriage imposes. In Banks's telling, the low marriage rate for men is a result of their strong bargaining power; the low marriage rate for women is a result of their weak bargaining power. He argues: "The failure of so many black men increases the value of successful black men—and that power seems to be intoxicating: a currency used to avoid commitment rather than to attract a wife" (62).

Finally, sex ratios may affect how children grow up. Most studies of within-household bargaining in general indicate that women want to spend relatively more on children's well-being than men do. Women seem to use their bargaining power for two purposes: to reduce their hours of market labor and to increase the well-being of their kids. (In most of these studies, women's work is not a glamorous and fulfilling career.) Generally, when women's bargaining power is greater they work outside the house less, more money is spent on child nutrition, and less money is spent on adult goods such as alcohol. You would expect more money to be spent on education too, but I don't know of any studies that have shown this directly.

In this interpretation, the low ratio of marriageable men to marriageable women can show up in lower investment in children, and we don't particularly care about the exact legal mechanism under which that happens. Remember we started talking about a continuum of support and investment by the father. The implication is that scarcity of marriageable men should show up in reduced well-being of mothers, reduced investment in children, and perhaps in the test score gap. As far as African Americans are concerned, this is speculation, but it puts together two implications with considerable empirical and theoretical support. Notice that the sex ratio effect goes into the coefficient on race in a regression, not into the coefficient on lone parenthood, since the effects are across the board.

Interracial Marriage Revisited

The serious objection to the marriageable pool hypothesis is that it ignores the possibility of intermarriage. The previous section was written as if the different races were on different planets, or at least on different continents. This is not true. If black women lack attractive black male partners, why don't they look for white male partners?

Consider the 25–29-year-old age group. Here's the basic picture from the March 2011 Current Population Survey (the household population). Black males numbered 1.41 million and 17.3 percent of them were married (with spouse present; I'll just say "married"). Black females numbered 1.53 million and 19.9 percent were married with spouse present. You see the low ratio of men to women here. On the other hand, 32.9 percent of the 6.48 million NHW men in this age range were married, as were 44.3 percent of the 6.32 million NHW women. Notice both the higher ratio of men to women and the much higher proportion of women who were married.

What would it take in terms of NHW mates to raise black women's marriage rate to the same level as NHW women? A little calculation: you would need $(0.443 - 0.199)*1.53 = 0.37$ million black women to get married. They would need 0.37 million mates. If all of these additional 0.37 million mates were NHW men who would not otherwise be married (no one is breaking up any marriages here; these are all marriages between people who would otherwise be single), the number of married NHW men would rise by 0.37 million. This would increase the marriage rate for NHW men from 32.9 percent to 38.6 percent.

Has the marriage rate of NHW male 25–29-year-olds ever been as high as 38.6 percent, or am I asking for an unprecedented historical change? In fact it has been that high as recently as 2007, when it was 40.5 percent; in 2008 it was 38.2 percent. So the black-white marriage gap for women could be wiped out with only a historically tiny increase in marriage among NHW men if that increase were directed to black women. You can do similar calculations for other age groups. We're not talking about a lot.

Recall that interracial marriages in general are rare, interracial marriages involving blacks are rarer, and interracial marriages involving black women and NHW men are extraordinarily rare. The vast majority of interracial marriages involving blacks are black men and NHW women—which is the exact opposite of what the sex ratios would lead us to expect. Our reasoning in the previous section, moreover, suggests that this paucity of marriages between black women and white men might have detrimental consequences for black children in general.

So the big question for this section is this: Why is there so little intermarriage, and in particular why is there so little marriage between white men and black women? Banks also comes to this question.

I'm not trying to assign blame; economics is not in that business. I'm trying to understand why black women and white men don't more often find mutual comparative advantage from marrying each other.

I don't know the answer. Several reasons, though, are worth considering.

1. Until very recently, there was little demand for mixed-race children. The prospect of mixed-race children was daunting to prospective parents not because of the nineteenth-century theory that they would be genetically messed up but because of the twentieth-century theory that they would have a hard time adjusting, so they would never amount to anything. (This may also explain partly why black-white interracial adoption is rare.) Fryer, Kahn, and Levitt (2008) provides some evidence that adjustment is a problem for mixed-race kids. The success of mixed-race individuals in politics and sports in the twenty-first century may change this perception. But this difficulty applies equally to marriages between black men and white women and marriages between black women and white men; it answers only half of the question.

2. Belot and Fidrmuc (2010) emphasize the importance of height for prospective marriage partners. Generally, men are taller than their wives. Thus intermarriages between two specific racial groups should usually include men from the taller group and women from the shorter group. Since Asians are shorter than whites, we should expect to see more marriages between Asian women and white men than between Asian men and white women—and that's what we see. Since black women are taller than Asian women, height may explain partly why Asian women are more likely to marry white men than black women are. But black and white men are about the same height, and black women are somewhat shorter than white women (see Chapter 4), so height probably explains only a small part of the rarity of intermarriage between black women and white men.

3. Relationships between white men and black women have a history of being exploitive. People today may shy away from them for that reason. But the Gallup Poll results in Table 8.9 indicate no such sentiment. For blacks, where this argument would be most salient, the difference in public approval for black women dating white men and for white men dating black women is not statistically significant. Whites appear to look more favorably on black women dating white men than on white women dating black men. So community approbation or disapprobation does not seem to explain anything.

Table 8.9. Percentage of whites, blacks, and Hispanics favoring interracial dating, 2005.

	White woman and black man	Black woman and white man
Whites	65	72
Blacks	83	82
Hispanics	86	84

Source: Jones (2005).

4. The one-drop rule may still matter. The woman may doubt that the man will love or invest in her child if the child's race is different from the man's. A mother loving or investing in her child is less of an issue than the father doing so. Thus this reason would give rise to gender asymmetry. Why doesn't this apply to Asian intermarriage, which has the opposite gender balance, or Hispanic intermarriage? I don't know—possibly because of the one-drop rule, possibly because white attitudes toward Asian children are different from white attitudes toward black children. American whites seem much more likely to adopt Asian children (even from overseas) than black children, and the adoption data that Baccara et al. (2014) analyzed indicate that many NHWs are extremely reluctant to bring up black children.

5. Marriages are unions between families, not just individuals. Blacks may fear that a white family they are joining might include malevolent racists or people who would make family occasions miserable for them and refuse to help them. Whites may fear that a black family will include similar racists or criminals. But what about gender asymmetry? It could be that wives are more reliant on good relationships with their in-laws than husbands are. Wives may care more about family occasions than husbands do or count on in-laws for more support in raising children. This is, of course, speculation.

In short, I can't explain the pattern of intermarriage, but there are a number of interesting possibilities. The final possibility is that there is no good reason for the low number of marriages between black women and white men and that the question will disappear on its own in a few years. Notice, however, how this question ties the chapter together: we can't understand the way that children grow up unless we understand social interactions among adults.

Conclusion

Washington and Du Bois probably got it wrong: social relations matter a lot. The world is far from color blind in the social sphere, and the consequences, especially in how children are prepared for the world, are profound. If these activities are not conducted in a color-blind way, is it really desirable that every other activity be color-blind too?

9

Housing and Neighborhoods

When you buy a house or rent an apartment, you acquire a bundle of goods—shelter, neighbors, voting and trash disposal rights, land, parking spots, landline telephone connections, cable TV or a satellite dish, Internet connections, electrical wires, closets, bathrooms, furnace, sewer and water connections or facilities, propinquity to various medical facilities, protection from various dangers. Housing takes a large and growing fraction of the average American's budget; shelter is over 30 percent of the total weight in the latest revision of the consumer price index. Housing is a complement to many other goods; owning a kayak, for instance, is a lot easier if you own someplace where you can store it easily. The kind of access minorities have to housing therefore is an important question.

This chapter concentrates on buying, not selling. For most people, the biggest piece of their income comes from work (this is why we had a long chapter on labor markets); the biggest piece of their income goes to housing.

In particular, the housing you buy has a big influence on your child's friends and where they go to school; how well you're protected from extreme cold and extreme heat and marauding animals; how long your commute to work is and where you look for a job; your exposure to certain crimes such as robbery, burglary, and motor vehicle theft; your opportunities as a child for studying and playing; your exposure to contagious diseases, mold, and various allergens; your access to sunlight; which doctors you see and what hospitals you visit, especially in emergencies; what stores you shop at and what kinds of food are available in them; what neighbors you leave the key with and ask to water your plants when you go away; what pollutants you and your children are exposed to during the many hours you and they stay home; whom you marry and whether you marry; and what people think of you when they see your address.

A number of these issues have been studied. Notice that some of these factors depend on location (for example, your child's friends) and some depend on structure (your exposure to sunlight and mold). Issues of location have been studied more than issues of structure.

Minorities appear to consume housing in different ways from NHWs, and since housing affects so many other aspects of life these differences may have consequences. Discrimination appears to play some role in these differences. Current housing arrangements, moreover, may generate large social costs and large social waste.

The classic writers took very different positions on housing, especially housing location. Washington didn't care where black people lived (within the South); for him, these types of social questions were "gewgaws." For Malcolm X, housing segregation was implicitly a good thing because it forms the basis of separatism and political power. For the Kerner Commission, where minorities live was a huge problem—possibly the source of all evil. Indeed, since the Kerner Commission, a strand of thought in the social sciences has maintained that housing location is *the* key problem in race; we'll have to assess that.

This chapter will begin with general facts that look at the question of how minorities consume housing differently. The next section will look into explanations for these general facts, followed by a section that will try to assess whether or not the current situation is socially desirable. The section after that is about policy. I postpone discussion of homeownership to the next chapter.

General Facts

This section describes a few ways that the way minorities, especially African Americans, consume housing is different from the way NHWs consume housing. The main concerns are segregation, centralization, housing quality, housing prices, and homeownership. The last two issues are discussed only briefly.

Segregation

Segregation means separateness; the definition of the word doesn't necessarily have anything to do with discrimination or animosity. You can have discrimination without segregation—examples are the experiences of women today or the experiences of slaves in the nineteenth century. You can have segregation without discrimination—Californians or Columbia students, for instance. It's neither good nor bad by itself; we'll have to think about it and look at evidence.

Within metropolitan areas, minorities are highly segregated from NHWs and still segregated from each other, but less so than they are from NHWs. There are identifiable minority neighborhoods. If you know what neighborhood someone lives in, you can make a pretty good guess about her race or ethnicity.

Measuring segregation.   How do you measure segregation? Three different measures are used extensively and several others have been developed but are seldom used. The popular measures are not perfect, but they're what we have.

The index of dissimilarity (D[A, B]).   This is the oldest measure. It comes from the 1950s and 1960s, when people thought there were only two races and information technology was rudimentary.

It's a two-way measure: it compares two races, A and B, and answers the following question: what is the minimum percent of group A that would have to move so that they would be spread over neighborhoods the same way group B is? It turns out that the answer to this question this also answers the question where you reverse A and B.

Consider extreme examples first. Suppose all Hispanics live in East Harlem and all Asians live in Flushing or, more generally, that no neighborhood in the New York City area includes both Asians and Hispanics. This is perfect segregation. Every Hispanic would have to move to a different neighborhood if Hispanics were to be distributed among neighborhoods the same way Asians are, and every Asian would have to move if Asians were to be distributed among neighborhoods the same way Hispanics are. Then D(Hispanic, Asian) = D(Asian, Hispanic) = 1.

At the other extreme, suppose Hispanics are 30 percent of the total population and Asians are 10 percent of the total population and that distribution holds in every neighborhood. Then Hispanics and Asians are distributed among neighborhoods in the exact same way. This is perfect integration: nobody would have to move. Then D(Hispanic, Asian) = D(Asian, Hispanic) = 0.

Calculating D(Hispanic, Asian) is simple, which is why it was used, especially in the days before cheap computing power. First, throw out anybody who isn't Hispanic or Asian. From our example above, that leaves a total population that's 75 percent Hispanic and 25 percent Asian. Then divide all the neighborhoods into 2 categories: those disproportionately Hispanic (more than 75 percent) and those disproportionately Asian (more than 25 percent). Obviously the sets are disjoint and exhaustive.

Now add up the number of Hispanics in disproportionately Hispanic neighborhoods. If you're going to have no segregation, then there can be no disproportionately Hispanic neighborhoods. If you want to get rid of segregation by moving Hispanics to other neighborhoods, you have to go to every disproportionately Hispanic neighborhood and move enough Hispanics out of it so that the proportion of Hispanics in that neighborhood is 75 percent. When you've gone to all of those neighborhoods (and only those neighborhoods) and figured out how much that is, add those figures up, divide them by total Hispanic population, and you have the index of dissimilarity.

Or you could do these same steps but use Asians (and disproportionately Asian neighborhoods) instead of Hispanics. You would get the same number.

Here's the algebra. Index neighborhoods by n. Index totals by omitting subscripts. Then h_n Hispanic population in neighborhood n and a_n is the Asian population in neighborhood n; h is the total Hispanic population in the city or metropolitan area and a is the total Asian population.

A neighborhood n is disproportionately Hispanic if

$$h_n / (h_n + a_n) > h / (h + a),$$

which is equivalent to

$$h_n / h > a_n / a.$$

Call the set of neighborhoods that are disproportionately Hispanic H and the set of neighborhoods that are disproportionately Asian A.

Suppose neighborhood n is disproportionately Hispanic. To reduce the population of neighborhood n so it would no longer be disproportionately Hispanic, you have to reduce the Hispanic population (relative to the total Hispanic population) by

$$(h_n / h - a_n / a)$$

so that

$$h_n / h = a_n / a$$

when you get done moving people.

Do that for every Hispanic neighborhood and add those amounts up and you get the index of dissimilarity D(Hispanic, Asian):

$$D \ (Hispanic, \ Asian) = \sum_{n \in H} \left(\frac{h_n}{h} - \frac{a_n}{a} \right).$$

Restricting these calculations to disproportionately Hispanic neighborhoods is very important. If you just take the sum over all neighborhoods, you will end up with zero—guaranteed.

You can prove that D(Hispanic, Asian) $= D$(Asian, Hispanic). It's pretty easy:

$$D(Hispanic, Asian) - D(Asian, Hispanic) = \sum_{n \in H} \left(\frac{h_n}{h} - \frac{a_n}{a} \right) - \sum_{n \in A} \left(\frac{a_n}{a} - \frac{h_n}{h} \right)$$

$$= \sum_{n \in H} \left(\frac{h_n}{h} - \frac{a_n}{a} \right) + \sum_{n \in A} \left(\frac{h_n}{h} - \frac{a_n}{a} \right)$$

$$= \sum_{n} \left(\frac{h_n}{h} - \frac{a_n}{a} \right) = \sum_{n} \frac{h_n}{h} - \sum_{n} \frac{a_n}{a}$$

$$= 1 - 1 = 0$$

The index of exposure (E[A, B]).   This measure is binary (it deals with two races) but not symmetrical: $E(A, \ B)$ does not equal $E(B, \ A)$. It answers the question: What is the proportion of race B in the neighborhood that the average member of group A lives in? What is the probability that a His-panic person's neighbor will be Asian?

Although the index of dissimilarity doesn't depend on the size of the groups, the index of exposure does.

Here's the algebra: Use the same notation as before but let T_n denote the total population of neighborhood n, not just Hispanics and Asians. Then the proportion of Asians in neighborhood n is a_n / T_n, and that's also the probability (approximately) that your neighbor is Asian if you live in neighborhood n.

Now the probability that a Hispanic person lives in neighborhood n is h_n / h. And that's the probability that a Hispanic person will have the type of exposure to Asians that prevails in neighborhood n.

To get the average exposure, you add these up, with weights determined by the size of the Hispanic population in each neighborhood:

$$E(H, A) = \Sigma (h_n / h)(a_n / T_n)$$

where the sum is over *all* neighborhoods n.

Notice that size matters for the index of exposure, unlike the index of dissimilarity. Generally if there are more Asians around, the exposure of His-panics to Asians will be greater. That's why the index of exposure is not symmetrical. If there are a lot more Hispanics than Asians in the metro-politan area, the average Asian is more likely to meet a Hispanic than the average Hispanic is to meet an Asian.

When we look over the last few decades, the increasing size of the His-panic and Asian populations will generally raise the exposure of every group to Hispanics and Asians.

The index of isolation (I[A]). This is the proportion of same-race neigh-bors for the average member of group A. It's easy to define: $I(A) = E(A, A)$. Isolation is the exposure of a group to itself. So in general it depends on the size of the group.

The growing size of Hispanic and Asian populations should lead us to expect that index of isolation will rise.

Of course, all of these measures depend on how you define neighborhoods. Smaller neighborhoods imply higher values of segregation indices. If every neighborhood is just one person, segregation is very high (that is, total segregation, except for multirace people). If there's only one neighborhood and it's the whole world, integration is perfect. For some purposes, there are natural "neighborhoods" and this isn't a problem. Examples are classrooms, schools, names (you can compute indices of dissimilarity for first names, treating individual names as neighborhoods). Other times, neighborhood boundaries are not clear and can make a difference. For example:

x x x
0 0 0
x x x

If you form three neighborhoods vertically, perfect integration between x's and 0's prevails in this "city." If you form three neighborhoods horizontally, perfect segregation prevails.

As a practical matter, most studies use census tracts as neighborhoods. These are areas that the census has been using as surrogates for neighborhoods. Each has 2,000–8,000 people and tries to conform with "natural boundaries" such as rivers, highways, and railroads. A few studies use census blocks.

These indices also don't take into account the geographic relationships of neighborhoods to each other. Suppose all neighborhoods are totally of one color, either black or white. Then segregation on these indices is total. But a city where these neighborhoods are arranged like a checkerboard should really be considered more integrated than a city where all the black neighborhoods are in one corner. Some more sophisticated but not heavily used measures try to consider this aspect of segregation.

What do we know about segregation? What do we know about segregation? First, there's a lot of it—especially from NHWs. Table 9.1 shows the average indices of dissimilarity between races and ethnic groups in metropolitan areas. The averages are weighted by the population of the group listed in the table row heads in the metropolitan area, so they are not symmetric.

For blacks in major U.S. metropolitan areas, the average index of dissimilarity was 0.591 in 2010, down from 0.73 in 1980. The metropolitan areas with the greatest black-NHW indices of dissimilarity were Detroit and Milwaukee with 0.796, New York with 0.791, Newark with 0.780, and Chicago with 0.759. In these metropolitan areas, over three-quarters of blacks

Table 9.1. Average indices of dissimilarity in metropolitan areas weighted by population listed in row heads, 2010 census.

	Non-Hispanic white	Black	Hispanic	Asian
Non-Hispanic white	—	53.5	42.8	37.2
Black	59.1	—	45.9	56.9
Hispanic	48.5	43.2	—	47.7
Asian	40.9	50.6	45.8	—

Source: Logan and Stults (2011).

Table 9.2. Indices of dissimilarity for large metropolitan areas, 2010, ten largest cities and Detroit.

	Black-white	Hispanic-white	Asian-white
New York	79.1	63.4	49.5
Los Angeles	65.0	63.1	47.6
Chicago	75.9	57.0	41.7
Houston	60.6	52.5	48.7
Philadelphia	73.7	58.8	41.8
Phoenix	41.3	49.3	29.9
San Antonio	47.7	46.1	36.1
San Diego	48.4	49.6	44.3
Dallas	55.1	51.9	44.4
San Jose	38.6	47.6	43.0
Detroit	79.6	51.8	46.5

Sources: Logan (2011a); Logan and Stults (2011).

(or NHWs) would have to move to achieve perfect integration. Even for the least segregated metropolitan areas, the indices of dissimilarity are high: 0.408 in Charleston, South Carolina, 0.369 in Las Vegas. Table 9.2 shows more detail for large metropolitan areas.

For African Americans, average isolation was 0.452, down from 0.61 in 1980 (see Table 9.3). The greatest isolation was in Detroit (0.809) and Memphis (0.691). In these cities, black people almost always have black neighbors.

Table 9.3. Indices of dissimilarity of blacks, Hispanics, and Asians with non-Hispanic whites by income, large metropolitan areas, 2000.

	Blacks (all)	Mid-income blacks	Hispanics (all)	Mid-income Hispanics	Asians (all)	Mid-income Asians
New York	83	83	65	62	47	51
Los Angeles	70	72	60	59	47	49
Chicago	81	81	58	58	43	49
Houston	67	69	52	49	48	52

Source: Logan (2002).

For Hispanics, the average index of dissimilarity from NHWs was 0.49 in 2010, down only slightly from 0.51 in 1980. Hispanic-NHW dissimilarity was highest in Los Angeles (0.634) and New York (0.631) and lowest in Laredo (0.307). Isolation for Hispanics was very high in South Texas, where the population is predominantly Hispanic. Average Hispanic isolation rose nationally from 0.382 in 1980 to 0.460 in 2010; it's now higher than average African American isolation.

For Asians the index of dissimilarity from NHWs was 0.41 for the average metro area in 2010, about the same as 1980. Asian-NHW dissimilarity was highest in Edison, New Jersey (0.537); New York (0.495); and Houston (0.487). The greatest Asian isolation was in Honolulu (0.747), San Jose (0.454), and San Francisco (0.422).

This segregation is not mainly due to income; income explains only a small proportion of the segregation we observe (see Table 9.3). This table looks at dissimilarity between middle-income minorities and NHWs. If income were the story behind segregation, then middle-income minorities and middle-income NHWs would live in the same neighborhoods; the index of dissimilarity between them would be pretty close to zero. Instead, Table 9.3 shows that middle-income segregation is almost the same as total segregation, and sometimes greater. Sethi and Somanathan (2009) calculated what the index of dissimilarity would be if income were all that mattered in determining where people lived. If income were all that mattered, D(black, white) for 1990 in metropolitan areas would be between 0.08 and 0.18, with an average of 0.12. This is much less segregation than actual segregation in 1990.

The dominant time trend in segregation since 1970 has been decreasing for African Americans. Segregation of African Americans increased in every census from 1900 to 1970, and it has decreased in every census since then. Glaeser and Vigdor (2012) argue that for African Americans, segregation in 2010 had fallen to the level of segregation in 1910. For Hispanics and Asians there has been no trend in segregation.

Why has African American segregation decreased? The trend has three chief components.

First is the shift in population generally to the Sun Belt. Except for retirement communities, Sun Belt cities are less segregated than Frost Belt cities. As the proportion of Americans who live in the Frost Belt decreases, average segregation decreases.

Second is a drastic decrease in the number of neighborhoods that are essentially all white. In 1970, 62.6 percent of metropolitan whites lived in census tracts that were less than 1 percent black. By 1990, this proportion had decreased to 35.6 percent. By 2010, only 424 census tracts out of 22,000 were all white.

Third: integration is much more stable in many neighborhoods than it used to be. Integration used to be called "the time between when the first black family moves in and when the last white family moves out." But since 1980, quite a few neighborhoods with sizable proportions of both blacks and whites have stayed that way for a long time. Between 1980 and 1990, 76 percent of tracts that were integrated at the start of the decade were still integrated at the end; in 53 percent of them, the white population grew (Ellen 2000a).

Two better-publicized phenomena had much smaller effects: gentrification and Katrina. Gentrification is definitely occurring in a few places such as Harlem and Washington, D.C., but these few neighborhoods do not weigh heavily in the general scheme of things. Similarly, Katrina led to a drastic decrease in segregation in New Orleans, but New Orleans is only one city.

Immigrant segregation.   Cutler, Glaeser, and Vigdor (2008) follow immigrant segregation since 1910. Immigrant segregation is somewhat different from racial and ethnic segregation because immigrants often share households with non-immigrants: their native-born kids. At the height of the European immigration wave in 1910, segregation was not as great as racial segregation is now (see Table 9.3). Immigrant segregation decreased until 1960 and has increased since then. Changes in the composition of immigrants (those who speak languages further from English (in the "family tree" of languages—so Dutch and French are close to English but Mandarin and Basque are not) and those who are from poorer countries and from Africa and African diaspora countries always tend to be more segregated, and there are more of such immigrants now), and changes in urban form (places where you can rely on mass transit are rarer) seem to be a lot of the story.

Centralization

Not only do minorities have an unusually high propensity to live in neighborhoods with other minorities, they also have an unusually high propensity to live in neighborhoods that are close to historic centers of cities, or the central business districts. Minority neighborhoods, particularly African American neighborhoods, are much closer to the central business district, on average, than white neighborhoods. That's why the adjective "inner-city" is a synonym for "minority."

The measurement of centralization is similar to the measurement of segregation in the index of dissimilarity. The question for the measurement of centralization is what proportion of minorities would have to move, at a minimum, if minorities were to end up having the same distribution of residences by distance from the central business district as whites have. The difference is that moves out (away from the central business district) are counted as positive, moves in are counted as negative. So the index of centrality equals one if all minorities live closer to the central business district than all whites; it equals zero if minorities have the same distribution of distance to the central business district as whites do; and it equals minus one if all minorities live farther away from the central business district than all whites.

In 2000, the average index of centrality (over 380 metropolitan areas) was 0.685 for blacks, 0.613 for Hispanics, and 0.683 for Asians (Woo 2012, table 1).

Income doesn't explain much about why minority housing is so centrally located. In fact, income is not very well correlated with distance from the central business district—in many old cities such as New York and Chicago, some of the wealthiest neighborhoods are immediately adjacent to the central business district. And even if distance from the central business district were perfectly correlated with income, the index of centrality would still be below 0.30.

Land near the central business district is one of the most valuable resources in any metropolitan area, and it is a resource in fixed supply. Apparently race is an important determinant of who uses that land. This is strange, since there is no obvious connection between skin color, hair texture, and the benefits or costs of living next to a central business district.

The optimal allocation of people to neighborhoods—and the allocation that a well-functioning market would accomplish—assigns to each neighborhood the people who benefit the most from being there. In order to argue that concentrating minorities in inner cities is a good idea, then, you have to argue both that they derive benefits from being there and that no one else would derive more benefit than they do. Since cities are great places, the former proposition is probably true, even though some evidence (which we will see below) raises some doubt about it. The latter proposition is more dubious.

You would expect that because they live so close to the central business district, minorities would have lower commuting times than whites do. Lower commuting time is the main benefit that people get from living near the central business district, so almost any argument in favor of the current arrangement has to start with the benefits that minorities get from being close to their jobs. Giving minorities greater access to the central business district makes sense only if access to the central business district is differentially valuable to minorities.

It turns out, though, that minorities have longer commuting times, not shorter. On average, minorities have longer commutes than whites and the more centralized minority groups, blacks and Asians, have longer commutes than Hispanics. The reason is not solely that minorities are more likely to use public transportation, which is usually slower than private cars. Holding transportation mode constant, minorities still have longer commutes. Table 9.4 provides some detail. The jobs that minorities have appear to have decentralized to a much greater extent than their residences.

Table 9.4. Mean travel time to work, 2009 (minutes), by racial/ethnic group, residents of metropolitan areas.

	Total	Drove alone	Public transit
White	24.4	23.5	46.9
Black	27.3	24.5	50.0
Hispanic	26.3	24.1	46.0
Asian	28.0	25.7	48.8

Source: McKenzie and Rapino (2011), supplemental table C.

If minorities gain more than whites from living near the central business district, it's not clear how they do so.

Housing Quality

Race and ethnicity also make a difference in the quality of housing that people purchase.

Unconditionally, black and Hispanic households have worse houses in worse neighborhoods. The median black household in 2005 had 670 square feet per person; the median Hispanic household had 485 square feet per person; and the median household in the United States had 752 square feet per person. Table 9.5 provides data on other neighborhood and structural characteristics. Blacks and Hispanics live in dirtier, noisier, more dangerous neighborhoods in houses that are older and have fewer rooms.

Some of this difference is due to income, region, size of household, and age, of course, but probably not all. Among households below the poverty level, median square feet per person was 586 for blacks, 363 for Hispanics, and 701 for the total population. Table 9.6 shows that among households

Table 9.5. Self-reported neighborhood and housing characteristics by race/ethnicity, 2005 (percent).

	Black	Hispanic	Everybody else*
Street noise or traffic present	32.4	26.8	25.0
Neighborhood crime present	24.6	19.2	13.0
Poor city or county services	1.7	1.1	0.6
Police protection unsatisfactory	11.0	11.8	6.6
Trash, litter, or junk on street: major accumulation	4.7	4.0	2.0
Structure characteristics: 2005			
Unit built 1990 or after	15.7	16.9	22.7
2 or more baths	32.3	40.0	51.9
Separate dining room	44.8	39.9	50.3

Sources: U.S. Census Bureau (2006) for structure characteristics; U.S. Census Bureau (2008), table 963 for neighborhood characteristics.

*Includes non-Hispanic whites, Asians, American Indians and Alaskan Natives, Native Hawaiians and Pacific Islanders, and other groups.

Table 9.6. Housing characteristics for households below poverty level, 2005 (percent).

	Black	Hispanic	Everyone else
Unit built 1990 or after	10.5	12.5	15.8
2 or more baths	19.7	23.3	30.9
Separate dining room	35.4	28.6	36.5

Source: U.S. Census Bureau (2006).

Table 9.7. Percentage of poor households in neighborhood where the average affluent household lives, 2005–2009.

Non-Hispanic whites	8.9
Non-Hispanic blacks	13.9
Hispanics	13.0
Asians	8.7

Source: Logan (2011b), table 2.
Note: The average poor non-Hispanic white household lives in a neighborhood that is 12.9% poor.

below the poverty level, minorities live in older households with fewer amenities.

DiPasquale and Kahn (1999) have constructed an index of structure quality and an index of neighborhood quality for Los Angeles County in 1990. They found that black and Hispanic recent movers on average lived in neighborhoods that were considerably worse than the neighborhoods of whites with the same income, age, household composition, and nativity status. Minority renters move to structures with about the same quality as comparable white renters move to, but minority owners buy houses of somewhat lower quality than comparable white owners. Even with owners, the neighborhood difference is much larger than the structure difference.

Another measure of quality is neighborhood income. Whatever your income is, there are generally advantages to living around richer people. It appears, though, that both high-income blacks and Hispanics have considerably poorer neighbors than high-income NHWs do. Table 9.7 shows that the average affluent black or Hispanic household is more likely to have a poor neighbor than is the average poor NHW household.

Housing Prices

Very little is known about differences in what races pay for *equal-quality* housing in the modern era (since 1970), and it's even very hard to think about what equal-quality means in this context. Blacks (not Hispanics in recent years) pay less for housing, but the housing they buy is of lower quality. Correcting for quality is difficult, because few whites live in the sort of neighborhoods (with high murder rates, for instance) that many minorities live in.

The best recent study, Bayer et al. (2012), corrects for housing quality by looking at resales of the same house. They found that blacks and Hispanics pay about 3 percent more than NHWs for the same house. The premium that minorities pay appears to be bigger in metropolitan areas that are more segregated.

Housing Discrimination and Other Explanations for the Differences

Several different kinds of discrimination in housing markets have been discussed and studied. Some are current (as W. E. B. Du Bois would argue) and some are in the past (as Booker T. Washington would argue). They all may matter today. Many different actors may discriminate in the housing market: sellers of homes, landlords (when they select or evict tenants), realtors, consumers (when they decide where to live and make offers on homes or apartments), neighbors, and local governments.

Discrimination by landlords and realtors is now illegal and various kinds of discrimination by neighbors has always been illegal—burning crosses and throwing firebombs, for instance. Other kinds of discrimination by neighbors are legal—being really inconsiderate, for instance. Discrimination by sellers is a murky legal area about which I'll say something later. Similarly, discrimination by local governments is a murky legal area, although it's generally impermissible. Discrimination by buyers is legal and probably pervasive.

History apparently matters because segregation measures are serially correlated: cities with high segregation in 1960 usually also have high segregation in 2010. Actions that are now illegal made cities segregated, and they stayed segregated because of (legal) consumer discrimination (and maybe other kinds of discrimination too).

So I'll begin with history.

History

Methods of discrimination in the past were both legal and illegal. The earliest attempts to enforce segregation were a series of ordinances adopted by towns near San Francisco around 1880 to prohibit Chinese people from residing in them. The Supreme Court struck these laws down, but shortly thereafter the towns responded by banning laundries. The laundry ban was upheld.

In the early 1900s a number of cities (Baltimore and Louisville, for instance) in states close to the South (and a few cities in southern states too) passed laws prohibiting African Americans from living in certain parts of town. The Supreme Court struck these down in 1917 in *Buchanan v. Warley*.

As the Great Migration of southern blacks to the urban north intensified in the 1920s, whites in northern cities and suburbs established racial covenants. A covenant is a restriction in the deed to a property that restricts how the owner and subsequent owners can use the property. If I sell you a house, I can put a covenant in the deed that says you must allow the neighbor to share the driveway or allow the cable company to run its wires through the backyard. The restriction passes down from owner to owner. A racial covenant is a provision that says if you sell the house, you have to sell it to a white person—or often, a white Christian. In some areas, 80 percent of homes had covenants in the 1920s and 1930s. Putting a racial covenant in a deed is (theoretically) a voluntary action on the part of a seller—usually the developer of a subdivision—not a government action. (Not quite voluntary, though—apparently realtors often inserted covenants into deeds without the owners' consent.) However, enforcing a racial covenant *is* a government action. The states enforced racial covenants throughout the 1920s, 1930s, and 1940s, and racial segregation increased. In 1948, the Supreme Court ruled in *Shelley v. Kramer* that racial covenants were unenforceable.

Realtors were another factor well into the 1960s. Realtors have a code of ethics and if you don't follow it, you can get into trouble: you can lose your license or other realtors can refuse to deal with you (in which case you won't be very successful). Parts of the code were incorporated into the regulations of federal agencies like the Home Owners' Loan Corporation, the Federal Housing Administration, and the Veterans Administration; these were the agencies created during the New Deal and after World War II to rescue the housing market in and after the Great Depression. Up until the 1960s, the code, even in the North, said that an ethical realtor did not sell houses in a white neighborhood to blacks.

The totally extralegal enforcement of segregation was a lot simpler. Blacks who walked around in white neighborhoods got beaten up, and the homes of blacks who bought houses in white neighborhoods were often firebombed. The 1919 Chicago riots started when blacks went to a white beach: after six days of rioting, 38 were dead, hundreds were injured, and a thousand were homeless. Most of the victims were blacks. Sugrue (1996) gives several accounts of racist violence in 1950s Detroit. He also describes retaliation against whites who sold to blacks and left the neighborhood.

Many apartment owners also refused to rent to minorities, but we know very little about this history.

Local governments got into the act in various ways. Sometimes they joined in the harassment of blacks who tried to buy in white neighborhoods (by issuing violations, demanding excess documentation, or arresting guests, for example); this was particularly true for white suburbs that wanted to stay white. Cities planned public housing in ways to enforce segregated patterns and often operated public housing projects in discriminatory ways (certain housing projects were off limits to black tenants, for example).

It should be no surprise, then, that segregation increased in every decade from 1900 to 1970. Since segregation is serially correlated, this has an effect on segregation today. When we look at the theory of consumer discrimination, we'll understand the linkage better.

The 1968 Civil Rights Act outlawed discrimination by landlords with more than a certain number of apartments and by realtors.

Local Governments Today

We don't know much about the racially discriminatory practices of local governments today. Many local governments discourage construction of multifamily housing that is covered in fair housing laws, preferring instead single-family housing and housing for the elderly. There were many news stories in the early 2000s about harassment of Hispanics in different suburbs, both in housing (inspections) and the use of public spaces (areas where day laborers gathered to arrange work). All these actions can be justified in nonracial terms and may be tied to issues such as income and immigration status instead of race. But they may not be. These are disparate impact issues.

Realtors and Landlords Today

There is considerable audit evidence of discrimination (disparate treatment) by realtors and by landlords. The U.S. Department of Housing and Urban Development (HUD) has authorized a series of housing discrimination audits (the most recent was in 2012) that show continuing but declining discrimination. The other studies were 1977 and 1989.

Remember audits? In this case, the auditors respond to advertisements (including online advertisements in 2012) of houses for sale or apartments for rent. All of the auditors tell stories that indicate that they easily have enough money to live in the units they're interested in (so the procedure misses discrimination that may affect marginally and ambiguously qualified consumers). They record whether they were shown or offered the house, whether the realtor (in the case of houses) tried to interest them in other houses, what sort of comments the realtor made, what sort of neighborhoods the realtor tried to interest them in. In 2012, audits were done with black, Hispanic, and Asian auditors.

What were the results? No apparent discrimination occurred in 2012 in terms of getting a foot in the door: almost every time that one auditor could see an agent, the other auditor could too, and almost every time one auditor was shown at least one unit, the other one was too. This was true of all three minority groups and for both rental and sales markets. "Door slamming" had all but disappeared by 2012, at least for obviously qualified consumers. But as recently as 1977, door slamming was a significant phenomenon. In that year, the net difference between the times the advertised unit was available to the white auditor and the times it was available to the black auditor was about 20 percent in the rental market and 10 percent in the sales market.

The differences come in how eager agents appear to be to get the auditors' business. Whites learn about more units and are shown more units. In the rental market, white auditors learn about more units than minority auditors do about 28 percent of the time and are shown more units about 19 percent of the time. Minorities (with no significant differences between the groups) learn about more units than the white auditor is shown about 17 percent of the time and are shown more units about 14 percent of the time. In the sales market, Hispanics and whites seem to be treated about the same in terms of units learned about and shown, but white auditors are considerably more likely to learn or be shown more homes than the black or Asian auditors they are paired with.

In the 2012 audit, the racial composition of neighborhoods that were recommended to minority homebuyers was "very similar to the composition of those recommended to equally qualified whites" (Turner et al. 2013, xvii). In the previous audits, however, considerable "racial steering" was found.

Hanson, Hawley, and Taylor (2011) is another modern audit. The authors sent e-mails to people listing apartments on Craigslist—some from "respondents" with African American–sounding names, some from "respondents" with white American–sounding names. Landlords responded with longer, more polite e-mails that used more descriptive language to the "white" auditors. They also replied faster and were more likely to invite further correspondence. But there was no difference in terms of negative responses such as asking for references. All of the differences were small—about 1 percent in most cases, because usually landlords respond the same way.

Two questions arise about this sort of discrimination: (1) why does it happen? (and why don't nondiscriminatory folks put the discriminators out of business?); and (2) what are the consequences? I don't have good answers for either question.

On the why question for landlords, the picture is probably similar to restaurants: some of them may be afraid of losing white tenants or they may statistically discriminate against minority tenants (thinking that they may be dirty or noisy or criminal or not pay their rent on time). Pure Beckerian discriminators would probably get out of the business.

For realtors, the steering may have been statistical discrimination too: they might ask why should they waste their time showing houses in neighborhoods they don't think their customers are interested in? Adverse treatment is harder to explain: why should they let business walk out the door? Part of the reason may be that pure Beckerian realtors could survive in the business in a region with enough whites because real estate is often more of a hobby than a business: they will make less money than nondiscriminatory realtors but they won't be put out of business. People for whom realty is a part-time job, almost a hobby, may indulge their preferences about not spending too much time with people they don't like.

What are the consequences? As Ross (2008) points out, this sort of discrimination by itself doesn't seem to be enough to cause the massive segregation that continues. And the patterns of discrimination that audits find do not match the patterns of segregation that we find: black segregation is much greater than Asian or Hispanic segregation, but realtors or landlords do not discriminate against blacks more than they discriminate against Asians or Hispanics, and they may do it less often. The huge decrease in realtor discrimination from 1977 to 2012 was not accompanied by a comparable decrease in segregation.

But segregation is not the only issue. The possibility of discrimination makes moving more costly. This implies that minorities are more likely to be mismatched with their housing. It may inhibit job mobility.

The higher search costs that minorities face in the housing market may also be responsible for the higher prices they pay for houses. Much as we saw in Chapter 5 with the wages employers pay minorities, a seller will ask for a higher price and bargain more aggressively with a prospective buyer whom she thinks has worse alternative options than with one she thinks has better alternative options. Continued search is the usual alternative option that prospective buyers have, so statistical discrimination should lead sellers to ask more from minority prospective buyers. (Perhaps racial animus rather than statistical discrimination prompts sellers to bargain more aggressively, but the evidence from Bayer et al. [2012] suggests otherwise. Minority sellers get the same premium from minority buyers that NHW sellers do.)

Consumers Today

The big issue for segregation is discrimination by consumers. Many people take the racial composition of neighborhoods into account when they decide where to live. Sometimes this is Beckerian discrimination—they don't like to have neighbors of certain races—and sometimes it's statistical discrimination—they think that neighborhoods with different racial compositions have different hard-to-observe characteristics (such as crime and bad schools). Ellen (2000a) shows that statistical discrimination may be the main story: when the white population of a neighborhood goes down, it's generally not because the rate at which whites move out increases but because the rate at which whites move in decreases. Presumably people from outside don't know as much about the neighborhood as people who have lived there for a while. Similarly, families with kids respond more than families without kids.

People may also have more subtle reasons for wanting to live near many people of their own race. Comfort may be an issue. Anderson (2011), for instance, describes how some blacks don't trust whites because of American history and personal experience (Malcolm X expressed this sentiment). Even whites who act kindly and generously may just be hiding their true nature, and other whites may be too quick to react to stereotypes. In a neighborhood with many whites, blacks with these views would not be able to relax—they would have to be on their guard at all times against both racist attacks and reactions to stereotypes (as, for instance, Trayvon Martin should have been). They may be willing to work with whites but seek an island for themselves at home. Some whites may feel the same way about living in a neighborhood with many blacks.

Every race may fear the worst elements of other races. Being the victim of a racist incident can be disturbing at best and fatal at worst, and the more people of a different race living in your neighborhood, the more likely you may be to encounter the wrong people at the wrong time.

Elements of Myrdal's vicious circle may be at work in producing these attitudes. People who grow up with few pleasant encounters or friendships with people outside their own race may be inclined toward distrust or even hatred. Distrust or hatred in one race can feed distrust or hatred in another. Segregated societies produce attitudes conducive to future segregation.

Once you concede that racial composition matters to some consumers, you introduce externalities, so you give up a lot of the properties we normally associate with markets. My moving into a neighborhood changes the racial composition and therefore changes how other people value houses in that neighborhood: my moving in is an action with an externality. The market will not (necessarily) produce the optimal assignment of people to houses, and equilibrium may not be unique.

Schelling (1978) was the first economist to think about neighborhoods this way. He emphasized that outcomes are not good reflections of preferences. For instance, if there are two neighborhoods and two races and each wants to be the majority but is willing to accept being in a slight minority, the only equilibrium is two completely segregated neighborhoods. Schelling's models, however, don't have prices.

Card, Mas, and Rothstein (2008) have a simple version of a Schelling model with prices. But it's partial equilibrium, not general equilibrium: they look at one neighborhood with everything about other neighborhoods fixed.

They consider a particular neighborhood with a fixed number of houses (for our purposes). Call that number n. The "bid-rent curve for whites" for houses in this neighborhood is $b^w(n^w, m)$, where n^w is the number of whites living in the neighborhood and m is the percent of minorities in the neighborhood.

What is the bid-rent curve? Suppose there are n^w whites already living in the neighborhood—the whites who are willing to pay the most—and the neighborhood is m percent minority. The question the bid-rent curve answers is: How much money is the marginal white willing to pay to live there? The marginal white is defined as the white not living in the neighborhood who is willing to pay the most to live there.

Similarly, $b^m(n^m, m)$ is the bid-rent curve for minorities.

Start with something you know: standard supply and demand without factoring in racial composition. Bid-rent curves in this case are shown in Figure 9.1.

Bid-rent curves slope down from standard heterogeneity: you line up buyers of each race in order of willingness to pay and the demand curve has elasticity because some people are willing to pay more than others. As the white population increases, the marginal white is willing to pay less because all higher valuers are already taken care of. Similarly, as the minority population increases, the marginal minority is willing to pay less because all higher valuers among minorities are already taken care of.

The internal equilibrium condition is $b^w([1-m]N, m) = b^m(mN, m)$, and m^* is the equilibrium in Figure 9.1. At m^*, the marginal minority buyer and the marginal white buyer are willing to pay the same for a house in the neighborhood.

Because the bid-rent curves both slope down, the equilibrium is always unique.

It's also stable. Suppose that the minority percentage in the neighborhood is less than m^*. Then the marginal minority buyer is willing to pay more than the marginal white buyer, so any house on the market will go to the minority bidder and the minority percentage will rise. If the minority percentage is

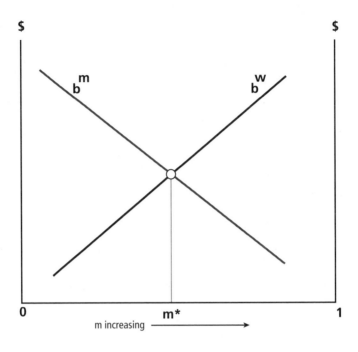

Figure 9.1.

greater than m^*, the marginal white bidder is willing to pay more than the marginal minority bidder and the minority percentage will fall. Either way, the market will force the minority percentage toward m^*.

And finally, it's going to be optimal: the people from both races who value the neighborhood the most will live there.

Are there also segregated equilibria? Yes: if the highest valuer of one race values the neighborhood less than the lowest valuer of the other race when everyone is taken care of. Figures 9.2 and 9.3 show how this could happen.

These equilibria are also unique, stable, and optimal. Remember that these are classical equilibria where nobody cares about race.

To understand Schelling's insights, go to the opposite extreme and suppose that *only* racial composition matters. In particular, suppose that everyone (or everyone in a race) has the same willingness to pay for the nonracial characteristics of the neighborhood and everyone within a race has the same reaction to racial composition. Whites like m to be low and minorities like m to be high. Figure 9.4 illustrates.

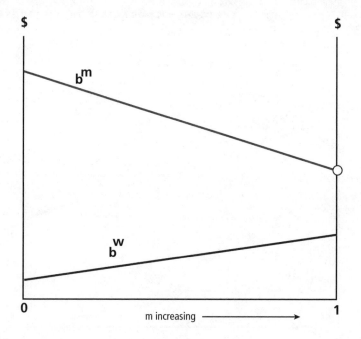

Figure 9.2. All-minority-segregated equilibrium.

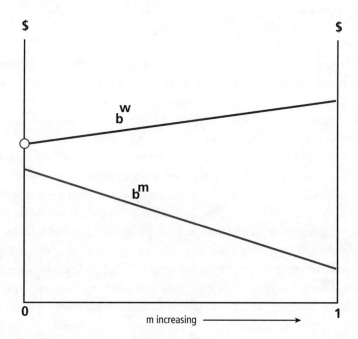

Figure 9.3. All-white-segregated equilibrium.

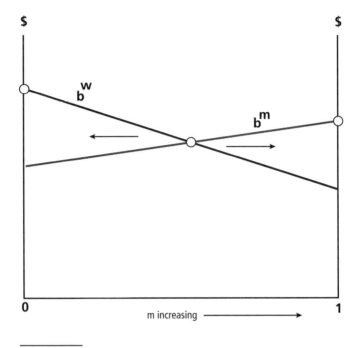

Figure 9.4.

In Figure 9.4 there are three equilibria, which I've circled: all white, all minority, and an integrated equilibrium. The two segregated equilibria are stable: if for some reason a small number of race-discordant people enter the neighborhood, they will be outbid and soon leave. The integrated equilibrium is unstable; sometimes it's called a tipping point. If the minority percentage is a tiny bit below this equilibrium amount, minorities will be slightly lonely and whites will outbid them to live in the neighborhood. The minority percentage will decrease, and that will make whites even more willing to outbid minorities. This process will continue until no minorities are left in the neighborhood. Similarly, if the minority percentage is slightly above the integrated equilibrium, whites will leave the neighborhood and continue to leave until all are gone. The unstable equilibrium is called a tipping point because if the population starts with more minorities, the neighborhood will tip into the all-minority category and if it begins with more whites, it will tip into the all-white category.

As I drew them in Figure 9.4, the welfare of residents in both segregated equilibria is superior to the welfare of residents in the integrated one, but

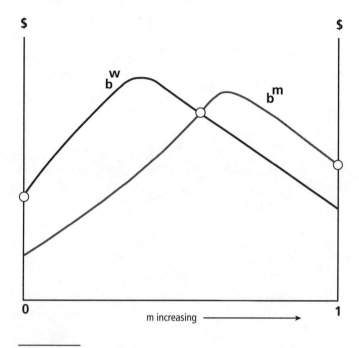

Figure 9.5.

that is just because I was particularly mindless and wanted everything to be monotonic. So consider Figure 9.5.

In this figure, people like some variety but don't like to be in the minority. The integrated equilibrium is unstable and the only stable equilibria are pretty lousy.

In general, even if the curves are monotonic and there's no taste for variety, there's no guarantee that a stable equilibrium will be optimal. You can end up at a suboptimal but totally stable equilibrium. That's why history matters and why the current arrangement of people could be really bad.

But is the Schelling model a good model of cities since the 1960s? Card, Mas, and Rothstein (2008) looked at the data and concluded that the Schelling model is not a good description of what has been happening. This model predicts no stable integration and tipping in both directions. Card, Mas, and Rothstein looked at a huge array of census tracts for long periods of time and found some stable integration and almost no tips where the minority share had gone down. Ellen (2000a) found similar behavior.

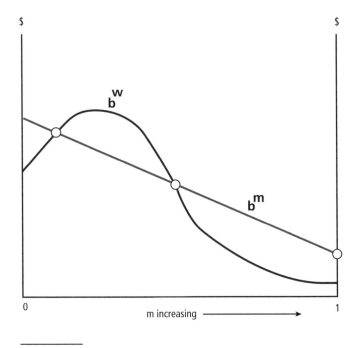

Figure 9.6.

Card, Mas, and Rothstein therefore propose a different way of drawing bid-rent curves that fits the data better. *Both* racial composition and heterogeneity in normal nonracial preferences come into play. Figure 9.6 illustrates a fairly simple version.

These bid-rent curves are drawn on the assumption that minorities don't care much about racial composition and whites care about both racial composition and neighborhood-specific amenities. More complicated and realistic versions are possible. Figure 9.6 has two stable equilibria: one all minority and one integrated. It has an unstable equilibrium too—a tipping point.

Why did I draw the curvy white bid-rent curve in Figure 9.6? The easy way of thinking about it is that all whites have the same reactions to race but different willingness to pay for the particular neighborhood, given racial composition. (Having only one kind of heterogeneity makes thinking about the problem easier.) There is a lot of heterogeneity in this willingness to pay (perhaps for job access). If the neighborhood is heavily white, you will

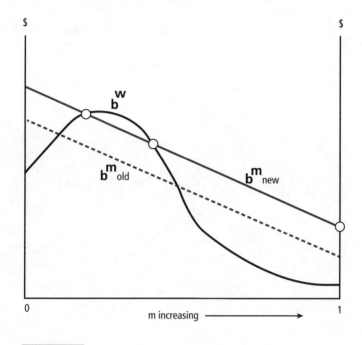

Figure 9.7.

run out of whites who are willing to pay a lot to live there, in normal fashion, and the bid rent curve slopes downward. But if the proportion of minorities is high, then even whites who value the neighborhood highly on nonracial grounds are not willing to pay much because they don't like the racial composition of the neighborhood.

Since there are two stable equilibria, some neighborhoods like this will be stably integrated and some will be all minority. History matters, and as I drew it, the all-minority equilibrium is not optimal, even within the class of stable equilibria.

Card, Mas, and Rothstein think about a different kind of tipping process. They think about minority demand rising or stochastically fluctuating over time. As the minority bid rent curve rises, the minority share in the stable integrated equilibrium rises and the minority share in the unstable equilibrium falls. Figure 9.7 illustrates. If the neighborhood started out heavily white and is now at the integrated equilibrium, the minority share will increase slowly as minority demand increases.

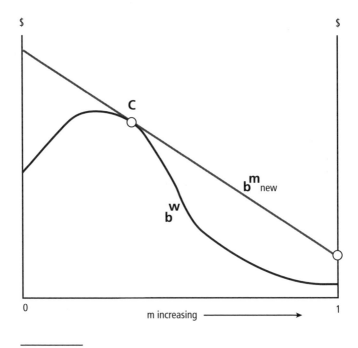

Figure 9.8.

But then as minority demand grows even further, the stable and unstable equilibria converge, as shown in Figure 9.8. The minority share is still increasing slowly.

But when the minority bid-rent curve increases a little bit more, the integrated equilibrium disappears, as shown in Figure 9.9. Minority share increases drastically as the integrated equilibrium disappears and the neighborhood becomes totally minority. Minority demand becomes so great that even the whites who have the strongest nonracial motives to live in the neighborhood are outbid by minorities who do not mind the neighborhood's racial composition.

For Card, Mas, and Rothstein, the tipping point is the last stable integrated equilibrium before minority demand gets so high that there are no more integrated stable equilibria—point C in Figure 9.8. Card, Mas, and Rothstein calculate these tipping points and find them around 10–13 percent minority. They also find that the tipping point seems to be higher in later years than it was in earlier years.

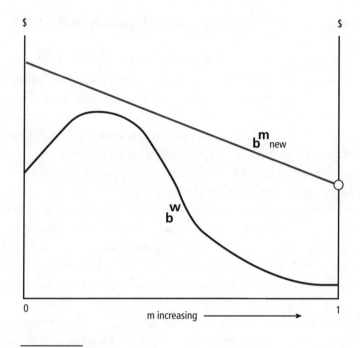

Figure 9.9.

Thus, in this example, segregation increases in a particular neighborhood when minority demand increases. Why might minority demand increase? Three reasons may be historically relevant: migration to a metropolitan area (Hispanics and Asians to the urban centers of the United States in recent decades or blacks to northern cities in most of the twentieth century), rising income (if the neighborhood was previously out of reach for most minorities), and reduced discrimination by realtors. Naively, you might think that both income convergence between minorities and NHWs and a reduction in discrimination among realtors would promote integration. But both trends *may* (not must) promote segregation. Outcomes are not always simple reflections of fundamentals; that's why economics is useful and "common sense" is not.

Remember that this is partial equilibrium. Willingness to pay depends on prices and conditions in other neighborhoods. The more nice neighborhoods minority buyers can enter, the less they will be willing to pay for this neighborhood. These considerations are not modeled explicitly.

Consequences of Segregation and Discrimination

In the last chapter and the previous section of this chapter, we've seen good evidence of massive discrimination in social relationships and in housing. Some of it is illegal, but most of it is not. Most of it we don't even think about as immoral—we don't call a person who considers the race of his or her spouse or adopted child or the racial composition of the neighborhood where she is buying a house a racist. Both minorities and NHWs probably practice such discrimination, although possibly to different degrees. And there are no serious proposals to ban such discrimination, such as allowing someone to sue prospective spouses or prospective house purchasers for discrimination. The two areas reinforce each other, since neighborhoods lead to friendships and friendships lead to neighborhood choices. The activities in question are far from trivial—getting married and buying a house are the most consequential things I've done in my life, and I'm not unusual in this regard.

This discrimination raises a basic question: Does it have any effects? Remember that disparate treatment discrimination can occur with little if any disparate impact, and what we've shown so far has been only disparate treatment, for the most part.

The other reason why we want to know the effects is the controversy over segregation. Is segregation (or centralization) the root of all evil, as the Kerner Commission argues, or is it the source of black community's strength, as Malcolm X implies? Or is it something in between? Californians and Columbia students are segregated and nobody cares—should we care whether minorities are segregated?

Several possible impacts have been investigated in the literature. I'll start with what seems more certain and go to areas where results are not very clean. Almost all the literature on this question is about African Americans and a little bit is about NHWs. The consequences for Hispanics and Asians have been studied little.

Education and Job Mobility

We've already seen two consequences of discrimination in housing markets: higher search and mobility costs for minorities and more segregated classrooms.

The result about search and mobility costs was only about disparate treatment when it came from the audits. But African Americans have less mobility both across and within metropolitan areas. This may be one reason for the wage gap, a good example of disparate impact.

We found that African Americans from families with high socioeconomic status were hurt by being in predominantly African American schools (although they might have more friends), and because most schooling is based on neighborhoods, school segregation results from housing segregation. Card and Rothstein (2006) also showed an independent effect of neighborhood segregation on minority cognitive achievement—neighborhoods might matter.

Commuting Time

Another easy-to-understand finding is about commuting time, as we saw in Table 9.4. African Americans who live in central cities have really long commuting times—longer than practically anyone else. This is bizarre, since one of the benefits of living close to the center of the city is supposed to be lower commuting cost. It's like finding that people who live in Florida disproportionately suffer from frostbite.

The higher commuting costs are a real cost—several hours a month of time and probably further costs out of pocket. In essence, the wage gap is really bigger than it appears. In the current world, these higher commuting costs are probably tied to centralization: the neighborhoods that were great places for African Americans to live in in the 1930s are not great today because these neighborhoods are no longer close to unskilled jobs; they are not great today because in the multiple-equilibrium world of segregation, changing which neighborhoods are minority neighborhoods is really hard. The problem is ossification more than anything else. But even in a world where minority neighborhoods could move quickly, there would be fewer of them, so many job matches would not work out well for minorities.

Crime

Segregation and centralization may contribute to the concentration of crime among minorities, particularly African Americans. Chapter 11 discusses the mechanisms and evidence. Black murder rates are higher in more segregated metropolitan areas.

Health

Probably the best evidence is about health. Living in a segregated city or a poor, heavily minority neighborhood is not good for your health.

Two studies that I know of deal with health effects, but they take entirely different approaches. Both grow out of other literatures. The first is Ingrid Ellen's study (2000b) of low birth weight (LBW). She asks whether mothers in more segregated cities are more likely to have LBW babies, everything else being equal. Segregation is endogenous, and the same things that are causing segregation might be causing low birth weights. (Someone might propose a different explanation for the correlation: for instance, if the minority population of a city was poorer and wilder than the minority population of another city, whites might avoid them more; segregation would be higher and simultaneously more babies would have LBW.) So she uses instrumental variables to isolate the causal effect of segregation. She does this in a way that has become fairly standard: segregation in 1960 and the number of rivers a city has. Cities that were more segregated in 1960 tend to be more segregated in every subsequent census. Cities with more rivers tend to be more segregated, probably because they have more natural boundaries. (Essentially, she finds the effect that 1960 segregation and number of rivers has on LBW births, and from this backs out the effect that segregation caused by these two instruments has on LBW births.) She finds that white women in more segregated cities are not more likely than white women in less segregated cities to have LBW babies, holding all the usual other variables constant, but that black women in more segregated cities are more likely to have LBW babies. Centralization is an even more powerful determinant of low birth weight than segregation.

These results are about the effect of metropolitan segregation on blacks who grow up anywhere in the metropolitan area; they don't compare blacks who grew up in segregated neighborhoods with blacks who grew up in integrated neighborhoods. If you find them convincing and are living on the South Side of Chicago, they tell you to move to Las Vegas, not to an integrated neighborhood in Chicago.

Without an experiment, making a comparison of the effects of different kinds of neighborhoods in the same metropolitan area is tough. Families choose what neighborhood to live in; they don't normally have location randomly imposed on them. If you observe two otherwise identical families living in different kinds of neighborhoods, the unobserved characteristics that made one family live in the integrated neighborhood could very well affect directly how healthy they are and what health practices they follow. Thus, to compare the effects of neighborhoods, you need an experiment.

The other big health result comes from a controlled experiment called Moving to Opportunity (MTO). We discussed the results of this experiment briefly in Chapter 4 in the context of health. In the 1990s and early 2000s, the federal government conducted this experiment in several cities in which randomly selected inner-city housing project residents were subsidized to encourage them move to private apartments in wealthier neighborhoods (census tracts with less than 10 percent poverty). A control group of similar residents did not receive this encouragement. Both the experimental and the control group were followed for several years.

The subsidy took the form of a section 8 certificate (these are now officially called Housing Choice Vouchers but everyone still says section 8). A family with a section 8 certificate can choose its own apartment, provided that it meets certain structural standards. The family pays 30 percent of its income as rent and the government pays the rest, up to an administratively determined fair market rent, which is the same everywhere in the metropolitan area. So with a section 8 certificate, a family has the same out-of-pocket expenses in any apartment anywhere that accepts fair market rent or less.

As we saw in Chapter 4, the people who moved to better neighborhoods enjoyed considerable health benefits, both physical and mental. Adult mental health improved on such measures as distress and calmness; these improvements were about as big as those produced by the most effective clinical and pharmacological interventions. Mental health also improved for young women. Obesity fell for adults too, but this result may have been a statistical aberration.

Both of these health results are direct contradictions to Malcolm X's ideas about the benefits of separatism.

Human Development

Children who grew up in more segregated cities seem to have developed more poorly, at least in the twentieth century: they were less likely to graduate from high school or to finish college and they were more likely to become unwed mothers. Cutler and Glaeser (1997) first made this argument. They compared young adults in 1980 based on their residence in 1975. Blacks in more segregated metropolitan areas did worse; segregation made no difference to whites. Ananat (2011) improved on Cutler and Glaeser's work by finding a really strong instrument for segregation (configuration of rail lines in 1910) and repeated most of their results for 1980, except for college graduation. Ananat also found greater black poverty and inequality in 1990 in more segregated cities, which she attributed to less human capital development among African Americans in these cities. However, Echenique and Fryer (2007) raise some questions about whether these effects persist in later censuses, particularly the 2000 census.

These are results about the metropolitan segregation, not about different neighborhoods. The results about different neighborhoods are similarly inconsistent. While only MTO is the basis for health results, development results can also be found in an earlier quasi-experiment.

The earlier program grew out of a civil rights lawsuit that was decided in Chicago in 1976. A group of public housing residents claimed that the Chicago Housing Authority had discriminated against minorities in site selection—concentrating projects in minority neighborhoods—and in tenant placement—concentrating minority tenants in certain projects in minority neighborhoods. They won their case. As a result, the Chicago Housing Authority (with help from the federal government) had to set up the Gautreaux Assisted Housing Program (Dorothy Gautreaux was the lead plaintiff).

Under the program, which lasted more than a decade, low-income families from Chicago housing projects received section 8 vouchers to move to neighborhoods that were richer and whiter. The Gautreaux program also advertised to landlords in desirable neighborhoods and counseled families intensely to encourage them to move to those neighborhoods. In many cases, families had little choice over where to move: apartments were assigned as they came up, and if they refused an apartment they moved down the queue. In the end, about half of the families in the program moved to wealthy, mainly white neighborhoods; the other half did not.

Among the group who stayed in minority neighborhoods, the children of those who moved were more likely to attend college, more likely to have jobs if they did not attend college, and more likely to have good jobs. (Pretty good evidence indicates that Gautreaux participants didn't increase crime or decrease property values in the neighborhoods they moved to [Yinger 1995, 152–153, 235–236].)

But Gautreaux wasn't really an experiment; while luck had something to do with who moved where, the families who moved out of minority neighborhoods weren't selected independent of any desire to move. The encouraging results from Gautreaux therefore led researchers and the government to establish the MTO program. Because of its greater scientific rigor, MTO could answer the questions it asked much better than the Gautreaux project could. But Gautreaux might have asked better questions.

While the MTO program demonstrated that moving to a better neighborhood improved health, it did not find that such a move improved many other outcomes. Children's cognitive achievement showed no gain, and teenage boys were more likely to exhibit problem behavior and to be arrested for property crimes. However, delinquency and problem behavior among teenage girls did decrease (Brooks-Gunn et al. 2004; Kling, Ludwig, and Katz 2004; Orr et al. 2003). To those who thought that breaking up the ghetto would be a magic bullet, MTO was a big disappointment.

What explains the difference between the Gautreaux results and the MTO results? Three elements could matter.

First is the selection issue I've already emphasized. Whatever it was that made the Gautreaux families willing to move to white neighborhoods may have also made them more effective at raising their children for life in contemporary America.

Second is time. Recall that Echenique and Fryer found metropolitan-wide effects in 1980 but not in 2000. Gautreaux occurred around 1980 and MTO occurred around 2000. The world changed a lot between 1980 and 2000. For instance, crime fell considerably and information technology (how people communicate and learn about the world) improved.

Finally, Gautreaux and MTO were really testing two different "treatments"; MTO wasn't simply a later and more rigorous test of the "treatment" Gautreaux examined. The two programs differed in two ways, one obvious and the other not.

The obvious difference is that Gautreaux defined a good location by race, not by income. The treatment in Gautreaux was moving to a neighborhood with less than 30 percent minority population; the treatment in MTO was moving to a neighborhood with less than 10 percent poor population.

The less obvious difference is how people found the place where they were to live. On paper, MTO and Gautreaux look the same: "section 8 with housing counseling." But "housing counseling" appears to me to be a lot different in the Gautreaux project in the late 1970s than it was in the MTO project in the late 1990s. Housing counseling in the 1970s was much more paternalistic than housing counseling in the late 1990s.

To understand why this matters, think more rigorously about how section 8 works, since both programs were financed by section 8. Section 8 regulations emphasize the structural issues of a potential home; they almost completely ignore location. By ignoring location, they implicitly encourage bad location.

Now think about the section 8 formula. The amount of rent the landlord gets is the fair market rent. The fair market rent for an apartment is based on the size of the family and the distribution of rents in the metropolitan area. An apartment's location within a metropolitan area doesn't matter.

The surplus that a landlord-tenant pair gains from a section 8 relationship is the following sum:

The tenant's willingness to pay for the apartment
+ fair market rent − market rent.

Now suppose that the rate at which the tenant's willingness to pay for location increases more slowly than the market rent as location improves. Then surplus is maximized in the worst possible location. Since surplus is pretty fungible between a landlord and a tenant in ways that are unobservable to an outside observer or regulator, you would expect the partnerships that actually form to be those that generate the greatest surplus for their members, if people get matched with apartments in something like a market process. Section 8 tenants are going to live in the worst possible locations.

In rough terms, if HUD pays the same amount for an apartment in a lousy location as it pays for an apartment in a great location and the market doesn't, HUD will get the lousy-location apartments and the market will get the good ones.

Now think about MTO. MTO was a section 8 experiment, not a generic neighborhood-effects experiment. MTO added a constraint on location—neighborhood income. It didn't add constraints on any other dimension of location—safety, pollution, schools, job access, integration. So what you should expect is for MTO participants to take the apartments in the worst locations in the neighborhoods they were allowed to move to: the worst schools, the worst job access, the most pollution, the most crime.

Gautreaux, on the other hand, happened before the Internet, when good local maps were hard to come by and information was scarce. The counseling agency found the apartments, then it gave each family a choice of apartments: "Counselors accompanied applicants on visits to available units. Generally, two or three such visits were made in one trip in order to provide the families with some basis for comparison. . . . If the clients wished to apply for a unit they had visited, a meeting was arranged between the owner and the clients" (Peroff, Davis, and Jones 1979, 38). In all, 95 percent of clients took the first unit offered; the threat was that if they didn't, they would go to the bottom of the queue. The counselors seemed to dominate the process by vetting all the units and then deciding which ones the clients would get to visit and negotiate for. Unless landlords were making side payments to counselors, it would have been difficult for tenants and landlords to sort themselves to maximize surplus.

But in MTO in the late 1990s, when access to information was a lot better, counselors seemed to think of themselves as providing information about the world, not about specific units, with actual housing search being almost an afterthought: "Also, the counseling agencies could require that some of the extra time be spent on preparation for housing search" (Orr et al. 2003, 2n6). Clients seemed to have been prepared to search for housing and then set loose to search on their own. The opportunities to maximize surplus seem to have been much better. Thus I expect that MTO families would have moved to worse locations within the permitted area than Gautreaux families did. This is speculation, of course.

What do the data show about the neighborhoods that constituted the MTO "treatment"? They weren't a lot different from the neighborhoods that constituted MTO "controls." Alliprantis (2011) found that poverty was significantly lower in the average treatment neighborhood than in the average control neighborhood, since the rules were based on poverty, but for many other indicators of neighborhood quality, MTO produced little or no improvement: in school quality, female high school graduation rate, and share of lone-parent households, for instance. Families who had MTO vouchers lived in neighborhoods that on average were 38 percent black; families without a voucher lived in neighborhoods that on average were 48 percent black (Goering 2003).

MTO thus tells us a lot about what programs like MTO could do, but it gives us only hints about how neighborhoods actually affect people.

Jobs

The location of African American neighborhoods may cost their residents jobs, not just lengthen the commutes of those who have jobs. Like longer commuting time, this would be an implication of centralization, not segregation. If low-skill jobs are now far away from where African Americans live, they may never find out about them or be able to get to an interview. The cost of commuting may be overwhelming. This idea is called the *spatial mismatch hypothesis.*

John Kain first proposed this hypothesis in the 1960s, and it figures prominently in the Kerner Commission report. William Julius Wilson popularized the idea in the 1980s in *When Work Disappears* (1996). Although many excellent studies have been published on the topic, empirical economics has reached no clear verdict on the importance or existence of spatial mismatch.

Two problems make it difficult to test the spatial mismatch hypothesis. First is selection: people choose where they live. People may live far from jobs because they don't have jobs, not the other way around. Everything else being equal, people who have jobs want to live near those jobs and people with little chance at employment will live far from jobs, since good job access is expensive. Owning hammers is correlated with being a carpenter, but if you gave everybody a hammer you wouldn't make everybody into a carpenter.

The second problem is finding a relevant measure of job access. Essentially, you have to ask where the people in a neighborhood who are not working would be working if they were working. There is no unique or obvious way of answering this counterfactual question, and studies that answer it in different ways arrive at different conclusions about spatial mismatch.

Gautreaux found that adults who moved to white neighborhoods worked more and received welfare less, while MTO found that moving to a richer neighborhood had no effect.

At least one good natural experiment, however, shows that neighborhood location has a noticeable effect on black employment patterns, although that effect has diminished in recent decades. The natural experiment looks at postal service jobs.

Working for the post office has long been attractive to African Americans, post office employment (particularly that of postal clerks) is fairly heavily concentrated in historical city centers, and post office locations are not primarily governed by considerations of profit maximization.

Across metropolitan areas, Boustan and Margo (2009) found that the relative odds (black versus white) of working for the post office were unrelated to segregation in 1940 and 1950, strongly positively correlated in 1960 and 1970, and less strongly correlated after 1980. Even in 2000, the correlation is positive but substantially smaller than in 1980. This result is driven by postal clerks; it does not hold for postal carriers, who work throughout the metropolitan area.

The story these results tell is that at least between 1960 and 1980, the constraints that segregation and centralization (which are strongly correlated) placed on black employment opportunities were real and affected the lives black people led. In this time, blacks could not reach suburban jobs and whites could. The other opportunities for low-skill employment downtown were meager. So they went to work for the post office in disproportionate numbers. In 1940 and 1950, inner-city jobs were plentiful, so centralization didn't affect the kinds of opportunities outside the post office that blacks had. After 1980, information technology improved, African American access to automobiles rose, and the correlation between segregation and centralization may also have fallen. Notice that this declining influence of neighborhood is consistent with the comparison of the impacts of Gautreaux and MTO.

Boustan and Margo thus demonstrate that segregation and centralization have affected the working lives of black people in a serious way. We can't be sure that the effect on total employment has been big, but we know that there has been an effect on the kind of jobs blacks get. The effect, however, is getting smaller.

City Decline

One of the great questions of U.S. urban economic history is why many northern and Midwestern cities declined so precipitously in the decades after World War II: why places like Chicago, Detroit, Newark, Cleveland, and New York City started to lose population after many decades of almost uninterrupted growth, why large parts of the middle class abandoned them, and why their image (among whites) changed from glamorous to gritty. Many factors contributed to this decline: automobiles, frozen food (it was no longer necessary to shop every day), the baby boom (transporting three little kids on a bus is a big challenge), rising incomes, and federal homeownership subsidies, for instance. But this urban decline also coincided with the Great

Migration of African Americans out of the rural South to many of these same cities. Did blacks go to the wrong places? Was the timing of this migration just a sad coincidence?

It probably wasn't. Black migration caused white flight. When blacks moved in, whites left cities, not just neighborhoods.

Showing a causal link between black entry and white exit is tough. Boustan (2010) solved this problem by looking at blacks pushed out of the South by farming conditions. Different parts of the South specialized in different crops, so the rate of black migration from different parts of the South varied as crops mechanized at different rates or experienced demand and supply shocks. Northern cities also differed in where the blacks who came to them moved from: people from Mississippi, for instance, tended to go to Chicago, while people from North Carolina went to New York City. So a shock to tobacco farming that pushed blacks out of North Carolina would increase migration to New York, while a shock to cotton farming in Mississippi would increase migration to Chicago.

So if Boustan sees more whites leaving Chicago than New York when Mississippi cotton farming mechanizes and North Carolina tobacco farming booms, she can be fairly confident that blacks are pushing whites out of cities. That's what she saw in a large data set covering three decades, 1940–1970. Her best estimate is that every black person who arrived in a northern city during this time caused about 2.3 white people to leave. Given how housing markets worked then, how urban governments were financed and chosen, and how prejudice operated, black migration and the white reaction to it caused a substantial part of the urban decline that hollowed out U.S. cities after World War II.

Information, Interaction, and Prejudice

Segregation may affect the kind of people who live in a metropolitan area. Many of our interactions, especially those that we don't plan, happen with people in our neighborhoods, and many of the people we like and trust most are our neighbors. This is especially true for children. People who lack these neighborly interactions with those of differing race or ethnicity may never learn what those people are like and may be more prejudiced, consciously or not, as a result. As information technology changes, however, these interactions may become less important.

Taste for Integration

A final cost is possible but has not been extensively studied. It could be that a lot of people like some degree of integration, but we have seen that markets aren't good at producing a lot of integration, even if people wanted it. Polls show that both whites and blacks say they prefer integrated neighborhoods, and substantial numbers of people of all races go out of their way to enjoy the cultures associated with other races. Markets in this case may fail to produce what people want.

Compensation through Lower Prices?

One question that the results about commuting, health, and schools raise is whether African Americans pay lower housing prices as a result. This would be compensation. For instance, if you observed two towns populated by otherwise identical people and one were more polluted than the other and people could freely move between the towns, then in equilibrium everyone would have to be indifferent about which town they live in. Thus the nastier town would have lower housing prices. You could not feel sorry for the people in the nastier town; the lower housing prices would compensate them for the pollution. Does this reasoning carry over?

No. Everyone isn't identical, and you can't go back and forth between being white and being black. There is no force to equalize utility across races. Even if housing prices for blacks are lower in some sense, we're not interested in feeling sorry anyway.

What about Hispanics and Asians?

So far this section has been all about African Americans. What about Hispanics and Asians? Not a lot is known. Hispanics and Asians are new immigrants, so it's unlikely that they've been ossified into terribly wrong neighborhoods. Some evidence indicates that immigrant enclaves can be helpful, especially when immigrants have high human capital. But like African Americans, they have direct problems from hindrances to job mobility and mobility in general, exacerbated by language and culture problems.

Policies

For all the belief in the 1960s that housing was the key to solving the race problem, remarkably few policies to improve housing outcomes have been proposed, fewer have been implemented, and still fewer have been evaluated. And the best-evaluated program—MTO—turned out to be a disappointment (although the gains in mental health would have made it seem a success if proponents had not built up expectations in so many other areas). In this section, I'll examine several other policy approaches but will be able to say very little that is backed by hard evidence.

Fair Housing Laws

The federal government has long supported making moving to mainly white neighborhoods easier for minorities. In the beginning, this support took the form of sporadic Supreme Court decisions that struck down particular exclusion practices. In 1886, in *Yick Wo v. Hopkins,* the Supreme Court struck down a San Francisco ordinance regulating laundries that was intended to make it impossible for Chinese to live in the city; this is probably the first application of disparate impact reasoning. We've already seen *Buchanan v. Warley* in 1917, striking down racial zoning laws, and *Shelley v. Kramer* in 1948, declaring racial covenants unenforceable. The common wisdom is that these decisions did little to reduce segregation, but nobody has tried to figure out what would have happened without them.

Similarly, in 1962, President Kennedy issued Executive Order 11063, which required action against discrimination in all federal housing programs. For several years, this executive order appears to have been largely ignored.

Housing was not part of the Civil Rights Act of 1964. The major piece of federal law is title 8 of the Civil Rights Act of 1968, called the Fair Housing Law. It prohibits realtors from racial steering, blockbusting (using comments about racial change to encourage panic selling), and discrimination in advertising. Sellers and landlords cannot discriminate in their decisions to sell or rent or in the terms and conditions they offer. But single-family homes and buildings with fewer than five units are exempt. In addition, the law places no restrictions on buying. So it exempts 80 percent of the selling side and 100 percent of the buying side. Many states also passed fair housing laws around this time, and some passed such laws earlier.

Empirical work indicates that fair housing laws have a very modest effect on segregation. That's consonant with theory.

But fair housing laws, if enforced, do make it easier for minorities to move and to find places to live. So they help reduce mobility costs, improve matches of jobs with employees, and make it easier to switch jobs, as did the civil rights laws on public accommodations. They may also reduce the premium that minorities pay for owner-occupied housing. But there's no evidence about these possible effects because nobody has looked for them.

Low-Income Housing Policy

The federal government has a number of policies for housing low-income people. All of them have rationed admissions, so they never have trouble finding people who want their benefits. Some of them supply housing directly—and so choose its location—while others subsidize private landlords. Many minorities are housed through these programs. As we've seen with section 8, these programs generally have very weak incentives to house people in better locations. Usually the landlords don't get more money if the neighborhood is more accessible to jobs or has better schools or is more healthful. Increasing the pressure for better neighborhoods in these programs would probably make the experience better for residents and might decrease segregation; better neighborhoods would make the programs work better in any case. Doing this would be simple: the federal government could increase subsidies for apartments in better locations. With section 8, for instance, the fair market rent would vary with neighborhood conditions such as job access, quality of schools, and quality of air.

Alternatively, the federal government could pay directly for integration.

Integration Maintenance

Integration maintenance refers to a wide array of activities in a small number of places that have the goal of promoting integrated communities. They include mortgage subsidies for whites moving into heavily minority neighborhoods, mortgage subsidies for minorities moving into heavily white neighborhoods, housing counseling to encourage integrative moves, bans on for-sale signs and on active solicitation of potential sellers by realtors, building and zoning code enforcement, advertising the advantages of integration, enhanced public services for "transitional" areas, programs to promote intergroup understanding, separate waiting lists by race and quotas for each floor in subsidized housing projects, equity assurance programs (programs that try to assuage white homeowners' fears that their investments will lose value if they stay in an integrated neighborhood by reimbursing 80 percent of their losses in home value after five years; the colloquial name is "black insurance").

These are local programs (there is nothing at the state or national level) that operate now mainly in upper-middle-income and middle-income suburbs near heavily minority cities: Oak Park and Forest Park (Chicago), Shaker Heights and Cleveland Heights (Cleveland), Park Hill (Denver), West Mount Airy (Philadelphia), and Maplewood and South Orange (Newark). Note all the trees and hills in these names. These are older, leafy suburbs where the residents are often quite liberal in politics. Starrett City (now officially called Spring Creek Towers), a federally subsidized housing project in Brooklyn, also had an integration maintenance program (racial quotas by floors and buildings) from 1974 to 1988, when the practice was declared unconstitutional.

There's great variety in these programs that would call for a variety of analyses. Some make sense (promoting intergroup understanding), some are stupid (banning for-sale signs, which is also unconstitutional). They would all probably work best, however, on a regional or national basis. The more kinds of integrated environment are available, the more likely you are to find one you like.

Integration maintenance programs sometimes slip over into being programs to keep minorities out of an area. The Starrett City quotas, for instance, were always in fact quotas on minority entry and priorities on white entry. Programs to encourage whites to move to a neighborhood or stay there are in fact programs to make it harder and more expensive for minorities to move there. This may be the only way to produce a few integrated neighborhoods in a metropolitan area where it is difficult for minorities to enter almost all predominantly white neighborhoods. Therein lies the other advantage of metropolitan-wide programs. As long as there are only a few integrated neighborhoods, there is a great danger that minority demand for those neighborhoods will overwhelm white demand. The way to reduce minority demand for specific neighborhoods without reducing minority welfare is to produce many integrated neighborhoods simultaneously. (In some ways this resembles the question of the integration of multiple restaurants in Chapter 8.)

Gentrification

Gentrification refers to a process in which richer people enter a neighborhood that was originally poorer and the neighborhood becomes richer over time. The neighborhood goes from being gritty to being trendy. Gentrification is thus a process, not a policy, but it's easy enough to think of government policies that either encourage gentrification or discourage it.

Most gentrification to date has been brought about by rich whites moving into poorer white neighborhoods (there are no poor white neighborhoods in major American cities). Some gentrification has been brought about by rich blacks moving into poor black neighborhoods. The 2010 census saw some gentrification in the form of rich whites moving into middle-class black neighborhoods—Harlem, parts of Brooklyn, the District of Columbia, and maybe some parts of the North Shore of Staten Island. If integration per se is good, that would seem to be desirable. Clearly minorities are better off if everybody else doesn't run away from them, and predominantly minority neighborhoods are more likely to flourish if more whites think about them as places to buy houses, not places to buy drugs. But renters might lose if demand for Harlem real estate increases without any corresponding easing of opportunities outside Harlem. Most of the evidence is that not a lot of people lose too much from gentrification, but this evidence is not about interracial gentrification, because to date there has been very little of it.

Conclusion

Race matters a lot in housing markets, and housing matters in how people live and raise their children. Discrimination and segregation for African Americans have been decreasing over time, but segregation has not been decreasing for Hispanics and Asians. How much housing matters may also be decreasing as transportation and information technology improve. Neither the robust integration the Kerner Commission sought nor the robust segregation Malcolm X sought seems to have large scholarly or political support these days. Nor does the last great public enthusiasm of the twentieth century, increasing minority homeownership rates (I discuss this in Chapter 10). Housing markets are very large and function poorly. Making one or two of them work better won't save the world, as some people believed in the twentieth century, but is still worth doing.

10

Homeownership, Mortgages, Bubbles, and Foreclosures

Minorities are less likely to own their own homes than NHWs and more likely to rent. At the beginning of 2014, 72.9 percent of NHW households were homeowners, compared to 45.8 percent of Hispanic households and 43.3 percent of African American households. The homeownership rate for "all other races," who are mainly Asians, was 55.8 percent.

Ownership and renting are just two different ways of accomplishing the same thing—acquiring a place to live—so it is not immediately obvious that these disparities should concern us. But they receive a lot of attention, and many people do care about them.

Minority homeownership rates get a lot of attention because they rose in the housing boom that preceded the Great Recession, then fell after 2006 for blacks and after 2007 for Hispanics. The Great Recession has been tied in both popular and scholarly writing to this rise and fall. Indeed, in one crude popular view, the Great Recession happened because too many blacks and Hispanics came to own homes. One goal of this chapter is to understand this historical incident—both as a question of fact and as an opportunity to learn more about how race and ethnicity work in the twenty-first century. In particular, I'll try to explain why minorities ended up with so many subprime mortgages, why the mortgages took the forms that they did, and what policy issues this debacle presents.

The other reason why homeownership draws a lot of attention is because for the majority of American households, their house is their largest investment. Homeownership and wealth are linked (although it's hard to say whether either causes the other, and if so, which causes which). So changes in house prices lead to changes in wealth. When we look at wealth directly in Chapter 13, homeownership will be a big part of the story.

The first section of this chapter looks at homeownership in general and whether we should care about it, and then at minority homeownership. The second section looks at mortgages in general and then at how minorities were treated in mortgage markets in the twentieth century. The third section tries to understand the credit and housing boom at the beginning of the twenty-first century and what it meant for minorities. Then we look at what happened in the Great Recession and its aftermath.

Homeownership

Some households own the place where they live and some rent it. In a world without tax distortions, the buy/rent decision would be based on transactions cost. If your use of a particular space for living didn't affect many other people and you were not going to share many services, you would own the property all by yourself: for instance, a farmhouse in Iowa. If your use affected many other people and they affected each other and you were going to share many services such as heat and air conditioning and elevators, then common ownership minimizes transactions costs, internalizes externalities, and reduces bargaining costs every time the elevator needs to be repaired; for instance, a dorm room at Columbia. The more goods and services you have that don't affect other people, the more likely you are to own your home; and the more goods and services you share with others, the more likely you are to rent. This is a simple, nonemotional decision. People who are richer and have bigger families and want to control more house should be more likely to own, and people in more densely populated places should be more likely to rent.

If this were all there were to homeownership, there would be no reason to be concerned about minority homeownership, any more than there is reason to be concerned about the racially different consumption of New-port and Marlboro cigarettes. There should be concern about the quality, location, and size of housing, but not much about ownership. To the extent that ownership is useful for access to certain types of housing, then it's nice to know about it, but the extent of homeownership is not a burning issue. If minorities can get access to great schools and nice neighborhoods without owning, ownership is no big deal. Conversely, the benefits of ownership can be measured directly in the quality of housing and life that people enjoy.

But that's not all there is, especially in the minds of many social commentators and politicians. Homeownership is said to be "the American dream."

Should We Care about Homeownership?

In some ways, consuming owner-occupied housing does create certain positive externalities in ways that consuming, say, pistachio ice cream does not.

Homeowners have different incentives to maintain the property they live in than renters do, and there is some evidence to indicate that they maintain it better, even though owners of big apartment complexes are more competent than owners of single-family homes. But homeowners may not do better than big landlords on property that other people use—for instance, shoveling snow in the winter.

Homeowners have different incentives to participate in civic life and local activities. They join more organizations and are more likely to vote in local elections than renters are. They are better informed. On the other hand, because of the way many of them are leveraged, owners may be overly risk averse, so their active civic participation may result in poor collective decisions. Owners, not renters, are usually the ones to exhibit a "NIMBY" (not in my backyard) reaction to any proposed change in the neighborhood environment.

Owners are more stable than renters. Since moving from an owner-occupied house is more costly than moving from an apartment, we don't know how much of the excess stability is due to selection (people don't buy a house unless they think they'll stick around for a while) and how much is due to treatment (if you selected people to be homeowners randomly, would they move less frequently than renters?). Probably both forces are operating. Moving, especially during the school year, is bad for kids, so stability is good for kids. On the other hand, stability slows down labor market adjustment.

High homeownership rates may lead to high unemployment rates (Blanch-flower and Oswald 2013).

A number of studies have found that children of owners do better in school than children of renters; these studies have tried to test for causality. The jury is still out on whether there is an effect beyond stability and selection.

Thus there is a plausible argument that homeownership might be a so-cially good thing. I said "plausible," not "definitive." We could achieve all of these goals in ways other than promoting homeownership. For incentives, we could enforce codes or give tax breaks for well-shoveled walks. For civic participation, we could subsidize access to Internet news. For stability, we could tax moving vans or establish rent control. For better citizenship or forced savings, we could (further) subsidize ownership of less risky assets, such as retirement accounts.

We could, but we don't. Instead, the federal government has established a series of large subsidies for owner-occupied housing. This book is not the place for a full description, but these subsides are substantial, hundreds of billions of dollars a year. Fannie Mae, Freddie Mac, and the Federal Housing Administration (FHA) are part of that system of subsidies, but the biggest subsidies are in the income tax code. Several studies (for example, Glaeser and Shapiro 2002) show that these subsidies don't affect the homeowner-ship rate, but they encourage people to buy larger houses (with some serious environmental consequences).

So we should be concerned about low homeownership by minorities be-cause minorities may gain from homeownership, given the subsidies taxpayers provide, and because of the possible external benefits that homeownership may create.

An equally valid reaction is that we should get rid of the subsidies (this is close to a consensus position among economists). Minorities would almost certainly gain from such a move in purely pecuniary terms, and there would be large efficiency gains for the economy as a whole. Don't hold your breath.

Minorities and Homeownership

Minorities are less likely than whites or NHW to own homes and have been for a long time. Figures 10.1 and 10.2 give some recent history.

In the long run, the gap has been closing, as you would expect. But since 2000 there has been little change on net in the gap for African Americans

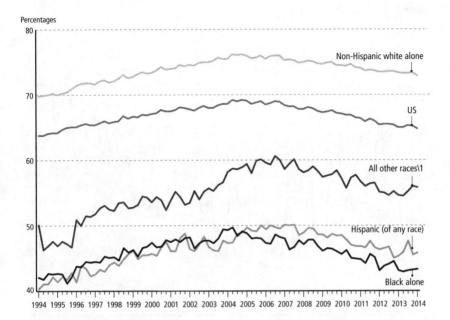

Figure 10.1. Homeownership rates.

and Asians, although there was strong growth in homeownership by Hispanics for a few years before the Great Recession began. Contrary to what you would expect from stories about subprime mortgages turning huge numbers of unqualified minorities into homeowners, Figure 10.1 shows little growth in the minority homeownership rate during the housing boom of the early twenty-first century, especially for blacks. The annual average homeownership rate for blacks rose from 47.2 percent in 2000 to only 47.8 percent in 2006, while the rate for Hispanics rose more substantially, from 46.3 percent to 49.7 percent. Relative to NHWs, blacks actually fell behind in homeownership—the gap between NHWs and blacks increased from 26.7 percent in 2000 to 28.0 percent in 2006—while Hispanics gained on NHWs a little—that gap decreased from 27.5 percent in 2000 to 26.2 percent in 2006. The NHW-Hispanic homeownership gap was 26 percent in almost all of 2007. (Since the number of minority households was rising much faster than the number of NHW households in this period and since minorities leave homeownership faster than NHWs, one part of the popular story

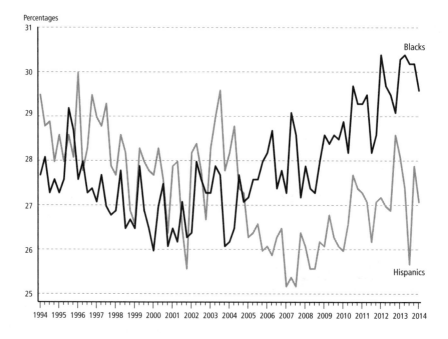

Figure 10.2. Gap between NHW homeownership rate and minority homeownership rates.

about the Great Recession is probably true: the majority of first-time home-owners in this period were almost certainly minorities.)

Of course, we know now that you have to run regressions with controls, not just look at raw differences. What are the results when we look at home-ownership and hold all the appropriate things constant?

Trying to hold all the appropriate variables constant is more difficult with homeownership than it is with labor and education because many of the variables need to be handled very carefully and some variables that we really want are not available in the data sets we have. And labor and education were not easy.

The variables that researchers almost always know and that are impor-tant are income, age, household size and composition (although it could be endogenous), and region (although it could be endogenous). These explain something about homeownership, but not a lot. The problem variables are credit score, wealth, and parental wealth. These three variables are good predictors of homeownership, but they are missing from many data sets on homeownership, and they may be endogenous. People who know that they can easily buy a house, for instance, may put more effort into maintaining a good credit score than people who think they are barred from homeownership (or think that they would have to pay a premium to become a homeowner).

Wealth can be endogenous too, in a way that can lead you astray if you are not careful. If the way you build wealth is by owning a house (because of weakness of will, for instance, when it comes to saving money) and if whites can buy houses and minorities can't, then whites will have wealth (and live in houses) and blacks won't do either, if you look at the cross-section. You may conclude that blacks don't own houses because they don't have wealth, when in fact the story is that blacks don't have wealth because they don't own houses.

In empirical work, Margo and Collins (2011) showed a large but declining unexplained gap throughout the twentieth century, and some early 1990s studies showed unexplained gaps in homeownership. But some of the more recent studies have suggested that the gap was declining during the 1990s. For instance, Gabriel and Rosenthal (2005), looking at the period up to 2001, found that about two-thirds of the gap was due to household characteristics and less than 5 percent was due to credit barriers.

Boehm and Schottman (2009) is probably the most sophisticated study about this period. They looked at renters and calculated transitions to and from homeownership and from first to second house in the 1990s and early 2000s. They used basic demographic information plus income and net wealth and household composition as controls. They didn't know credit scores. They fit separate equations for blacks and whites for all of the transitions I've mentioned.

The most convenient summary is the probability of being a homeowner at the end of eleven years. For households with average racial characteristics this probability was 21 percent for African Americans and 65 percent for whites. Then they did the equivalent of the two Blinder-Oaxaca decompositions. The civil rights experiment (white coefficients and black characteristics) raised the black homeownership rate after eleven years, but only to 36 percent. The enrichment experiment (black coefficients and white characteristics) was more powerful; it raised the black homeownership rate to

61 percent, which was below the white homeownership rate, but not by much. So the relevant contribution from race (civil rights experiment) was considerable, but it was far from the whole picture.

Theoretically, why should there be a gap, assuming the right variables are entered? Discrimination by realtors or mortgage companies would cause a gap. Blacks live (for reasons of history) in centralized neighborhoods with more apartments and may be stuck to some degree in those neighborhoods. The likely lower price of land in many minority neighborhoods could work in the opposite direction: owner-occupied houses may be cheaper in these neighborhoods than in much of the rest of the metropolitan area.

Mortgages

Most people have to get a mortgage to buy a house. In the United States, a mortgage is a loan with real property, like a house, as collateral. Mortgages in many states approximate being "non-recourse," but not in all states. "Non-recourse" means that if you default, that's the end of the story: the mortgage holder can't come after you for the difference between the outstanding amount on the mortgage and what it thinks the house is really worth. In finance terms, a non-recourse mortgage is a "put": it gives you the right to give your house to the mortgage holder at any time in return for a price equal to the outstanding amount of the mortgage.

If minorities have problems getting mortgages, they'll have problems buying houses. If they pay more for mortgages, they'll be less inclined to buy houses, and if they do buy houses, they'll enjoy the experience less.

What do we know about mortgage discrimination? A lot. But the studies are about a world that has disappeared (but may return).

We need to do a quick history of mortgages over the last century and see how the opportunities and setting for possible discrimination have changed.

Mortgage History

In the old days—before 1930—banks were local operations, often local monopolists. They had personal relationships with borrowers and held the mortgage after they originated it. Mortgage decisions were subjective and not especially competitive: they probably discriminated (but black banks did not flourish). Fisman, Paravisini, and Vig (2012), for instance, found with recent data from banks in India that cultural affinity, including caste, induced loan officers to make more loans (and the loans were more likely to be repaid).

The banks that made the loans held the mortgages until they were paid off (which was usually around five years in those days). If the homeowner defaulted, the bank that thought the deal was good was on the hook. Under this system, the bank had to confront many other types of risk: for instance, if interest rates went up, it would have to pay more money to its depositors but it would not be able to get more money from its borrowers. If house prices went down when the mortgage came due in five years, the homeowner might not be able to pay off the mortgage and the bank would have to take a house that was worth less than the mortgage.

The secondary market for mortgages started in the 1930s with the Federal National Mortgage Administration, now known as Fannie Mae. The federal government wanted to encourage long mortgages (at first twenty years but later thirty years), but banks didn't want the risks associated with tying up their money like this for such a long time. Fannie Mae, which was then part of the federal government, bought mortgages that met its standards from the banks so the banks would be free to adjust their holdings quickly. At that time, Fannie Mae sold its own bonds to raise the money to buy mortgages.

Securitization began with the Fannie Mae in the late 1960s (and later its younger sibling Freddie Mac) to get more funding to house the baby-boom generation. Instead of selling simple bonds, they promised to pay investors back based on how a group of mortgages actually performed. If the homeowners defaulted, Fannie or Freddie would absorb the loss, but if the homeowner paid off the mortgage before it was due, investors would get the principal but the interest would stop. With simple bonds, Fannie and Freddie had interest rate risk: if interest rates fell and homeowners refinanced their mortgages they would have to keep paying investors at the old higher rates even though they were not earning at those rates. But with securitization, the investors who buy the securities bear this risk.

While secondary markets improve the division of labor and securitization spreads uncorrelated risks better, they also have weaknesses. The secondary market raises moral hazard problems, and securitization creates risks when defaults are correlated. If I'm writing a mortgage I'm not going to hold,

I have less incentive to write a good mortgage—if it falls apart, someone else is going to take the hit.

That's obvious, so the secondary market was limited. Fannie and Freddie had rules and punishments for the banks they bought mortgages from. They were limited, for instance, to 30-year self-amortizing mortgages with low loan-to-value ratios to people with enough income and good credit scores. And if too many of a bank's mortgages defaulted, Fannie and Freddie could force it to buy all of its mortgages back. Many other types of assets have these same problems but have been successfully securitized for many years without blowing up the world financial system—student loans and credit card debt, for instance. And many loans were still held in banks' portfolios.

Automated underwriting developed in the 1980s and 1990s. This made it a lot easier for the secondary market to operate: decisions on mortgages came close to being made by machines, not by humans whose motives might be suspect—but who could also understand nuances and judge character (maybe).

Mortgage Discrimination in the 1990s

The apparent end of relationship banking for mortgages should also have been good news for minorities. Machines can't discriminate and none of the automatic underwriting programs included race; that would have been illegal. Banking became much more competitive as restrictions on interstate banking and usury laws were dropped. But automatic underwriting doesn't guarantee nondiscrimination: algorithms can place too much weight on variables correlated with race and thus engage in de facto statistical discrimination, which is illegal. Many human activities still surround the application process; discrimination can happen with them.

Two claims have been made about discrimination in mortgages: personal discrimination against minority applicants and geographic discrimination against minority neighborhoods—this is called redlining. These are distinct questions. Both of these claims are about denials, not rates. Denials are conditional on application, of course: if you don't apply, you can't be denied. I'll talk more about this in a little while.

The first good studies of mortgage discrimination date from the early 1990s, when automatic underwriting was first widely used, when banks and Fannie Mae and Freddie Mac still dominated the lending business, when banks still held many of the mortgages they originated, and when subprime was a word nobody knew.

The most ambitious and complete study of mortgage discrimination was conducted by the Boston Federal Reserve Bank. A team of researchers from that bank, led by Alicia Munnell, decided that they would stop listening to complaints from banks about errors due to variables that had been left out in previous studies that found mortgage discrimination. So they asked the bankers in New England to tell them what variables they used when making loan decisions. Then they asked the banks to give them all their files for minority applicants and a large sample of files of NHW mortgage applicants. They didn't ask for a few variables; they asked for everything. They're the Fed; they can do that.

Then they regressed the probability of loan denial on everything the banks had and everything that the banks said mattered. The conclusion was that race mattered considerably: a white applicant with the average characteristics of whites in the sample had an 11 percent chance of being turned down; a minority applicant with the exact same set of characteristics had a 17 percent chance of being turned down.

They found no evidence of redlining—race mattered, not space.

This work has stood up well under a torrent of challenges. Could it be because of sorting? Ross and Yinger (2002) checked different banks and rejected this explanation: there was not much difference between banks in denial rates. (Black-owned banks were somewhat worse than white-owned banks and definitely no better.)

The most plausible interpretation of these results is that loan officers, perhaps unconsciously, provide extra help to some white applicants—perhaps to their friends. They solicit additional information about their credit histories, find their explanations more credible and put them in better order, hint at how to put a slightly better face on their failings. Most applicants are clearly eligible or ineligible, of course, and friendly nudges can't help them, but for some applicants on the borderline, friendly nudges can be decisive. In a number of court cases about mortgage discrimination by particular banks, such friendly assistance was found to be the chief reason for racial disparity.

That was what happened after applicants applied. Audit studies from this period found differences in how people were treated before they applied. Studies in Pontiac, Louisville, Chicago, and Los Angeles found that before minorities could file applications, lenders showed them less enthusiasm than they showed whites. They seemed less interested in giving information; they urged blacks more frequently to go to other lenders or to secure an FHA loan; and they warned more often that the application process was arduous. Minorities got less coaching. Since these are audit studies, we don't know whether any of this mattered, but the first reaction is that it should have made minorities less likely to move, apply for mortgages, and own rather than rent. But we don't know.

On the other hand, a number of studies from this period found that blacks were more likely to default, even conditional on a lot of observable characteristics. This is the opposite of what the Jackie Robinson effect would tell you to look for. What's going on? Discrimination produces the Jackie Robinson effect if minorities and whites are drawn from the same distribution, given observable characteristics. If minorities have a worse distribution of unobservable characteristics, their average outcome can be worse, even if they are being discriminated against.

What unobservable characteristics could make minorities more likely to default, given observable characteristics? First, something could be different about minority neighborhoods. Loss in house values is a very good predictor of default (if your house retains its value but you don't have any money to pay the mortgage, you can sell the house, prepay the mortgage, and avoid default). Minority neighborhoods may have had different patterns of appreciation or depreciation in house prices in the time being studied.

Second, default isn't a simple process. It takes time and there are many ways to avoid default—selling the property, renegotiating the loan, arranging a second mortgage, finding a friend or relative to kick in. When things are going wrong, sophistication and friends with resources and sophistication help a lot. So does being liked by the loan officer. The other thing that helps in a time of trouble is a belief that others will help you. If minorities get less support in the job market, given observable characteristics, get worse medical care, given observable characteristics, and so on, why should I as a loan officer think that other people are going to cut them more slack? And if I don't think that other people will cut them more slack, I might as well foreclose and get my money now.

This behavior by 1990s banks was discrimination and was illegal. (As usual, I have no idea whether it was immoral.) It may also have been profit maximizing. What banks would have liked to do even more, maybe, would have been to charge minorities higher rates. This would also have been illegal if they did it directly and openly.

Mortgages and Houses in the Early Twenty-First-Century Boom

While economists were debating whether or not the mortgage market of the 1990s was discriminatory, the mortgage world changed and a lot of the debate became moot. Maybe. A few years ago I was tempted to stop talking about the 1990s because it seemed like ancient history. But it may very well be how the mortgage market is operating today or may be operating soon.

Mortgages in the Early 2000s

Between 2000 and 2007, household debt in the United States doubled, from $7 trillion to $14 trillion, and the household debt-to-income ratio increased from 1.4 to 2.1 (Mian and Sufi 2014, 4). Mortgages on houses led this increase.

These mortgages were both for purchases and for refinancing. Almost half of the credit expansion went to reduce the home equity of existing owners, not to finance changes of ownership (Mian and Sufi 2014, 87–88). Refinancing often led to greater consumption; many households that refinanced did not even pay down credit card debt.

Why household debt rose so fast over this period is somewhat controversial, but the most plausible and widely accepted explanation is that central banks and households in Asia had a great demand for safe, dollar-denominated assets. The central banks were reacting to the 1998 financial crisis, which may have taught them that the only way they could protect their autonomy against "hot money" was through massive defensive stockpiles of such assets.

Several new mortgage market institutions became prominent as debt rose. Most had first appeared on a small scale in the 1980s or 1990s, and probably none of them could have existed earlier, because they rely on information technology that developed late in the twentieth century. But the credit boom vastly expanded the scale on which they operated.

Monoline mortgage originators.   Monoline mortgage originators were companies such as Countrywide, New Century, and Ameriquest, almost all of which are out of business now. Unlike banks (and savings and loans), which both take deposits and give mortgages, these companies did no business other than originating mortgages. If you're going to sell the mortgages you originate into the secondary market anyway, why do you need a bank? Moreover, because they were not banks, they were not subject to bank regulation (including the Community Reinvestment Act). These new companies were nimbler than banks and could move faster to take advantage of profit opportunities. The moral hazard problem grew, of course, but the secondary market thought it could combat moral hazard with forced buyback provisions and automated underwriting.

Mortgage brokers.   With deregulation in the 1980s and 1990s and the proliferation of mortgage companies came a proliferation of mortgage products. When there are thousands of different ways to get a mortgage, you may want a guide, especially if you think you'll be turned down if you go to the wrong person. The guide you want is someone you trust. So people started to go into business as mortgage brokers—paid guides to the world of mortgages. Brokers were paid when the mortgage was granted, and they were in essence paid by the originator, not the homeowner. Both circumstances create moral hazard by giving brokers incentives to push their clients to accept disadvantageous deals.

Private-label securitization.   Wall Street firms started getting into the same business as Fannie and Freddie. But they did it somewhat differently, since they didn't think they had the same backup from the federal treasury.

The private companies took a pool of mortgages and sold several different tranches of securities against it. A tranche is a set of securities subject to the same rules. The most senior tranches got the first payments that came in every month from the mortgages in the pool. Whatever money was left over after the senior tranche got what it was due went to the next most senior tranche, and so on. A lower tranche got something only if every more senior tranche had been satisfied. So the most senior tranches were thought to be very safe and the least senior tranches were thought to be risky.

With private-label securities, then, investors in the junior tranches (often hedge funds) in essence guaranteed the investors in the more senior tranches. But the guarantee was limited.

The safety of the senior tranches relies on the independence of the risks in the pool. In the extreme, suppose that whenever one mortgage in the pool defaults they all do and all are worthless. This is an extreme example of correlated risks. Then the senior tranches are just as risky as the junior ones. To guard against correlated risks, Wall Street firms assembled pools that were geographically diversified, since the postwar United States had seen only regional housing crashes, never anything on a national scale (until 2006).

Subprime mortgages.   There are many different definitions of "subprime" mortgages, but the basic idea is that these are mortgages that few banks would want to write in the old days. They had features such as a high loan-to-value ratio, a high ratio of debt to income, little or no documentation of income or assets, very slow reduction of principal, or homeowners with poor credit scores. The characteristics of both the house and borrower matter, since the house is the collateral and the ultimate guarantee of the value of the mortgage.

Private-label securitization and subprime mortgages are tied together. Suppose private-label securitization doesn't exist and I write a subprime mortgage. What am I going to do with it? Fannie Mae and Freddie Mac bought few such mortgages except at the height of the housing bubble, so selling it to one of them would be difficult. If I'm a bank it's not going to be wise for me to hold them in my portfolio, partly because banks aren't supposed to hold a lot of risky stuff and partly because housing risk is geographically correlated. If I'm a monoline mortgage originator I don't have any way of funding it over the long term. So while a few subprime mortgages could be written before private-label securitization was robust, the market was limited.

The credit expansion was not uniform across cities and neighborhoods. It was strongest in zip codes where average credit scores were lowest and where mortgages had been denied in the past. Zip codes with these characteristics are often heavily minority. Mortgages to buy houses rose 30 percent a year in low credit-score neighborhoods from 2002 to 2005 but only 11 percent a year in high credit-score neighborhoods (Mian and Sufi 2014, 77). In low credit-score neighborhoods, the denial rate fell from 42 percent to 30 percent, although the application rate soared. This expansion occurred even though income was falling in low credit-score neighborhoods and rising in high credit-score neighborhoods (Mian and Sufi 2014, 79).

The Housing Bubble

Largely as a result of the credit boom, house prices rose sharply at the beginning of the twenty-first century, especially in the low credit-score zip codes where the lending expansion had been concentrated. From 2002 to 2006, house prices went up 80 percent in low credit-score neighborhoods and 40 percent in high credit-score neighborhoods (Mian and Sufi 2014, 81).

Rising house prices made every loan look safe. Lenders started offering loans designed to take advantage of rising home prices. These were loans with little or no buildup of equity unless prices kept rising: 3/27 and 2/28 adjustable rate mortgages (ARMs), no-interest loans, very long loans, pay-option loans. (A 3/27 ARM has a fixed low interest rate for three years, then the interest rate resets for 27 years to a higher level that depends on the current prevailing rate of interest. A 2/28 ARM is the same, except that the reset occurs after two years, not three. In a pay-option loan, the borrower has great flexibility in making payments; whatever she doesn't pay is automatically added to principal.) If default occurred, the lenders would get a house more valuable than the original loan because of appreciation. If renegotiation happened because the monthly payments were high, there would be more fees. Owners were just vessels through which anticipated house price appreciation would pass through to lenders. Their characteristics didn't matter.

Moral hazard played a role here too. As long as the secondary market was buying these loans (because some of the tranches would be safe and because serious nationwide depreciation of house prices was seen as almost impossible), all the originators and the brokers at the front end cared about was volume: they made their money on fees. So they needed more and more business.

Since rising house prices can cause easier credit and easier credit can cause rising house prices, some controversy exists over which came first. Mian and Sufi (2014, 83) argue convincingly for the credit explanation. Because of how topography affects the degree of ease with which new homes can be built, some cities (such as Houston) did not experience much of a housing price boom, while others (such as San Francisco) had huge housing price rises, partly because supply could not increase rapidly. It's a lot easier to expand housing supply in Houston than in San Francisco. If housing prices were the driving force, you would not expect to see much expansion of credit in cities such as Houston. But credit expanded in those cities too.

Of course, the importance of credit expansion does not mean that nothing else could have affected house prices. The number of Hispanic and Asian households grew considerably in this period. From 2000 to 2007, the number of Hispanic households grew by 35 percent and the number of Asian households grew by 42 percent (by contrast, the number of black households increased by 11 percent and the number of NHW households increased by only 4 percent). Because of this, demand probably increased in neighborhoods where Hispanics and Asians wanted to buy houses and could buy houses, and if housing supply had not responded strongly, house prices would have risen even more in these neighborhoods.

Subprime Loans and Minorities

Subprime loans, however you define them, went disproportionately to minorities, and minorities seem to have received loans with worse terms than similarly situated NHWs. Several empirical studies and an important legal document show this. But nobody has perfect data.

This is a conclusion you might already expect from all of the results about low credit-score neighborhoods and the concentration of blacks and Hispanics in these neighborhoods.

Avery, Brevoort, and Canner (2006) looked at loans that originated in 2005, the height of the bubble. Even though only a fifth of the loans that NHWs got were subprime, a majority of the loans that blacks got were subprime. Hispanics were also disproportionately likely to get subprime loans, rather than prime ones; Asians were less likely. The borrower characteristics that Avery and his colleagues had access to explained very little of the racial difference in subprime loans. They had information on income but not on credit scores or wealth. Who originated the loan was what mattered most in determining what kind of loan was made. Blacks and Hispanics got subprime loans because they dealt with lenders who gave subprime loans. But we don't know why they dealt with these lenders.

Mayer and Pence (2008) had different data—the proprietary data that investors had on privately securitized loans. They didn't know the race of borrowers, but they knew important underwriting information such as credit scores. Because they didn't know the borrowers' race, they used census tracts as their unit of observation. Census tracts with greater black population and greater Hispanic population in 2000 had more (privately securitized) subprime loans, relative to both total housing units and total reported mortgages.

Calem, Gillen, and Wachter (2004) combined both approaches on somewhat older data, but they looked only at Philadelphia and Chicago. They regressed the probability that a loan was subprime on both race of the borrower and neighborhood racial composition and found that both mattered. Holding borrower income, neighborhood foreclosure rates, and neighborhood credit scores constant, both having a minority owner and being in a minority neighborhood made a loan more likely to be subprime. However, they lacked important control variables such as loan-to-value ratio, so the finding was not definitive.

Reid and Laderman (2009) merged several different data sets to estimate the probability of receiving a subprime loan (rather than a prime loan) in California from 2004 to 2006. They knew borrower race and almost all the usual underwriting variables. They found that black and Hispanic borrowers were significantly more likely to get subprime loans than Asian or NHW borrowers. The effect of being black or Hispanic was like losing 100 points on a FICO score. For blacks, working through a mortgage broker greatly increased the probability of getting a subprime loan; for whites, the effect was considerably smaller.

Thus although no single study was definitive, several different approaches pointed in the same direction: either minority borrowers or borrowers from minority neighborhoods were more likely to get subprime loans, holding important variables constant. Some minority borrowers or borrowers from minority neighborhoods got subprime loans when otherwise identical NHW borrowers or borrowers from NHW neighborhoods got prime loans. Since subprime loans generally had less attractive terms than prime loans (higher interest rates, for instance, and stiffer prepayment penalties), this meant that minority borrowers had less attractive, more expensive loans.

Within the class of subprime loans, it's unclear in the academic literature whether minority borrowers or borrowers from minority neighborhoods were treated better or worse than other borrowers. Haughwout, Mayer, and Tracy (2009) looked at a particular type of subprime loan (2/28 ARMs) originated in a particular month (August 2005) and sold in the private secondary market. They found essentially no difference between minorities and NHWs in loan terms, holding the usual controls constant. Ghent, Hernandez-Murillo, and Owyang (2011), however, found that minority borrowers received somewhat worse terms on a variety of subprime products, not just 2/28 ARMs. Their data covered only California and Florida.

Probably the most detailed look at how the subprime market operated comes from a legal complaint that Justice Department filed against Countrywide, a now-defunct monoline originator, in December 2011. Countrywide was probably the largest subprime originator during the housing bubble, and the Justice Department analyzed all its records. The complaint alleged discrimination against minorities. Countrywide's successor organization, the Bank of America, settled the complaint almost immediately. We can learn a lot by examining this complaint.

First, the complaint is about disparate impact, not disparate treatment. When you run regressions, minorities get worse loan terms, holding everything else constant. It includes no hypotheses about individuals treating people of different races differently.

Second, the complaint is mainly about the treatment of Hispanics, since Countrywide was based in California. Many African Americans are involved, but the majority of cases are Hispanics.

Where did the Justice Department find disparate impact? Three areas: discrimination in the form of higher rates for minorities when minorities applied to Countrywide employees for mortgages; discrimination in the form of higher rates for minorities when they applied through brokers; and discrimination in the form of Countrywide employees steering minorities into subprime mortgages, which are more expensive, when similar NHWs were getting prime mortgages.

This discrimination took place through the discretion of individual employees or brokers; there were no company-wide policies. But company-wide compensation schemes may have been rewarding employees/brokers for this discrimination (or maybe not).

To see this, let's examine the first claim—rate discrimination by employees. The other two claims are similar in this regard. Every day Countrywide sent out a rate chart—what rates you were supposed to offer to each applicant for each type of mortgage, based on relevant characteristics of the applicant and the house. But employees had discretion in how they used this rate chart. They could offer higher or lower rates. If they offered higher rates and the applicant accepted, it was called an overage, and they were rewarded in their pay. If they offered lower rates and the applicant accepted, it was called a shortage, and they lost money in their pay. Their pay also depended on the number of mortgages they sold, and they were compensated more for subprime than for prime mortgages.

Disparate impact rests on the finding that minorities consistently ended up with more overages than shortages, even though all the relevant underwriting characteristics were supposed to be in the rate sheet. The Justice

Department essentially said that Countrywide did the relevant disparate impact regression without a race variable to make up the race sheet and that the average overage or shortage would be the coefficient on race in a full regression. Just to make sure, the Justice Department regressed the overage/shortage on a large group of characteristics in the file, and once again found that minorities paid more relative to the rate sheet and holding all the relevant characteristics constant again. The Justice Department didn't commit itself on what these regressions mean.

So what's going on here? Why were employees and brokers using their discretion to offer worse terms to minority borrowers? The fact that they were compensated more if the mortgages are worse is important, but it's not sufficient to explain this behavior. They were rewarded for offering bad mortgages to NHWs too, but they did not do so to the same extent. And they did not offer infinitely bad mortgages, as dumb greedy people would.

Consider the alternatives. It's unlikely that they were statistical discriminators. They didn't lose money if the mortgage defaulted; that's not in their compensation schemes. Countrywide didn't think it would lose money either—Countrywide was going to sell the mortgage into the secondary market within a few weeks of its origination, and as far as I know, mortgages to minorities did not carry a discount in the secondary market.

Secondary market buyers could not identify the race of the borrower and probably didn't look at the zip code. Indeed, considerable evidence suggests that investors and rating agencies were not simply race blind, they were totally blind, or totally fooled by the securitizers. Piskorski, Seru, and Witkin (2013) found that in private-label securitization pools, a tenth of mortgages were misclassified as owner-occupied when in fact the mortgages were taken out by investors. Investors are considerably more likely to default than owner-occupants, and securitizers blatantly withheld this relevant, perfectly legal information from investors. Ashcraft, Goldsmith-Pinkham, and Vickery (2010) showed that ratings agencies systematically ignored simple information such as credit scores when rating mortgage-backed securities when that information could have helped predict defaults. In an atmosphere where legal information that should have been used was hidden or ignored, it is unlikely that a lot of attention would have been paid to making inferences about race.

And in this era foreclosures were rare (because a borrower with personal difficulties could easily sell the house and pay the mortgage off) and not very costly (because the lenders would get a house that was probably at least as valuable as the mortgage).

Were Countrywide employees Becker-style taste discriminators? This is possible, but it doesn't seem overwhelmingly plausible. The contact between borrower and lender is a few hours of time; it's not like being an employee or a spouse. Countrywide advertised itself as a company that was opening up homeownership to minorities; it doesn't seem likely that people who disliked minorities would be eager to work for this company. Brokers were overwhelmingly people drawn from the minority community and they were selected for their ability to get along with co-ethnics and establish rapport with them, so of course they were disproportionately minorities themselves.

The most plausible explanation to me is that they were discriminatory monopolists. This is like the theory we saw in Chapter 5 about how search in labor markets with some discriminatory employers leads all employers to discriminate. The employees and brokers were worried that if they raised the margin too much they would lose the sale. But they were less afraid to lose the sale with minorities—maybe because minorities were more likely to be denied at the banks that held the mortgages in their portfolios (although Washington Mutual held loans in its portfolio and made lots of minority loans, most of them of terrible quality), maybe because minorities thought they would be denied loans at traditional banks even if that belief was incorrect, maybe because minorities tended to be more gullible or more trusting or less sophisticated. Or possibly because minority neighborhoods were less competitive or minority borrowers were less likely to search for mortgages online. So employees and brokers thought they could offer worse terms to minorities and get away with it—and they were right.

In a sense you can look at companies such as Countrywide as taking advantage of discrimination elsewhere in the market. Traditional lenders deny loans to minorities, so Countrywide could offer loans at terms that are very favorable to Countrywide and unfavorable to the borrowers. And it could sell those loans into the secondary market, which didn't recognize race.

Homeownership in the Boom

With all this financing activity directed at minorities and minority neighborhoods, why was the rise in the homeownership rate so anemic, especially for blacks? Gerardi and Willen (2009) give several possible reasons. The most obvious one is that most of the activity was refinancing. Refinancing doesn't raise the homeownership rate. The second answer is the decrease in FHA lending. Because subprime originators took the FHA's core borrowers, it withered in this period (and hardly anybody in Washington cared that it withered). From 1996 to 2005, the FHA market share for all origination mortgages fell from 19 percent to 6 percent, but its share among minority borrowers fell much more precipitously, from 32 percent to 7 percent.

The final reason is that turnover increased: people entered homeownership at a higher rate, but they also left it at a higher rate (as might be expected with subprime mortgages and personal problems).

It may make more sense to ask this question differently, since homeownership is not valuable in itself; it is valuable only as a tool for furthering other, more fundamental goals—stability, wealth accumulation, a stake in the community, and access to better schools and neighborhoods, especially integrated schools and neighborhoods. Intuitively, the type of lending that Countrywide was doing does not seem to further these goals. But little empirical work has been done on this yet. Segregation for blacks decreased in the 2000s, which might indicate that subprime lending promoted segregation, but segregation for Hispanics didn't and Hispanics appear to have been the focus of lending.

Homeownership is often thought of as a way for people to build wealth. But reducing the credit market constraints that hindered minority homeownership did little to reduce the wealth gap. Hispanics gained considerable wealth during the boom, as you might expect with their strong rise in homeownership, but blacks gained little and fell behind Hispanics. The bust wiped out all wealth gains, and by 2011 neither Hispanics nor blacks had more wealth than they did in 1999 (Gorbachev and Sethi 2014).

The Great Recession

The housing market started to fall in 2006, and the subprime monoline originators mainly went bankrupt in summer 2007, as the securitizers asked them to buy back mortgages and they couldn't. The rest of the story you know. House prices fell an average of 30 percent—much more in the places where they had risen the most. $5.5 trillion in presumed housing value evaporated (Mian and Sufi 2014, 19, 21). Defaults and foreclosures occurred at rates unseen since the Great Depression.

What do we know about defaults? Many, many different pieces—nobody has a perfect data set. But in almost every data set, minorities appear to be a larger share of defaults than of homeowners.

Perhaps the best early study was of Cleveland. Coulton et al. (2008) did a full census of defaults in Cuyahoga County. African Americans were much more likely to default in both prime and subprime loans, and homeowners with brokered loans were even more likely to default.

Many other studies with securitized mortgages show that either minority neighborhoods or minority borrowers are more likely to default, holding a lot of other variables constant.

The most recent study is Bayer, Ferreira, and Ross (2013), which looked at a large number of mortgages over seven metropolitan areas, and merged three different data sets, holding a large number of other variables constant. They found that blacks and Hispanics were considerably more likely to default and be foreclosed on than NHWs, and that Asians were slightly more likely. This was especially true for loans that originated at the height of the boom; for earlier or later loans, race and ethnicity didn't appear to matter.

Why? We know that the many minority borrowers who had the same observable underwriting characteristics as the NHW borrowers who got prime loans got subprime loans. So if the probability of default is the same for minorities and NHWs given observable underwriting characteristics, minorities should be less likely to default on both prime and subprime loans (although perhaps more likely to default overall). This is the Jackie Robinson effect applied twice. But the opposite is true in the Bayer, Ferreira, and Ross data, although their measure of "subprime"—"high cost loans" in HUD's comprehensive mortgage origination data—is crude.

Why? I don't know. Here are three possibilities.

First, the distributional argument—minorities and buyers in minority neighborhoods might have worse unobserved characteristics conditional on observed characteristics. We've examined this already in the discussion of the 1990s.

Second, minorities may have received worse loans contingent on observed characteristics. This is the implication of the first two counts of the Countrywide complaint and the consistent finding that minorities were more likely to get subprime loans. To simplify, think of loans as three-year balloons, which is close to what they were. "Worse loan" in this case means that minority borrowers have to repay more at the end of three years than NHW borrowers (points, rate, overappraisal, prepayment penalty, and so on). Then for the same shock to house prices, minority-owned homes would be more likely to be under water and hence more likely to default. Bayer, Ferreira, and Ross controlled for whether a loan was "high cost" or not and found that this does not predict default.

Third, minorities may have been hit harder by the Great Recession. This could have happened in either the labor market or the housing market. Hoynes, Miller, and Schaller (2012) show that minorities did worse than whites in the labor market, and when Bayer, Ferreira, and Ross added *race-specific* county-level unemployment rates to their regressions, the minority effect on delinquency and default fell sharply but didn't disappear. Controlling for county-level housing prices and possible negative equity doesn't reduce the effect of race, but Hoynes, Miller, and Schaller didn't have data on whether house prices in minority neighborhoods fell more or less than house prices in other neighborhoods in the same county.

Fourth, minorities may have had less cushioning to deal with the shocks they received. Cushioning would mean other sources of income and wealth, other sources of borrowing, and in general ways of mitigating the loss of income or home equity. Wealthy relatives would be a good example of cushioning. There is not a lot of direct evidence on this question. Bayer, Ferreira, and Ross interpret the concentration of defaults on borrowers who got loans peak of the boom by surmising that the borrowers who were drawn in at the peak were the most vulnerable. This is plausible, but as of yet there is no direct evidence.

What is well known is that defaults cause major neighborhood externalities. Some of these externalities are physical—crime and neighborhood deterioration. So minority neighborhoods are now suffering from these costs and are likely to continue to do so.

Neighborhood effects bring up another possible reason for the high minority default rate: contagion. If very bad loans are concentrated, defaults are also going to be concentrated, which leads to loss of house values in the neighborhoods where these loans are concentrated, which leads to more defaults. Some studies show some concentration of defaults, but it might be particular brokers rather than a dynamic like this. Bayer, Ferreira, and Ross didn't have neighborhood level data or data on broker involvement.

The Aftermath

After the Great Recession ended, minority homeownership rates continued to fall. By early 2014, the black homeownership had fallen all the way back to where it was in 1995 and the Hispanic rate had fallen to where it was in 2000. By 2013, the gap between NHWs and blacks was bigger than it had ever been since consistent data started being collected in 1994, and the gap between NHWs and Hispanics was back to about where it had been in 2000. Part of the reason for these disproportionate declines was defaults, but there were many other reasons why minorities left homeownership or failed to enter it.

House prices too continued to fall for several years after the Great Recession, especially in the minority neighborhoods where they had risen most steeply. As we will see in Chapter 13, the modest gains in wealth that minorities had made in the housing boom were wiped out or more than wiped out by the recession. By 2013 and 2014, almost all the relevant numbers looked like the 1990s again.

Many of the housing market institutions that flourished in the early 2000s also all but disappeared. Monoline mortgage originators, private-label securitization, and even the word "subprime" became all but invisible. The big question that has not been studied is whether the discriminatory practices in mortgage denial that characterized the 1990s returned along with the rest of the generally more conservative lending practices that characterized that decade.

Conclusion

The common story in the media about the early-twentieth-century credit and housing boom is misleading. That story is something like this: for unknown reasons, lenders let a bunch of minorities buy houses even though they were not qualified to buy houses. Of course they screwed up, because not everyone is qualified enough to own a house. When they screwed up, the markets crashed and we all got caught in the Great Recession.

The more left-wing common story is also misleading: things are always worse for minorities no matter what.

My view is something like this. The expansion of subprime loans and se-curitization (and the belief that house prices would never go down) decreased discrimination against minorities in one part of the mortgage market. The gains to minorities from this good news were limited by minority distrust of traditional banks, which allowed brokers and originators to act like dis-criminating monopolists and get minorities to accept worse mortgage prod-ucts. (This distrust was clearly warranted in earlier decades, but we don't know about the first decade of the twenty-first century.) The gains were also limited by other continuing problems in the housing market. For instance, no matter how great a mortgage you can get, you still may not want to live in a neigh-borhood where you will be treated as an outcast and your son might be shot for wearing a hoodie. Finally, the gains from new, less-discriminatory lenders came partly at the expense of a lender that was already less discriminatory—the FHA.

The story then is an example of Myrdal's virtuous circle not working. De-creased discrimination in one market did not set off a round of improve-ments in other markets; instead, any improvements in minority well-being were constrained by other markets.

When the bubble burst, defaults hit hardest in minority neighborhoods for a variety of reasons that we don't quite understand, including worse mortgage products, weaker support networks, the great reluctance of most people (that is, NHWs) to buy houses in minority neighborhoods, and con-tagion. Investors in minority neighborhoods would have done really well (partly at the expense of minority borrowers) if house prices had kept rising. When house prices instead fell, most of them appear to have done rather poorly.

The lesson I take from this is that creating a single color-blind market (secondary mortgages) is unlikely to do much for anyone as long as race mat-ters in almost all other related markets. This is especially true when color blindness is based on a false belief; in this case, that house prices would keep rising. Magic bullets don't work (especially when they're poorly aimed).

The U.S. housing finance system will have to be rebuilt in the next de-cade or so, and it's possible that a lot of this book's readers will participate in this process. The policies the United States has used to improve minority access to capital markets have not worked very well, and there's almost zero talk of alternative policies (including from me). But there ought to be.

The deeper question is how people confront the financial decisions they have to make and not get swindled—not just with mortgages but also with medical insurance, student loans, retirement savings, and long-term care insurance. This question would be hard enough in a homogeneous society where common trust was not an issue. But when you combine U.S. history with the type of poor outcomes that just happened in the subprime market, the question becomes a lot more difficult.

11

Crime

Even though crime has declined tremendously since 1991, it's still a central concern in how Americans think about race. (Perhaps Barack Obama would not have been elected president in 2008 without this crime decline.) For African Americans in particular, the costs of crime are enormous; the costs of crime for other minority groups are not so well known.

The most obvious costs of crime are those of being a victim. Minorities are disproportionately crime victims.

Then there are the costs of avoiding becoming a victim: locks, keys, security guards, taxicab rides, and so on. David Anderson (1999) estimated these costs at around $130 billion a year in the 1990s. The researchers who studied the Moving to Opportunity project attributed the stress and other psychological costs of living in a low-income neighborhood to rampant crime.

Your costs of avoiding crime are not limited to the steps you take. Especially if you're an African American male, the costs to you include the steps that others take to avoid you out of fear of crime. As Elijah Anderson (2011, 255) writes: "Many Americans feel apprehensive about encountering anonymous black people in public places. A strange black man can be viewed as criminal or crime prone until he can prove he is not, which is difficult to do in the split-second interaction that occurs in public places." Stereotypes about African Americans and crime may explain much of the reluctance of NHWs to move to minority neighborhoods or send their children to school there and some of the discrimination many black men report while shopping. Employers may also fear and distrust black men. In the extreme, some innocent black men such as Trayvon Martin may die because of the stereotype of black men as criminals.

The costs of crime also include the costs of running the police, judicial, and correctional systems. U.S. taxpayers shelled out about $258 billion for these systems in 2009 (Kyckelhahn 2012).

But taxpayers aren't the only ones who pay for these agencies' operations. African Americans and Hispanics are disproportionately stopped on highways or on city sidewalks when police are looking for criminals, and these stops carry significant costs in terms of time and humiliation. Incarceration also imposes great costs, not only on prisoners and inmates themselves who give up freedom and the opportunity to make a living, but also on their families, children, neighbors, and employers. It affects women's bargaining power, as we argued in Chapter 8. Prisoners are disproportionately minorities.

And the costs of prison do not end when you walk out the gate. Parole and probation impose strong restrictions on individual freedoms, and a criminal record follows you for life. A record deprives you of some formal rights—voting in many states, eligibility for public housing and student loans, ability to qualify for many licensed occupations. Landlords and employers often turn away people with criminal records.

Michelle Alexander (2012, 141) points to an interesting analogy:

Today a criminal freed from prison has scarcely more rights, and arguably less respect, than a freed slave or black person living "free" in Mississippi at the height of Jim Crow. . . . The "whites only" signs may be gone, but new signs have gone up—notices placed in job applications, rental agreements, loan applications, forms for welfare benefits, school applications, petitions for licenses, informing the general public that "felons" are not wanted here. A criminal record today authorizes precisely the forms of discrimination we supposedly left behind—discrimination in employment, housing, education, public benefits, and jury service.

No one has tried to quantify all these costs. But they are so large and so concentrated on African Americans—and Hispanics to a somewhat lesser extent—that a serious study has to be made of how the United States handles crime. That's the goal of this chapter, although I fall quite a bit short of attaining it.

The chapter will be economics, because this is a question of costs and benefits for the entire society. Often discussions of crime policies ignore the costs to people who have done something wrong and to their families and people who look like them; often discussions of punishment ignore the benefits that the threat of punishment brings from reducing crime. Neither approach is good economics. You can't be a good economist if you ignore either group or the costs they bear.

The first three sections of the chapter will ask why costs are so concentrated. The first is about traditional crimes with victims, the second section is about illicit drugs, and the third section is about incarceration and corrections. The last section is about policy: Are there good ways to reduce the total crime costs that minorities bear?

Most of the emphasis in this chapter will be on African Americans. Criminal justice data about Hispanics tend to be unreliable (since few data are self-reported), and Hispanic and Asian involvement with the criminal justice system appears to be smaller than African American involvement. In looking at data in this chapter, however, you should remember from Chapter 3 that reports of peoples' races are not always stable and that being labeled a criminal sometimes changes the racial labeling people carry from white to black. We don't know how big a problem this is.

Index Crimes

Index crimes are seven serious crimes about which the FBI collects data for its crime index. These crimes are murder, rape (and sexual assault), robbery, aggravated assault (these are called personal crimes or crimes of violence), burglary, theft or larceny, and motor vehicle theft—these are called property crimes. (By an act of Congress, arson has been legally considered an index crime since 1979, but because it is rare and poorly reported we will not pay much attention to it.) The index crimes have immediate easily identifiable victims, and they are pretty bad. They are also crimes where the offender and victim, or the offender and the victim's house, have to be in close physical proximity. Across history, there have been some cultural differences about what constitutes these crimes, but consensus in the United States today about these crimes is quite strong, although not perfect (the definition of rape, and the distinction between justifiable homicide and murder are the major areas of difference).

The index crimes do not include crimes without immediate victims (such as drug abuse or maybe prostitution), white-collar crimes (such as fraud and embezzlement), and computer crimes. The amount of money transferred by white-collar crimes dwarfs the amount transferred by index crimes (Bernard Madoff alone took more than all the robbers in the United States have stolen in the past half-century), but the kind of steps you take to avoid being a victim of white-collar crime are different from the steps you take to avoid being a victim of index crime. People who are afraid of black men are usually not afraid that they will plant viruses on their computers.

Crime is an emotional topic. Being labeled a criminal is much more emotionally powerful than being labeled, say, poorly educated. For obvious reasons, we don't really know who commits index crimes. I'll start with information that's fairly good and work up to more controversial and speculative areas. In this listing, I'll include information about many dimensions of crime: who victims are, where victims live, who is punished for committing crimes, and who actually commits crimes. These categories are conceptually distinct, but we have to look at all of them in order to get a full picture of the basic disparities in crime.

Fairly Good Facts

Victimization.   Blacks and Hispanics are more likely than whites to be victims of index crimes. For six of the index crimes, these data come from the National Criminal Victimization Survey (NCVS). This is a household survey that the federal government takes every year. Surveyors ask a sample of households whether they were crime victims last year, and if they were, they ask a lot of questions about the crime. The NCVS doesn't have information about murder (of course). Murder data come from the FBI, which compiles reports from most police departments in the nation. The race of murder victims is not self-identified and is subject to error (this is especially true for Hispanics). (Medical examiners also provide vital statistics for homicide victims, but their racial and ethnic classifications aren't highly reliable either.)

Table 11.1 gives information on victimization. Minorities are considerably more likely to be victims of crime than whites.

Table 11.1. Victimization rates by race and ethnicity.

	Black	Hispanic	White	
Murder	19.6		3.3	per 100,000 people, 2008
Rape	1.1*	0.8*	0.7	per 1,000 people aged 12 and up, 2010
Robbery	3.6	2.7	1.4	
Aggravated assault	4.4	3.0	3.2	
Burglary	42.0	34.3	23.6	per 1,000 households, 2008
Theft	99.6	141.4	96.3	
Motor vehicle theft	12.6	11.7	5.4	
	9.4		3.7	per 1,000 vehicles

Sources: U.S. Federal Bureau of Investigation (2009) for murder data from Uniform Crime Reports; U.S. Bureau of Justice Statistics (2011) for other crimes from National Criminal Victimization Survey.
*Indicates very small sample.

The big difference for blacks is murder. Murder victimization rates are especially high for young men: over the period 2002–2011, the murder victimization rate for black males peaked at age 23 at 100.3 per 100,000; the peak for white males was age 20 at 11.4 (Smith and Cooper 2013). Recall from Chapter 4 that homicide was responsible for a major portion of the racial difference in life expectancy.

Blacks and Hispanics are also especially likely to be robbery victims and motor vehicle theft victims. Housing markets may have a lot to do with motor vehicle theft, since minorities are more likely than NHWs to live in housing that doesn't have garages. For rape, burglary, and theft, the racial differences don't appear to be too big, and a lot of it could be explained by income. But murder appears to be off the charts.

The big difference in murder rates is in metropolitan areas. The racial gap in murder rates is much bigger in metropolitan areas than in rural areas; some studies have found a fairly small gap or even none at all in rural areas. Within races, metropolitan areas have higher murder rates than rural areas and bigger metropolitan areas have higher rates than smaller ones.

Neighborhoods. Crime is not spread randomly over the face of the earth; it's concentrated in a small number of locations. In a famous study of where crime occurred in Minneapolis, Sherman et al. (1989) found that 45,561 places (addresses or intersections) had no police calls in a year and 3,841 had more than fifteen. The 3,841 places with more than fifteen calls generated 50.4 percent of the calls police received, even though they were only 3.3 percent of the places in Minneapolis.

The places with a lot of crime tend to be in minority, especially African American, neighborhoods. In the Newark metropolitan area, for instance, six towns have heavily African American populations (they usually have African American mayors, for instance). Those towns had 24.9 percent of the metropolitan area's population in 2011. Even though they covered only 2.6 percent of the land area, 85.6 percent of the metropolitan area's murders, 79.9 percent of its robberies, 77.4 percent of its motor vehicle thefts, and 73.4 percent of its aggravated assaults were committed there (burglary [51.8 percent] and theft [34.9 percent]) were not so heavily concentrated) (O'Flaherty and Sethi 2015). The MTO project showed that living in a high-crime neighborhood is bad for mental and physical health, even if one is not a direct victim of crime.

Arrests.   Blacks are disproportionately likely to be arrested for most crimes, but some crimes stand out. Blacks represent about a quarter of young men in poverty, so their arrest rates for burglary and theft do not seem surprising. But the relative rates for murder and robbery are high. The relative black arrest rate is high for gambling too; Asians are also arrested disproportionately for gambling. On the other hand, whites seem to dominate arson and driving while intoxicated. The data on arrests are in Table 11.2.

Incarceration.   Since 1980, the population in American jails and prisons has grown very quickly. Minorities are the overwhelming majority of inmates and prisoners (see Tables 11.3 and 11.4).

Almost all prisoners are men. Black men are roughly six times as likely to be incarcerated as NHW men on a given night, and Hispanic men are more than twice as likely. About 4.6 percent of black men were incarcerated on July 1, 2007. Slice more thinly and you get very big numbers: among black men without high school diplomas between 26 and 35 years old, about a third are incarcerated on any given day. Petit and Western (2004) estimate that of African American men born between 1965 and 1969, the proportion

Table 11.2. Percentage of arrestees by race and crime category, 2010.

	White	Black	Asian
Murder	49.3	48.7	0.9
Rape	65.7	31.8	1.2
Robbery	43.3	55.0	1.0
Aggravated assault	63.7	33.5	0.9
Burglary	67.4	30.8	0.9
Theft	68.9	28.3	1.4
Motor vehicle theft	63.3	34.0	1.4
Arson	75.2	22.6	1.1
Weapons possession	58.2	40.1	1.0
Prostitution	54.3	42.4	2.6
Drug	66.6	31.8	0.8
Gambling	28.8	67.5	3.3
Driving while intoxicated	85.7	11.5	1.5

Source: University at Albany (2014).

Table 11.3. Number of inmates at midyear, 2009.

Jails	767,620
Federal prisons	206,577
State prisons	1,410,901
Total	2,385,098

Sources: Minton (2010) for jails; West (2010) for prisons.

Table 11.4. Inmates per 100,000 population in prisons and jails by gender, race, and ethnicity, 2008.

	Non-Hispanic white	Non-Hispanic black	Hispanic
Jails, 2008	167	831	274
Prisons and jails, 2010, male	678	4,347	1,775
Prisons and jails, 2010, female	91	260	133

Sources: Minton (2010) for jails, 2008; estimated for 2010 from Glaze (2011).

who had been to prison by 1999 was 20.5 percent overall, 58.9 percent for dropouts. Both the proportion of prisoners in the population and the share of prisoners who are black have declined slightly since 2007.

The proportion of immigrants in the prison population is extremely low (Butcher and Piehl 2007, 2008). This is part of the reason why Hispanic incarceration rates are lower than African American incarceration rates. Why are immigrants so law abiding? The main reason appears to be selection, but deportation and the threat of deportation also matter. It might be that opportunities to be a criminal are relatively better in the countries from which many immigrants come than in the United States; police forces in Latin America, for instance, are generally less professional than those in the United States.

What do people go to prison for? Table 11.5 has the basic information. The racial disproportions for murder and robbery stand out once again, a little more strongly than they do for arrests. For the first time in this chapter, we now see racial disproportionality in drug offenses.

Was it always like this? Table 11.6 shows that it was not. At the beginning of the twentieth century, the black incarceration rate was much lower, both absolutely and relative to the white incarceration rate. This is strange: society was clearly more racist and chain gangs were prevalent in the Jim Crow South (remember how Du Bois complained about convict labor). So the black incarceration rate must have been very low. No—the opposite is true. Why? The South probably ignored black-on-black crime. Good economics considers both victims and offenders; it doesn't try to minimize either the prison population or the number of crimes.

Murder clearances.   Most murders are resolved, and Table 11.7 shows how offenders match up with victims. Murder is overwhelmingly intraracial. Blacks are disproportionately murder victims because they are being killed by other blacks. Blacks kill whites a little more than whites kill blacks, but both numbers are small.

Victim reports.   For violent crimes, the NCVS asks victims about the characteristics of their assailants. Table 11.8 summarizes what victims say. Rape numbers are difficult to interpret, but they don't seem to contradict the arrest and prison data that show that blacks commit rapes, but not in the same

Table 11.5. Total number of state prison inmates and percent inmates by offense charged and race, 2009.

	Total prisoners	Percent white	Percent black	Percent Hispanic
Total	1,365,800	39.0	42.6	15.5
Murder	179,000	31.1	46.9	18.0
Rape/Sexual assault	167,400	53.5	33.6	10.0
Robbery	185,700	24.3	59.2	14.3
Assault	138,100	33.7	42.2	15.1
Burglary	131,000	48.3	36.7	12.5
Larceny	49,900	49.5	36.3	11.8
Motor vehicle theft	19,800	42.9	21.7	30.8
Drug offenses	242,900	30.4	50.4	17.0
Public order	121,000	45.0	38.3	13.2
Jail inmates	751,100	42.5	39.2	16.2

Source: Guerino, Harrison, and Sabol (2011).

Table 11.6. Incarceration rate per 100,000 population by geographic location and race, 1920–1996.

	Non-South		South		Black/Nonblack Ratios	
	Black (A)	Nonblack (B)	Black (C)	Nonblack (D)	Non-South (A/B)	South (C/D)
1920	734	77	217	50	9.51	4.37
1930	722	117	352	118	6.17	2.99
1940	1,132	163	553	176	6.95	3.15
1950	867	108	409	123	7.98	3.32
1960	822	98	493	142	8.40	3.46
1970	611	72	460	113	8.56	4.06
1980	671	84	631	146	7.96	4.33
1996	1,846	268	1546	260	6.89	5.95

Sources: Data to 1980, Myers and Sabol (1988); data for 1996, U.S. Census Bureau (1997). 1996 data do not include jails; other years do.

Table 11.7. Percentage of homicides by race of victims and perpetrators, 2010 (single-offender only).

	Offender			
	White	Black	Other/ Unknown	Total victims
Victim:				
White	44.2	7.1	1.6	52.9
Black	3.5	39.1	0.7	43.2
Other/unknown	1.1	0.7	2.0	3.8
Percentage of offenders	48.7	46.9	4.3	99.9

Source: U.S. Federal Bureau of Investigation (2011).

Table 11.8. Percentage of crimes of violence (excluding murder) by race of victims and offenders (single-offender crimes only), 2008.

	Offender			
	White	Black	Other/ Unknown	Total victims
Rape				
Victim:				
White	53.6	11.7	6.2	71.6
Black	0	21.2	7.1	28.4
Percentage of offenders	53.6	33.0	13.4	100.0
Robbery				
Victim:				
White	32.0	24.9	13.0	70.0
Black	2.5	20.5	7.1	30.0
Percentage of offenders	34.5	45.4	20.1	100.0
Aggravated assault				
Victim:				
White	58.4	11.7	14.8	84.9
Black	2.9	9.5	2.7	15.1
Percentage of offenders	61.3	21.2	17.5	100.0

Source: National Criminalization Victimization Survey data from U.S. Bureau of Justice Statistics (2011).

proportions as robberies and murders. Similarly, the aggravated assault victim reports are in line with the arrest numbers. Robbery is different: victim reports indicate a lot of black-on-black robbery and a lot of robberies of whites by blacks.

Notice that very few whites rob blacks. 2008 is actually a big year for white-on-black robbery; some years it's zero. This runs counter to most of what people think they know about race and crime. If whites dislike blacks, if law enforcement undervalues black safety, if courts are reluctant to accept black testimony against whites, then whites should rob blacks in large numbers. But they don't. (This information comes from black victims whose anonymity has been guaranteed.) Blacks rob whites much more often than whites rob blacks.

Criminological studies.   The consensus among criminologists is that arrests for serious crimes with victims are unbiased. This may be wrong, but it is approximately equally wrong in all directions. This consensus doesn't rule out bias in the criminal justice system. Notice that discrimination can go both ways, by both ignoring minority victims (like undocumented aliens who are robbed or gang-member kids who are killed) and mistreating alleged minority offenders.

Tonry (1997) and Lauritsen-Sampson (1999) went to great lengths to review the research that looks for discrimination in the criminal justice system. Mainly what they found was that there was little discrimination in the normal places—sentencing (when you consider severity of crime and prior criminal record), arrest, and so forth. For violent index crimes, there was not much left to explain after you control for severity and previous record.

But there were some areas where race seemed to matter (leaving aside drugs for now). Juvenile dispositions were stricter for blacks. Whether this feeds into criminal record is a possibility that Lauritsen and Sampson raised but don't resolve. Bail is another area of possible discrimination. Ayres and Wald-fogel (2001) provided evidence from Connecticut that bail was set higher for blacks, given severity of charge and likelihood of flight. If bail is nondiscriminatory, then bondsmen should expect the same profit from the marginal black arrestee and the marginal white arrestee. Ayres and Waldfogel found that expected profit is higher for blacks than for whites.

These findings are old now, but not much seems to have changed. Kutateladze et al. (2012) reviewed more recent studies. Some studies found that blacks and Hispanics were treated more punitively in a variety of settings, a few found the opposite, and some found no difference. Bail again, however, was an area where minorities, especially Hispanics, were treated worse.

Summary.   The index crimes that are the biggest problem in the black community—and the biggest puzzle—are murder and robbery. I'll concentrate on those two crimes in the rest of this section.

Explaining the Racial Disparity in Robbery and Murder

Why are robbery and murder so prevalent? It will take some time to work out an answer.

Bad Explanations for Racial Disproportionality in Crime for Murder and Robbery

I'll start by showing that the easy and obvious answers don't work very well.

Characteristics.   The most popular way to explain racial disparities is to point to some characteristic, assert that the characteristic causes a disproportionate propensity to commit crime, and show that minorities, especially African Americans, are more likely to have this characteristic. The characteristics usually cited are being poor, growing up in a lone parent household, being poorly educated, or having guns. Blacks are seven or eight times as likely as whites to be arrested or incarcerated for robbery and murder, but black kids are only about 2.5 times as likely as white kids to live with a lone parent, blacks aged 18 to 35 are only about twice as likely to be poor, and blacks are less likely than whites to own guns.

Lochner and Moretti (2004) find that equalizing black and white educational attainment would eliminate only about 23 percent of the racial gap in incarceration (and murder and robbery have much higher gaps than average).

Rogers et al. (2001) is the only study that looks at probability of being a murder victim. They have a lot of variables such as education, age, gender, marital status, region, and rural or not. These characteristics explain about 35 percent of the racial murder victimization gap. In metropolitan areas it's worse: blacks are 8.8 times as likely to be murder victims as NHWs, but if you hold characteristics constant, they're 6.6 times as likely.

Characteristics may explain a large part of the gap in burglary and theft and maybe even rape and assault, but not murder and robbery.

Underdeterrence.   Since both the certainty and severity of expected punishment reduce crime, perhaps blacks commit more of these crimes because they're less likely to be punished or expect less severe punishment if they're caught. They commit crimes, in other words, because they think they can get away with them. This explanation has two major problems.

First, almost no evidence indicates that blacks are less likely to be arrested or face less severe punishment than NHWs, except in a few small situations. None of the studies that Lauritsen-Sampson cite, for instance, have a conclusion like this, and only a few studies that Kutadeladze et al. cite. Second, if blacks were less likely to be punished or more likely to receive a light sentence, you would expect that the racial disproportion in the arrest statistics would be larger than the racial disproportion in the incarcerated population. But it isn't. Black arrestees are more likely to be in prison than white arrestees.

Second, the elasticities of crime with respect to punishment are too small to support the prison disproportions we see, even if blacks are treated somewhat more leniently (which the criminological literature does not find). Deterrence has two dimensions: probability of arrest and punishment conditional on conviction.

Most empirical studies find an elasticity of crime with respect to arrest rate of 0.3–0.5: if arrests go up 10 percent, crime goes down 3 to 5 percent. Suppose the black arrest rate went up by 10 percent. Then black crimes would go down by 3 percent. As a result, black arrests would go *up* by 7 percent. So if blacks were more likely to be arrested than they are now, the gap in arrests would be bigger, not smaller. That makes the unexplained portion bigger, not smaller.

Most studies of punishment show that the elasticity is even smaller. Let's say the elasticity is 0.3: a sentence 10 percent more severe reduces crime by 3 percent. How much more severe do white sentences have to be to make the crime rate of blacks seven times as high?

This is an elasticity problem. Let p = punishment of blacks and ap = punishment of whites. Then a is the ratio between white punishment and black punishment; it's what we want to find.

Let $C(r)$ denote per capita crimes by race r: $C(b) = 7\ C(w)$.

By definition of elasticity e:

$$\ln C(b) = A - e \ln p$$
$$\ln C(w) = A - e \ln ap = A - e \ln a - e \ln p.$$

Subtract the bottom equation from the top:

$$\ln C(b) - \ln C(w) = e \ln a.$$
$$\text{But } \ln C(b) - \ln C(w) = \ln 7.$$

Hence

$$\ln 7 = e \ln a$$

Let $e = 0.3$. Then $a = 656$.

In order to produce a black crime rate seven times the white crime rate, whites would have to be punished 656 times more severely than blacks. If this were happening, somebody would notice it.

Culture of violence.   Perhaps African American culture inclines people to violence. This claim is dubious. Blacks are more pious and religiously observant than whites and less likely to use alcohol, which is very strongly linked to violence. Blacks also appear to be less likely to be victims of violent crimes by family members. Are gambling and drug trafficking really more violent than arson, rape, and driving while intoxicated? In the rural South, where black culture should be strongest, there is almost no racial gap in murder rates. (Nor does southern culture appear to be the story. Black murder rates are highest in the West, not the South.)

Size.   Perhaps African American men rob and kill because they are big and strong. But African American men are no larger on average than white men of the same age. For 20–39-year-old men, the average weight for NHWs was 189.7 pounds; for blacks, 189.1 pounds. The average height was 70.9 inches for NHWs, 70.2 inches for blacks. There was no difference in BMI either.

Carrying money (for robbery).   Maybe blacks rob whites because whites are richer and carry more money. In fact, whites are richer but they don't carry more money; they carry more plastic (possibly because whites are more likely to have bank accounts). The median black robbery victim over the last decade lost more than the median white robbery victim.

What Explains the Racial Disparity in Robbery?

What explains the racial disparity in robbery? In a word, stereotypes. That's the argument Rajiv Sethi and I make in several studies (O'Flaherty and Sethi 2007, 2008, 2009).

Robbery is an interaction where decisions have to be made quickly on the basis of poor information. A robber has to decide whom to threaten. In many cases, all the information he has is a quick visual scan. After the robber threatens, the victim has to decide whether to comply or resist; the victim usually has even less information and may not even have a full view of the robber. If the victim resists, the robber has to decide whether to retaliate. In all of these decisions, statistical discrimination is highly likely, because race is something Americans see (and hear) quickly and have notions about.

Suppose robbery victims believe that black robbers are more likely to use violence when the victim resists. Then more victims will comply with black robbers than with white robbers. So robbery will be more lucrative for blacks and more blacks will engage in robbery. But not too many more, because if too many blacks who truly are not willing to use violence become robbers, the stereotype will fail.

Similarly, suppose that robbers believe that white victims are less likely to resist than black victims (ethnographic studies confirm that robbers believe this). Then robbers will prefer white victims to black victims and rob more of them.

This can be an equilibrium if there are real fundamental differences. Suppose that people who are poorer are more likely to be violent as robbers and more likely to resist as victims. Then since blacks are poorer than whites, we can start off with the stereotypes. But the stereotypes mean that if you take two people, one black and one white, equally poor and equally inclined to violence, the black person has better prospects as a robber and is more likely to become a robber. Similarly, the white person is more likely to be robbed. The stereotypes exacerbate the fundamental differences.

This theory has predictions about disparities in resistance and violence that are reasonably borne out by the data.

Notice that discrimination is occurring: people are drawing conclusions based on race. This discrimination is totally legal and totally understandable, if we care about that. But it has consequences. In particular, it contributes to the incarceration gap and the fear that some people have of associating with young black men. And then there are consequences for employment, marriage, and childrearing. The world is not color blind.

The process of robbery—the interplay between beliefs and reactions—thus takes a small fundamental difference between blacks and whites and amplifies it. Amplification of differences is a recurring theme in this chapter.

What Explains the Racial Disparity in Murder?

Some murders are robberies gone bad; that blacks are engaged in robberies more than whites explains some of the racial disparity in murder. But robbery-murders are only a small fraction of total murders.

We need to start with some theory of murders. Murder differs from most other index crimes in two relevant ways. First, most people most of the time have no reason to kill someone else. This makes murder different from robbery, say, where most people would like a little bit more money so they might be willing to rob if they were not constrained by conscience or law. Second, killing someone can reduce your probability of being killed. This makes murder different from, say, burglary: if I think you're going to break into my house and steal my computer, no one would suggest that I break into your house and steal your TV set first.

Hence, murder has what game theorists call strategic complementarity: if we are in a society where people might kill us, we are more likely to kill people. Very high murder rates can only be achieved if you have some spiral like that going on, since there usually is no other good reason to kill someone.

Once again, then, if black neighborhoods have more people who want to kill someone for reasons other than preemption and if those numbers are high enough, strategic complementarity can cause very high murder rates. People who under other circumstances would not murder (or would not develop the weaponry to murder, like a very quick and horrible temper) find themselves doing so in order to maintain their safety. This is like the robbery result: small fundamental differences between races get exacerbated.

The missing piece is that I have not said why black neighborhoods are different in the number of murders that would occur for reasons other than preemption. The short answer is anonymous drug dealing and other street vice. Understanding that is the subject of the next section.

Why Are Murder and Robbery Different from Other Index Crimes?

The short answer, then, to the question of why murder and robbery are different from other index crimes is that in a race-sighted world, they are crimes where small differences between groups get amplified.

Illicit Recreational and Occupational Drugs

We saw that African Americans and Hispanics were much more likely to be in state prisons on drug charges than NHWs. The same is true for federal prisons. The question for this section is why.

We also saw that while African Americans were overrepresented among people who are *arrested* on drug charges, the disproportion is nowhere near the disproportion in prison. No good arrest data are available for Hispanics. Black people were three to four times as likely as whites to be arrested on drug charges; but were six to seven times as likely to be in prison.

The Simple Accounting Answer

Why the disparity? Some of it probably arises because a higher proportion of NHW arrests are for simple possession. In 1998, 57 percent of those convicted of drug-trafficking felonies were African American; 53 percent of those convicted for drug abuse felonies were African American. If the conviction is for a felony, it may not be for possessing an amount designed for personal consumption. It seems, then, that African Americans and perhaps Hispanics are being put in prison for selling drugs, not using drugs.

Next let's look at who uses drugs. There are two reasons to do this: to see if it supports the notion that the reason for disparity is sales, not use, and to ask why African Americans and Hispanics are such good salespeople. Table 11.9 gives data on drug use from the National Household Survey of Drug Abuse (NHSDA). This is a household survey, so it leaves out prisoners.

Table 11.9. Percentage of household population aged 12 and over that used illicit recreational and occupational drugs in the previous 30 days by race/ethnicity, 2010.

	Non-Hispanic white	Non-Hispanic black	Hispanic	Non-Hispanic Asian
Any illicit drug	8.8	9.6	7.9	3.7
Marijuana	7.0	8.6	5.8	2.6
Powder cocaine	0.6	0.7	0.6	0.4
Crack cocaine	0.1	0.4	0.1	0
Hallucinogens	0.4	0.6	0.7	0.2
Inhalants	0.3	0.2	0.4	0.1
Psychotherapeutics*	3.0	2.0	2.5	1.0
Tobacco	28.4	29.5	21.9	12.5

Source: Substance Abuse and Mental Health Services Administration (2012).
*Nonmedical use of prescription psychotherapeutics.

Table 11.10. Coefficients in regression equation for past-year drug use, 1988–1991.

	Black	Asian	Hispanic
Marijuana	−0.105*	−0.414*	−0.271*
Cocaine	−0.035	−0.428*	−0.068*
Heroin	0.026	−0.130	−0.147

Source: Saffer and Chaloupka (1999).
*Significant at 5% level. Other variables include price (decriminalization), income, gender, marital status, and youth.

But that's appropriate for our purposes: prisoners aren't incarcerated for using drugs while incarcerated, their supply networks are different, and they probably don't use drugs as much as people who are not imprisoned. Table 11.10 shows some results about drug use conditional on other characteristics; once again, African Americans are in fact less likely to use illicit drugs, controlling for obvious characteristics.

The basic message is that rates of use don't differ much by race. Not enough to support even a 2-to-1 ratio, much less a 4-to-1 or 6-to-1 ratio.

Since blacks and Hispanics are not a huge proportion of users, are they then a huge proportion of sellers? That is, do they dominate sales to whites?

It's not clear that this is true either. In surveys of adolescents in 1980 and 2000, low-income white kids were more likely to say that they had sold drugs than low-income black kids (Weiman and Weiss 2009). In the NHSDA, only 43 percent of those who used marijuana in 2006 bought it and most of them bought it from friends, who are likely to be of the same race. So it appears that most whites get drugs from other whites.

The most plausible story for why minorities are arrested and imprisoned so much is that they dominate a particular kind of selling: what Rajiv Sethi and I call street vice, by which we mean illegal transactions between a willing buyer and willing seller in which the seller deals with many buyers and has ongoing relationships with few buyers. Selling drugs to people you don't know, in other words. Most drugs are not sold this way, but one explanation for the overrepresentation of minorities among arrestees and prisoners is that minorities are overrepresented in this part of the industry.

Why are arrests concentrated in this part of the market? Tonry (1995) gives the standard answer: that's where arrests are easy. If you need customers to see your business, then cops can see it too. If you sell to people you don't know, you may be selling to cops. In Tonry's view, the easy arrests for drugs are in minority neighborhoods, of minority sellers. He thinks that people buy drugs in white neighborhoods too, from white sellers, but that this business is much more secretive and it's much more difficult for police to make arrests. Drug selling in minority neighborhoods is much more open and blatant. So police who want to make arrests will do so in minority neighborhoods.

This is probably not the whole story of police motivation. Blatant drug selling is much more destructive of neighborhoods than clandestine sales; the external costs are greater. It's not entirely laziness that causes the police to focus on blatant sales.

Considerable ethnographic evidence supports this conclusion. Hagedorn (1998) studied drug markets in Milwaukee. He found flourishing street-drug markets in minority neighborhoods but didn't find anything like that in white neighborhoods. He described suburban drug selling as basically a word-of-mouth operation.

I don't want to imply that there's no street vice in white neighborhoods. Beckett et al. (2006) described an open-air heroin market in a white area of

Seattle. But arrest and incarceration statistics suggest that such markets are relatively rare. I'm aware of no ethnographic reports of minorities traveling to white neighborhoods to buy drugs.

Booker T. Washington (1915, 113) predicted that this would happen in a famous essay about segregated black neighborhoods: "A segregated negro community is a terrible temptation to many white people. Such a community invariably provides a certain type of white men with hiding-places—hiding places from the law, from decent people of their own race, from their churches and their wives and their daughters."

Why Is Street Vice Concentrated in Minority Neighborhoods?

The obvious next question is why street vice is concentrated in minority neighborhoods. The answer comes from location theory, a branch of urban economics. Many types of retail businesses don't have much presence in these places; what makes illicit drugs different?

First, customers have high transportation costs. Either their physiology or the police or robbers may catch up to them while they are shopping. They make frequent trips to buy drugs because home storage is dangerous. They want to buy at all times of day and night, even when public transportation is poor.

Second, drug sellers have high fixed costs. They need to protect their businesses and themselves from police and from robbers.

Third, demand is thin. With fixed costs, this means that not every neighborhood can support its own drug dealer. (Wedding gown dealers, for instance, also face thin markets, since a lot of people don't buy wedding gowns in the average year.)

Fourth, drug-dealing firms specialize. Many stores make money selling commodities in thin demand through economies of scope: you sell many different things to cover your overhead: milk, M&Ms, and birthday cards, for instance. But because drugs are illegal, this is usually not a good strategy, because if the police confiscate your drugs they'll probably confiscate your birthday card inventory too.

Fifth, drug selling uses unskilled labor intensively. Not a lot of MBAs and PhDs are employed in this field and a lot of high school dropouts are.

Sixth, workers usually don't commute very far. If you have to take the money or the drugs home after work (they can't be locked up at the street corner), travel is costly. If you don't, there are still great advantages to neighborhood familiarity.

Seventh, you don't pay for the space you use, thus you don't have to outbid competing users.

What does this imply about the equilibrium location of street vice (not clandestine word-of-mouth operations)?

First, let's suppose that customers can't shop outside their own neighborhoods. Suppose also that the proportion of the population that buys drugs anonymously is the same everywhere. Then neighborhoods that are more densely populated will have more customers per acre and so will have more drug sellers and lower prices, partly because there are more buyers over whom to spread overhead costs and partly because of more competition. Similarly, neighborhoods where low-skilled labor is available at a lower wage will have lower drug prices and more drug-selling businesses.

Thus on these two counts you would expect to see more drug dealers and lower prices in minority neighborhoods than in NHW neighborhoods, because minority neighborhoods have greater population density and lower wages.

But the story doesn't end there. Suppose people can travel out of their neighborhoods to buy drugs, but at a cost. Since prices are lower in minority neighborhoods, nobody will travel from minority neighborhoods to white neighborhoods. If the price difference is great enough (because the density or the wage difference is great enough), then some whites will buy drugs in minority neighborhoods. When whites buy drugs in minority neighborhoods, demand in white neighborhoods falls. This means that drug firms will charge higher prices and locate farther apart in white neighborhoods. That would make drug buying in white neighborhoods less attractive for the remaining white buyers, and some of them will opt to buy in minority neighborhoods.

If the original price difference is great enough the process can unravel, and all the (street vice, anonymous) drug-selling firms in the white neighborhoods will go out of business (even though the white neighborhoods might be dense enough to support some of them if the minority neighborhoods were not nearby). So in many (but not) all metropolitan areas, all of the street vice will be concentrated in minority neighborhoods, and so will the arrests that accompany it. (The exceptions, white neighborhoods with street vice, will be densely populated neighborhoods with high drug use in metropolitan areas with small minority populations—Seattle, in other words.)

Once again, small fundamental differences get amplified—this time by markets.

An Alternative Story

An alternative story about why blacks are arrested and imprisoned so often for drug crimes is that the police stereotype of a drug criminal is a black person, and even though that stereotype is false, nothing dispels it. This stereotype, according to proponents of this story, is not self-confirming; instead, it survives because nothing challenges it.

The stereotype arose for historical and political reasons. As Alexander (2012, 104–105) describes it:

> The Reagan administration launched a media campaign . . . to publicize horror stories involving black crack users and crack dealers in ghetto communities. Although crack cocaine had not yet hit the streets when the War on Drugs was declared in 1982, its appearance a few years later created a perfect opportunity for the Reagan administration to build support for its new war. . . . Early in the 1980s, the typical cocaine-related story focused on white recreational users who snorted the drug in powder form. These stories generally relied on news sources associated with the drug treatment industry . . . and emphasized the possibility of recovery. By 1985, however, . . . this frame was supplanted by a new "siege paradigm," in which transgressors were poor, nonwhite users and dealers of crack cocaine.

In this view, since drug users are in fact ubiquitous and drug use is a victimless crime, the police can concentrate anywhere with equally good results. So there is no penalty for acting on their mistaken belief that blacks are the people who should be arrested for drug dealing, even though white drug dealing is just as prevalent.

This story, in my view, has two major flaws. First, the type of anonymous, open-air drug markets that are at issue here are a public nuisance; neighbors don't like them, and many black neighbors complain. If such markets were present in large numbers in white neighborhoods (as opposed to clandestine markets), white neighbors would complain loudly and often. Police could not maintain their mistaken belief without some cost.

Second, the stereotypes proposed here are not in fact neutral; they're self-destroying. Suppose otherwise identical anonymous markets existed in both black and white neighborhoods but that only the market in the black neighborhood was subject to police raids and arrests. The drugs would then have to be more expensive in the black neighborhood and business, especially white business, would shift to where drugs were cheaper. Over time, the black business would shrivel and the white business would boom. As a steady number of arrests were launched against a shrinking business, prices would go up further and the business would shrink further. If police made arrests only against anonymous markets in black neighborhoods, why would anyone do business there?

Notice that the stereotype argument cuts two ways. If the general public believes that drugs are available anonymously only in black neighborhoods, then people who want to buy drugs anonymously will believe this too, since they're part of the general public. So they will search in black neighborhoods for drug outlets. (The Reagan administration, in this interpretation, was providing black drug dealers with free advertising.) Realizing that, drug entrepreneurs will locate their businesses in those neighborhoods. The stereotype will be confirmed.

Customer stereotypes, then, are self-confirming, while police stereotypes are in fact self-destroying. Both stereotypes bring those who hold them into black neighborhoods to seek drug sellers, but only the customer stereotype makes drug sellers want to be there.

Consequences of the Concentration of Street Vice

The incarceration and neighborhood disruption that street vice causes are pretty bad by themselves. But they're not the whole story.

Consider robbery, for instance. Street vice makes minority neighborhoods an inviting place to carry on a robbery business. People employed in the business often have lots of cash and lots of valuable drugs; they don't call the police when they're robbed. So they're inviting targets, except that they're violent themselves. People seeking drugs are an even better target, since they're carrying money and are not eager to explain to the police or anyone else why they had that money. So the presence of many drug users makes robbery a good business and robbers will think there is a high probability that the average person they encounter is an easy mark. This will encourage them to rob people, and they will often be wrong. So street vice can increase the probability of robbery for people (especially whites) who are totally unconnected to the enterprise.

That's speculation. There are several better documented connections.

Remember Moving to Opportunity: contrary to expectations, boys who moved to wealthier neighborhoods did not decrease the amount of crime they committed relative to the control group. Most of this crime is not serious. There were five different cities and a variety of neighborhoods, and the crime response to moving was not the same everywhere. So Ludwig and Kling (2007) went back to the data to try to see what correlated with increases in crime and what correlated with decreases across cities and neighborhoods. They looked at the obvious things, such as segregation and poverty, which did not perform well in the regression. The best explanatory variable was whether kids said that they saw drug dealing in the neighborhood. If kids moved to neighborhoods with visible drug dealing, crime did not go down. If kids moved to neighborhoods without visible drug dealing, crime tended to go down.

So street vice may in fact be linked to how kids grow up and the amount of nondrug crime committed. This hypothesis is not well developed now.

The connection with murder is better studied.

First, consider murders rates over long periods of time or great distances. Miron (1999) looks at the time series of murder rates in the United States. There are two humps: the 1920s and the 1980s to early 1990s. What do they have in common? Strenuous efforts to suppress recreational drugs: prohibition in the first case, and the War on Drugs in the second. More rigorously, Miron has regressed murder rates in the twentieth century on age structure and expenditures on drug and alcohol enforcement and many other variables. He found that only age structure and drug and alcohol enforcement matter. He also checks for the direction of causality and finds that drug and alcohol enforcement causes murder, at least in the temporal sense, and not the other way around. He does something similar with a world cross-section of murder rates.

Second, Fryer et al. (2005) constructed an index of crack use for most cities for most years from 1980 to 2000. They found that crack is a good predictor of murders of black teenagers, especially in the early part of the period. It's a less powerful predictor later on. Several other studies have used less sophisticated methods to reach similar conclusions.

What's the theory? Drugs could lead to murder in several ways. More specifically, several considerations imply that people in the drug business, especially in street vice, are more likely to kill and be killed.

First is the absence of any other means of contract enforcement. Legal companies have lawyers; but drug firms can't go to court to resolve business disputes. They use hit men instead of lawyers.

Second is the absence of basic protection. A jewelry store can call the police and expect them to try to arrest somebody who steals its wares or cash. A drug-selling business needs some other means to protect itself from robbers, and violence is the obvious way. Similarly, if Walmart wants to start competing with Pathmark in New Jersey, the police are around to dissuade it from sending out goons to break all of Pathmark's windows and to dissuade Pathmark from doing the same to Walmart. But the police don't provide this service to the Crips and the Bloods. Drug sellers have to be prepared for this sort of nonprice competition.

Of course, drug sellers can come to agreements with each other and live relatively peaceably, but these agreements are subject to disruption. The early period of crack that Fryer et al. found so deadly may have been such a period of disruption; so too may have been the bloodbath that ensued when Mexico tried to break up drug cartels in the period 2006–2012. (Dell [2012] shows rigorously that specific crackdowns in Mexico led to greater violence as rival organizations fought for control of territories with weakened incumbents.)

Third, the marginal penalties for murder are lower for drug workers than for other people. If I'm likely to go to jail for fifteen years for what I'm doing now, how much worse can it be if I also get convicted for killing someone? At the very least, you have to discount my prison time for this offense.

Fourth, the penalties for killing other people in the drug business are rather low. Juries don't get upset about people who kill drug dealers; many police may not be particularly upset either.

So where you have a lot of street vice, you can usually expect a lot of homicide.

Murder Revisited

Earlier in this chapter, I wrote about murder and how preemption could cause large differences in murder rates due to small differences in fundamentals. I didn't say what could start such a spiral that would make the black homicide rate so different from the white. Now I have an answer to that question.

Take an ordinary population, and drop a bunch of street-vice workers into it. First you get more occasions when people want to kill unconditionally; that is, to protect their businesses, not to keep from being killed. You also get people who don't have much to lose from killing. More subtly, you have people whose killers are not likely to be treated harshly; such people want to protect themselves preemptively.

What happens when ordinary people find themselves encountering more and more people employed in street vice in their ordinary lives—people ready to kill on little provocation? First, the ordinary people start getting killed—in cross-fires, in mistakes, on occasions when tempers flare over nondrug business. Second, some ordinary people start thinking that they must preempt too. And so on. The contagion spreads. Not infinitely far, but it spreads.

Notice that amplification works twice here: small fundamental differences in neighborhoods give rise to larger differences in street vice, and these differences in turn produce the observed differences in murder and robbery.

Summing Up Illicit Drugs

I've said nothing in this whole section about the pharmacological properties of illicit drugs. That's because practically nothing depends on them (the high travel costs of customers in part, but that's all). This whole sordid tale works because these drugs are illegal, not because they're bad.

Costs of Crime Fighting

In this section, I'll look at several costs of crime fighting (as opposed to crime) that are concentrated on minorities, especially African Americans.

Mass Incarceration

The United States of the late twentieth and early twenty-first centuries is unusual in the extent of its correctional system. No other country today imprisons such a high proportion of its population and in no period of U.S. history was the proportion higher. (The proportion of the U.S. population that was incarcerated peaked in 2009 and has fallen slightly since then.) The Soviet Union under Stalin imprisoned a higher proportion of its population than the United States does today, but that's not good company.

Before the 1970s, the U.S. incarceration rate was stable for many years at less than 200 per 100,000 residents (Raphael and Stoll 2009a). At its peak in 2009, the U.S. incarceration rate was 756 per 100,000. Most rich countries incarcerate far fewer than 200 per 100,000, and many incarcerate fewer than 100 per 100,000 (Norway, France, Germany, and Japan, for instance) (O'Flaherty and Sethi 2015).

Prison and jail don't account for the entire correctional population. In 2010, about 4.1 million Americans were subject to probation and 840,000 were subject to parole. Probation "is a court-ordered period of correctional supervision in the community, generally as an alternative to incarceration. . . . Parole is a period of conditional supervised release in the community following a prison term" (Glaze and Bonczar 2011). Probation and parole are less severe penalties than imprisonment, and minorities are less dominant in these populations than in the prison population. Table 11.11 shows these data.

Table 11.11. Racial and ethnic composition of individuals in state prisons, on parole, and on probation, 2009 and 2010 (percent).

	State prisons 2009	Parole 2010	Probation 2010
Non-Hispanic white	39	42	55
Black	43	39	30
Hispanic	16	16	13
Other	2	3	2
Total	100	100	100

Sources: University at Albany (2014), table 10.5 for data on state prisons; Glaze and Bonczar (2011) for data on probation and parole.

The large rise in the U.S. prison population began around 1980 (probation and parole populations started to rise about this time too), the same time that the war on drugs was proclaimed. In some popular accounts, the prison population grew because prisons filled up with drug offenders. This is not wholly accurate. The number of people incarcerated on drug charges rose from about 41,000 in 1980 to about 539,000 in 2008 (O'Flaherty and Sethi 2015). This is a huge increase. But it's only about 30 percent of the 1,738,000 increase in incarceration over this period. Minorities are somewhat more likely than NHWs to be held on drug charges—in 2009, 17.8 percent of the state prison population had been committed for drug offenses, 21.0 percent of the black prison population and 19.5 percent of the Hispanic population. But this small disproportion is not enough to change the basic picture. A lot of people are in prison for drug offenses, and a lot more people are in prison now for drug offenses than were in prison for them in 1980, but prisons are mainly filled with index crime offenders. Of course, these data don't pick up any indirect effects of the war on drugs.

However, because drug sentences are usually shorter than sentences for violent crime, the proportion of former drug prisoners in the population of former prisoners is higher than the proportion of current drug prisoners in the population of current prisoners at any point in time. (If a four-year college and a two-year college both have 1,000 people attending every year, the two-year college will have twice as many alumni.) The importance of drug incarceration in explaining why there are more *former* prisoners is therefore greater than its importance in explaining why there are more *current* prisoners.

Understanding imprisonment.   Why is so much punishment being meted out? The easy answer is to reduce crime. And it probably does reduce crime. The two major accounts of the great American crime decline of the 1990s (Levitt 2004 and Zimring 2007) both give the rising prison population some credit (although Zimring notes that crime fell by a comparable amount in Canada without any rise in incarceration). But many things can reduce crime: blizzards, for instance, do a good job overall, and recessions cut illicit drug consumption and possibly murder. The policy questions are whether imprisoning large numbers of people, especially minorities, is the least socially expensive way of reducing crime, and if so, whether the crime reductions it brings about are worth more than the cost.

These questions are somewhat muddled because no one ever makes a policy decision to have a certain level of incarceration. Instead, decisions about policing, sentencing, and parole policies interact in a complex way with criminal motivations, witness cooperation, victim self-protective efforts, and history to produce a prison population at any moment.

It's useful to see how this fits together in the simplest possible case. First ignore parole failures—people who are released on parole but then return to prison because they violated some of the conditions. In the long run, the number of prisoners per capita will depend on the crime rate (the average crimes per person per year), the certainty of punishment (the proportion of crimes that result in a conviction and a prison sentence), and the severity of punishment (the number of years the average prisoner stays imprisoned). The relationship in the long run (steady state) is just:

$$\text{Prisoners per capita} = \text{crime rate} \times \text{certainty} \times \text{severity}.$$

(This equation is only approximately accurate. The exact equation has the ratio of prisoners to nonprisoners on the left hand side, not the ratio of prisoners to all people. But since prisoners are only a small percentage of the U.S. population, the equation is accurate to within a few percentage points.)

Government policies affect only certainty and severity of punishment, but of course certainty and severity also affect the crime rate. (The prison population doesn't go to its long-run value immediately after any of these variables changes, just as snow doesn't immediately vanish when the temperature rises above freezing.)

With the possibility of parole failure, the formula is slightly different:

$$\text{Prisoners per capita} = \text{crime rate} \times \text{certainty} \times \text{severity} \\ \times (1/\text{parole success rate}).$$

"Parole success rate" is the proportion of parolees who end their parole periods without returning to prison. (This is the easiest case, where all prisoners leave on parole and all processes are exponential.) The parole success rate depends both on the behavior of parolees and on policy decisions about how strict parole terms are, how closely parolees are monitored, and what conditions trigger return to prison.

Table 11.12. Percentage of total increase in steady-state population per capita attributable to nondrug crimes, drug crimes, and parole violations, 1984–2002.

All sources	100.0
Index and other nondrug crimes	38.0
Greater expected time	17.8
Other changes (net)	20.2
Drug crimes	28.8
Greater expected time	1.6
Other changes	27.2
Parole violators	33.2
Greater expected time	1.3
More prisoners	10.4
Other changes	21.5

Sources: O'Flaherty and Sethi (2015); Raphael and Stoll (2009b).

Raphael and Stoll (2009b) used this framework to understand why the state prison population rose from 1984 to 2002 (the majority of prisoners are in state prisons). Rajiv Sethi and I (2015) recategorized their work into a simple table (see Table 11.12).

The rise in state prison population is divided into roughly equal parts of index crime offenders, parole violators, and drug offenders; index crime offenders are responsible for the largest piece of the increase.

About half of the increase in imprisoned index crime offenders is due to greater time served; time served is not a major factor for the other parole violators or drug offenders. Policy changes such as mandatory minimum sentences and truth-in-sentencing laws caused the increase in time served (Raphael and Stoll 2013, chapter 4). The increase in prisoners per crime is due almost entirely to more prison admissions per arrest: more crime was not being committed and police were not catching more criminals, but those they caught were more likely to go to prison (Raphael and Stoll 2013, chapter 2).

The rise in admissions for drug crimes is also almost entirely due to policy changes. Illicit drug consumption was not rising during this period, but per capita prison admissions went up a lot.

Finally, about a third of the increase in parole violators is due to a bigger prison system: more prisoners implied more parolees and more parolees implied more people who could violate parole. But most of the increase is due to a higher rate of parole revocation, which is also probably a policy change.

So the basic story is that state prison populations grew because state policies became more punitive along many dimensions, not because more crimes were committed or police became better at catching criminals (except drug offenders).

The basic story for the federal system is the same: policy changes made it grow (Raphael and Stoll 2013, chapter 4). The federal system grew faster than state prisons did; the number of federal prisoners per capita increased sixfold from 1980 to 2010. Most of the increase was attributable to drug inmates, whose share of federal prisoners rose from 28 percent in 1974 to 55 percent in 2004. Overall, the rate of admission to federal prisons doubled and the average length of stay tripled. The number of federal crimes also grew, and federal courts started handling many matters that state courts had handled before. Part of the federal prison growth was diverted state prison growth.

It would be good to decompose the racial differences in imprisonment rates in a similar way, but no one has tried. The problem, as I discussed above, is that we really don't know crime rates, especially for drugs. Presumably the increase in imprisonment of minorities at the end of the twentieth century came about the same way the total increase did, but I don't know that for sure.

Collateral effects of imprisonment.   Prison affects the families of current prisoners, former prisoners, and the neighborhoods to which prisoners return.

We have already speculated on the effect of sex ratios on women's bargaining power. Studies of how children are directly affected are more common. Johnson (2009) estimated that about 21 percent of black children had a father with an incarceration history, compared with 11 percent for white children. Among black children whose father was a high school dropout, 35 percent had fathers with an incarceration history. Parental prison spells appear to be bad for kids. A parental prison spell, especially for a preschool child, greatly increases the incidence and severity of behavioral problems, even holding parental prison spells before the child's birth and many other background variables constant (Johnson 2009). This regression result doesn't establish causality, but it suggests it. Incarceration thus contributes to the educational achievement gap. Wildeman (2010) also finds that paternal incarceration is associated with greater aggressive behavior by boys.

Former prisoners, even those who have completed parole, lose a variety of rights and opportunities, both legally and informally. Everywhere, for instance, most are barred from public housing and Section 8, and many are barred from student loans. In twelve states former felons can't vote, and ten states restrict some people with a misdemeanor conviction from voting (ProCon 2012).

Audit studies have found considerable disparate treatment discrimination against former prisoners in terms of employment, but disparate impact is more controversial. People are usually not randomly selected to be prisoners or former prisoners, so finding the effect of imprisonment is difficult. Holzer (2009) reviews many studies and concludes that incarceration reduces black men's employment by 4–9 percent and their wages by 3–16 percent. Since 25 to 30 percent of young black men have criminal records, these effects are substantial. However, some recent very rigorous studies (Kling 2006 and Loeffler 2013) have shown no employment or earnings effects of imprisonment for various groups of former prisoners.

Prison may also change people's personalities—both those of the prisoners themselves and those who come into frequent contact with former prisoners. Prisons are dangerous and inhospitable places, full of many people who are not nice and who have few incentives to be nice. Being in prison may encourage people to be violent, aggressive, distrustful, and quick-tempered in order to survive. The wikiHow article "How to Deal with Being in Prison," for instance, advises:

> Stick up for yourself or you will be turned into a punk. It's better to get into a fight and lose than to be seen as cowering or placating (even better to win). Your reputation is more important than your desire to avoid pain, so guard it with your life. Ultimately you should avoid any confrontation whenever possible, but if an altercation is unavoidable, react quickly and with aggression. If conflict is inevitable, swing first. If you happen to get beat down, NEVER, ever call for the correctional officers. Doing so will get you a label as a punk, resulting in more fights down the road.

Similarly, the wikiHow article "How to Survive in Federal Prison" says:

> Don't trust anyone. That goes for guards, prison officials, and the person in the cell next door. If someone is being nice to you, ask "What's in it for him

or her?" They almost always have some hidden motive that you don't know about. In prison, nothing is free.

A personality developed for coping with prison life may not be well suited to normal civilian life. The traits these wikiHow articles say prisoners should cultivate—aggression, preemptive violence, mistrust—can easily lead to violence and criminality in civilian life.

Moreover, people who often interact with violent, aggressive, mistrusting people, even in civilian life, may find it optimal to adopt these traits themselves. If you are surrounded by aggressive, preemptively violent people it may be best for you to aggressive and preemptively violent yourself, even if you are not a former prisoner. So neighborhoods with many former prisoners, as some minority neighborhoods appear to be in the age of mass incarceration, may become neighborhoods full of violent people. What happens in prisons does not necessarily stay in prisons.

That is why criminologists (for instance, Clear 2007) have begun study how incarceration affects neighborhoods. These neighborhood effects may be part of the reason why some of the recent studies of the effect of imprisonment on employment have found nothing. As Loeffler (2013) writes: "If many prisons are simply extensions of high-disadvantage neighborhoods, then the effects of moving between the environments might be smaller than previously thought."

Police Stops

The other crime reduction costs imposed primarily on minority people are from traffic stops and stop-and-frisk operations. The costs here are humiliation and lost time, and the people who bear these costs have not been convicted of any crime (and almost always have not committed any crime). Elijah Anderson (2011, 249–252) describes an incident where police held, handcuffed, and verbally abused a black law student in front of his professors and other students because of a totally unfounded link to a shooting incident. Five years later, the student, now a practicing lawyer, told Anderson: "Never a day goes by that I don't think about what happened back then. That incident was traumatic for me, and now I feel somewhat jaded. It has taken a while for me to get over what happened. The incident was part of my education as a young black man."

Racial profiling by law enforcement agencies first became an issue in the 1990s on major eastern toll roads, as data revealed that police, mainly searching for drugs, were stopping a far higher proportion of minority motorists than anyone could imagine were driving poorly. On the New Jersey Turnpike, for instance, African Americans drove 15 percent of the cars exceeding the speed limit by more than six miles per hour (98 percent of all drivers were at least six miles per hour above the speed limit), but they were between 35 and 44 percent of the motorists who were stopped (U.S. General Accountability Office 2000).

Stop-and-frisk operations, particularly on the streets of New York, have also been cited in racial profiling discussions. These operations are particularly targeted toward reducing violent crime. New York police officers stop over half a million people a year, and blacks were over nine times as likely as whites to be stopped (Fagan 2010). The police found guns in only .15 percent of stops—15 out of 10,000.

This racial disproportionality in surveillance operations prompted economists to ask two questions: Why were police operating like this? and What effect does this racial profiling have on crime?

The first question, unfortunately, has drawn more attention from researchers. Usually this question is phrased in this way: Are police taste-based discriminators or statistical discriminators? Several different approaches have been taken: comparing hit rates (proportion of stops that discover contraband) across the races of motorists (Knowles, Persico, and Todd 2001); comparing stops by officers of different races (Antonovics and Knight 2009; Anwar and Fang 2006); and comparing activities in the daytime—when officers can see the driver's race—and at night—when they can't (Grogger and Ridgway 2006). Many (but not all) of these studies have concluded that officers were statistical discriminators, not taste-based discriminators, but the tests they use depend on specific assumptions about what officers know and what they try to do.

For instance, if officers observe only the driver's race and almost nothing else informative about whether he's carrying contraband, then in equilibrium the proportion of stopped motorists carrying contraband will be the same in each race if officers are pure statistical discriminators. (If the proportion of guilty people were higher in either race than in the other, then police would stop only members of the higher-proportion race, so only the lower-proportion race would carry contraband. This is contradictory, so it could not be an equilibrium.) Knowles, Persico, and Todd (2001) found that the proportion of guilty motorists in traffic stops on I-95 was about the same for all races, except Hispanics. Because it would not be in their model if police were taste-based discriminators, they concluded that only statistical discrimination was occurring. Sanga (2009), however, looked at both I-95 and other Maryland roads and found that both blacks and Hispanics had lower hit rates on the other Maryland roads.

However, this result need not hold if police can observe other nonracial signals of guilt—a more realistic assumption. Erratic driving, tinted windows, high speeds, very cheap or very expensive cars may all be signals—nonracial signals—that drugs are being transported. Police who want to stop as much contraband as possible will therefore set a lower threshold for stopping a car of a member of a group that is more likely to be carrying contraband, even if these police are not taste-based discriminators. So, for instance, for minority drivers police might stop and search any convertible, but for white drivers they might stop only red convertibles playing gangsta rap. If guilt is correlated with the strength of the signal, then the proportion guilty among stopped minority drivers might end up being lower than the proportion guilty among stopped white drivers because some of the stopped minority drivers were emitting weak signals about guilt. "Might" is a carefully chosen word here; in general, the proportion could be higher or lower or the same. So when police can observe nonracial signals, the proportion guilty among stopped drivers doesn't say anything about whether police are taste-based discriminators or not.

(This result is like the arguments we've seen already about cardiac surgery in Chapter 4 and mortgage defaults in Chapter 10. A statistically discriminating police officer makes the *marginal* stopped minority motorist's probability of guilt equal to the *marginal* white driver's probability of guilt. "Marginal" here means the stopped motorist with the weakest signal of guilt. But the distributions of probability of guilt among stopped motorists who are not marginal—motorists who are more likely to be guilty than the marginal ones—differ by race, so comparisons of the average probability of guilt among stopped motorists don't imply much about police behavior or motivation.)

The more important question is whether racial profiling reduces crime—whether the costs in humiliation produce any benefits. Taste-based discrimination almost certainly does nothing to reduce crime, but what does statistical discrimination do? Put it the other way: How can you expect police to do their jobs better if you forbid them from using all available information?

Bjerk (2007) explored this question and his answer is somewhat surprising: the effect of statistical discrimination on crime is ambiguous. Requiring police to be color blind may either increase or decrease crime or have no effect at all. The fundamental reason is that police are trying to find as many guilty drivers as possible; they aren't explicitly trying to minimize crime and aren't considering all the incentive effects of their efforts. Suppose the police are at the statistically discriminatory equilibrium and are stopping minority drivers with weaker signals than white drivers. If police ease up a little on minority drivers and tighten up a bit on white drivers (which is what they would do if they became a little color blind), then minorities will be deterred less and whites will be deterred more. Minorities will be more likely to transport contraband and whites will be less likely. The net effect could be either more crime or less.

Bjerk gives some rough guidelines about when color-blindness is likely to increase or decrease crime. The smaller the share of drivers minorities represent, the more likely color-blind behavior is to reduce crime. That's because if whites are very numerous, the crime increase among whites will be bigger than the crime decrease among minorities. If the proportion of drivers stopped is very small, then the change in deterrent effect will be very small, so the effect on crime is likely to be small, no matter which direction it goes.

Bjerk's analysis thus implies that racial profiling on highways might actually increase the transport of contraband, since the overwhelming majority of motorists on these highways are white. In any event, since only a tiny fraction of motorists are stopped, color-blind policing is likely to have little effect on the total transport of contraband on these roads. And since drugs can reach their destinations in many, many ways, the effect on drug consumption is likely to be even smaller.

For stop-and-frisk operations on city sidewalks, the picture may be different. Minorities are a larger share of New York City's population today than they were of motorists in the 1990s, and the crimes targeted are more serious.

The missing element from the analysis of crime reduction through surveillance is a serious accounting for the costs of being stopped to people who are stopped. If police don't internalize these costs, they'll make too many stops (more than the optimal number), even in the best case, and if they reduce crime it will be at the expense of the people stopped. The remedy for this problem is obvious: require police to make a payment (say, $20) to every innocent person who is stopped. Random innocent people shouldn't be forced to fight crime for free; it's inefficient. (One problem with this policy, aside from police officers stopping their friends, is that it may encourage people to act in suspicious ways—which may reduce the ability of police to use suspicious activity as information about crime.)

Policies

Crime and crime fighting thus impose enormous costs on minorities. Is there a better way?

You might be tempted to think about strong generalizations such as "Get tougher," or "Reduce sentences." These general statements don't recognize that crimes are different and should be thought about separately. What works for rape is not necessarily the best policy for driving while intoxicated.

So in this section I'll discuss the three crimes we identified as affecting minorities disproportionately: murder, robbery, and drug dealing. These activities probably account for the majority of costs borne by minority communities. I'll also look at programs designed to change how people approach life.

Murder

Probably the most important response authorities can make to murder is to take it seriously. Nationally, the ratio of arrests to murders was about 0.76 in 2010, according to the FBI's Uniform Crime Reports (this isn't precisely the proportion of murders that are solved, because murders and arrests don't necessarily happen in the same year or with one victim and one offender, but it's an easy approximation; the official "clearance rate" was 65 percent). That's far higher than the ratio for any other index crime. But many murders are isolated crimes of passion or madness that are easy to solve and pose no problems of contagion.

Some jurisdictions, however, especially some with high proportions of African Americans, don't have such high ratios of arrests to murders. For instance, the ratio was below 0.45 for many years in the early twenty-first century for Essex County, New Jersey (Newark, Irvington, and East Orange). In these jurisdictions, substantial numbers of murders are escalated disputes, fights over drugs, and gang activities—the kind of activities that lead to contagion. They may be more difficult to solve than isolated flare-ups, but the victims are also usually less appealing to police than the victims of isolated flare-ups. Most of these victims are African American and many of them have criminal records.

Substantial evidence indicates that the criminal justice system punishes murderers who kill black victims less harshly than murderers who kill white victims. Glaeser and Sacerdote (2000), for instance, show that civil penalties for deaths of black people are smaller than civil penalties for deaths of white people, holding many variables constant. The implications with contagion and preemption are far reaching: if I think that you won't be punished for killing me, then I need more than ever to kill you before you kill me. If the state won't protect me, I'll have to protect myself.

Strong enforcement actions and dedicated detective work for all murders—not just the murders of "good people"—are therefore an obvious way to reduce homicide among minorities. Most studies (though not all) find that traditional variables—arrest rates, police strength, prison population—reduce the rate of murder (for a review and analysis, see O'Flaherty and Sethi 2010).

Some of the methods that produce large estimates are revealing. Levitt (2002) uses firefighter employment as an instrument for police employment, on the reasoning that cities with stronger public safety cultures will have more of both police officers and firefighters. He finds a very strong effect of police strength on murder—stronger than the effect on any other crime, and stronger than the effect most other methods find. This is consistent with a world where a public safety culture promotes large expenditures on homicide squads and specialized training, which in turn affect murder. Since most police don't work on murder, it shouldn't be surprising that more transient measures of total police bodies—year-to-year variation as city budgets go through good times and bad, for instance—show little or no effect.

Programs designed to reduce murder also seem to work when they send public messages that all parties to a dispute will face higher penalties and everyone knows that everyone else faces higher penalties and when they focus resources on murders of people who aren't necessarily upstanding citizens. Whether these programs can be interpreted as "hug-a-thug" or "bricks-and-sticks" doesn't seem to matter as much.

Thus both Operation Ceasefire (in Boston) and Project Exile (in Richmond, Virginia) may have cut murder rates, although the evidence is weak (see O'Flaherty and Sethi 2010). Operation Ceasefire told gang members directly (in front of each other) that violence would not be tolerated. In a series of meetings, police, prosecutors, and community leaders sent the same message: "We're here because of the shooting. We're not going to leave until it stops. And until it does, nobody is going to so much as jaywalk, nor make any money, nor have any fun" (Kennedy et al. 2001, 27–28). Project Exile involved sentence enhancements for violent and drug crimes involving guns. The harsh sentences were announced with a media blitz, including billboards and ads on buses.

If strategies like these together with enhanced detective work became more widespread, the number of people incarcerated for murder would probably go up. Even though total murders would go down, the percentage response of crime is almost always smaller than the percentage change in certainty or severity of punishment. But for minority communities, this tradeoff could very well be worthwhile.

What about capital punishment? Deterrence is only one of many issues relevant to capital punishment, but it's probably the one most susceptible to empirical resolution. Many studies of capital punishment have been completed and published. What do they find? Some find that the prospect of capital punishment increases murders, some find that it decreases murders, and some find no effect. The National Academy of Sciences (2012, 2–3) reviewed the studies since the mid-1970s and conclude that "research to date on the effect of capital punishment on homicide is not informative about whether capital punishment decreases, increases, or has no effect on homicide rates. . . . A lack of evidence is not evidence for or against the hypothesis."

The studies reviewed had two fundamental flaws: they didn't control well for variation in noncapital punishment (maybe states that have capital punishment also treat imprisoned murderers more harshly—or less harshly), and they didn't develop plausible and verifiable theories about how potential murderers estimate the probability of capital punishment. Sometime in the future these flaws may be mended. Until then, claims about what the evidence shows about what capital punishment would or would not do to minority homicide rates can't be evaluated.

Robbery

Robbery may be on its way to becoming an obsolete crime, like horse theft or witchcraft. People don't carry as much cash as they used to, and many of the valuable things that they do carry, such as smartphones and tablets, are either personalized or so easily traceable that they have little resale value (or can be configured to have little resale value). Around 2013, there was an upsurge of smartphone robbery and theft, but changes to smartphone features such as kill switches, which render the devices unusable after they have been stolen, appear to be reversing this trend (Chen 2014). Cell phones and surveillance cameras also mean that potential victims are never as alone as they were in the 1980s. In looking at how robberies changed at the end of the twentieth century, Rajiv Sethi and I (2009) attributed a lot of the drop to "victim hardening." From 1990 to 2009, robberies went down by 84 percent in New York City; the median decline in the next nine biggest cities was still a whopping 49 percent (Zimring 2012). You should not encourage your kids to become robbers.

But robbery is still a sizeable business, even if it's not a growth industry. Are there good ways to reduce its costs?

Subsidies to reduce use of cash may be helpful. People who move away from cash provide an external benefit: because robbers can't tell exactly who they are, everyone else becomes a less inviting target. Many landlords in poor neighborhoods, for instance, want to be paid in cash or by money order. If cash payments were taxed or noncash payments were subsidized, robbers would find fewer prospects. Similarly, subsidizing low-balance transaction accounts may be a good crime-fighting tool.

(A similar argument has sometimes been made for allowing concealed weapons: if some people carry concealed weapons, robbers will fear everyone and all potential victims will benefit [Lott 1998]. Concealed weapons, of course, can also lead to problems, unlike credit cards. Empirically, laws allowing concealed weapons seem to increase crime [Duggan 2001]. So more empirical studies of substitutions away from cash—through the implementation of Electronic Benefit Transfer technology, for instance— would be helpful.)

New technologies are embedding chips in cell phones that will allow people to make and receive payments without either plastic or paper. Network effects matter here: you won't get the chip to make payments unless a lot of the stores you do business with accept it, and they won't accept it unless a lot of their customers have it. Adopting these technologies has external benefits and should be encouraged, especially in minority communities.

Some evidence has also shown that business improvement districts can reduce street and property crime, largely without increases in incarceration (Cook and MacDonald 2011). Business improvement districts are private associations that largely consist of businesses who join together to tax themselves to provide common services such as advertising, street sweeping, and security guards. (They are often traditional stores that want to be surrounded with amenities, like stores in malls.) Business improvement districts in minority neighborhoods might be able to reduce robberies, but state laws often make it difficult for them to be set up—somebody has to force all the property owners who benefit from a BID to contribute to its operations.

On the more traditional public law enforcement side, Cook and Ludwig (2010) argue for more certainty and less severity for most crimes—essentially, shifting resources from prisons to police. We saw above that certainty and severity of punishment determined prison population in the long run, given the crime rate, but certainty and severity also affect the crime rate.

Certainty and severity work both through deterrence—discouraging potential criminals from committing crimes when they have the opportunity to do so—and through incapacitation—keeping potential criminals from committing crimes by making it impossible to do so. Crime is less attractive to potential criminals when punishment is more likely or more drastic, so the criminals will be deterred. The more potential criminals are incapacitated by being in prison, the fewer the crimes they can commit.

The marginal crime reduction returns to severity probably decrease as punishment increases; raising a sentence from 20 years to 25 probably reduces crime very little. The additional years are very far in the future and may be difficult for potential criminals to imagine. Career criminals may also believe (rationally) that they are likely to be imprisoned for the additional years regardless of whether they commit this particular crime because they are likely to commit other crimes. Additional years may also be relatively small punishment if the criminal record itself is the source of long-term stigma. Kling (2006), for instance, found that incarceration *length* had no impact on post-incarceration earnings. Most people decrease criminal activity as they age;

this is especially true of a physically demanding activity like robbery. Long sentences mean old prisoners, so small incapacitation benefits.

Certainty, on the other hand, probably yields no such decline in crime-reduction benefits and currently is fairly low for robbery anyway. Raphael and Stoll (2009) estimated that there were six prison admissions for each hundred robberies in 1984 and seven in 2002. Many robberies are punished by arrest or probation instead of prison and some individuals commit many robberies before they are imprisoned, but still the majority of robberies probably go unpunished.

On the other hand, as we noted above, the severity of punishment for index crimes increased considerably after 1980 and is quite high. Cook and Ludwig (2010) ask what would happen if the severity of punishment were rolled back from 2009 levels to 1984 levels. They conclude that the prison population would fall by about 400,000 and governments would save about $12 billion a year (not to mention the benefits to potential prisoners and their families). They estimate that this modest emptying of prisons would result in about 26,000 more violent crimes a year (mainly robberies and assaults). But because certainty matters more than severity at the margin, if you took the $12 billion from prisons and used it to hire police, violent index crimes would decrease by about 156,000. So on net, violent crime would decrease by 156,000 − 26,000 = 130,000. That would be significant for minority communities. On top of this, the reduction in prison population would be a major benefit to would-be prisoners and their families.

Raphael and Stoll (2013) provide a slightly different version of this thought experiment. They note that imprisonment appears to have "diminishing marginal returns" in crime reduction. As the prison population grows, the prisoners who are added are increasingly less dangerous and their imprisonment contributes increasingly less to crime reduction. Some empirical work (Piehl, Liedka, and Useem 2006) in fact indicates that once the prison population hits around 325 to 425 per 100,000, adding prisoners no longer reduces crime. Recall that the United States in 2009 had 756 prisoners and inmates per 100,000. Instead of rolling back the prison population to 1980 levels, they suggest rolling it back to 1990 levels and project that this reduction would have almost no effect on crime.

Something like these thought experiments may have been carried out in New York City from 1990 to 2009. As I noted, crime, especially robbery, fell dramatically in this period, much more than in the rest of the United States, but the prison population remained essentially flat (there was a small rise at the beginning of the period, followed by a long gradual decline after 1997). However, the size and efficacy of the police department increased greatly (Zimring 2012).

Similarly, California recently reduced its prison population to something close to 1990 levels. A modest increase in property crime, particularly motor vehicle theft, appears to have resulted, but no increase in murder and rape. The effect on robbery may have been small and positive, but it was difficult to measure. If a small fraction of the money saved by reducing the prison population had been used to expand police forces, all of these crime effects could have been countered (Lofstrom and Raphael 2013).

The same logic of substituting certainty for severity has also been applied successfully to probation violations. As Kleiman (2009) describes them, most current probation programs test for drugs occasionally and sporadically but invoke a harsh sanction if they find them: probation revocation, which usually implies a substantial period of incarceration. In a controlled field trial in Honolulu, the experimental group was subjected to frequent random drug tests with immediate but brief jail terms in the case of failure. The control group received the usual low-certainty, high-severity program. The experimental group committed less crime and spent fewer days incarcerated. More certainty and less severity reduced both crime and punishment.

Illicit Drugs

Illicit drugs are the most controversial of the major crime areas; no one seriously argues for decriminalizing murder and robbery. But we've already seen probable links from drug policies to both murder and robbery.

One possible policy would be to make the currently illicit drugs legal in some form. A similar policy with better public health consequences would be to allow pharmaceutical companies to develop and sell recreational and occupational drugs that met certain standards for safety and moderate side effects (O'Flaherty and Gowda 2004). In either case, drug consumption would probably increase and some serious problems would ensue (which would be more serious with the legalization of current worse drugs than with the legalization of future better drugs): traffic and workplace accidents, health complications, violence in homes and recreational venues, and possibly suicide. Alcohol is implicated in all these problems today, and while other legal recreational and occupational drugs might substitute some for alcohol consumption, the substitution is unlikely to be total.

Herein lies the fundamental racial unfairness of current drug policy. If illicit drugs were legalized, NHWs would be the overwhelming majority of users (just as they are today) and the external costs of added drug use would fall mainly on NHW communities. But aside from government expenditures, which are substantial, the costs of keeping drugs illegal (violence, corruption, and incarceration) falls mainly on minority communities (and Latin American nations).

To be clear, external costs are what concern me here. The direct costs of incarceration and violence on minority workers in the drug industry are to a large extent passed on to customers in the form of higher drug prices. These higher prices make NHW drug consumers worse off but presumably make NHW nonconsumers better off. But the market doesn't account for the external costs of the War on Drugs in minority communities, including the violence that spills over to nondrug encounters, the indignities of racial profiling, the effects of stereotypes on hiring and shopping, the hardships that befall families of the incarcerated, and the problems of lopsided sex ratios. The external benefits of drug prohibition accrue mainly to NHWs, while the external costs fall mainly on minorities.

The best estimates, moreover, indicate that the costs of prohibition far exceed its benefits. Kuziemko and Levitt (2004) estimate that imprisoning drug offenders in the late twentieth century reduced drug consumption by 9–15 percent. Citing Harwood (1998), they say that the costs of cocaine consumption are about $50 per gram of pure cocaine, and the majority of these costs are not external. But the cost to the government of incarcerating drug offenders at that time was about $270 to reduce pure cocaine consumption by one gram. Even without considering the external costs of incarceration, then, imprisonment for drug crimes is inefficient. (Kuziemko and Levitt find that it reduces property and violent crime but the effect is small on net.) It might be that separating costs from benefits in drug policy allows such inefficiency to continue.

If drugs were legal, a high enough tax could reduce consumption to almost any desired level, including the level we see today with the current prohibitions on certain drugs. If there were a tax high enough to keep drug consumption at current levels, the external costs of drug consumption would be no higher than they are now and the government would be collecting significant revenue instead of spending money on chasing and imprisoning drug offenders. More important, since this policy would not be enforced primarily by arresting minority drug sellers, the external costs of the War on Drugs in minority communities would largely disappear. Becker, Murphy, and Grossman (2006) give a fuller description of how this policy would work.

Within a regime where the usual illicit drugs are still illegal and untaxed and pharmaceutical companies can't compete, other policies can still mitigate some of the problems. Perhaps the cheapest would be to reduce enforcement efforts against clandestine drug sales, especially in affluent communities, and against the marketing of drugs over the Internet. Reducing demand in anonymous open-air markets should reduce the external costs of these markets and the heavy minority involvement. It will make sellers look more like users. The cost, however, would probably be somewhat higher drug consumption.

Zimring (2012) argues that the New York Police Department followed a variant of this strategy during the late twentieth and early twenty-first centuries, when crime declined precipitously. They attacked open-air markets viciously and more or less ignored clandestine drug sales and use. In the early 1990s they launched a major campaign against open-air drug markets and essentially put them out of business. But then the narcotics unit shrank and drug use was ignored. Their goal was not to reduce drug use; it was to reduce drug violence. To support this position, Zimring shows that over this two-decade period of aggressive and amazingly successful policing, drug consumption in New York City hardly changed at all. Despite the tough rhetoric, New York engaged in a harm reduction program.

Misdemeanor marijuana arrests rose during this period (but not marijuana consumption), but these were targeted at the people carrying the marijuana, not the marijuana itself. They were "pretextual arrests": the police were using the marijuana laws as tools to arrest people they thought were likely to commit or had committed more serious crimes. That was why the arrestees were overwhelmingly minority males, even though women use marijuana almost as much as men do.

Another alternative would be to concentrate enforcement efforts on consumers—not sellers or producers—perhaps even going so far as to prohibit the use of drugs but not their sale. Use, after all, is what generates the harms that drug prohibition strives to prevent, not sales or possession. Punishing consumers rather than sellers would allow drug markets to operate peacefully and normally and would spread the external costs of punishment more evenly across the population.

Punishing users would also spur them to seek treatment. Seeing their neighbors and relatives punished severely might also spur more affluent and influential citizens of all races to seek less severe punishment and more heavily subsidized treatment.

The difficulty with this policy, of course, is that setting up a system with legal sales (presumably taxed) and illegal consumption presents considerable logistical problems. It's not impossible that information technology could rise to this challenge. The rapid growth of unauthorized use of prescription drugs—possibly soon to be the largest category of illegal drug use in the United States—demonstrates that such an arrangement is not impossible.

Changing What People Are Like

Instead of changing the payoffs people get from crime through deterrence or changing their opportunities through incapacitation, another set of programs aims to reduce crime by changing what people's goals are and how they approach life. Although there is no reason to think that the distribution of personality traits is responsible for the vast interracial gulf for the three crimes this chapter concentrates on, these programs might still be worthwhile. A number of these programs have been evaluated rigorously, and some appear to reduce crime by as much per government dollar as incarceration does. Since almost all of these programs produce benefits that go beyond crime fighting, this test is far more stringent than it needs to be or should be.

Donohue and Siegelman (1998) tried to find programs that pass this too-stringent test. High-quality preschool with lots of parental involvement passed it. Residential Job Corps programs—intensive vocational training for young adults in camp-like settings—came close. The other social programs that had been rigorously evaluated before 1998 didn't pass the test. (On the other hand, Donohue and Siegelman's test may have been too lenient: they looked only for a reduction in crimes committed by program participants, not total crimes. If preschool alumni stopped selling drugs, for instance, their place may have been taken by other youngsters.)

Since then, a number of programs that work on the social-behavioral skills of young men and their families have been evaluated and seem to work well (Cook and Ludwig 2010). These are skills such as self-control and the ability to resolve conflicts peacefully. Examples of generally successful programs are Functional Family Therapy, Multisystemic Therapy, and Multidimensional Treatment Foster Care. Raising the school-leaving age to 18 has also been evaluated favorably.

Even programs that meet these very high standards have political drawbacks. The first drawback is that most take a long time to have an effect. The effects of preschool on crime rates, for instance, may not show up for more than a dozen years. A high-quality preschool program can't help a mayor or governor whose constituents are complaining about crime happening now or who herself is worried about reelection next year.

The second problem is that to be effective at reducing crime the programs have to be targeted narrowly at children or young adults who are likely to commit crime when they grow up. The best preschool in the world won't reduce the number of crimes that would be committed by a girl who otherwise would never commit a crime. Race is a strong predictor of who commits murder and robbery even holding family income and family structure constant. For all crimes, gender is a very strong predictor. Intelligently targeted social programs to reduce crime can't be race blind (or gender blind).

Conclusion

In 1849, Thomas Carlyle's famous "Occasional Discourse on the Negro Question" spoke about how compulsion was a necessary part of the racial etiquette in the West Indies (675–677):

> Quashee, if he will not help in bringing out spices, will get himself made a slave again (which state will be little less ugly than his present one), and with a beneficent whip, since other methods avail not, will be compelled to work. . . . You are not "slaves" now; nor do I wish, if it can be avoided, to see you slaves again: but decidedly you will have to be servants to those born *wiser* than you, that are born lords of you,—servants to the whites, if they *are* (and what mortal can doubt they are) born wiser than you.

Today, many people think that others—a subset of black men in particular—should be subject to compulsion because of what they are. As Cook and Ludwig (2010, 13) phrase it:

> Much of the public conversation about crime . . . focuses on just one aspect . . . , the character of youths. In the simplistic version, the population consists of good guys and bad guys. The bad guys commit crimes and the good guys do not. . . . Crime control is then a matter of locking up as many bad guys as possible (or, when the bad guys are immigrants, deporting them). Public opinion polls suggest that much of the public believes that offenders are made not born, so the number of "bad guys" can also be reduced through better parenting.

In 1850, John Stuart Mill responded to Carlyle with an essay called "The Negro Question," and attacked (29) "the vulgar error of imputing every difference . . . among human beings to an original difference of nature"—or parenting, he would probably add today.

> As well might be said, that of two trees, sprung from the same stock, one cannot be taller than another but from greater vigour in the original seedling. Is nothing to be attributed to soil, nothing to climate, nothing to difference of exposure—has no storm swept over the one and not the other, no lightning scathed it, no beast browsed on it, no insects preyed on it, no passing stranger stript off its leaves or its bark? If the trees grew near together, may not the one which, by whatever accident, grew up first, have retarded the other's development by its shade? Human beings are subject to an infinitely greater variety of accidents and external influences than trees, and have infinitely more operation in impairing the growth of one another; since those who begin by being strongest, have almost always hitherto used their strength to keep the others weak.

Mill's intellectual descendants, the practitioners of the "dismal science" (the term Carlyle coined in the "Occasional Discourse on the Negro Question," as I noted in Chapter 1), continue to look for the vast variety of influences that affect human behavior and think about reducing crime through a wide variety of tools. That is the approach I tried to introduce you to in this chapter. Because crime and crime fighting are so expensive, especially for minority communities, and because the line between legitimate compulsion and tyranny is often so difficult to discern, that seems like a sensible approach. The huge decline in crime since 1991, a decline that experts are unanimous in not being able to attribute to even a small number of causes, shows that inherent character traits must be of minor importance and gives me a lot of hope.

12

Businesses and Entrepreneurs

Y ou should care about whether minorities are setting up businesses and becoming entrepreneurs for several reasons.

The most boring is the simple question of efficiency. Some people have comparative advantage at running businesses; others have comparative advantage in working in other people's businesses. Deadweight losses occur if people end up in the wrong positions. We'll see that many Asians and few African Americans are entrepreneurs. Maybe some Asians are really better at working for other people and some African Americans are really better at running their own businesses. Of course, this presumes that we can identify what comparative advantage at being an entrepreneur consists of and that it's independent of other social conventions.

The most exciting reason to study entrepreneurship is that it's the source of really great fortunes, and perhaps really great fortunes have an important impact on our society. The first part of the story is true: entrepreneurs have a hugely disproportionate share of U.S. wealth, and famous rich people such as Bill Gates and Warren Buffett are entrepreneurs. The second part of the story is more questionable because it has not been studied at all. Do the personal characteristics of billionaires matter to the whole society? Have white men been the dominant demographic group in this country because the richest people are white men or does causality run the other way: Are the richest people white men because white men have been the dominant demographic group? These are interesting questions, but I don't know any answers.

The third reason is more directly relevant to this book. Nobody stops anybody from being self-employed: self-employment has no gatekeeper like the ones that tell you that you're not hired or you're not going to get the loan or you should not have coronary artery bypass grafts or you can't go to Columbia. Thus if you're an enterprising minority person who faces discrimination in other realms of life, perhaps entrepreneurship will give you the way to realize your ambitions and use all your talents. I call this the romantic view of entrepreneurship.

The final reason to study entrepreneurship is also directly relevant to this book. Many kinds of discrimination can become disparate treatment without disparate impact if minorities can go into business for themselves. What other people see as discrimination, minority entrepreneurs should see as opportunity, and the process of converting that opportunity into profit should eliminate any disparate impact that the discrimination might otherwise create. Thus, for instance, if white employers were Becker-style discriminators, minority entrepreneurs could hire minority labor cheaper than their white competitors and do well while doing good. Minority doctors could advertise themselves as having more rapport with minority patients and improve health care while becoming rich. If other realtors don't treat minorities well, then minority realtors should be able to step in, get minority buyers better homes, get sellers more money, and become rich. Minority banks could similarly make a fortune from good minority borrowers if majority banks discriminated. Minority entrepreneurs, in other words, could solve many of the problems we identified in other parts of the book. Why don't they ride to the rescue?

For all these reasons, entrepreneurship is worth studying.

Basic Facts

Counting Problems

Counting business owners is not easy. The difficulty is caused by the people at the bottom—the folks who sell jewelry during their lunch hour, for instance. The federal government produces many different data sets with many different definitions. Users have to be careful to understand the specific definition of entrepreneurship in the data set they're using. Apparently, these problems are most serious for Hispanics in some of the most commonly used specialized data sets.

Not Heaven

Self-employment doesn't appear to be a growing trend in the U.S. economy, unless it's spurred by a recession, and many countries with high self-employment rates, such as Haiti, are not beacons of prosperity. Self-employed people generally work very long hours, most of them don't make an outlandish amount of money, and a very large proportion of businesses fail.

What nonracial characteristics make people likely to become entrepreneurs? Basically the same kind of characteristics that make people likely to make a lot of money as workers: being educated, being old but not too old to have some energy left, being married, being wealthy, and being male. Conditional on being self-employed, these are also the same characteristics that make you more likely to have a large, successful, enduring business. Wealth is tricky in this setting, since it can be endogenous: for people who are already self-employed, wealth may be high because they are self-employed; for people who are on the verge of becoming self-employed, wealth may be high because they are saving up in order to go into business. Similarly businesses that have higher start-up costs are more successful, but this again could be endogenous: people may be more willing to give money to a start-up company if they think its prospects are better. We have to be careful.

Blacks and Hispanics Don't Do Well in Business

Table 12.1 shows data on the proportion of workers who are self-employed (outside of the agricultural sector). Black and Hispanic self-employment is well below Asian and NHW self-employment. Black and Hispanic self-employment rates have been rising slowly since the 1980s, but NHWs show no trend. Moreover, the businesses blacks and Hispanics do set up are smaller and less successful. Table 12.2 shows how businesses compare by race or ethnicity of owner. Hispanic businesses appear to be somewhat more successful

Table 12.1. Self-employment rates by ethnicity and race, 2006.

	Percent self-employed
Non-Hispanic white	11.1
Black	5.1
Hispanic	7.5
Asian	11.8

Source: Fairlie and Robb (2008), table 2.1, from Current Population Survey outgoing rotation sample.

Table 12.2. Business outcomes by ethnicity and race.

	Sales	Paid employees	Closing rate (%)	Positive profit (%)
Non-Hispanic white–owned	$440	2.8	22.6	75.1
Black-owned	74	0.6	26.9	60.7
Hispanic-owned	141	1.0	22.2	73.6
Asian-owned	292	2.0	17.9	72.5
Indian (Asian)	395	2.7		
Chinese	367	2.3		
Filipino	113	1.1		
Japanese	354	2.4		
Korean	298	2.0		
Mexican	138	1.0		
Puerto Rican	113	0.7		
Cuban	234	1.4		

Source: Fairlie and Robb (2008), tables 2.5, 2.6, 2.8, 2.9, 2.10.

Notes: Sales are in thousands of 2002 dollars. Data on paid employees is from 2002. The closing rate is the percent of firms that were in business in 1992 that were no longer operating in 1996. Data on percent of firms with positive net profit is from 1992.

than black businesses, but neither are as successful as NHW and Asian businesses. Maybe that's why blacks and Hispanics don't set up so many businesses.

Asians Do Fairly Well

Asians are slightly more likely than NHWs to be entrepreneurs, and those who are entrepreneurs enjoy some success. Tables 12.1 and 12.2 provide the basic data. No time trend in Asian self-employment rates is apparent. Nor do self-employment rates differ markedly among Asian ethnic groups. About 80 percent of Asian business owners are immigrants, as compared with about 69 percent of the total Asian population in 2000. So the proportion of immigrant business owners is only a little higher than the proportion of immigrants in the adult population.

Explanations

These data suggest two questions: Why are so few blacks (and Hispanics) business owners? Why are so many Asian business owners? In both cases, I'll try to answer the question by making comparisons with NHWs.

Comparing Blacks (and Maybe Hispanics) with NHWs

As usual, we can distinguish between explanations that emphasize history and those that emphasize current discrimination. Although, as we have seen, Hispanics look a lot like blacks when it comes to self-employment, much less research has been done on Hispanics, partly because one of the best data sets for studying self-employment, the 1992 Characteristics of Business Owners data set, has inconsistent results about Hispanics in ways that researchers have been unable to reconcile.

Current discrimination—W. E. B. Du Bois explanations. If you run regressions on the probability of becoming self-employed or on various measures of business success, you almost always get a racial residual or unexplained gap. This is a standard disparate impact result. Comparing blacks and NHWs, when you run regressions for opening a business in the next few years or for self-employed status, education matters, but you don't get much of the gap explained. For instance, for Current Population Survey data in the late 1980s, the Blinder-Oaxaca decompositions for the proportion of self-employed looked like this:

Black: 3.4 percent
White characteristics and black coefficients (enrichment experiment): 4.5 percent

Black characteristics and white coefficients (civil rights experiment):
8.2 percent
White: 10.0 percent

These Blinder-Oaxaca decompositions don't use wealth as an explanatory variable because of the endogeneity issues. Similarly, Fairlie and Robb (2008) explain 8 percent of the gap in profits and 20 percent of the gap in sales with standard variables (these variables don't include start-up costs, once again because of endogeneity issues).

There is also evidence of discrimination in lending. Bostic and Lampani (1999) and Cavaluzzo et al. (1999) show that blacks get turned down more than whites for business loans, holding constant everything you can find. Black business owners are also more likely than white to say that they didn't apply for loans because they thought they would be turned down.

Researchers have made a number of attempts to measure consumer discrimination and its effects on minority entrepreneurship. I don't find any results especially convincing yet.

Past discrimination—Booker T. Washington explanations.   Some variables that reflect history have significant impacts on the racial entrepreneurship gap. The big ones are wealth and start-up costs. Wealthier people are more likely to start up businesses, and businesses with higher start-up costs do better. These two variables explain a lot of the black-white gap: Fairlie and Robb find that wealth explains about 15 percent of the gap in the rate at which people start businesses, and adding start-up capital to the model for business profit increases the proportion of the profit gap (whether the business has profits of at least $10,000) explained by characteristics from 26 percent to 42 percent. But as I mentioned before, wealth and start-up costs are not completely exogenous. Wealth and the ability to raise money matter, but maybe not as much as the regressions suggest. You need an instrument, such as family wealth during childhood.

Family history matters too, but not a lot. If your parents were entrepreneurs, you're more likely to be one too, and if you had experience in a similar business before you started yours, you'll do better too. These differences, however, don't explain a lot of the black-white gap (partly because entrepreneurship is less heritable for blacks) and they explain none of the Asian-white gap.

"Ethnic tradition" probably doesn't matter much, even though it was once a favorite story of sociologists. At the turn of the century the self-employment rate of African Americans was far higher than it is now—they owned lots of farms in the South, many of them with employees. At that time, the black self-employment rate was about the same as the white self-employment rate.

Self-employment rates of immigrant groups have little to do with self-employment in the home country. India is not full of gasoline stations, and Korea is not wall-to-wall delis and dry cleaners.

Comparing Asians and NHWs

For Asians, regressions on the probability of being or becoming self-employed sometimes show a positive coefficient and sometimes don't. Remember that Asians are better educated than NHWs and education is positively correlated with business ownership and success. Asians also have more wealth than NHWs.

Whether Asian businesses are more successful than NHW businesses is controversial and unclear. In the Fairlie and Robb data, Asian businesses unconditionally are more likely to survive, to have profits of at least $10,000, and to have employees; they also have larger sales on average. But is this because Asians invest more financial and human capital? To find out, Fairlie and Robb first try to explain these gaps without including start-up capital in the regressions. Characteristics—the most powerful one is education and the second is region—explain about 90 percent of the profit gap, but less than a quarter of the other gaps. Holding these standard variables constant, Asian business are more successful than NHW businesses, at least on these measures.

But then they added start-up capital and the industry that the business is in to the regression. These variables together with the others explain about 100 percent of the survival and sales gaps and about 150 percent of the profit and employee gaps. In other words, given start-up capital, Asian businesses perform no better than NHW businesses in terms of survival and sales and they perform worse in terms of profit and number of employees.

Notice that we're talking about *accounting* profit. That leaves out the opportunity cost of the owner's labor, the owner's family's labor, and the owner's capital. Asian businesses raise more of their larger capital from the owner

Table 12.3. Profits per hour of owner time by race and level of education, around 1990.

	College-educated	No college
Indian and Filipino	$5.63	$3.59
Korean and Chinese	6.02	3.40
African American	6.41	4.76
Nonminority	7.52	6.39

Source: Bates (1997).

and the owner's family. Self-employed Asians work longer hours than self-employed NHWs. Fairlie and Robb use a very crude measure of profits, but everything here suggests that Asian businesses really are less profitable than NHW businesses.

In an earlier book that drew on older data, Bates (1997) tried to look more closely at economic profit. He calculated accounting profit per hour for various businesspeople. The results are in Table 12.3.

This seems to me to be the right way to look at it, even though it's out of date and the Fairlie and Robb data indicate somewhat stronger performance by Asian firms. But the goal is to make economic profit, not to have a big operation or to make more than $10,000 in accounting profit. After all, $10,000 a year in accounting profit is a very low hurdle for a business run by a college-educated person working 60-hour weeks who has invested $50,000 of his own money. Asian businesses don't seem to be more economically profitable than NHW businesses.

For the most part, Asian businesses do not rely on Asian customers. In general, having a co-ethnic customer base does not appear to be the key to business success in the United States: if it were, black and Hispanic businesses would be much more plentiful than Asian businesses, since black and Hispanic customers are much more plentiful. For Hispanics, customer base appears to be a minor consideration, as the self-employment rate appears to be somewhat higher in metropolitan areas with greater proportions of Hispanics. For blacks, no such correlation appears to be present, either in the numbers of businesses or in their success (Fairlie and Robb 2008, 25; Bates 1997).

Analysis

How do you put these two sets of results together—results about becoming self-employed (or staying self-employed) and results about business success? It's challenging, and no one except Borjas and Bronars (1989) has really attempted to do so. When you look at the self-employed, you're looking at a self-selected group and you need to understand the basis for selection.

I'll use a very simple model to try to understand what is going on. Suppose there are two ways of earning money: salaried employment and self-employment. Each person has an expected amount that she could make in each if she chose to work in that sector—net of everything else and including utility or disutility of the job. This takes into consideration any discrimination she might face, any special abilities she has, and any particular enjoyment she might get from being her own boss or from getting a regular paycheck. So each person is a point in two-dimensional space, as in Figure 12.1.

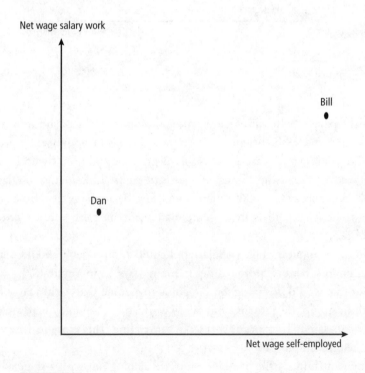

Figure 12.1.

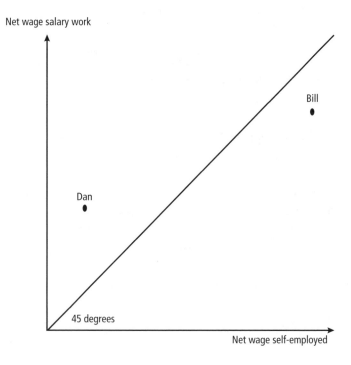

Figure 12.2.

If the payoff from self-employment is greater than the payoff from salaried employment, she becomes self-employed, and the converse. So people who are salary workers are above the 45-degree line and people who are self-employed are below the 45-degree line, as in Figure 12.2. Dan is in salaried employment because he makes more from being an employee than from being an entrepreneur; Bill is in self-employment because his returns are the opposite.

To think about a whole population, I could and probably should draw a cloud of dots, because people differ in many ways, as in Figure 12.3.

But that would be taxing. So I'm going to assume that within any racial or ethnic group, the returns from salary work and self-employment are perfectly correlated. That means that I can draw a line. This is not realistic, but it's a helpful simplification.

You can think of the line being upward sloping but with a slope of less than one. The positive correlation arises because many of the same talents

Net wage salary employed

45 degrees

Net wage self-employed

Figure 12.3.

that make you good at salaried employment also make you good at self-employment—education and intelligence, for instance, and ability to concentrate for long hours. The slope is less than one because the returns to the most valuable talents can be realized only as an entrepreneur and the returns to the least valuable talents can be realized only as a salary employee. To found the next Google, I have to be an entrepreneur; to empty wastebaskets, I have to be a salary employee. Thus we have the line in Figure 12.4. So the people who actually become entrepreneurs are the most able at making money and they make more on average than salary employees. The opportunity to become self-employed exacerbates inequality.

Now think of two groups and how the lines for the two groups could compare. I'll try some easy and obvious stories first and see if they tell us anything about the real world.

The easiest case is when the two groups are the same: the same line applies for both. Then both groups have the same proportion of entrepreneurs,

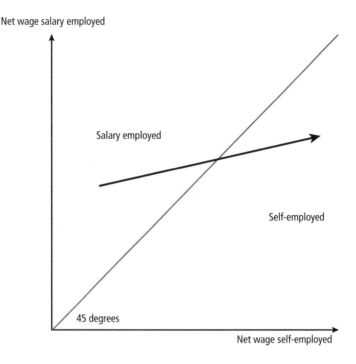

Figure 12.4.

the businesses in the two groups are equally successful, and the members of both groups earn equal wages in the salary world. Empirically, this might almost match the situation for NHWs and Asians, although language issues suggest that the two lines really aren't the same.

Now let's try out the romantic story of entrepreneurship: minorities face discrimination in the salary world but can operate unhindered by discrimination in the self-employment world. So if you take two people (one NHW and one minority) who would make the same as salaried workers, the minority will make more as an entrepreneur. That gives us Figure 12.5. Some predictions of Figure 12.5 are borne out empirically: lower earnings for black entrepreneurs, lower earnings for black salary workers. But the romantic view also implies that black entrepreneurs will be more common (within the black population) than white entrepreneurs. This doesn't hold empirically. So the romantic story doesn't work for blacks.

Figure 12.5. The romantic view.

Does it work for Asians? It implies a big difference in salary earnings, which we don't see. The romantic view seems wrong for both blacks and Asians.

What story works for blacks? Discrimination (or lower returns given observable characteristics) in both domains, but a bigger difference in self-employment than in self-employment. I show this in Figure 12.6. If you consider a black person and a white person with the same skills, the black person would make less in both salaried employment and self-employment, but the gap in earnings is bigger for self-employment than for salaried employment.

What are the empirical implications of the relationships in Figure 12.6? There are fewer black entrepreneurs and they do worse. Notice that because fewer of the top blacks are drawn out of salaried employment the measured salary gap shrinks, but it can still be positive. The salary gap in earnings is likely to be smaller than the entrepreneurship gap in earnings, which seems right.

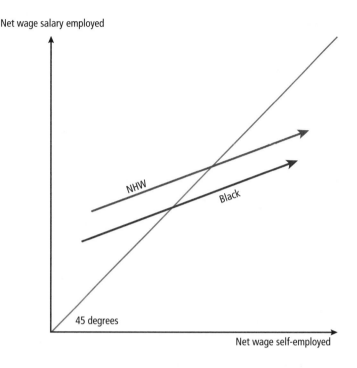

Figure 12.6.

What about Asians? Think about wealth. Investable wealth doesn't help you in the salary market, but it helps you in self-employment. Similarly, having a family that is willing to work in your store helps if you're self-employed but not if you're a salary worker. Language may be more of a hindrance in salaried employment than in self-employment.

These ideas suggest that the correlation between potential earnings in self-employment and potential earnings in salaried employment may be much smaller for Asians than for NHWs. That would make the lines in the figures less steep.

To simplify, then, let's draw the Asian line completely flat, as in Figure 12.7. This arrangement gets us a possible explanation. As I drew it, a greater proportion of Asians are self-employed, earnings in salaried employment are about the same on average (although NHWs have greater wage inequality), and average Asian earnings in self-employment are slightly lower. Figure 12.7, then, captures the major differences in the empirical literature now.

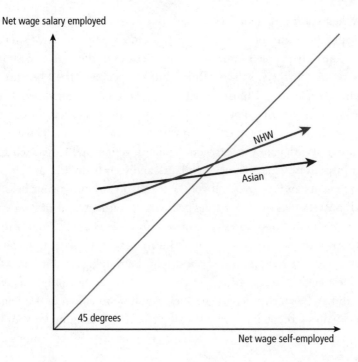

Figure 12.7.

I think the other good alternative is that whites and Asians are pretty similar—in keeping with Fairlie and Robb. Obviously more work is needed on this issue with data sets that include the whole population, not just entrepreneurs.

Conclusion

Remember that this is an economics book, not a talk show, so my job is understanding what people do, not condemning them or praising them for it. So I couldn't praise Asians for opening up businesses or condemn African Americans for not doing so if I wanted to.

Let's get back to the first question I raised, and one that I think is the most important one: Are the right people entrepreneurs? That's the real economics question.

When you think about what small businesses are like, the fact that few African Americans (or Hispanics) are self-employed is not surprising or terrible. The only people I know who post pictures of themselves with important people on their walls are small businesspeople. That's because small businesspeople are the most vulnerable, most interconnected people in our society, not the least. They're not lone-wolf prospectors testing themselves against Mother Nature in the north woods. If you run a small business, you have to deal with your workers, your landlord, your suppliers, your customers, your inspectors, your parking attendants, and your financiers and keep them all happy. As an employee, all you have to worry about is your boss. For a small businessperson, if anything goes wrong with any one of your constituents, you're in trouble and your other constituents are in trouble too. If I go to work for you and you go out of business next week because you failed to deal with the restaurant inspector right, I am in big trouble and I should not have gone to work for you in the first place. So not only must you be able to handle all these constituencies, you have to convince everyone that you can do so. If you have trouble hailing a cab or arranging for your health care, then why should anyone believe you can do all these things almost flawlessly?

Given our current world and the current discrimination in this world and the current stereotypes, self-employment is not a great idea for most African Americans or Hispanics. This would be different in a different world, but that doesn't matter now. Lefties could play shortstop if the bases were arranged in reverse, but it's still not a good idea for a lefty to play shortstop today.

One of the costs of the other kinds of discrimination is that too few African Americans and Hispanics become entrepreneurs. But that is a reason for dealing with other kinds of discrimination.

What does this say about separatism? My interpretation is that separatism works as a radical proposition or not at all. African American entrepreneurship is necessary for separatism, but it can thrive only in a world that's otherwise almost totally color blind (in which case there would be no disparate treatment for entrepreneurs to keep from becoming disparate impact) or in a world where most other spheres (such as government, education, and finance) are already separatist. Piecemeal separatism makes as much sense as a piecemeal transition from driving on the right to driving on the left (trucks this year, cars next year).

On the other hand, I'm not sure that the large numbers of Asians in retail businesses represent a wise allocation of resources. The data indicate that many of these people are highly skilled and highly diligent. Maybe they should be running corporations, not delicatessens. It's more interesting to think about why they aren't running corporations than to praise them for arranging apples nicely.

13

Wealth

Blacks and Hispanics hold a lot less wealth than NHWs and Asians. This chapter is about why and whether that condition is likely to persist.

Since capital markets aren't perfect, wealth makes a difference in what you can do. Wealth helps in getting a good education for kids. Wealth also matters for mortgages and homeownership and for businesses and entrepreneurship, as we've seen. If blacks and Hispanics had more wealth, they would own more homes and start more businesses (although we can't really say how many more because part of wealth comes from owning a home and running a business).

Wealth is also great to have in an emergency. If you need money fast to pay for an operation, bail yourself out of jail, fix a broken water pipe, or take advantage of a wonderful business opportunity, you can move quickly and discreetly if you have a savings account or a portfolio of stocks.

A lot of people think of wealth as power too: you don't have to beg or borrow if you can buy. I'm not so sure: if you have wealth you need somebody to protect it for you. Modern forms of wealth, moreover, are pretty much dependent on complex webs of inference and confidence and may in some cases make you less powerful. What use, exactly, is the trillion dollars in U.S. debt that China holds?

While wealth is good stuff, it's not the be-all and end-all of economic life. If you inherit $100,000 and choose to donate all of it to charity or spend it all on your children's education or on your quest to climb Mount Everest, who am I to say that you did something wrong or should be stopped from doing it? If minorities are living the types of lives they want to lead and have little wealth, so what? Consumption is what economic life is about, not wealth—wealth is valuable only to the extent that it permits consumption by you or someone you care about. But since wealth often permits consumption, we need to study it.

Measuring Wealth

Wealth is not very well measured or very often measured. A large proportion of wealth is held by the top 1 percent of households, and they don't share a lot of information about what they own. The chief source of information about wealth is the Survey of Consumer Finances, which the Federal Reserve takes every three years. The sample size is small—only about 4,500 households—and while rich households are oversampled, their response rate is low. Because rich households are oversampled and few blacks or Hispanics are rich, blacks and Hispanics are undersampled.

Wealth is a stock, not a flow. The basic identities are

Wealth now = wealth last year + savings this year + return on wealth
        + bequests received this year

Savings this year = income this year − consumption this year.

With income, by contrast, you don't start with income last year; income is a flow, not a stock.

In most published sources, wealth or net worth is defined as:

Bank accounts + money market accounts + IRAs, 401ks, and defined contribution pension plans + bonds + home equity + stocks + value of business − nonhousing debt

Home equity = value of house − mortgage outstanding and other debt backed by the house

Sometimes net value of vehicles is also included in net wealth and sometimes it isn't. Two items are left out that usually should be there: defined benefit pension wealth and social security wealth. Minorities have proportionately more of these three forms of wealth, and they did not lose as much value in the Great Recession as houses, stocks, and bonds did. These forms of wealth may be somewhat less liquid than other forms and so are somewhat less helpful in emergencies; they may also be less useful for setting up businesses.

Credit cards are also usually omitted. Balances on credit cards give you quick access to cash, so credit cards serve the same precautionary purpose as financial wealth, but outstanding credit card debt is subtracted from your net worth. Blacks and possibly other minorities have less access to credit cards and credit lines than whites do, even holding most other observable variables constant (Bertaut and Haliassos 2006; Cohen-Cole 2011), so their measured wealth may understate their ability to capitalize on opportunities and react to emergencies.

Wealth is distributed much more unequally than income in almost all developed countries. In the United States now, for instance, the top 1 percent accounts for about 20 percent of income but 35 percent of wealth; in Western Europe the comparable figures are 10 percent of income and 25 percent of wealth. These are not necessarily the same households. The bottom 50 percent of households hold almost no wealth: about 5 percent of total wealth in both the United States and Western Europe (Piketty 2013, tables 7.2 and 7.3). Many households have zero or negative wealth (their debts are greater than their assets), while very few households have zero or negative income.

Because the distribution of wealth is like this, it probably is not appropriate to compare the intergroup differences in wealth with intergroup differences in other things with strikingly different distributions. For instance, suppose that all minorities have zero wealth and all NHWs have wealth of one dollar. Then the ratio of NHW wealth to minority wealth would be infinitely great. But it really would not be appropriate to compare this distribution with the actual distribution of income and say that wealth was distributed more unequally than income.

Similarly, changes in intergroup gaps over time are also difficult to interpret. Suppose that all minorities have one dollar in wealth and all NHWs except one, "the king," have two dollars in wealth. The king has a huge amount of wealth that fluctuates with the stock market. Everyone else's wealth is constant over time. The ratio of median minority wealth to median NHW wealth will be stable at one-half, but the ratio of mean minority wealth to mean NHW wealth will fluctuate wildly. The two obvious measures of the intergroup gap give conflicting answers about how it is changing over time, and it is not clear which answer is the right one.

Racial Disparities in Wealth

The basic fact is that African Americans and Hispanics on average have a whole lot less wealth than NHWs. (Very little data on Asian wealth are available.) The conventional measures of the wealth gap, which we know can be misleading, have not narrowed in the last several decades. Very few minorities are at the top of the distribution, where wealth is concentrated, and a large number are concentrated at the bottom. In the Forbes 400 list of richest Americans, there is only one African American (Oprah Winfrey), probably only one Hispanic (Jorge Pérez), and maybe a dozen Asians. (About 4.4 percent of households were headed by an Asian in 2012, so even Asians are underrepresented in the Forbes 400.)

Table 13.1 shows standard summaries of wealth by race and ethnicity since 1989. The distribution of wealth is highly skewed—the upper tail is much further from the mode than the lower tail is—so the mean is considerably bigger than the median. As the example with the king suggests, whether you

Table 13.1. Median and mean net worth of non-Hispanic whites and Hispanics, 1989–2010, in constant 2010 dollars (thousands).

	Median			Mean		
	Non-Hispanic white	Hispanic	Ratio	Non-Hispanic white	Hispanic	Ratio
1989	120.0	11.3	10.6	383.6	106.0	3.6
1992	105.7	18.2	5.8	337.2	117.5	2.9
1995	108.5	22.4	4.8	355.5	109.3	3.3
1998	127.8	22.2	5.8	450.6	134.1	3.4
2001	150.4	22.0	6.8	599.0	144.1	4.2
2004	162.2	28.5	5.7	648.3	176.2	3.7
2007	179.4	29.7	6.0	727.4	240.3	3.0
2010	130.5	20.4	6.4	654.5	175.9	3.7

Source: Bricker et al. (2012), internal data, table 4.

want to look primarily at the mean or the median depends in large part on your attitude toward the richest households' wealth. If you want to think a lot about the richest households and believe that their wealth is reasonably well measured, then you want to look at the mean. If the richest 1 percent of NHW households doubled their wealth and everyone else stayed the same, the mean of NHW wealth would go up but the median would stay the same. On the other hand, if you seriously distrust the measurement of the richest households' wealth in the Survey of Consumer Finances, then you might want to pay more attention to the median, since it's not affected by measurement problems at the top (or the bottom). The median may also be a better picture of a "typical household." But you should be aware that both standard measures have shortcomings.

Table 13.1 shows that NHW wealth is considerably greater than minority wealth, regardless of whether you look at the median or at the mean. Median NHW wealth is 5–7 times as great as median minority wealth; mean NHW wealth is 3–4 times as great. (The discrepancy between mean and median probably arises because the median NHW household owns a house while the median minority household does not; the mean puts some weight on the fairly numerous minority households who own homes, while the median doesn't.)

Wealth doesn't appear to be converging over time. The ratios between NHW and minority wealth move up and down quite a bit but mainly stay in a band. For instance, relative minority wealth rose in the subprime boom (especially in the mean, where minority homeowners count) and fell in the dotcom boom (since many NHWs owned stocks and few minorities did). But except for the unusual 1989 median ratio (which is probably attributable to counting issues), there is no clear trend.

An alternative measure is to ask where the median minority household was in the total wealth distribution. During the time covered in Table 13.1, the median minority household was usually very close to the 25th percentile of the total distribution. The exception was 2010: because large numbers of NHWs had negative wealth in that year, the median minority household moved up in the total wealth distribution. This will probably turn out to be a transitory occurrence.

In the Federal Reserve reports, the category "non-white and Hispanic," which we translate as "minority," includes African Americans, Hispanics, Asians, and Native Americans. Because of the small sample size, the official reports do not provide more detail than this. Wolff (2012), however, has reanalyzed the Survey of Consumer Finances data to estimate net worth for African Americans and Hispanics separately. The results are presented in Tables 13.2 and 13.3. The sample sizes are small, so the numbers have considerable sampling error.

The basic picture doesn't change: NHWs have a lot more wealth than African Americans or Hispanics, and there is no clear trend. Generally, African Americans have greater median net worth than Hispanics, but Hispanics have greater mean net worth. Tables 13.2 and 13.3 show very starkly how the collapse of the housing market and the Great Recession hammered Hispanics and African Americans, Hispanics especially. Between 2007 and 2010, Hispanic mean wealth fell by half and median wealth fell by close to 90 percent. Relative to NHWs, Hispanics are worse off than they have been since at least 1989.

Table 13.4 shows that minority households hold their wealth in different forms than NHW households do. Minorities are less likely to hold almost any asset, but the differences are greatest for stocks, mutual funds, and bonds of almost all types, assets that often have high rates of return. Life insurance seems to be the big investment for minorities.

Table 13.2. Median and mean net worth of non-Hispanic whites and African Americans, 1989–2010, in constant 2010 dollars (thousands).

	Median			Mean		
	Non-Hispanic white	Non-Hispanic African American	Ratio	Non-Hispanic white	Non-Hispanic African American	Ratio
1989	113.6	2.9	39.2	393.2	65.9	6.0
1992	95.3	16.0	6.0	380.5	70.7	5.4
1995	87.3	10.5	8.3	346.8	58.3	5.9
1998	109.3	13.4	8.2	429.3	78.0	5.5
2001	131.0	13.1	10.0	573.5	81.7	7.0
2004	136.6	13.7	10.0	616.4	117.1	5.3
2007	151.1	9.7	15.6	685.8	129.0	5.3
2010	97.0	4.9	19.8	593.3	84.5	7.0

Source: Wolff (2012), table 12.

Table 13.3. Median and mean net worth of non-Hispanic whites and Hispanics, 1989–2010, in constant 2010 dollars (thousands).

	Median			Mean		
	Non-Hispanic white	Hispanic	Ratio	Non-Hispanic white	Hispanic	Ratio
1989	113.6	2.4	47.3	393.2	64.7	6.1
1992	95.3	5.7	16.7	380.5	84.6	4.5
1995	87.3	7.2	12.1	346.8	73.4	4.7
1998	109.3	4.0	27.3	429.3	106.0	4.1
2001	131.0	3.6	36.4	573.5	98.6	5.8
2004	136.6	6.4	21.3	616.4	132.1	4.7
2007	151.1	9.6	15.7	685.8	179.2	3.8
2010	97.0	1.3	74.6	593.3	90.3	6.6

Source: Wolff (2012), table 13.

Table 13.4. Percentage of families holding various financial assets by race, 2009.

	Nonwhite or Hispanic	Non-Hispanic white
Transaction accounts	84.9	95.5
Certificates of deposit	7.4	19.4
Savings bonds	8.2	16.7
Bonds	0.8	3.4
Stocks	9.1	22.5
Pooled investment funds	5.4	13.1
Retirement accounts	42.3	62.0
Cash value of life insurance	20.8	25.8
Other managed assets	2.1	7.3

Source: Bricker et al. (2012).

Digression on History

Even though history is embedded in wealth, the Booker T. Washington story about the long reach of history is probably not very important, at least for the average household. Only relatively recent history matters much. It's implausible that the disparity in wealth today is due mainly to slavery per se or the absence of reparations in 1865 per se. Intertemporal connections are just too weak for almost all the population. To see why, consider the basic equation about how bequests in one generation are related to bequests in the next generation:

$$\text{Bequests from } t \text{ to } t+1 = \text{bequests from } t-1 \text{ to } t + \text{return on bequest} + \text{income of } t - \text{consumption of } t.$$

If you got \$1 in added bequests in t, you would increase your consumption some. So the increment in your bequest to the next generation would be less than \$1. Suppose you split the dollar in half—half for your increased consumption and half for your heirs. Then over five generations, that only gets three cents from the dollar received by the first generation and possibly nothing. If we think of five generations as roughly the time that has passed since 1865, we see that reparations if they had been paid then would not have a major impact on the wealth of African Americans today. And this three cents forecast is optimistic because inheritance is a chain and a chain is only as strong as its weakest link: if one generation decided to leave a bequest of zero or had bad luck (lived too long, for instance), the chain would be broken and the additional money in 1865 would not trickle down to you at all. Even today, only roughly 20 percent of black households receive bequests or inter vivos transfers. And the best studies of the marginal propensity to bequeath find numbers much less than 50 percent: Altonji and Villanueva (2007) estimated 2 percent, not 50 percent (if I gave your parents \$100, how much of that would you expect to see?) If ex-slaves had received modest reparations in 1865, most of them would probably have consumed all or almost all of it in their lifetimes or their grandchildren would have lost it in the Great Depression. And they would have been perfectly justified in consuming all of it.

A gruesome natural experiment suggests that this theoretical conclusion—wealth doesn't last very long for ordinary people—has some empirical support. In 1838, the state of Georgia and the U.S. Army forced the Cherokee Nation out of its ancestral home in Georgia; the resulting "Trail of Tears" brought the survivors to Oklahoma. The state had legally expropriated the land several years before. It divided this land into 160-acre parcels (four times the famous "forty acres" but without a mule), and held a lottery in 1832 to distribute these parcels among white male Georgians. Virtually every white adult male participated in the lottery, and 15,000 won.

The land came with no strings attached and lottery winners could sell their claims immediately if they wished. Winning was a big deal; the value of winning was about equivalent to the mean wealth of the time. This is a natural experiment because it lets us see what happens when randomly selected white men get big surprise additions to their wealth (at the expense of the Cherokees).

Bleakley and Ferrie (2013) compared descendants of lottery winners and losers in 1870 and 1880. Children of winners had no more wealth than children of losers in 1870; the wealth effect disappeared in one generation. (There were no indirect effects either: winners' children were no more likely to be able to read and did not enjoy higher occupational status; winners' grandchildren were in fact less likely to be attending school in 1880.) Someone might object that the disruption caused by the Civil War and emancipation made this period unrepresentative, but among losers the correlation between fathers' wealth in 1850 and children's wealth in 1870 is not far from modern levels. For the rich it may be different, but for ordinary Americans wealth appears to dissipate in a few generations.

These results for whites with the Cherokee land lottery have the same flavor as results for blacks with the end of slavery, although the natural experiment was nowhere near as clean and direct data on wealth are not available. When slavery ended in 1865, the black population of the United States was divided between individuals who had been born free and those who had been born as slaves. As you would expect, blacks who had been born free were much better off than former slaves: in the 1880 census, for instance, 65 percent of the free blacks in their twenties were literate, compared with only 22 percent of the former slaves of this age (which was probably an overstatement). But Sacerdote (2005) found that by 1920 the grandchildren of free blacks and the grandchildren of former slaves had virtually the same levels of literacy, schooling, and occupational status.

Booker T. Washington really did not have the full story.

What's Going On?

The two big questions are: How can we explain the gap? And how do wealth dynamics differ among racial groups? The two questions work together. You really want to know dynamics to get a full picture of the gap, but the information is sparser and static pictures are more common.

If we're looking at wealth at a snapshot in time, what households should have more of it than others?

> *Age and life cycle.* People save for retirement and for contingencies, so wealth should usually increase at least until retirement. Overall, you see this. In 1998, households with a head 55–64 years old had net worth 8.7 times as great as households with a head less than 35 years old. Wealth usually decreases after retirement as households start using up their savings.
>
> *Income.* If you make more money, you can put away more money. What really matters is permanent income: how much you usually make. If you had a bad year (like Warren Buffett did in 2008), you still might have a lot of money. But the relationship is nonlinear: up to some point, you're not going to save anything.
>
> *Education.* Besides the relationship with permanent income, you might be more sophisticated or more patient.
>
> *Life expectancy.* If you don't think you have long to live and you don't have a strong bequest motive, you have little reason to accumulate wealth. So women might be expected to save more than men, everything else being equal, and whites might be expected to save more than blacks.
>
> *Kids.* Children use up money when you're young, but if you're old and have kids you have a stronger bequest motive. Or you might be counting on them when you're middle-aged to provide pension or insurance to you when you're old.

Putting all these considerations together to see how much of the racial gap in wealth they explain is not easy.

Altonji and Dorazelski (2005) probably do the best job. They used a data set called the Panel Study of Income Dynamics; it's like the National Longitudinal Survey of Youth (see Chapter 5) but has been around longer and follows households instead of individuals.

Altonji and Dorazelski calculated permanent income and then run separate regressions for wealth as a function of permanent income, higher powers of permanent income and age, and other characteristics. They didn't have data on inheritances. They ran a white regression and a black regression and they primarily reported on Blinder-Oaxaca decompositions. I'll pay attention to just plain wealth, although they also have results on log wealth and wealth/income. (Because many households have zero or negative wealth, it's difficult to run regressions on log wealth, and when you run regressions on wealth you have many technical problems because many factors are probably additive and not multiplicative.)

The first important finding is that black wealth is much less sensitive to the explanatory variables, especially permanent income, than white wealth. More income doesn't increase black wealth the way it increases white wealth. This sort of result should be familiar by now: we've seen something similar for test scores and school attainment.

Thus if you look at the civil rights experiment, you find that very little of the gap is due to differential treatment. Seventy-nine percent of the wealth gap is due to differences in characteristics when you treat characteristics the white way. If you look at the enrichment experiment, however, you see that giving blacks white characteristics would not do much: it would account for 25 percent of the gap when characteristics pay off in the way that coefficients in the black regression indicate. At white mean characteristics, 75 percent would be unexplained.

Figure 13.1 shows how you can reconcile these apparently divergent findings.

One of the explanatory variables that Altonji and Dorazelski used is self-employment. The coefficients on the dummies for self-employment for whites are large: $150,000 more wealth when the household head is self-employed and $48,000 more when the spouse is self-employed. The coefficients for blacks are much smaller: self-employment for the head appears to add only $57,000 in wealth and self-employment for the spouse appears to subtract $3,000. These coefficients are a major part of the story, but causality may run the other way. Among people with the same observable characteristics, those with larger wealth have an easier time setting up a business for themselves. So the 79 percent on the share of characteristics valued the white way is probably an overstatement.

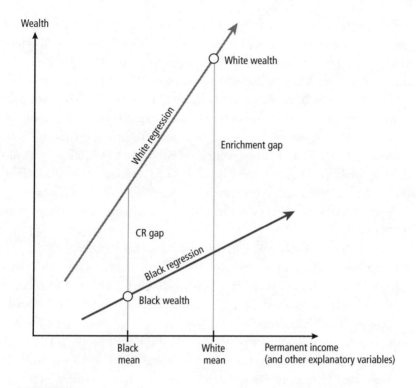

Wealth

White wealth

Enrichment gap

White regression

CR gap

Black regression

Black wealth

Black mean

White mean

Permanent income
(and other explanatory variables)

Figure 13.1.

The situation seems to be similar for Mexican Americans. In Cobb-Clark and Hildebrand's (2004) study, income doesn't explain much of the gap. Mexicans have more young children and younger household heads, and this contributes as much to the gap as the difference in permanent income. Education also plays a big role, even holding permanent income constant: more educated people held riskier assets with higher returns.

Mexican Americans born in the United States hold more wealth than blacks; the difference is mainly attributable to the richer 50 percent of households in each group. The functions don't appear to be a lot different.

The major thing that Altonji and Dorazelski left out is inheritances; they didn't have data. Potentially, inheritances could explain the differences in slopes. *Potentially*. How? Suppose that whites get inheritances and blacks don't—a reasonable assumption. And suppose that inheritances are correlated with permanent income (not a bad assumption either). So if you're white and get a high income you'll get an inheritance along with that income. If you're black, you get the income but not the inheritance, so the higher income will appear to have less effect with blacks. This is possible, but not necessarily so.

To see how much this matters, Altonji and Dorazelski looked at siblings. They assumed that siblings get similar bequests because the vast majority of parents split things up evenly (good empirical evidence supports this presumption). So they ran the same regressions but put in a fixed effect for families: this picks up bequests and whatever else is common in families. That makes the coefficient on permanent income show how wealth differs among siblings with different permanent income (and presumably no difference in inheritance).

Accounting for inheritances in this way causes no big change in the picture. So Altonji and Dorazelski think that inheritances explain little of the gap. But their sample is small and their argument is indirect. Others who have used different methods find that at most 20 percent of the racial gap in average wealth is due to inheritances. Inheritances explain even less for median wealth, since inheritances are very small for most people. Of course, schooling and other investments in human capital could be the way that advantages are passed from one generation to the next, not transfers of financial wealth.

Why Do Income and Age Produce Less Wealth for Minorities?

Arithmetic says that if age and permanent income are less powerful at producing wealth for minorities than for NHWs, then either minorities are saving less or getting a lower rate of return on their investments, or some combination of those two causes. Even if you believe that inheritances are important, these two causes have to be at work at some point in history.

So the next step is to look at changes in wealth over time. Altonji and Dorazelski reported some results for looking at how wealth changes for some periods in the late 1980s and early 1990s. We saw in Table 12.1 that white mean wealth was increasing faster than minority during that period. Perhaps the dotcom boom was responsible.

Altonji and Dorazelski ran the same sort of models with change in wealth as the dependent variable. The results have the same flavor. On the civil rights experiment, the unexplained gap is 26 percent and characteristics account for 74 percent of the racial disparity. On the enrichment experiment, the unexplained gap is 49 percent.

What's going on?

First, in this period, blacks held assets with low returns, not stocks, and white real estate may have done better. But these differences in rates of return don't seem to be enough to explain the full gap.

Second, blacks and Hispanics may have lower savings rates than NHW, holding current income constant or holding permanent income constant, at least during the periods the data come from. The world might change.

Minority Savings Rates, Given Income

The question of whether blacks and other minorities save more, given income, has a long history. Very little of that history concentrates on Hispanics. In the 1950s, blacks saved more than whites and this difference gave rise to a lot of discussion in the development of modern theories about savings. Duesenberry (1949) said that people spend in order to keep up with their reference group. The reference group for blacks was other blacks, and since blacks didn't have much to spend, you could look rich in this group without spending much. Friedman (1957) developed the permanent income hypothesis; he argued that blacks with high incomes usually had much lower permanent incomes so should be expected to consume less. While both of these explanations were brilliant, they were probably wrong. Using much better data, Galenson (1972) found that the reason blacks saved more between 1940 and 1960 was that it was much more difficult for them to dissave. If you can't borrow, you can't dissave. (We've seen that blacks still have less access to consumer credit than whites do, but the disparity is now probably less than it used to be.)

Wolff (2001) has some more current results where blacks have lower savings rates than whites given permanent income and some results where blacks have about the same savings rate.

Why might blacks save less? A few stories have been advanced in the literature. One possibility is poor relatives and friends. Suppose you have a bunch of poor relatives who will ask for money whenever they need it, which is quite often. The more you give them, the less you have available to save. Moreover, if you save up some money, they are likely to mooch it away from you because you can't say no. Better to spend it on yourself now than to save it and give it to them later.

Second, there is the effect of defined benefit pensions. In the United States, there are two kinds of pensions. Defined benefit pensions are traditional: the employer and worker both pay money into an independent pension fund for a large group of people, and when a worker retires she has a pension that's set by rules about length of service and final salary, no matter what happens to the stock market or the investment return for the collective pension fund. Defined contribution pensions are newer: the employer and the worker pay into an individual account for the worker, and when she retires she gets whatever is in the account, no matter how long she served or what she made. Defined benefit pensions make the pension fund bear the investment risk; defined contribution funds make the worker bear that risk. (The most common defined contribution pensions are usually called 401(k)s.)

Defined benefit pensions are more prevalent in large industrial companies, such as General Motors, and in governments. Blacks are disproportionately employed in both sectors. If you have a defined benefit pension, you don't have to save as much in the forms that most surveys count as wealth. Defined contribution pensions get counted as wealth, but not defined benefit pensions.

Third, lower life expectancy. The longer you expect to live, especially the longer you expect to live after retirement, the more you want to save. We know that blacks have lower life expectancy, both at birth and at age 60. So they have less reason to save. But this doesn't apply to Hispanics, which runs counter to the smaller wealth accumulation by Hispanics.

Fourth, distrust of the mechanisms for saving. To save in a modern society, you don't put your money under a rock; you enter into some complex contract, generally with a large institution, that has to cover many years or decades. If minorities distrust physicians (whom they can see) who want to perform CABG, why should we be surprised if they also distrust Bank of America and the New York Stock Exchange? Table 13.4 provides some support for this idea. Life insurance companies, particularly the minority-owned companies, have spent many decades building trust with minorities (through the employment of minority agents, for instance), so the large share of savings through life insurance is consistent with the idea that trust matters for saving and investment behavior.

Finally, Charles, Hurst, and Roussanov (2009) have written about conspicuous consumption. They define this as consumption motivated by a desire to show one's income to one's peers and impress them. They argue that conspicuous consumption explains in part why blacks and Hispanics save less.

First, let's look at their data. Charles, Hurst, and Roussanov operationalize conspicuous consumption as spending on clothing, cars, and jewelry (or personal items)—stuff you can carry around and other people can see. Holding total expenditures constant (and hence holding permanent income constant), minorities spend considerably more than NHWs on these things and on nothing else (except possibly housing, which might also be conspicuous consumption, but where the market is so strange that Charles, Hurst and Roussanov don't want to say anything). This added spending on conspicuous consumption has to come at the expense of something else, and they show that it comes at the expense of some current items (like educational spending) and possibly at the expense of saving.

They also show that holding your income constant, you spend more on conspicuous consumption if the average income of your reference group is lower. By reference group they mean people of the same race or ethnicity in the same state. They find that differences in reference group income explain most or all of the racial difference in conspicuous consumption spending.

If you spend more on jewelry, you are likely to save less, everything else being equal. They show that holding your permanent income constant, you have less wealth if your reference group is poorer. This is consistent with the idea that you spend more on conspicuous consumption and therefore save less (conspicuous consumption declines with age). But it's consistent with many other stories about wealth too (for instance, you inherited less or you're afraid of friends and relatives mooching). They find that differences in income of reference group explain a lot of the racial difference in wealth in the Panel Study of Income Dynamics.

Second, let's look at Charles, Hurst, and Roussanov's theory. Essentially they stand Duesenberry on his head. Let's say that the only purpose of spending on these things is to signal your income to your peers and your peers are impressed by how much income you have. If the average income in your circle is $10,000, then an extra $500 in your presumed income will be more impressive to your peers (it will raise you past more people in the income distribution) than if average income in your circle is $1 million. If you hang around with $10,000 people, a Rolex watch or a designer jeans impress people more than they would if you hung around with $1 million people. So if you hang around with $10,000 people you get more status bang for your buck when you buy designer jeans than if you hang around with $1 million people. Everything else being equal, then, you will spend more on conspicuous consumption.

This argument uses a lot of steps, and is not totally convincing, but something is probably going on.

An alternative story about conspicuous consumption is that it arises from male bargaining power. Women may want to spend on education and to save, since they are going to live a long time. Men want to have a good time, and if men are in short supply, women are going to have to dress very well. So you can get something like the conspicuous consumption result from male-female ratios too. This alternative explanation has not been tested empirically yet.

The story is also sensitive to the definition of conspicuous consumption. Charles et al. use expenditures for education as an example of nonconspicuous consumption, but couldn't sending your children to very expensive private colleges and putting the corresponding decals on your car rear window count as conspicuous consumption too?

Conclusion

If Booker T. Washington had the whole story right in 1895, then the racial gap in wealth would be purely the product of observable individual characteristics today: race would not matter when you regressed wealth or changes in wealth on permanent income and age. That is the simple story of catching up from slavery and it is the simple story of minorities as white people who don't happen to have as much income.

Once again we see that that is not the whole story (although it's part of the story). Race matters today. Reparations in 1865, which would have solved everything if Washington had been right, would really not have solved much. But that doesn't mean that they should not have been paid. That question is the subject of the next chapter.

14

Reparations

Reparations are controversial. But you need to think about them if you claim to have thought about race in the United States. One reason to study reparations is to think about who we are. The book began with a discussion of who we are in a biological sense and what we inherit from the past biologically. This chapter is about what we inherit from the past morally. Some of you may think the answer is nothing. Don't be too sure.

The chapter is about whether reparations are good and just, not whether they are good politics. Loury (2006), for example, makes a very strong case that pushing for reparations is lousy politics. This is not a book about politics. We should be clear in our own minds about what's right and wrong. A lot of stuff that's right and good seems to have no chance politically. Fooling other people may sometimes be okay; fooling yourself is not.

Reparations have often been paid or received: Germany and Japan, for instance, paid reparations for events in World War II, and the families of September 11 victims received compensation from the U.S. government. There are other precedents where bad things were not followed by reparations: the South African reconciliation process, for instance. These actions may have been good or they may have been bad; you should know how to decide. The issue of reparations is not closed. If climate change inundates Bangladesh, for instance, will reparations be due?

I'll proceed cautiously. First I'll discuss reparations in general. Then I'll say something about slavery. Then I'll apply the general ideas about reparations to slavery and Jim Crow. An appendix will examine the argument for affirmative action in higher education as a form of reparations. This chapter will be light on facts. Many facts are important, but I'd rather concentrate on pointing out what facts we need to know and let historians concentrate on resolving what those facts are.

Payment and Receipt of Reparations

The most basic and strange idea that I want to start with is that payment of reparations is a separate issue from receipt of reparations. The legal system sometimes confuses this because a lot of it works from the incentives lawyers have to sue. But we often pay fines without victims receiving anything— for littering or illegal parking, for instance—and sometimes there are receipts without anybody paying anything—the payments to 9/11 victim families, for instance. So I'm going to consider the arguments for payment and receipt separately and not require them to balance. It's not all right to kill ten-year-old orphans, and the case for paying reparations would not be weakened if all Africans had perished on the Middle Passage.

Why Pay Or Receive Reparations?

We can divide reasons into reasons for paying and reasons for receiving. Here are some of the reasons I've seen:

Possible Reasons for Paying

Deterrence.   An obligation to pay can promote efficiency. If I can take an action that harms someone else, then I won't take that action inefficiently if I have to pay for the amount of harm I cause. Ex post enforcement sends a message ex ante, otherwise nothing would ever be enforced.

Retribution.   Sometimes wrongdoing must be punished regardless of the consequences because it is wrongdoing.

Possible Reasons for Receiving

Insurance.   If I get compensated when bad things happen to me, then there is less variance in my life. Notice that insurance implies moral hazard: I may not take appropriate steps to avoid harm if I don't bear the full amount of harm.

Investment.   People won't invest appropriately if the fruits of their investment can be lost without compensation.

Corrective justice.   Consider the flip side of retribution: Rights that are violated should be restored. This is often the libertarian argument from the importance of property rights.

So it's possible that good arguments can be made for reparations under various circumstances.

What Sort of Events Should Reparations Be Due For?

Obviously, very bad events where some parties (maybe one) did something wrong and other parties (maybe one) suffered as a result justify reparations. Examples are the standard torts that lawyers work on, World War I, the Holocaust, slavery and Jim Crow, the Mexican American War, the Tulsa riots, the Opium Wars, and so on. Unfortunately, it's easy to compile a list of outrages.

I'll call the party doing something wrong the *wrongdoer,* and the party suffering the wrong the *victim.*

Notice that in these cases the wrongdoer didn't do harm merely in the sense of not conferring a benefit. The government of France caused U.S. slavery in the sense that it could have put together an army in 1790 and invaded the South and freed the slaves, but it didn't. But nobody argues that France should pay reparations for this failure. Or that the United States should pay reparations for the Holocaust because it didn't act decisively enough to stop it or to prevent it. (Or that the person who introduced Hitler's maternal grandparents to each other should pay reparations for the Holocaust.)

Instead, the wrongdoer must have had some duty that he or it failed to perform. For instance, in the Tulsa riot the police had a duty to protect the black citizens of Tulsa. The southern states had a duty to assure all U.S. citizens the right to vote and live a decent sort of life and not get lynched. Slave-owners had a duty not to interfere in other people's lives and a duty to respect their choice of occupation or spouse or continent to live on. So a claim for reparations must be based on an argument that the wrongdoer had a particular duty.

What are duties? How does one make an argument that a particular person has a particular duty? These are deep philosophical questions beyond the scope of this book. Duties have something to do with "normal behavior." Most of us think we have a duty not to litter but not a duty to pick up litter on the sidewalk, even though both duties are consequentially equivalent. (If you drop a candy wrapper on the ground and I see it and walk by without picking it up, both of us are causes of the unsightly condition; either one of us could have ended it but didn't.)

Wrongdoers can be either human or corporate or government (government is a species of corporate). There can be more than one wrongdoer in the same incident: slave-owners or state governments or the federal government might all be wrongdoers; in Tulsa, the rioters and city government were both wrongdoers.

Wrongdoers must also take actions that are causes of the bad outcome. If you had done your duty, the bad thing would not have happened. Given what the others did, was your action a crucial cause of the harm? So it's possible for there to be many wrongdoers, each fully responsible. Or none (firing squads mean that no individual soldier is a cause of the death). This is a major reason why payment doesn't have to equal receipt.

Victims are also defined relative to duties. Owners of land in Egypt and India were harmed by U.S. slavery, but I can think of no reason why they should be compensated. (Slave labor in the United States reduced the world price of cotton and made land on which cotton could be grown in these two countries less valuable.)

Who Benefits Doesn't Matter

People have no obligation to disgorge gains that came their way through the malfeasance of others. Consider the new spouses of 9/11 widows and widowers. Some of them may be spectacularly happy. Do these second spouses owe reparations to anyone? Their happiness is irrelevant for deterrence, retribution, insurance, investment, and so on.

In passing, who as a matter of fact gained from slavery? It's a complex general equilibrium question that Fogel and Engerman (1974) investigate. Probably not the later slave-owners, since they paid market prices. Most likely the big gainers were consumers of cotton and owners of industrial land in Manchester and Liverpool. But it doesn't matter.

Nor does it matter how much the gainers gained. Most of the things such as slavery and the Holocaust were probably inefficient. If you limited reparations to gains, they would be too small from the deterrence perspective and probably from the investment perspective and maybe from the other perspectives too.

Who today gained and lost from slavery and how much? That's incalculable. In the absence of slavery we would not be us.

What Recipients Do with Reparations Doesn't Matter

It's also irrelevant what recipients do with reparations and whether it will solve any other problem. It's theirs; they can do with it what they wish. The racial wealth gap probably would not have been affected by reparations in 1865.

How Does This Apply to Slavery? The View from 1865

Suppose it's 1865. Is there a case for payment of reparations? For receipt of reparations?

Payment

Slave-owners could have emancipated the slaves they owned and didn't. Did they have a duty to do so? State governments could have emancipated the slaves, and many of them did so. The federal government may not have been able to emancipate the slaves, but both the Dred Scott decision and the Fugitive Slave Act could have gone the other way.

How much compensation? The possibilities in the literature are willingness to accept (how much money slaves would have had to be paid to be willing to accept slavery) and loss of output (the value of what slaves produced). Willingness to accept is the argument that people and state governments had a duty not to enslave. Loss of output is the argument that slaveowners had a duty not to take output. Willingness to accept is a much bigger figure, partly because slaves were living on the owner's land and eating his food (see Fogel and Engerman for a calculation of loss of output). Willingness to accept is the more natural figure for a neoclassical economist to compute; loss of output is the more natural figure for a Marxian economist.

How about corporations such as Aetna that insured slaves? I don't see them as a significant cause. If Aetna didn't insure slaves, somebody else would have, and if nobody did, Aetna's refusal would still cause only one small deviation from the actual history of slavery.

Maybe there are other people too who were wrongdoers. But I don't see an argument for "all white people."

Receipt

Who should receive payments? Clearly people who had been slaves, in proportion to the length of time and any particular hardship. (Notice that the loss of output standard implies that slave children owe compensation to former owners.) The argument against such receipt is moral hazard: payment reduces the incentive to escape. But since escape is a large investment that is not directly productive, probably the moral hazard problem is small. The insurance argument is fairly strong. I don't know about the investment argument.

What Form of Reparations?

While we're still in 1865, there are as usual two questions—form of payment and form of receipt.

On payment, form doesn't matter on deterrence grounds: the dollar value to the wrongdoer must equal the dollar value of harm to the victims. It doesn't matter what form it takes.

On receipt, the basic presumption should be cash. The idea in all versions is to raise the utility of victims, and in general the cheapest way of doing so is cash. There's no reason not to raise utility in the cheapest way.

Cash is not *always* the cheapest way to raise utility: maybe the federal government could buy mules cheaper than the freedmen could. That's a market failure. Sometimes market failures make programs better ways than cash to raise utility. But showing that a particular program is better for the recipients than cash in a particular instance is almost always challenging.

It's Not 1865 Anymore

All of the wrongdoers and victims are dead. Many crimes have statutes of limitations. In general, in criminal law you get total immunity by dying. You also can't collect your debts after a certain point. The passage of time presents real problems.

I'll approach this problem by breaking it up four ways: payment, receipt, humans, corporations (governments).

Payments and Corporations

Corporations don't die, so if they're still around they're still liable. So the federal government or the state of Alabama owe money for slavery. Now you say that there's no such person as the state of Alabama, so it's really the taxpayers of today who are going to have to pay and that's not fair. What did a person who migrated from China to Alabama in 1995 ever do that she would have to pay for slavery?

Think of the debt as running with the land. If you buy land in New York City, you are responsible for all the bad stuff the city government does. When the city government had to pay damages for the wrongful shooting of Amadou Diallo, Al Sharpton, who led the protests against the shooting, was one of those who had to pay. If you buy stock in R. J. Reynolds or Dow Chemical or Citibank or British Petroleum, you get to share in the responsibility for all the bad things that come with the stock. If you buy BP stock today and then tomorrow a court decision comes down that BP has to pay $5 billion because of the Gulf Oil spill in 2011, you can't say you had nothing to do with it. Nobody has to buy BP stock; similarly, nobody has to move to New York City or Alabama.

Notice that this has the right deterrent effect. If I run a corporation and am contemplating buying slaves, my stock gets shot to pieces. If I run a government and am contemplating invading Mexico or letting my cops sodomize suspects, my constituents are going to realize that nobody's going to buy their property because of the debt that goes with it, so they're going to oppose my unjust actions—on prudential, not moral, grounds.

So this case is pretty easy.

Payment and Humans

Humans die, and for American slavery, all the human wrongdoers are dead now.

One argument is to treat a family like a corporation. I'll be worse off if I have to contemplate my grandchildren paying a huge fine, so I'll be deterred if I know that my action will make my grandchildren sufficiently unhappy. This is a possible scenario, but it argues for payments only from people appropriately linked to actual wrongdoers. So Chinese Americans in Alabama today don't pay and probably a lot of African Americans who have slave-owner ancestry do.

This makes some sense for deterrence, but it doesn't make a lot of sense for retribution. It's not clear that we want to treat families like corporations. Even on deterrence grounds, why should people with kids be more deterred than people without kids, people who love their kids a lot be more deterred than people who don't care much about their kids?

In criminal cases, we don't visit the crimes of the parents on the children. Nobody proposed punishing Osama bin Laden's children when the United States couldn't find him. Is using the pain of the descendants of wrongdoers to deter them really a moral maneuver—holding them hostage, in other words?

Another possibility with humans is to pay attention to land, not families. Maybe the debt should run with the land in this case too—like an oil spill. If you own the land, you owe the debts that may have accumulated through misuse of the land. This works for deterrence purposes, since landowners then have an incentive to keep moral outrages from happening on their property. It may be a little surprising to invoke this principle after 150 years. But it's probably not all that more surprising than finding an old leaky oil tank under your front lawn.

So the case for payments by people is not as clear as the case for payments by governments.

Receipts and Corporations

Mexico might be owed reparations for the Mexican American War. This seems to be similar to the payments and governments case, and it works that way for investment. But it's not clear that this is good insurance or good corrective justice.

Receipts and Humans

One approach is to be symmetrical and treat families as corporations. How does this work for insurance? "If something bad happens to me, my great-grandchildren will get something nice." Not too far-fetched, although not absolutely sensible. For investment? "I'll plant this tree because if somebody cuts it down or steals the fruit, they'll have to compensate my great-grandchildren, which will make me happy." Not too terrible. So the idea has some plausibility.

But it doesn't seem to be widely accepted in reparations practice. Often there is a rush to compensate the survivors before they die: this was the case with survivors of the Holocaust and the atom bomb in Japan (but it was descendants who were compensated for the Rosewood, Florida, riot of 1923). Why isn't the idea of compensating descendants widely accepted?

One possible problem is getting the right amount. Should descendants of people who cared little for their offspring get more so that the compensation is worth the same for everyone who was directly affected? Second, is it legitimate to compensate person B for harms suffered by person A? (That is, does this provide corrective justice?) Suppose somebody owes me $10 and person X is a friend of mine—not my best friend, just a friend. Should I be happy, though, and consider the debt discharged, if my debtor paid $100 to person X?

An alternative argument for payments to descendants of slaves might be that slave-owners and southern governments hurt them directly by not emancipating their ancestors. A decent case can be made that African Americans today would be better off if their ancestors had been emancipated earlier, although this is not an airtight case—we saw in Chapter 13 that by 1920 the grandchildren of black people who were born free were no better off on some important measures like education and occupation than the grandchildren of former slaves. But for reparations to be due to the twenty-first-century descendants, the argument has to be made that the slave-owners had a duty to the twenty-first-century descendants. What sort of duty? The twenty-first-century descendants have the basic rights of American citizens and receive wages for what they produce. They may have less income, less wealth, and worse health, for instance, but did the slave-owners have a duty to maintain a certain standard of living for the descendants of their slaves?

For an analogy, suppose that A robs B of $100. B is a generous sort of person, and there is some reason to think that if the robbery had not occurred, B would have donated $10 to charity C. Does A have a duty to charity C?

Notice that none of these arguments require descendants—just people the slaves might care about. How do you know that the slaves would have cared more for their great-great-grandchildren living totally different lives than, say, for slaves in Sudan, farm workers in Latin America, or Indian peasants? We're telling a story about what people would have wanted—why does it have to be a bloodline story? Or is it racial essentialism? In more of an accounting sense, many slaves have no living descendants. Should they be treated differently from slaves who were lucky enough to have living descendants?

Jim Crow, Too

Although slavery is usually the subject of reparations discussions, it is probably not the only gross violation of the rights of black people that has occurred in U.S. history. Jim Crow must also be considered, as Bittker (1973) and Kennedy (2013) have argued. We already mentioned particular incidents during this period—the Tulsa and Rosewood riots—and seen that governments and individuals violated their duties to black citizens on these occasions. The more general duties to provide basic education and security, to allow travel, to permit people to choose heterosexual marriage partners, and to treat citizens with dignity in public spaces may also have been violated. These are duties that were widely acknowledged outside the South and with respect to whites. Hispanics and Asians who lived at that time also experienced Jim Crow laws and policies. The big difference between Jim Crow and slavery is that many of the people who experienced Jim Crow are still alive (although none of them are young).

Conclusion

Some people think of reparations as a really hot, really divisive topic. Perhaps that's true if you think of reparations as a yes-or-no question, especially if the subtext is who is to blame. But I don't think of it that way at all.

Maybe that's because I'm weird. Or maybe I'm just trying to demonstrate that economics can take any simple emotional issue and make it complex and boring.

The lesson I want you to take from this chapter is that paying and receiving reparations are very complex issues that include many tough and intricate questions and allow many and varied types of answers. There are hundreds of possible conclusions, not just one. You don't have to be for or against reparations. It's a question for analysis and one that you need to grapple with to understand who you are.

Appendix: Reparations and Affirmative Action in Higher Education

In Chapter 7, the chapter on education, I noted that reparations were among the leading arguments for affirmative action in higher education but did not have the tools to examine that argument. In this appendix, I examine that argument.

In the 1960s, when this type of affirmative action began to be practiced, and for several decades thereafter, many of the people who directly benefited had been victims themselves of Jim Crow policies that are generally recognized today as unjust. Today and in the future, most possible direct beneficiaries will not be people who experienced Jim Crow, although they may be children or grandchildren of such people. The arguments about reparations for the two groups are different. I will concentrate on the latter group, since our interest is today and the future.

Begin by assuming that African Americans (and possibly some Hispanics and Asians) with direct experience of Jim Crow are victims, state and local governments that enforced Jim Crow are wrongdoers, and that reparations are owed from the latter to the former. The U.S. government may be a wrongdoer too, to the extent that it did not adequately enforce the Fourteenth Amendment and the Civil Rights Act of 1866 and it could have. If this is the case, then the straightforward, obvious procedure would be for these governments to pay cash to the surviving victims—all of them.

The main argument for using affirmative action rather than cash to compensate these victims, as I understand it, is that affirmative action for certain current-generation African Americans would be more valuable to the surviving victims than cash (or any other means of compensation). Kennedy (2013, 85–86), for instance, acknowledges that affirmative action in higher education benefits directly only a handful of the best-off black students of the current generation but argues that it creates large external benefits: affirmative action, he says, "redounds to the betterment of the group as a whole by facilitating the emergence of a vanguard that will promote group uplift. . . . The enhanced opportunity that relatively privileged racial minorities receive redounds not only, and perhaps not principally, to their own personal benefit, but redounds to the benefit of their group and, more generally, to the benefit of society as a whole."

What are these benefits that minority communities as a whole (and especially Jim Crow survivors) might enjoy? In part they are the community leadership benefits I discussed in Chapter 7. But the interpretation is different. There I argued that the marginal benefits minority students would generate for minority communities were likely bigger than the marginal benefits NHW students would generate for their communities. In the reparations setting, the size of the benefits to nonminority communities doesn't matter. The question is all about benefits to minority communities—or the older members of minority communities—and whether admitting minority students or NHW students with special skills and affinities or giving cash or some other program provides more of the benefits that justice requires.

Minority communities and Jim Crow survivors may receive other direct benefits from affirmative action in higher education as well. They may simply be happy and feel pride when members of their race receive honors or high positions. They may receive excellent services from minority doctors or lawyers. And Jim Crow survivors may have links of family and friendship to direct beneficiaries of affirmative action.

The important question, though, is still the size of the benefits to the people who deserve compensation—quite a different question from the societal efficiency question we concentrated on in Chapter 7. Serious empirical work on reparations arguments for affirmative action would concentrate on estimating these benefits and the benefits of alternative programs such as cash (and subsidies to elementary and secondary education). At the very least, it would survey Jim Crow survivors about alternatives.

The other purpose of reparations is to punish wrongdoers. It is less clear how affirmative action in higher education accomplishes this. If affirmative action were found to be the best way to compensate the victims of Jim Crow or slavery, the straightforward approach would be to force the wrong-doing governments to subsidize additional slots reserved for minorities at the colleges and universities in question. Perhaps this is happening implicitly if affirmative action programs make public universities more popular with key legislators and they get larger appropriations as a result or private universities get more federal grants because they practice affirmative action. Whether this is happening is also an empirical question that has not been investigated.

However, Chapter 7 detailed many reasons why affirmative action helped universities, corporations, and other powerful institutions and pointed to their revealed support for the practice. Punishments don't get support like that. That is why I concentrated on forward-looking rather than backward-looking arguments for affirmative action.

It may also mean that if affirmative action in higher education is part of reparations, it would have to be considered as a receipt without payment, like the compensation of 9/11 victims.

15

Wrapping Up

I've left a lot out of this book: politics, consumer goods markets, most questions about Native Americans, transfer and insurance programs such as Social Security and Temporary Assistance for Needy Families, mental health, and homelessness, to name just a few of the more conspicuous absences. But enough may have been included to answer some of the important questions.

Looking Backward

The classic statements that began the book began left us with six major questions. Let's see how well these questions can be answered now.

Does Race Itself Matter Today or Is It Just a Proxy for History?

We've seen fairly clearly that both race *and* history matter; both Booker T. Washington and W. E. B. Du Bois are worth listening to.

I emphasized history at the beginning of the book and at the end: biology in the beginning and reparations at the end. History leaves a massive imprint on who we are, both physically and morally. Parents shape children's lives in innumerable ways. If no one could recognize race, the people who had a lot of slave ancestors would probably be worse off than the people who had few or none.

But history is not the whole story. Many people today use race in making decisions: whom to marry and what child to adopt, where to live, what pitches to swing at when two strikes have already been called, whether to resist a robber or give up their money, where to walk the dog, how to practice religion, what to name their kids, whom to believe about long-term care insurance, where to market subprime refinancings. Sometimes the discrimination is overt (marriage, adoption, and residential location, for instance); sometimes there are just subtle problems in communication and understanding (health care, education in the classroom, perhaps mortgage denial). Sometimes people use race to make inferences about themselves: whether they are smart, whether they are musical, whether they are likely to be good football players if they work hard enough. Loury (2006), in writing about reparations, points out that thinking in terms of race is probably a more important legacy of slavery than anything anyone could sue over. Race matters today.

How Independent Are the Spheres of Life?

Everything's connected. Washington had it wrong with his analogy of the fingers; Myrdal got at least part of the big picture right. Figure 15.1 shows all the connections; you can use this figure as a handy summary of the whole book. You can't think about jobs, for instance, without thinking about schools. But to think about schools, you have to think about residences and marriages. And so on. Discrimination or historical disadvantage in one sphere of life inevitably spills over to many other spheres of life. That's why I couldn't honestly write a simple, easy book like, say, *Race and Employment,* or *Race and Housing.*

What Sphere Is Key to Progress?

The book has not been kind to the idea of magic bullets. Figure 15.1 shows why. Different parts of life are like a web, not like a tree; causation is mutual, not unidirectional. Progress in any sphere is constrained by diminishing marginal returns because of other spheres. Eliminating all discrimination in employment, for instance, won't equalize earnings as long as educational

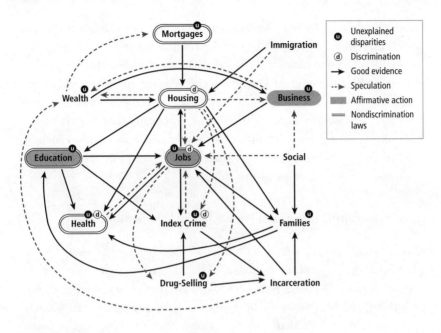

Figure 15.1. The big picture.

achievement varies by race, and educational achievement will vary by race as long as housing and marriage markets vary by race. No single sphere can pull every other sphere with it; the others hold it back. That's the bad news from Figure 15.1.

The possible good news from Figure 15.1, which Myrdal emphasized, is that sometimes improvements in one area can spill over into other areas. Better schools can lead to better jobs and better jobs in this generation can lead to better schools in the next. Virtuous circles might be possible—but vicious circles are possible too.

A major unresolved question is the extent to which different kinds of investments are substitutes or complements. If, for instance, parental income is a substitute for school input in educating children, then we are in a Myrdal-type world where changes in one sphere are amplified by the connections to other spheres; both virtuous and vicious cycles can occur. But if parental income is a complement for school inputs—if good educational results require both high parental income and enriching school inputs—then stasis in one sphere can check progress in other spheres: vicious circles are possible but virtuous circles are not. We don't have good enough econometric results yet to know which picture of the world is more accurate.

Experience, however, seems to suggest that complementarity is important. The triumph of the original Du Bois agenda (voting rights, public accommodations, and school access) in the 1960s did not trigger a swift, massive unraveling of discrimination in all areas of American life. As far as we can tell a half-century later, it set off no virtuous circle. Spheres don't seem to move in unison. When a black man was elected president in 2008, the black incarceration rate was at an all-time high.

How Important Is Interracial Friendship and Understanding?

King, Myrdal, and the Kerner Commission seem to have the answer to the question of the importance of interracial social relations right, although the evidence is not very strong. Many crucial transactions, from learning algebra to deciding whether to undergo open heart surgery, depend on trust and mutual respect of a type that only something like friendship seems strong enough to promote. So does the experience of forming and raising a family. Modern life is far too complex and information is far too dispersed to think we can get through it all without more than a little help from our friends. Friendship is a lubricant that allows a modern economy to function; the benefits of living in a large, diverse, dynamic innovative economy can't be realized without interracial friendship and understanding. Or so it seems.

Is a Society with Many Different Races, Especially a Society Where One Race Has Exploited Another, Possible and Desirable?

A multiracial society, even one where one race has exploited another, is obviously possible. But the book has really not been able to answer Malcolm X's question about desirability. We don't have a good experiment. Since the 1960s, more effort has gone into King's integration goals than into Malcolm's segregation goals. Would life be better if the United States had followed Malcolm instead of King? Since it didn't happen, no definitive answer is possible. The large flow of immigrants to the United States from more racially homogeneous societies, however, suggests that many new Americans have rejected Malcolm (while the political backlash against immigration suggests that many old Americans have embraced him).

Looking Forward

At any rate, since the United States has not followed Malcolm X's separatist path, policies on race will matter for many years to come. We've seen that policies sometimes work—anti-discrimination laws in the South in the 1960s, for instance, public accommodations laws, school desegregation, police expansion in the 1990s. When they do work, there are many good consequences. But sometimes policies don't achieve their intended results. Sometimes they produce nothing—No Child Left Behind seems to fit in to that category. Sometimes they produce undesired results—mass incarceration and drug prohibition, for instance. And sometimes they produce results that are opposite of what was intended—the Americans with Disabilities Act, for instance.

Policies don't have to be color blind to be a good idea, and sometimes the best policies are color sighted (although intermarriage in the future may make color harder to "see"). That's why studying these questions, not just emoting about them or throwing slogans at them, is desirable.

The America that Washington, Du Bois, Myrdal, King, Malcolm, and the Kerner Commission wrote about was much younger, sicker, whiter, dumber, and less exposed to the world economy than the America of the twenty-first century, and women had fewer rights and opportunities. The issues of the future are not going to be the issues of the past.

My guess is that health care will matter more in the twenty-first century than it did in the twentieth and that employment and housing will matter less. Crime and education will continue to be major issues. But emphases will probably change—increasing Hispanic educational attainment, for instance, will receive a lot more attention.

Race and age may become more intertwined when the NHW population is old, the minority population is young, and the entire United States looks like Florida today. Will Social Security and Medicare become "white people's programs," paid for grudgingly if at all by a working population that is overwhelmingly Hispanic, black, and Asian? I suspect not. In America, everyone can aspire to be old someday (although not everyone can realistically aspire to be rich).

Whom to believe and what to believe may become the big personal questions of the twenty-first century. These were not such crucial questions for the average person in the middle of the twentieth century: you could communicate easily with only a few hundred people, only a few major television networks and newspapers produced the definitive version of the news, pensions were defined benefit, so you didn't have to think about them too much, mortgages were all pretty much the same, long-term care insurance didn't exist, and health insurance was something your employer took care of. None of that is true today. You need sources of information and advice you can trust.

How will they be established? I don't know. But a strong possibility is that they will grow up along racial and ethnic lines. Perhaps people in the near future will define their racial and ethnic identities by how they get their news and who advises them about health insurance rather than where they live and who cuts their hair. Whether this arrangement is compatible with the smooth working of a modern economy I don't know; intuitively it seems superior to the ignorance and swindling that marked the first decade of the twenty-first century, even if it's not color blind. Maybe the presence of strong racial identities will turn out to be a source of strength for U.S. society.

Summing Up

In *The Souls of Black Folk* in 1903, W. E. B. Du Bois wrote that "the problem of the twentieth century is the problem of the color line." A century later, the color line looks a lot different than it looked then, but it hasn't gone away. To understand U.S. society and the U.S. economy in the twenty-first century (whether or not you are an American), you still have to understand race. If you are an American, to understand yourself in the twenty-first century you have to understand race. I hope this book has helped you do that.

References

Abdulkadiroglu, Atila, Joshua D. Angrist, Susan M. Dynarski, Thomas Kane, and Parag A. Pathak. 2011. Accountability and flexibility in public schools: Evidence from Boston's charters and pilots. *Quarterly Journal of Economics* 126(2): 699–748.

Acemoglu, Daron, and Joshua Angrist. 2001. Consequences of employment protection? The case of the Americans with Disabilities Act. *Journal of Political Economy* 109(5): 915–957.

Aizer, Anna, Laura Stroud, and Stephen Buka. 2009. Biology, stress, and the intergenerational transmission of economic status. Working paper, Department of Economics, Brown University.

Akerlof, George, and Rachel Kranton. 2000. Economics and identity. *Quarterly Journal of Economics* 115(3): 715–753.

Alexander, Michelle. 2012. *The new Jim Crow: Mass incarceration in the era of colorblindness.* Rev. ed. New York: The New Press.

Alliprantis. Dionissi. 2011. Assessing the evidence of neighborhood effects from Moving to Opportunity. Working paper 11-22, Federal Reserve Bank of Cleveland.

Almond, Douglas, and Kenneth Y. Chay. 2006. The long-run and intergenerational impact of poor infant health. Working paper, Department of Economics, Columbia University.

Almond, Douglas, Kenneth Y. Chay, and Michael Greenstone. 2003. Civil rights, the War on Poverty, and black-white convergence in infant mortality in Mississippi. Working paper, Department of Economics, Columbia University.

Altonji, Joseph, and Rebecca Blank. 1999. Race and gender in the labor market. In *Handbook of Labor Economics,* vol. 3, ed. Orley C. Ashenfelter and David Card, 3143–3259. Amsterdam: North-Holland.

Altonji, Joseph, and Ulrich Dorazleski. 2005. The role of permanent income and demographics in black/white differences in wealth. *Journal of Human Resources* 40(1): 1–30.

Altonji, Joseph, and Ernesto Villanueva. 2007. The marginal propensity to spend on adult children. *BE Journals in Economic Analysis and Policy* 7(1): 1–50.

Ananat, Elizabeth Oltmans. 2011. The wrong side(s) of the tracks: The causal effects of racial segregation on urban poverty and inequality. *American Economic Journal: Applied Economics* 3(1): 34–66.

Anderson, David A. 1999. The aggregate burden of crime. *Journal of Law and Economics* 42(2): 611–642.

Anderson, Elijah. 2011. *The cosmopolitan canopy: Race and civility in everyday life.* New York: Norton.

Anderson, Gary M., and Dennis Halcoussis. 1996. The political economy of legal segregation: Jim Crow and racial employment patterns. *Economics and Politics* 8(1): 1–15.

Angrist, Joshua D., Aimee Chin, and Ricardo Godoy. 2008. Is Spanish-only schooling responsible for the Puerto Rican language gap? *Journal of Development Economics* 85(1–2): 105–128.

Angrist, Joshua D., Susan M. Dynarski, Thomas Kane, Parag A. Pathak, and Christopher R. Walters. 2010. Inputs and impacts in charter schools: KIPP Lynn. *American Economic Review* 100(2): 239–243.

Antonovics, Kate L., and Brian Knight. 2009. A new look at racial profiling: Evidence from the Boston Police Department. *Review of Economics and Statistics* 91(1): 163–177.

Anwar, Shamena, and Hanming Fang. 2006. An alternative test of racial prejudice in motor vehicle searches: Theory and evidence. *American Economic Review* 96(1): 127–151.

———. 2012. Testing for the role of prejudice in emergency departments using bounce-back rates. *The B. E. Journal of Economic Analysis and Policy* 13(3): article 4.

Appiah, K. Anthony. 1995. Race, culture, and identity: Misunderstood connections. In K. Anthony Appiah and Amy Gutmann, *Color conscious: The political morality of race,* 30–105. Princeton, N.J.: Princeton University Press.

Arcidiacono, Peter, Esteban Aucejo, Patrick Coate, and V. Joseph Hotz. 2012. Affirmative action and university fit: Evidence from Proposition 209. Working paper, Department of Economics, Duke University.

Arcidiacono, Peter, and Jacob Vigdor. 2010. Does the river spill over? Estimating the economic returns from attending a racially diverse college. *Economic Inquiry* 48(3): 537–557.

Arias, Elizabeth. 2004. United States Life Tables, 2001. *National Vital Statistics Reports* 52(14): 1–40.

———. 2011. United States Life Tables, 2007. *National Vital Statistics Reports* 59(9): 1–61.

Ashcraft, Adam, Paul Goldsmith-Pinkham, and James Vickery. 2010. MBS ratings and the mortgage credit boom. Federal Reserve Bank of New York Staff Report no. 449, May.

Autor, David H., and David Scarborough. 2008. Does job testing harm minority workers? Evidence from retail establishments. *Quarterly Journal of Economics* 123(1): 219–277.

Avery, Robert, Kenneth Brevoort, and Glenn Canner. 2006. Higher priced home lending and the 2005 HMDA data. *Federal Reserve Bulletin* 92 (September): a123–a166.

Ayres, Ian. 2005. Three tests for measuring unjustified disparate impacts in kidney transplantation. *Perspectives in Biology and Medicine* 48 (1 Supplement): S68–S87.

Ayres, Ian, with Joel Waldfogel. 2001. A market test for race discrimination in bail setting. In Ian Ayres, *Pervasive prejudice? Unconventional evidence of race and gender discrimination,* 233–313. Chicago: University of Chicago Press.

Baccara, Mariagiovanna, Allan Collard-Wexler, Leonardo Felli, and Leeat Yariv. 2014. Child-adoption matching: Preferences for gender and race. *American Economic Journal: Applied Economics* 6(3): 133–158.

Baker, Bryan, and Nancy Rytina. 2013. *Estimates of the unauthorized immigrant population residing in the United States: January 2012.* Washington, D.C.: U.S. Department of Homeland Security, Office of Immigration Statistics. www.dhs.gov/sites/default/files/publications/ois_ill_pe_2012_2.pdf.

Banks, Ralph Richard. 2011. *Is marriage for white people? How the African American marriage decline affects everyone.* New York: Plume.

Bansak, Cynthia, and Steven Raphael. 2001. Immigration reform and the earnings of Latino workers. *Industrial and Labor Relations Review* 54(2): 275–295.

Bass, W. M. 2005. *Human osteology.* 5th ed. Columbia: Missouri Archaeology Society.

Bates, Timothy. 1997. *Race, self-employment, and upward mobility: An elusive American dream.* Baltimore: Johns Hopkins University Press.

Bayer, Patrick, Marcus D. Casey, Fernando Ferreira, and Robert McMillan. 2012. Price discrimination in the housing market. Working paper 18069, National Bureau of Economic Research.

Bayer, Patrick, Fernando Ferreira, and Stephen L. Ross. 2013. The vulnerability of minority homeowners in the housing boom and bust. Working paper 19020, National Bureau of Economic Research.

Becker, Gary. 1957. *The economics of discrimination.* Chicago: University of Chicago Press.

Becker, Gary, Kevin Murphy, and Michael Grossman. 2006. The market for illegal goods: The case of drugs. *Journal of Political Economy* 114(1): 38–60.

Beckett, K., K. Nyrop, and L. Pflingst. 2006. Race, drugs, and policy: Understanding disparities in drug delivery arrests. *Criminology* 44(1): 105–137.

Behrman, Jere, Mark Rozenzweig, and Paul Taubman. 1996. College choice and wages: Estimates using data on female twins. *Review of Economics and Statistics* 78(4): 672–685.

Belot, Michelle, and Jan Fidrmuc. 2010. Anthropometry of love: Height and gender asymmetries in interethnic marriages. *Economics and Human Biology* 8(3): 361–372.

Bertaut, Carol, and Michael Haliassos. 2006. Credit cards: Facts and theories. In *The economics of consumer credit,* ed. Giuseppe Bertola, Richard Disney, and Charles Grant, 181–237. Cambridge, Mass.: MIT Press.

Bertrand, Marianne, Dolly Chugh, and Sendhil Mullinathan. 2005. Implicit discrimination. *American Economic Review* 95(2): 94–98.

Bertrand, Marianne, and Sendhil Mullainathan. 2004. Are Emily and Greg more employable than Lakisha and Jamal? A field experiment on labor market discrimination. *American Economic Review* 94(4): 991–1013.

Billings, Stephen B., David J. Deming, and Jonah E. Rockoff. 2012. School segregation, educational attainment, and crime: Evidence from the end of busing in Charlotte-Mecklenburg. Working paper 18487, National Bureau of Economic Research.

Bittker, Boris. 1973. *The case for black reparations.* Boston: Beacon Press.

Bjerk, David. 2007. Racial profiling, statistical discrimination, and effect of a colorblind policy on the crime rate. *Journal of Public Economic Theory* 9(3): 521–545.

Black, Dan, K. Daniel, and J. Smith. 2001. Racial differences in the effects of college quality and student body diversity on wages. In *Diversity challenged,* ed. G. Orfield and M. Kurlaender, 221–231. Cambridge, Mass.: Harvard University Press.

Black, Dan, and Jeffrey Smith. 2006. Estimating the returns to college quality with multiple proxies for quality. *Journal of Labor Economics* 24(3): 701–728.

Black, Dan A., Amelia Haviland, Seth G. Sanders, and Lowell J. Taylor. 2009. The role of location in evaluating racial wage disparity. Working paper 2009-043, Federal Reserve Bank of St. Louis.

Blanchflower, David, and Andrew Oswald. 2013. Does high home-ownership impair the labor market? Working paper 19079, National Bureau of Economic Research.

Bleakley, Hoyt. 2007. Disease and development: Evidence from hookworm eradication in the American south. *Quarterly Journal of Economics* 122(1): 73–117.

Bleakley, Hoyt, and Joseph P. Ferrie. 2013. Shocking behavior: Random wealth in ante-bellum Georgia and human capital across generations. Working paper 19348, National Bureau of Economic Research.

Boehm, Thomas P., and Alan M. Schottman. 2009. The dynamics of homeownership: Eliminating the gap between African American and white households. *Real Estate Economics* 37(4): 599–634.

Borjas, George. 2003. The labor demand curve is downward-sloping: Reexamining the impact of immigration on the labor market. *Quarterly Journal of Economics* 118(4): 1335–1374.

Borjas, George, and Stephen Bronars. 1989. Consumer discrimination and self-employment. *Journal of Political Economy* 97(3): 581–605.

Borjas, George, Jeffrey Grogger, and Gordon Hanson. 2010. Immigration and the economic status of African-American men. *Economica* 77(306): 255–282.

Bostic, Raphael, and K. P. Lampani. 1999. Racial differences in patterns of small business finance: The importance of local geography. In Federal Reserve Bank of Chicago, *Proceedings of the conference on Business Access to Capital and Credit,* 149–179. http://www.chicagofed.org/webpages/events/1999/business_access_capital_credit.cfm#.

Boustan, Leah. 2010. Was postwar suburbanization white flight? Evidence from the black migration. *Quarterly Journal of Economics* 125(1): 417–443.

Boustan, Leah, and Robert A. Margo. 2009. Race, segregation, and postal employment: New evidence on spatial mismatch. *Journal of Urban Economics* 65(1): 1–10.

Bowen, William G., and Derek Bok. 1998. *The shape of the river: Long-term consequences of considering race in college and university admissions.* Princeton, N.J.: Princeton University Press.

Brewer, Dominic, Eric Eide, and Ronald Ehrenburg. 1999. Does it pay to attend an elite college? Evidence on the effect of college type on earnings. *Journal of Human Resources* 34(1): 104–123.

Bricker, Jesse, Arthur B. Kennickell, Kevin B. Moore, and John Sabelhaus. 2012. Changes in U.S. family finances from 2007 to 2010: Evidence from the Survey of Consumer Finances. *Federal Reserve Bulletin* 98(2) (February): 1–80. http://www.federalreserve.gov/pubs/bulletin/2012/pdf/scf12.pdf.

Brody, Howard, and Linda M. Hunt. 2006. BiDil: Assessing a race-based pharmaceutical. *Annals of Family Medicine* 4(6): 556–560.

Brooks-Gunn, Jean, J. Duncan, Jeffrey Kling, and Lisa Sanbonmatsu. 2004. Neighborhoods and academic achievement: Results from the Moving to Opportunity experiment. Working paper 492, Princeton University Department of Economics, Industrial Relations Section.

Burke, Mary A., and Frank W. Heiland. 2011. Explaining gender-specific racial differences in obesity using biased self-reports of food intake. Working paper 11-2, Boston Federal Reserve Bank.

Butcher, Kristin, and Ann Morrison Piehl. 2007. Why are immigrants' incarceration rates so low? Evidence on selective immigration, deterrence, and deportation. Working paper 13229, National Bureau of Economic Research.

———. 2008. Crime, corrections, and California: What does immigration have to do with it? *California Counts* 9(3). http://www.ppic.org/content/pubs/cacounts /CC_208KBCC.pdf.

Calem, P., K. Gillen, and S. Wachter. 2004. The neighborhood distribution of subprime mortgage lending. *Journal of Real Estate Economics and Finance* 29(4): 393–410.

Card, David. 1990. The impact of the Mariel boatlift on the Miami labor market. *Industrial and Labor Relations Review* 43(2): 245–257.

———. 2005. Is the new immigration really so bad? *Economic Journal* 115(507): F300–F323.

Card, David, Alexandre Mas, and Jesse Rothstein. 2008. Tipping and the dynamics of segregation. *Quarterly Journal of Economics* 123(1): 177–218.

Card, David, and Jesse Rothstein. 2007. Racial segregation and the black-white test score gap. *Journal of Public Economics* 91(11–12): 2158–2184.

Carlyle, Thomas. 1849. Occasional discourse on the Negro question. *Fraser's Magazine for Town and Country,* December, 670–679.

Carneiro, Pedro, James Heckman, and Dimitriy V. Masterov. 2005. Labor market discrimination and racial differences in pre-market factors. *Journal of Law and Economics* 48(1): 1–39.

Cavaluzzo, Ken, Linda Cavaluzzo, and John Wolken. 1999. Competition, small business financing, and discrimination: Evidence from a new survey. In Federal Reserve Bank of Chicago, *Proceedings of the conference on Business Access to Capital and Credit,* 180–266. http://www.chicagofed.org/webpages /events/1999/business_access_capital_credit.cfm#.

Chandra, Amitabh. 2003. Is the convergence of the racial wage gap illusory? Working paper 9476, National Bureau of Economic Research.

Chandra, Amitabh, and Jonathan Skinner. 2003. Geography and racial health disparities. Working paper 9513, National Bureau of Economic Research.

Chandra, Amitabh, and Douglas Staiger. 2010. Identifying provider prejudice in health care. Working paper 16382, National Bureau of Economic Research.

Charles, Kofi Kerwin, and Jonathan Guryan. 2008. Prejudice and wages: An empirical assessment of Becker's *The economics of discrimination. Journal of Political Economy* 116(5): 773–809.

Charles, Kofi Kerwin, Erik Hurst, and Nikolai Roussanov. 2009. Conspicuous consumption and race. *Quarterly Journal of Economics* 124(2): 425–467.

Charles, Kofi Kerwin, and Ming Ching Luoh. 2010. Male incarceration, the marriage market, and female outcomes. *Review of Economics and Statistics* 92(3): 614–627.

Chay, Kenneth Y., Jonathan Guryan, and Bhashkar Mazumder. 2009. Birth cohort and the black-white achievement gap: The roles of access and health soon after birth. Working paper 15078, National Bureau of Economic Research.

Chen, Brian X. 2014. Smartphones embracing theft defense. *New York Times,* June 20, B1.

Chen, J., S. S. Rathore, M. J. Radford, Y. Wang, and H. M. Krumholz. 2001. Racial differences in the use of cardiac catheterization after acute myocardial infarction. *New England Journal of Medicine* 344: 1443–1449.

Chiappori, Pierre-Andre, Bernard Fortin, and Guy Lacroix. 2002. Marriage market, divorce legislation, and household labor supply. *Journal of Political Economy* 110(1): 37–72.

Chin, Aimee, N. Meltem Daysal, and Scott Imberman. 2012. Impact of bilingual education programs on limited English proficient students and their peers: Regression discontinuity from Texas. Working paper 18197, National Bureau of Economic Research.

Chingos, Matthew M. 2012. The impact of a universal class-size reduction policy: Evidence from Florida's statewide mandate. *Economics of Education Review* 31: 543–562.

———. 2013. Class size and student outcomes: Research and policy implications. *Journal of Policy Analysis and Management* 32(2): 411–438.

Clarke, George, and Scott Wallsten. 2004. Do remittances act like insurance? Evidence from a natural disaster in Jamaica. Working paper, Social Science Research Network. http://papers.ssrn.com/sol3/papers.cfm?abstract_id =373480.

Clear, Todd. 2007. *Imprisoned communities: How mass incarceration makes disadvantaged neighborhoods worse.* New York: Oxford University Press.

Clemens, Michael A. 2011. Economics and emigration: Trillion-dollar bills on the sidewalk? *Journal of Economic Perspectives* 25(3): 83–106.

Clemens, Michael A., Claudio E. Montenegro, and Lant Pritchett. 2008. The place premium: Wage differences for identical workers across the U.S. border. Working paper 148, Center for Global Development.

Coate, Stephen, and Glenn C. Loury. 1993. Will affirmative action policies eliminate negative stereotypes? *American Economic Review* 83(5): 1220–1240.

Cobb-Clark, Deborah, and Vincent Hildebrand. 2004. The wealth of Mexican-Americans. IZA discussion paper 1150, Institute for the Study of Labor, Bonn.

Cohen-Cole, Ethan. 2011. Credit card redlining. *Review of Economics and Statistics* 93(2): 700–713.

Cohodes, Sarah, and Joshua Goodman. 2012. First degree earns: The impact of college quality on college completion rates. HKS Faculty Research Working Paper Series RWP12-033.

Cohodes, Sarah, Samuel Kleiner, Michael F. Lovenheim, and Daniel Grossman. 2014. The effect of child health insurance expansion on schooling: Evidence from public health insurance expansions. Working paper 20178, National Bureau of Economic Research.

Cook, Philip J., and Jens Ludwig. 1997. Weighing the burden of acting white: Are there race differences in attitudes toward education? *Journal of Policy Analysis and Management* 16(2): 256–278.

———. 2010. Economical crime control. Working paper 16513, National Bureau of Economic Research.

Cook, Philip J., and John MacDonald. 2011. Public safety through private action: An economic assessment of BIDs. *Economic Journal* 121(552): 445–462.

Costa, Dora L. 2004. Race and pregnancy outcomes in the 20th century: A long-term comparison. *Journal of Economic History* 64(4): 1056–1086.

Coulton, Claudia, Tsui Chan, Michael Schram, and Kristen Mikelbank. 2008. Pathways to foreclosure: A longitudinal study of mortgage loans in Cleveland and Cuyahoga County, 2005–2008. Center on Urban Poverty and Community Development, Case Western Reserve University, Cleveland, Ohio.

Cullen, Julie Berry, and Brian Jacob. 2007. Is gaining access to selective elementary schools gaining ground? Evidence from randomized lotteries. Working paper 13443, National Bureau of Economic Research.

Currie, Janet. 2011. Inequality at birth: Some causes and consequences. Working paper 16798, National Bureau of Economic Research.

Currie, Janet, and Duncan Thomas. 1995. Does Head Start make a difference? *American Economic Review* 85(3): 341–364.

Cutler, David, and Edward Glaeser. 1997. Are ghettoes good or bad? *Quarterly Journal of Economics* 112(3): 827–92.

Cutler, David, Edward Glaeser, and Jacob Vigdor. 2008. Is the melting pot still hot? Explaining the resurgence of immigrant segregation. *Review of Economics and Statistics* 90(3): 478–497.

Cutler, David, Ellen Meara, and Seth Richards. 2009. Induced innovation and social inequality: Evidence from infant medical care. Working paper 15316, National Bureau of Economic Research.

Dale, Stacy, and Alan Krueger. 2002. Estimating the return to attending a more selective college: An application of selection on observables and unobservables. *Quarterly Journal of Economics* 117(4): 1491–1527.

———. 2011. Estimating the return to college selectivity over the career using administrative earnings data. Working paper 17159, National Bureau of Economic Research.

Decker, Sandra, and Carol Rapaport. 2002. Medicare and disparities in women's health. Working paper 8761, National Bureau of Economic Research.

Dee, Thomas S. 2004. Teachers, race, and student achievement in a randomized experiment. *Review of Economics and Statistics* 86(1): 195–210.

———. 2005. A teacher like me: Does race, ethnicity, or gender matter? *American Economic Review* 95(2): 158–165.

Dee, Thomas S., and Brian Jacob. 2011. The impact of No Child Left Behind on student achievement. *Journal of Policy Analysis and Management* 30(3): 418–446.

Dee, Thomas S., Brian Jacob, and N. L. Schwartz. 2011. The effects of NCLB on school resources and practices. Unpublished manuscript.

Dell, Melissa. 2012. Trafficking networks and Mexican drug war. Working paper, Department of Economics, Harvard University.

Deming, David. 2009. Early childhood intervention and life-cycle skill development: Evidence from Head Start. *American Economic Journal: Applied Economics* 1(3): 111–134.

Dickens, William T., and James R. Flynn. 2006. Black Americans reduce the IQ gap: Evidence from standardization samples. *Psychological Science* 17(10): 913–924.

DiPasquale, Denise, and Matthew Kahn. 1999. Measuring neighborhood investments: An examination of community choice. *Real Estate Economics* 27(3): 389–424.

Dobbie, Will, and Roland G. Fryer Jr. 2011a. Exam high schools and academic achievement: Evidence from New York City. Working paper 17286, National Bureau of Economic Research.

———. 2011b. Are high quality schools enough to increase achievement among the poor? Evidence from the Harlem Children's Zone. *American Economic Journal: Applied Economics* 3(3): 158–186.

———. 2011c. Getting beneath the veil of effective schools: Evidence from New York City. Working paper 17632, National Bureau of Economic Research.

Donohue, John J., and James Heckman. 1991. Continuous vs episodic change: The impact of civil rights policy on the economic status of blacks. *Journal of Economic Literature* 29(4): 1603–1643.

Donohue, John J., III, and Peter Siegelman. 1998. Allocating resources among prisons and social programs in the battle against crime. *Journal of Legal Studies* 27 (January): 1–43.

Du Bois, W. E. B. 1897. *Conservation of races.* Washington, D.C.: American Negro Academy.

———. 1903. *The souls of black folk: Essays and sketches.* Chicago: A. C. McClurg and Company.

———. (1906) 1995. The Niagara Movement: Address to the country. In *W. E. B. Du Bois: A reader,* ed. David Levering Lewis, 367–369. New York: Henry Holt and Company.

———. 1913a. An open letter to Woodrow Wilson. *The Crisis* 5(5): 236.

———. 1913b. Another open letter to Woodrow Wilson. *The Crisis* 6(5): 232.

———. (1940) 2007. *Dusk of dawn.* Introduction by Kwame Anthony Appiah. Oxford: Oxford University Press.

Duesenberry, James S. 1949. *Income, saving, and the theory of consumer behavior.* Cambridge, Mass.: Harvard University Press.

Duggan, Mark. 2001. More guns, more crime. *Journal of Political Economy* 109(5): 1086–1114.

Dynarski, Susan, Joshua M. Hyman, and Diane Whitmore-Schanzenbach. 2011. Experimental evidence on the effect of childhood investments on postsecondary attainment and degree completion. Working paper 17533, National Bureau of Economic Research.

Echenique, Frederico, and Roland G. Fryer. 2007. A measure of segregation based on social interactions. *Quarterly Journal of Economics* 122(2): 441–485.

Ellen, Ingrid Gould. 2000a. *Sharing America's neighborhoods.* Cambridge, Mass.: Harvard University Press.

———. 2000b. Is segregation bad for your health? *Brookings-Wharton Papers on Urban Affairs* 1: 203–238.

Epstein, Richard. 1992. *Forbidden grounds: The case against employment discrimination laws.* Cambridge, Mass: Harvard University Press.

Evans, William N., Craig Garthwaite, and Timothy J. Moore. 2012. The white/black educational gap, stalled progress, and the long term consequences of the emergence of crack cocaine markets. Working paper 18437, National Bureau of Economic Research.

Fagan, Jeffrey. 2010. David Floyd et al., vs. City of New York et al., United States District Court, Southern District of New York, 08 Civ. 01034 (SAS): Report of Jeffrey Fagan, Ph.D. http://ccrjustice.org/files/Expert_Report_JeffreyFagan .pdf.

Fairlie, Robert W., and Alicia Robb. 2008. *Race and entrepreneurial success: Black-, Asian-, and white-owned businesses in the U.S.* Cambridge, Mass.: MIT Press.

Figlio, David N. 2005. Names, expectations and the black-white test score gap. Working paper 11195, National Bureau of Economic Research.

Figlio, David N., Jonathan Guryan, Krzyzstof Karbownik, and Jeffrey Roth, 2014. The effects of poor neonatal health on children's cognitive development. *American Economic Review* 104 (12): 3921–3955.

Finkelstein, Amy, Sarah Taubman, Bill Wright, Maria Bernstein, Jonathan Gruber, Joseph P. Newhouse, Heidi Allen, Katherine Baicker, and The Oregon Health Study Group. 2011. The Oregon health insurance experiment: Evidence from the first year. Working paper 17190, National Bureau of Economic Research.

Fisman, Raymond, Daniel Paravisini, and Vikrant Vig. 2012. Cultural proximity and loan outcomes. Working paper 18096, National Bureau of Economic Research.

Flegal, Katherine M., Margaret D. Carroll, Cynthia L. Ogden, and Lester R. Curtin. 2010. Prevalence and trends in obesity among U.S. adults, 1999–2008. *Journal of the American Medical Association* 303(3): 235–241.

Fletcher, Michael. 2001. Long division. *The New Crisis* (September–October): 26–31.

Floud, Roderick, Robert W. Fogel, Bernard Harris, and Sok Chul Hong. 2011. *The changing body: Health, nutrition, and human development in the western world since 1700.* Cambridge: Cambridge University Press.

Fogel, Robert W. 1989. *Without consent or contract: The rise and fall of American slavery.* New York: Norton.

Fogel, Robert W., and Stanley Engerman. 1974. *Time on the cross: The economics of American Negro slavery.* Boston: Little Brown.

Freeman, Richard B. 2006. People flows in globalization. *Journal of Economic Perspectives* 20(2): 145–170.

Friedman, Milton. 1957. *A theory of the consumption function.* Princeton, N.J.: Princeton University Press.

Fryer, Roland G., Jr. 2007. Guess who's coming to dinner? Trends in interracial marriage in the 20th century. *Journal of Economic Perspectives* 21(2): 71–90.

———. 2010. Financial incentives and student achievement: Evidence from randomized trials. Working paper 15898, National Bureau of Economic Research.

———. 2011. Creating "no excuses" (traditional) public schools: Preliminary evidence from an experiment in Houston. Working paper 17494, National Bureau of Economic Research.

Fryer, Roland G., Jr., P. S. Heaton, Steven D. Levitt, and Kevin Murphy. 2005. Measuring the impact of crack cocaine. Working paper 11318, National Bureau of Economic Research.

Fryer, Roland G., Jr., Lisa Kahn, and Steven Levitt. 2008. The plight of mixed race adolescents. Working paper 14192, National Bureau of Economic Research.

Fryer, Roland G., Jr., and Steven Levitt. 2004a. The causes and consequences of distinctively black names. *Quarterly Journal of Economics* 119(3): 767–806.

———. 2004b. Understanding the black-white test score gap in the first two years of school. *Review of Economics and Statistics* 86(2): 447–464.

———. 2004c. The black-white test score gap through third grade. Discussion paper, Harvard University.

———. 2006. Testing for racial differences in the mental ability of young children. Working paper 12066, National Bureau of Economic Research.

———. 2013. Testing for racial differences in the mental ability of young children. *American Economic Review* 103(2): 981–1005.

Fryer, Roland G., Jr., and Paul Torelli. 2010. An empirical analysis of "acting white." *Journal of Public Economics* 94(5–6): 380–396.

Gabriel, Stuart A., and Stuart S. Rosenthal. 2005. Homeownership in the 1980s and 1990s: Aggregate trends and racial gaps. *Journal of Urban Economics* 57(1): 101–127.

Galenson, Marjorie. 1972. Do blacks save more? *American Economic Review* 62(1): 211–216.

Garces, Eliana, Duncan Thomas, and Janet Currie. 2002. Longer term effects of Head Start. *American Economic Review* 92(4): 999–1012.

Gerardi, Kristopher, and Paul Willen. 2009. Subprime mortgages, foreclosures, and urban neighborhoods. Working paper series issue 1, Federal Reserve Bank of Atlanta.

Ghent, Andra, Ruben Hernandez-Murillo, and Michael Owyang. 2011. Race and subprime loan pricing. Paper presented at American Real Estate and Urban Economics Association mid-year meeting, Washington, D.C.

Gibbs, Chloe, Jens Ludwig, and Douglas L. Miller. 2011. Does Head Start do any lasting good? Working paper 17452, National Bureau of Economic Research.

Gibson, John, and David McKenzie. 2011. Eight questions about brain drain. *Journal of Economic Perspectives* 25(3): 107–128.

Gill, G. W. 1986. Craniofacial criteria in the skeletal attribution of race. In *Forensic osteology: Advances in the identification of human remains,* ed. K. Reichs, 143–159. Springfield, Ill.: Charles C. Thomas.

Glaeser, Edward, and Bruce Sacerdote. 2000. The determinants of punishment: Deterrence, incapacitation, and vengeance. HIER discussion paper 1894, Harvard University Department of Economics.

Glaeser, Edward, and Jesse Shapiro. 2002. The benefits of the home mortgage interest deduction. Working paper 9284, National Bureau of Economic Research.

Glaeser, Edward, and Jacob Vigdor. 2012. The end of the segregated century: Racial separation in America's neighborhoods, 1890–2010. Civic report 66, Manhattan Institute.

Glaze, Lauren E., 2011. Correctional populations in the United States, 2010. U.S. Bureau of Justice Statistics. http://www.bjs.gov/content/pub/pdf/cpus10.pdf.

Glaze, Lauren E., and Thomas Bonczar. 2011. Probation and parole in the United States, 2010. *U.S. Department of Justice Bulletin* (December). http://www.bjs.gov/content/pub/pdf/ppus10.pdf.

Goldsmith, Arthur H., William Darity Jr., and Jonathan R. Veum. 1998. Race, cognitive skills, psychological capital, and wages. *Review of Black Political Economy* 26(2): 9–21.

Goodman, Joshua. 2014. The wages of sinistrality: Handedness, brain structure, and human capital accumulation. *Journal of Economic Perspectives* 28(4): 193–212.

Gray, Bradford, Mark Schlesinger, Shannon Mitchell Siegfried, and Emily Horowitz. 2009. Racial and ethnic disparities in the use of high-volume hospitals. *Inquiry* 46(3): 322–338.

Green, Alexander, Dana Carney, Daniel Pallin, Long Ngo, Kristal Raymond, Lisa Lezzoni, and Nahzarin Banaji. 2007. Implicit bias among physicians and its prediction of thrombolysis decisions for black and white patients. *Journal of General Internal Medicine* 22(9): 1231–1238.

Grieco, Elizabeth M., Edward Trevelyan, Luke Larsen, Yesenia D. Acosta, Christine Gambino, Patricia de la Cruz, Tom Gryn, and Nathan Walters. 2012. The size, place of birth, and geographic distribution of the foreign-born population in the United States: 1960 to 2010. Working paper 96, U.S. Bureau of the Census, Population Division.

Grissom, Jason A., and Lael Keiser. 2011. A supervisor like me: Race, representation, and the satisfaction and turnover decisions of public sector employees. *Journal of Policy Analysis and Management* 30(3): 557–580.

Grogger, J., and G. Ridgway. 2006. Testing for racial profiling in traffic stops from behind a veil of darkness. *Journal of the American Statistical Association* 475(101): 878–887.

Guerino, Paul, Paige M. Harrison, and William J. Sabol. 2011. Prisoners in 2010. *U.S. Department of Justice Bulletin* (December). http://www.bjs.gov/content/pub/pdf/p10.pdf.

Guryan, Jonathan. 2004. Desegregation and black dropout rates. *American Economic Review* 94(4): 919–943.

Hagedorn, J. M. 1998. The business of drug dealing in Milwaukee. Thiensville: Wisconsin Policy Research Institute. http://www.csdp.org/research/drugdeal.pdf.

Hanson, Andrew, Zackary Hawley, and Aryn Taylor. 2011. Subtle discrimination in the rental housing market: Evidence from e-mail correspondence with landlords. *Journal of Housing Economics* 19(4): 276–284.

Hanushek, Eric, John Kain, and Steve Rivkin. 2002. New evidence about Brown v. Board of Education: The complex effects of school racial composition of achievement. Working paper 8741, National Bureau of Economic Research.

Harris, David R., and Jeremiah J. Sim. 2002. Who is multiracial? Assessing the complexity of lived race. *American Sociological Review* 67(4): 614–627.

Harwood, H., D. Fountain, and G. Livermore. 1998. *The economic costs of alcohol and drug abuse in the United States, 1992.* NIH Pub. 98-4327. Rockville, Md.: National Institutes of Health.

Haughwout, Andrew, Christopher Mayer, and Joseph Tracy. 2009. Subprime mortgage pricing: The impact of race, ethnicity, and gender on borrowing Federal Reserve Bank of New York staff report no. 368, April. http://www.newyorkfed.org/research/staff_reports/sr368.pdf.

Heckman, James. 1998. Detecting discrimination. *Journal of Economic Perspectives* 12: 101–16.

Heckman, James, and Brook S. Payner. 1989. Determining the impact of federal antidiscrimination policy on the economic status of blacks: A study of South Carolina. *American Economic Review* 79(1): 138–177.

Heron, Melonie, Donna L. Hoyert, Sherry L. Murphy, Jiaquan Xu, Kenneth D. Kochanek, and Betzaida Tejada-Vera. 2009. Deaths: Final data for 2006. *National Vital Statistics Reports* 57(14): 1–135.

Heron, Melonie P., Donna L. Hoyert, Jiaquan Xu, Chester Scott, and Betzaida Tejada-Vera. 2008. Deaths: Preliminary data for 2006. *National Vital Statistics Reports* 56(16): 1–52.

Herrnstein, Richard J. and Charles Murray. 1994. *The bell curve: Intelligence and class structure in American life.* New York: Free Press.

Hoekstra, Mark. 2009. The effect of attending the flagship state university on earnings: A discontinuity-based approach. *Review of Economics and Statistics* 91(4): 717–724.

Hoff, Karla, and Priyanka Pandey. 2006. Discrimination, social identity, and durable inequalities. *American Economic Review* 96(2): 206–211.

Holzer, Harry J. 2009. Collateral costs: The effects of incarceration on employment and earnings among young workers. In *Do prisons make us safer? The benefits and costs of the prison boom,* ed. Steven Raphael and Michael A. Stoll, 239–268. New York: Russell Sage.

Holzer, Harry J., and David Neumark. 2000. Assessing affirmative action. *Journal of Economic Literature* 29: 1603–1643.

Hoxby, Caroline M., and Sonali Murarka. 2009. Charter schools in New York City: Who enrolls and how they affect their students' achievement. Working paper 14852, National Bureau of Economic Research.

Hoynes, Hilary, Douglas I. Miller, and Jessamyn Schaller. 2012. Who suffers during recessions? *Journal of Economic Perspectives* 26(3): 27–48.

Hsieh, Chang-Tai, and Miguel Urquiola. 2006. The effect of generalized school choice on achievement and stratification: Evidence from Chile's voucher program. *Journal of Public Economics* 90(8–9): 1477–1503.

Illuminating BiDil. 2005. *Nature Biotechnology* 23(8): 903.

Jencks, Christopher, and Meredith Phillips. 1998. *The black-white test score gap.* Washington, D.C.: Brookings Institution.

Jepsen, Christopher, and Steven Rivkin. 2009. Class size reduction and student achievement: The potential tradeoff between teacher quality and class size. *Journal of Human Resources* 44(1): 223–50.

Johnson, Rucker. 2009. Ever-increasing levels of parental incarceration and the consequences for children. In *Do prisons make us safer? The benefits and costs of the prison boom,* ed. Steven Raphael and Michael A. Stoll, 177–206. New York: Russell Sage.

Johnson, William R., and Derek A. Neal. 1998. Basic skills and the black-white earnings gap. In *The black-white test score gap,* ed. Christopher Jencks and Meredith Phillips. Washington, D.C.: Brookings Institute Press.

Jones, Jeffrey M. 2005. Most Americans approve of interracial dating: Practice not uncommon in U.S. http://www.gallup.com/poll/19033/most-americans-approve-interracial-dating.aspx.

Kane, Thomas J. 2004. Racial and ethnic preferences in college admissions. In *The economics of affirmative action,* ed. Harry J. Holzer and David Neumark, 604–629. Northampton, Mass.: Edward Elgar Publishing.

Kaufman, Jay S., Thu T. Nguyen, and Richard S. Cooper. 2010. Race, medicine, and the science behind BiDil: How ACE-inhibition took the fall for the first ethnic drug. *Review of Black Political Economy* 37(2): 115–130.

Kennedy, David M., Anthony Braga, Anne M. Piehl, and E. J. Waring. 2001. *Reducing gun violence: The Boston Gun Project's Operation Ceasefire.* Washington, D.C.: National Institute of Justice.

Kennedy, Randall. 2013. *For discrimination: Race, affirmative action, and the law.* New York: Pantheon.

Kenney, Genevieve, and Douglas Wissoker. 1994. An analysis of the correlates of discrimination facing young Hispanic job seekers. *American Economic Review* 84(3): 674–683.

King, Martin Luther, Jr. 1963. I have a dream. American Rhetoric: Top 100 speeches. http://www.americanrhetoric.com/speeches/mlkihaveadream.htm.

Kirby, James B., and Toshiko Kanedo. 2010. Unhealthy and uninsured: Exploring racial differences in health and health insurance coverage. *Demography* 47(4): 1035–1051.

Kling, Jeffrey. 2006. Incarceration length, employment, and earnings. *American Economic Review* 96(3): 863–876.

Kling, Jeffrey, Jens Ludwig, and Lawrence F. Katz. 2004. Neighborhood effects on crime for male and female youth: Evidence from a randomized housing voucher experiment. Working paper 10777, National Bureau of Economic Research.

Knowles, John, Nicola Persico, and Petra Todd. 2001. Racial bias in motor vehicle searches: Theory and evidence. *Journal of Political Economy* 109(1): 203–229.

Komlos, John. 2010. The recent decline in height of African-American women. *Economics and Human Biology* 8(1): 58–66.

Kreider, Rose M., and Daphne Lofquist. 2014. *Adopted children and stepchildren: 2010: Population characteristics.* U.S. Bureau of the Census publication P20-572. http://www.census.gov/prod/2014pubs/p20-572.pdf.

Krishna, Kala, and Alexander Tarasov. 2013. Affirmative action: One size does not fit all. Working paper 19546, National Bureau of Economic Research.

Krogman, W. M., and M. Y. İşcan. 1986. *The human skeleton in forensic medicine.* 2nd ed. Springfield, Ill.: Charles C. Thomas.

Krueger, Alan, Jesse Rothstein, and Sarah Turner. 2006. Race, income, and college in 25 years. *American Law and Economics Review* 8(2): 282–311.

Krueger, Alan, and Pei Zhu. 2004. Another look at the New York City school voucher experiment. *American Behavioral Scientist* 47(5): 658–698.

Kutateladze, Besiki, Vanessa Lynn, and Edward Liang. 2012. Do race and ethnicity matter in prosecution? A review of empirical studies. New York: Vera Institute of Justice.

Kuziemko, Ilyana, and Steven D. Levitt. 2004. An empirical analysis of imprisoning drug offenders. *Journal of Public Economics* 88(9–10): 2043–2066.

Kyckelhahn, Tracey. 2012. Justice expenditure and employment abstracts, 2009—Preliminary. Data set. U.S. Bureau of Justice Statistics. http://bjs.ojp .usdoj.gov/index.cfm?ty=pbdetail&iid=4335.

Lang, Kevin, and Jee-Keon K. Lehmann. 2012. Racial discrimination in the labor market: Theory and empirics. *Journal of Economic Literature* 50(4): 959–1006.

Lang, Kevin, and Michael Manove. 2011. Education and labor market discrimination. *American Economic Review* 101 (June): 1467–1496.

Lauritsen, Janet, and Robert Sampson. 1997. Racial and ethnic disparities in crime and criminal justice in the U.S. In *Ethnicity, crime, and immigration: Comparative and cross-national perspectives,* ed. Michael Tonry, 311–374. Chicago: University of Chicago Press.

LaVeist, T.A., K. J. Nickerson, and J. V. Bowie. 2000. Attitudes about racism, medical mistrust, and satisfaction with health care among African American and white cardiac patients. *Medical Care Research and Review* 57(supplement 1): 146–161.

Levine, Philip B., and Diane Schanzenbach. 2009. The impact of children's public health insurance expansions on educational outcomes. *Forum for Health Economics and Policy* 12(1): 1–26.

Levitt, Steven D. 2002. Using electoral cycles in police hiring to estimate the effects of police on crime: Reply. *American Economic Review* 92(4): 1244–1250.

———. 2004. Understanding why crime fell in the 1990s: Four factors that explain the decline and six that do not. *Journal of Economic Perspectives* 18(1): 163–190.

Lillie-Blanton, M., M. Brodie, D. Rowland, D.Altman, and M. McIntosh. 2000. Race, ethnicity, and the health care system: Public perceptions and experiences. *Medical Care Research and Review* 57(supplement 1): 218–235.

Liu, J. H., D. S. Zigmund, M. L. McGory, N. F. SooHoo, S. L. Ettner, R. H. Brook, and C. Y. Ko. 2006. Disparities in the utilization of high-volume hospitals for complex surgery. *Journal of the American Medical Association* 296(16): 1973–1980.

Lochner, Lance, and Enrico Moretti. 2004. The effect of education on crime: Evidence from prison inmates, arrests, and self-reports. *American Economic Review* 94(1): 155–189.

Loeffler, Charles E. 2013. Does imprisonment alter the life course? Evidence on crime and employment from a natural experiment. *Criminology* 51(1): 137–166.

Lofstrom, Magnus, and Steven Raphael. 2013. *Public safety realignment and crime rates in California.* San Francisco: Public Policy Institute of California.

Logan, John R. 2002. Separate and unequal: Data set. http://mumford.albany.edu /census/data.html#home.

———. 2011a. Residential segregation. Data set. Project 2010, Brown University. http://www.s4.brown.edu/us2010/segregation2010/Default.aspx?msa=19804.

———. 2011b. Separate and unequal: The neighborhood gap for blacks, Hispanics, and Asians in metropolitan America. Census brief prepared for Project 2010, Brown University. http://www.s4.brown.edu/us2010/Data/Report/report0727 .pdf.

Logan, John R., and Brian Stults. 2011. The persistence of segregation in the metropolis: New findings from the 2010 census. Census brief prepared for Project 2010, Brown University. http://www.ncbi.nlm.nih.gov/pmc/articles /PMC3859616/.

Lott, John R., Jr. 1998. *More guns, less crime: Understanding crime and gun-control laws.* Chicago: University of Chicago Press.

Loury, Glenn. 2006. Trans-generational justice: Compensatory vs interpretive approaches. In *Reparations: Interdisciplinary inquiries,* ed. John Miller and Rahul Kumar, 87–113. New York: Oxford University Press.

Loury, Linda Datcher, and David Garman. 1995. College selectivity and earnings. *Journal of Labor Economics* 13(2): 289–308.

Ludwig, Jens, and Jeffrey Kling. 2007. Is crime contagious? *Journal of Law and Economics* 50(3): 491–518.

Ludwig, Jens, and Douglas L. Miller. 2007. Does Head Start improve children's life chances? Evidence from a regression-discontinuity design. *Quarterly Journal of Economics* 122(1): 159–208.

Lutz, Byron. 2011. The end of court-ordered desegregation. *American Economic Journal: Economic Policy* 3(2): 130–168.

Malcolm X. (1964) 2009. The ballot or the bullet. In *Let nobody turn us around: Voices of resistance, reform, and renewal: An African American anthology,* 2nd ed., ed. Manning Marable and Leith Mullings, 405–413. Lanham, Md.: Rowman & Littlefield.

Malone, Nolan, Kaari F. Baluja, Joseph M. Costanzo, and Cynthia J. Davis. 2003. The foreign-born population: 2000. Census 2000 brief. http://www.census .gov/content/dam/Census/library/publications/2003/demo/c2kbr-34.pdf.

Margo, Robert, and William Collins. 2011. Race and home ownership from the end of the Civil War to the present. *American Economic Review* 101(3): 355–359.

Marmaros, David, and Bruce Sacerdote. 2006. How do friendships form? *Quarterly Journal of Economics* 121(1): 79–119.

Mathews, T. J., and Marian F. MacDorman. 2011. Infant mortality statistics from the 2007 period linked birth/infant death data set. *National Vital Statistics Reports* 59(6): 1–31.

Mayer, Christopher, and Susan Pence. 2008. Subprime mortgages: What, where, to whom? Discussion paper 2008-29, Federal Reserve Board of Governors.

McDowell, Margaret A., Cheryl D. Fryar, Cynthia L. Ogden, and Katherine M. Flegal. 2008. Anthropometric reference data for children and adults: United States, 2003–2006. *National Health Statistics Reports* 10 (October 22).

McKenzie, Brian, and Melanie Rapino. 2011. *Commuting in the United States: 2009.* U.S. Bureau of the Census, American Community Survey Reports, report ACS-15.

Mian, Atif, and Amir Sufi. 2014. *House of debt: How they (and you) caused the great recession, and how we can prevent it from happening again.* Chicago: University of Chicago Press.

Mill, John Stuart. 1850. The Negro Question. *Fraser's Magazine for Town and Country,* January, 25–31.

Miniño, Arialdi M., Melonie P. Heron, and Betty L. Smith. 2006. Deaths: Preliminary data for 2004. *National Vital Statistics Reports* 54(19): 1–52.

Miniño, Arialdi M., Sherry L. Murphy, Jiaquan Xu, and Kenneth D. Kochanek. 2011. Deaths: Final data for 2008. *National Vital Statistics Reports* 59(10): 1–127.

Minton, Todd D. 2010. Jail inmates at midyear 2009—Statistical tables. Bureau of Justice Statistics. http://www.bjs.gov/content/pub/pdf/jim09st.pdf.

Miron, Jeff. 1999. Violence and the U.S. prohibition of drugs and alcohol. Working paper 6950, National Bureau of Economic Research.

Mobius, Mark, and Tanya Rosenblatt. 2006. Why beauty matters. *American Economic Review* 96(1): 222–235.

Model, Suzanne. 2008. *West Indian immigrants: A black success story?* New York: Russell Sage.

Monras, Joan. 2014. Immigration and wage dynamics: Evidence from the Mexican peso crisis. Working paper, Columbia University Department of Economics.

Moro, Andrea, and Peter Norman. 2004. A general equilibrium model of statistical discrimination. *Journal of Economic Theory* 114(1): 1–30.

Moss, Philip, and Chris Tilly. 2001. Why opportunity isn't knocking: Racial inequality and the demand for labor. In *Urban inequality: Evidence from four cities,* ed. Alice O'Connor, Chris Tilly, and Lawrence D. Bobo, 444–495. New York: Russell Sage Foundation.

Munnell, Alicia, Lynn E. Browne, James McEneaney, and Geoffrey M. B. Tootell. 1996. Mortgage lending in Boston: Interpreting HMDA data. *American Economic Review* 86(1): 25–53.

Murnane, Richard. 2013. US high school graduation rates: Patterns and explanations. *Journal of Economic Literature* 51(2): 370–422.

Murphy, Kevin, and Robert Topel. 2005. Black-white differences in the economic value of improving health. *Perspectives in Biology and Medicine* 48(1): S176–S194.

Myers, Samuel L., Jr, and William Sabol. 1988. Unemployment and racial differences in imprisonment. In *The economics of race and crime,* ed. Margaret C. Simms and Samuel L. Myers Jr, 189–209. New Brunswick, NJ: Transactions Publishers.

Myrdal, Gunnar. (1944) 1996. *An American dilemma,* vol. 1, *The Negro problem and modern democracy.* New Brunswick, N.J.: Transaction Publishers.

Nagel, J. 1995. American Indian ethnic renewal: Politics and the resurgence of identity. *American Sociological Review* 60(6): 947–65.

National Academy of Sciences, Committee on Deterrence and the Death Penalty. 2012. *Deterrence and the death penalty.* Washington, D.C.: National Academy of Sciences.

National Center for Education Statistics. 2005. *NAEP 2004: Trends in academic progress: Three decades of student performance in reading and mathematics.* Washington, D.C.: National Center for Education Statistics. http://nces.ed .gov/nationsreportcard/pdf/main2005/2005464_2.pdf.

National Commission on Civil Disorders. 1968. *Report of the National Commission on Civil Disorders.* Washington, D.C.: Government Printing Office.

Neal, Derek A. 2004. The measured black-white wage gap for women is too small. *Journal of Political Economy* 112(1): S1–S28.

Neal, Derek A., and William R. Johnson. 1996. The role of premarket factors in black-white wage differences. *Journal of Political Economy* 104(5): 868–95.

Newport, Frank. 2013. In U.S., 24% of young black men say police unfair. http:// www.gallup.com/poll/163523/one-four-young-black-men-say-police-dealings -unfair.aspx.

Novotny, V., M. Y. İşcan, and S. R. Loth. 1993. Morphological and osteometric assessment of age, sex and race from the skull. In *Forensic analysis of the skull,* ed. M. Y. İşcan and R. P. Helmer, 71–88. New York: Wiley Liss.

O'Flaherty, Brendan, and Vanita Gowda. 2004. Drugs, race, and technology: Winning the war on bad drugs. In *Racism, liberalism, and economics,* ed. David Colander, Robert Prasch, and Falguni Sheth, 275–284. Ann Arbor: University of Michigan Press.

O'Flaherty, Brendan, and Rajiv Sethi. 2009. Why have robberies become less frequent but more violent? *Journal of Law, Economics and Organization* 25(2): 518–534.

———. 2010. Peaceable kingdoms and war zones: Preemption, ballistics, and murder in Newark. In *The economics of crime: Lessons for and from Latin America,* ed. Rafael di Tella and Ernesto Schargrodsky, 305–358. Chicago: National Bureau of Economic Research and University of Chicago Press.

———. 2015. Urban crime. In *Handbook of urban and regional economics,* vol. 5, ed. Gilles Duranton, and Vernon Henderson, and William Strange. Amsterdam: North-Holland.

Ogbu, John. 1994. Racial stratification in the United States: Why inequality persists. *Teachers College Record* 96(2): 264–298.

Oreopoulos, Philip. 2009. Would more compulsory schooling help disadvantaged youth? Evidence from recent changes to school-leaving laws. In *The problems of disadvantaged youth: An economic perspective,* ed. Jonathan Gruber, 85–112. Chicago: University of Chicago Press.

Orr, Larry, Judith Feins, Robin Jacob, Erik Beecroft, Lisa Sabonmatsu, Lawrence F. Katz, Jeffrey B. Liebman, and Jeffrey R. Kling. 2003. *Moving to opportunity interim impacts evaluation.* Washington, D.C.: U.S. Department of Housing and Urban Development, Office of Policy Development and Research.

Oyer, Paul, and Scott Schaeffer. 2000. Layoffs and litigation. *Rand Journal of Economics* 32(2): 345–358.

Pager, Devah, Bruce Western, and Bart Bonikowski. 2009. Discrimination in a low-wage labor market: A field experiment. *American Journal of Sociology* 74 (October): 777–799.

Parsons, Christopher, Johan Sulaeman, Michael C. Yates, and Daniel S. Hamermesh. 2011. Strike three: Umpires' demand for discrimination. *American Economic Review* 101(4): 1410–1435.

Peroff, Kathleen A., Cloteal L. Davis, and Ronald Jones. 1979. *Gautreaux housing demonstration: An evaluation of its impact on participating households.* Washington, D.C.: U.S. Department of Housing and Urban Development, Office of Policy Development and Research.

Petit, Becky, and Bruce Western. 2004. Mass imprisonment and the life course: Race and class inequality in U.S. incarceration. *American Sociological Review* 69 (April): 151–169.

Phelps, Edmund S. 1972. The statistical theory of racism and sexism. *American Economic Review* 62(4): 659–661.

Piehl, Anne Morrison, Raymond V. Liedka, and Bert Useem. 2006. The crime-control effect of incarceration: Does scale matter? *Criminology* 5(2): 245–275.

Piketty, Thomas. 2013. *Capital in the twenty-first century.* Cambridge, Mass.: Harvard University Press.

Piskorski, Tomasz, Amit Seru, and James Witkin. 2013. Asset quality misrepresentation by financial intermediaries: Evidence from the RMBS market. Working paper, Columbia Business School.

Prakash, Nishith. 2009. Improving the labor market outcomes of minorities: The role of employment quotas. IZA discussion paper 4386, Institute for the Study of Labor, Bonn.

ProCon. 2012. State felon voting laws. Felon Voting: Pro and Con. http://felonvoting.procon.org/view.resource.php?resourceID=286.

Quillian, Lincoln. 2008. Does unconscious racism exist? *Social Psychology Quarterly* 71(1): 6–11.

Raphael, Steven, and Lucas Ronconi. 2008. Reconciling national and regional estimates of the effect of immigration on US labor markets: The confounding effects of native male incarceration rates. Working paper, Goldman School of Public Policy, University of California, Berkeley.

Raphael, Steven, and Michael A. Stoll. 2009a. Introduction. In *Do Prisons Make us safer? The benefits and costs of the prison boom,* ed. Steven Raphael and Michael A. Stoll, 1–25. New York: Russell Sage.

———. 2009b. Why are so many Americans in prison? In *Do prisons make us safer? The benefits and costs of the prison boom,* ed. Steven Raphael and Michael A. Stoll, 27–72. New York: Russell Sage.

———. 2013. *Why are so many Americans in prison?* New York: Russell Sage.

Ray, Debraj, and Rajiv Sethi. 2010. A remark on color-blind affirmative action. *Journal of Public Economic Theory* 12(3): 399–406.

Reid, Carolina, and Elizabeth Laderman. 2009. The untold costs of subprime lending: Examining the links among higher-priced lending, foreclosures, and race in California. Community affairs working paper 2009-09, San Francisco Federal Reserve Bank.

Rocha, R., and D. Hawes. 2009. Racial diversity, representative bureaucracy, and equity in multiracial school districts. *Social Science Quarterly* 90(2): 326–344.

Rodgers, William M., III, and William E. Spriggs. 1996. What does AFQT really measure? Race, wages, schooling and the AFQT score. *Review of Black Political Economy* 24(4): 13–46.

Rogers, Richard G., Rebecca Rosenblatt, Robert A. Hummer, and Patricia M. Krueger. 2001. Black-white differentials in adult homicide in the United States. *Social Science Quarterly* 82(3): 435–452.

Rooth, Dan-Olof. 2007. Implicit discrimination in hiring—Real world evidence. Discussion paper 05/07, Centre for Research and Analysis of Migration, London.

Ross, Stephen. 2008. Understanding racial segregation: What is known about the effect of housing discrimination? Working paper 2008-15, Department of Economics, University of Connecticut.

Ross, Stephen, and John Yinger. 2002. *The color of credit: Mortgage discrimination, research methodology, and fair-lending enforcement.* Cambridge, Mass.: MIT Press.

Rothstein, Jesse, and Nathan Wozny. 2011. Permanent income and the black-white test score gap. Working paper 17610, National Bureau of Economic Research.

Rothstein, Jesse, and Albert Yoon. 2009. Mismatch in law school. Working paper, Department of Economics, University of California–Berkeley.

Sacerdote, Bruce. 2005. Slavery and the intergenerational transmission of human capital. *Review of Economics and Statistics* 87(2): 217–234.

Saffer, Henry, and Frank Chaloupka. 1999. Demographic differentials in the demand for alcohol and illicit drugs. In *The economic analysis of substance use and abuse,* ed. Frank Chaloupka, Michael Grossman, Warren Bickel, and Henry Saffer, 187–211. Chicago: University of Chicago Press.

Saffer, Henry, Dhaval M. Dave, and Michael Grossman. 2011. Racial, ethnic, and gender differences in physical activity. Working paper 17413, National Bureau of Economic Research.

Saiz, Albert. 2007. Immigration and housing rents in American cities. *Journal of Urban Economics* 61(2): 345–371.

Sander, Richard. 2004. A systematic analysis of affirmative action in American law schools. *Stanford Law Review* 57(6): 1963–2016.

Sanga, Sarath. 2009. Reconsidering racial bias in motor vehicle searches: Theory and evidence. *Journal of Political Economy* 117(6): 1155–1159.

Saperstein, A., and A. Panner. 2010. The race of a criminal record: How incarceration colors racial perception. *Social Problems* 57(1): 92–113.

Schecter, A. D., P. J. Goldschmidt-Clermont, G. McKee, D. Hoffeld, M. Myers, R. Velez, J. Duran, S. P. Schulman, N. G. Candra, and D. E. Ford. 1996. Influence of gender, race, and education on patient preferences and receipt of cardiac catheterization among coronary care unit patients. *American Journal of Cardiology* 78(9): 996–1001.

Schelling, Thomas C. 1978. *Micromotives and macrobehavior.* New York: Norton.

Sedlis, S. P, V. J. Fisher, D. Tice, R. Esposito, L. Madmon, and E. H. Steinberg. 1999. Racial differences in performance of invasive cardiac procedures in a Department of Veterans Affairs Medical Center. 1997. *Journal of Clinical Epidemiology* 50(8): 899–901.

Sethi, Rajiv, and Rohini Somanathan. 2009. Racial inequality and segregation measures: Some evidence from the 2000 census. *Review of Black Political Economy* 36(2): 79–91.

Sherman, Lawrence W., Patrick R. Gartin, and Michael E. Buerger. 1989. Hot spots of predatory crime: Routine activities and the criminology of place. *Criminology* 27(1): 27–55.

Simanski, John F., and Lesley M. Sapp. 2013. *Immigration enforcement actions: 2012.* U.S. Department of Homeland Security, Office of Immigration Statistics. www.dhs.gov/sites/default/files/publications/ois_enforcement_ar_2012_1.pdf.

Simeonova, Emilia. 2008. Doctors, patients, and the racial mortality gap: What are the causes? Discussion paper 0708-13, Columbia University Department of Economics.

Slavin, Robert E. 2010. Can financial incentives enhance educational outcomes? Evidence from international experiments. *Educational Research Review* 5(1): 68–80.

Slavin, Robert E., Nancy Madden, Margarita Calderon, Anne Chamberlain, and Megan Hennessy. 2011. Reading and language outcomes of five-year randomized evaluation of transitional bilingual education. *Educational Evaluation and Policy Analysis* 33(1): 47–58.

Smedley, Brian D., Adrienne Y. Stith, and Alan R. Nelson, eds. 2002. *Unequal treatment: Confronting racial and ethnic disparities in health care.* Washington, D.C.: Institute of Medicine, National Academy Press.

Smith, Erica L., and Alexia Cooper. 2013. Homicide in the United States known to law enforcement, 2011. U.S. Bureau of Justice Statistics NCJ 243035. http://www.bjs.gov/content/pub/pdf/hus11.pdf.

Smith, James P., and Finis Welch. 1989. Black economic progress after Myrdal. *Journal of Economic Literature* 27(2): 519–564.

Steele, Claude M. 1997. A threat in the air: How stereotypes shape intellectual identity and performance. *American Psychologist* 52(6): 613–629.

St. Hoyme, L. E., and M. Y. İşcan. 1989. Determination of sex and race: Accuracy and assumptions. In *Reconstruction of life from the skeleton,* ed. M. Y. İşcan and K. A. R. Kennedy, 53–94. New York: Wiley Liss.

Stiefel, Leanna, Amy Ellen Schwartz, and Ingrid Gould Ellen. 2007. Disentangling the racial test score gap: Probing the evidence in a large urban school district. *Journal of Policy Analysis and Management* 26(1): 7–30.

Stratton, Leslie S. 1993. Racial differences in men's unemployment. *Industrial and Labor Relations Review* 46(3): 451–463.

Substance Abuse and Mental Health Services Administration. 2012. *Results from the 2010 National Survey on Drug Use and Health: Mental Health Findings,* NSDUH Series H-42, HHS Publication No. (SMA) 11-4667. Rockville, MD: Substance Abuse and Mental Health Services Administration. http://www.samhsa.gov/data/sites/default/files/2k10MH_Findings/2k10MH_Findings/2k10MHResults.htm.

Sugrue, Thomas J. 1996. *The origins of the urban crisis: Race and inequality in postwar Detroit.* Princeton, N.J.: Princeton University Press.

Todd, Petra, and Kenneth Wolpin. 2007. The production of cognitive achievement in children: Home, school, and racial test score gaps. *Journal of Human Capital* 1(1): 91–136.

Tomaskovic-Devey, Donald, Melvin Thomas, and Kecia Johnson. 2005. Race and the accumulation of human capital across the career: A theoretical model and fixed-effects application. *American Journal of Sociology* 111(1): 58–89.

Tonry, Michael. 1995. *Malign neglect: Race, crime and punishment in America.* New York: Oxford University Press.

Tucker, M. Belinda, and Claudia Mitchell-Kernan. 1995. Trends in African American family formation: A theoretical and statistical overview. In *The decline in marriage among African Americans,* ed. M. Belinda Tucker and Claudia Mitchell-Kernan, 3–26. New York: Russell Sage.

Turner, Joanna, Michel Boudreaux, and Victoria Lynch. 2009. A preliminary evaluation of health insurance coverage in the 2008 American Community

Survey. Working paper, U.S. Census Bureau. http://www.census.gov/content /dam/Census/library/working-papers/2009/demo/2008ACS_healthins.pdf.

Turner, Margery Austin, Rob Santos, Diane K. Levy, Doug Wissoker, Claudia Aranda, Rob Pitingolo, and The Urban Institute. 2013. *Housing discrimination against racial and ethnic minorities 2012.* Washington, D.C.: U.S. Department of Housing and Urban Development.

University at Albany. 2014. *Sourcebook of criminal justice statistics.* http://www .albany.edu/sourcebook/about.html.

U.S. Bureau of Justice Statistics. 2011. *Criminal victimization in the United States, 2008—Statistical tables.* http://www.bjs.gov/index.cfm?ty=pbdetail&iid=2218.

U.S. Bureau of Labor Statistics. 2009. Usual weekly earnings of wage and salary workers: Fourth quarter 2008. http://www.bls.gov/news.release/archives /wkyeng_01222009.pdf.

U.S. Census Bureau. 1997. *Statistical abstract of the United States: 1996.* Washington, D.C.: Government Printing Office.

———. 2002. *Statistical abstract of the United States: 2001.* Washington, D.C.: Government Printing Office.

———. 2005. *Statistical abstract of the United States: 2004.* Washington, D.C.: Government Printing Office.

———. 2006. *American Housing Survey for the United States: 2005.* Current housing reports series H150/05. Washington, D.C.: Government Printing Office.

———. 2008. *Statistical abstract of the United States: 2007.* Washington, D.C.: Government Printing Office.

———. 2010. *Statistical abstract of the United States: 2009.* Washington, D.C.: Government Printing Office.

———. 2011. America's families and living arrangements: 2011. Data set. https:// www.census.gov/population/www/socdemo/hh-fam/cps2011.html.

———. 2012a. Educational attainment in the United States: 2011—Detailed tables. Data set. http://www.census.gov/hhes/socdemo/education/data/cps /2011/tables.html.

———. 2012b. Hispanic origin and race of coupled households (CPH-T-4). Data set. https://www.census.gov/population/www/cen2010/briefs/cph-t-4.html.

———. 2012c. *Statistical abstract of the United States: 2011.* Washington, D.C.: Government Printing Office.

———. 2014. *America's families and living arrangements: 2004.* https://www.census .gov/population/www/socdemo/hh-fam/cps2004.html.

———. n.d. Infographic: America's foreign born in the last 50 years. http://www .census.gov/census-sis/index/research/By-Type/data-visualization/infographic ----americas-foreign-born-in-the-last-50-years.html.

U.S. Federal Bureau of Investigation. 2009. Crime in the United States: 2008. Data set. http://www2.fbi.gov/ucr/cius2008/index.html.

———. 2011. Crime in the United States: 2010. Data set. http://www2.fbi.gov/ucr/cius2010/index.html.

U.S. General Accountability Office. 2000. *Racial profiling: Limited data available in motorist stops: Report to the Honorable James E. Clyburn, chairman, Congressional Black Caucus.* GAO/GGD-00-41, March. General Accountability Office: Washington: D.C.

Van der Bergh, Linda, Eddie Denessen, Lisette Hornstra, Marinus Voeten, and Rob W. Holland. 2010. The implicit prejudiced attitudes of teachers: Relations to teacher expectations and the ethnic achievement gap. *American Educational Research Journal* 47(2): 497–527.

van Ryn, M., and J. Burke. 2000. The effect of patient race and socio-economic status on physician's perception of patients. *Social Science and Medicine* 50: 813–828.

Washington, Booker T. (1895) 2012. Address of Booker T. Washington at the opening of the exposition. In *Booker T. Washington rediscovered,* edited by Michael Scott Bieze and Marybeth Gasman, 60–64. Baltimore, Md.: Johns Hopkins University Press.

———. 1915. My view of segregation laws. *The New Republic,* December 4, 113–114.

Weiman, David, and Christopher Weiss. 2009. The origins of mass incarceration in New York State: The Rockefeller Drug Laws and the local war on drugs. In *Do Prisons Make Us Safer? The Benefits and Costs of the Prison Boom,* ed. Steven Raphael and Michael A. Stoll, 73–117. New York: Russell Sage.

West, Heather C. 2010. Prison inmates at midyear 2008—Statistical tables. U.S. Bureau of Justice Statistics. http://www.bjs.gov/content/pub/pdf/pim09st.pdf.

White, T. D., M. T. Black, and P. A. Folkens. 2011. *Human osteology.* 3rd ed. San Diego, Calif.: Academic Press.

Wildeman, Christopher. 2010. Paternal incarceration and children's physically aggressive behaviors: Evidence from the Fragile Families and Child Wellbeing Study. *Social Forces* 89(1): 285–310.

Wilford, John Noble. 2008. How epidemics helped shape the modern metropolis. *New York Times,* April 15.

Wolfe, Barbara L., and Jason Fletcher. 2013. Estimating benefits from university-level diversity. Working paper 18812, National Bureau of Economic Research.

Wolff, Edward N. 2001. Racial wealth disparities: Is the gap closing? Public Policy Brief 66A, Jerome Levy Institute, Bard College. http://www.levyinstitute.org/pubs/ppb66.pdf.

———. 2012. The asset price meltdown and the wealth of the middle class. Working paper 18559, National Bureau of Economic Research.

Woo, Han. 2012. Major "combination-patterns" of residential segregation based on five dimensions of segregation: Latent profile analysis. Working paper, Department of Sociology, Johns Hopkins University.

Wozniak, Abigail. 2014. Discrimination and the effects of drug testing on black employment. Working paper 20095, National Bureau of Economic Research.

Yang, Dean. 2011. Migrant remittances. *Journal of Economic Perspectives* 25(3): 129–152.

Yinger, John. 1995. *Closed doors, opportunities lost: The continuing costs of housing discrimination.* New York: Russell Sage.

Zimmer, Carl. 2013a. Rare genes cause common diseases. *Discover* 34(1): 72.

———. 2013b. Interbreeding with Neanderthals. *Discover* 34(2): 38–44.

Zimring, Franklin E. 2007. *The great American crime decline.* New York: Oxford University Press.

———. 2012. *The city that became safe: New York's lessons for urban crime and its control.* New York: Oxford University Press.

Acknowledgments

I've been lucky. A lot of people have helped me write this book, and only a few were conscious of what they were doing.

Several hundred Columbia students have taken the classes that eventually developed into this book. The first few times I taught this course I knew virtually nothing, and what I knew I wasn't able to express well. They pushed me to learn more (even topics that I had at first resisted and had rationalized as irrelevant), to rethink what I thought I knew, and to explain what I did know more clearly.

The most important lesson my students taught me is that a careful, inquiring, open, rigorous, and respectful discussion of race is possible in the twenty-first century. When some of my colleagues first learned that I was planning to teach a course on race, they asked me why I wanted to get my house picketed. I was a little worried about that, but I was more worried that the class would degenerate into a sticky morass of silent embarrassed staring and feel-good platitudes. Neither of my worries was realized, or anything close. I would not have persisted unless the students' attitudes had assured me that somebody was interested in a book like this. I've never wanted to be either a punching bag or a preacher.

One reason the classes went as well as they did is that I have always been helped by able teaching assistants, especially Allison Schrager, Ben Marx, Matt Flagge, and Harold Stolper, all of whom helped me for multiple semesters. The TAs made the class bearable to students, especially when I didn't know what I was talking about, and they kept me in line and corrected me when I was wrong.

My colleagues in the Columbia Economics Department supported both the class and the book; there are easier ways to fill classrooms. I'm especially grateful to Susan Elmes, Alessandra Casella, Don Davis, Ron Findlay, Mike Riordan, Bernard Salanie, and David Weinstein for their encouragement and forbearance. Angela Reid, Jodi Johnson, Afton Battle, and Shane Bordeau made sure that administrative duties did not swallow me up.

Jill Shapiro of the Columbia Department of Ecology, Evolution, and Environmental Biology taught me about the physical anthropology of race and the history of race in natural science. She gave me many comments and corrections on Chapter 3, and my debt to her is very great.

I've also been blessed to inhabit a vibrant intellectual community. In graduate school, Richard Freeman and Claudia Goldin showed me that serious empirical work could illuminate the workings of race in ways I had not thought possible. My frequent coauthors, Ingrid Gould Ellen and Rajiv Sethi, have patiently taught me many things, and their influence on the book is too pervasive to be limited by a simple list. Over the years, Dionissi Alliprantis, Leah Boustan, Steve Cameron, David Colander, Ceci Conrad, Olga Gorbachev, Rucker Johnson, Glenn Loury, George Sherer, Pablo Spiller, Bill Spriggs, and many others have talked to me about these topics; I doubt that I helped them much, but they helped the book.

The amount and quality of research that economists and others have done on race in the past decade or so is overwhelming; that provides the book's primary raw material. Learning these results has been a great experience, but it has also made me feel very, very parasitic.

The academic community is not the only community that has nourished this book. I grew up in Newark at a time when you not only *could* talk about race—you had to. My parents, Annette and Charles O'Flaherty, made sure that my brother and I lived in an integrated world, a rarity for the time. For instance, they never told me that there was anything bad or unusual about my being the only white kid in my first grade class (although they told me that the class size of forty-five was excessive).

I've learned a lot in Newark. During and after college and graduate school, I was taught by Mayor Kenneth Gibson, Senator John Caufield, and Harry Wheeler. In the past decade or so, I've been sustained by the Newark History Society, the Newark Water Group, Unified Vailsburg Services Organization, and Newark Emergency Services for Families. Richard Cammarieri, Bob Curvin, Regina Joseph, Mu'minah Oyeyemi, Archie Williams, and Zemin Zhang have been particularly attentive mentors, even if they didn't think they were. Newark is a wonderful place to learn about race in America. Perhaps I will write about that someday.

Compared with this preparation, writing the book was easy. I received detailed and extremely helpful comments from Jill Shapiro, Steve Raphael, and an anonymous referee. Michael Aronson and Kathleen Drummy shepherded the book through review and revisions and into production. Isabelle Lewis produced the figures, and Ally Federov provided many helpful comments.

Every day I've relied on Mary Gallagher for strength, for wisdom, for grounding, for support, and for putting up with the mess I have turned our home into in the process of writing this book. Whenever I panicked, she figured a way out of the problem. Niamh N. Gallagher and Nellie B. O'Flaherty have also helped in every way they could, and their assistance has been invaluable.

Errors in this book remain my responsibility, of course. The first error, I'm sure, is omitting someone from the list of those I've thanked explicitly.

Index